What Readers Are Saying About *Practical Programming*

I wish I could go back in time and give this book to my 10-year-old self when I first learned programming! It's so much more engaging, practical, and accessible than the dry introductory programming books that I tried (and often failed) to comprehend as a kid. I love the authors' hands-on approach of mixing explanations with code snippets that students can type into the Python prompt.

➤ **Philip Guo**
Creator of Online Python Tutor (www.pythontutor.com), Assistant Professor, Department of Cognitive Science, UCSD

Practical Programming delivers just what it promises: a clear, readable, usable introduction to programming for beginners. This isn't just a guide to hacking together programs. The book provides foundations to lifelong programming skills: a crisp, consistent, and visual model of memory and execution and a design recipe that will help readers produce quality software.

➤ **Steven Wolfman**
Professor of Teaching, Department of Computer Science, University of British Columbia

This excellent text reflects the authors' many years of experience teaching Python to beginning students. Topics are presented so that each leads naturally to the next, and common novice errors and misconceptions are explicitly addressed. The exercises at the end of each chapter invite interested students to explore computer science and programming language topics.

➤ **Kathleen Freeman**
Director of Undergraduate Studies, Department of Computer and Information Science, University of Oregon

Practical Programming, Fourth Edition

An Introduction to Computer Science Using Python 3.14

Dmitry Zinoviev

with Paul Gries
Jennifer Campbell
and Jason Montojo

The Pragmatic Bookshelf
Dallas, Texas

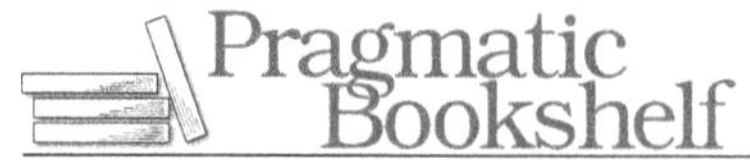

See our complete catalog of hands-on, practical,
and Pragmatic content for software developers:
https://pragprog.com

Sales, volume licensing, and support:
support@pragprog.com

Derivative works, AI training and testing,
international translations, and other rights:
rights@pragprog.com

The team that produced this book includes:

Publisher:	Dave Thomas
COO:	Janet Furlow
Executive Editor:	Susannah Davidson
Development Editor:	Adaobi Obi Tulton
Copy Editor:	Karen Galle
Indexing:	Potomac Indexing, LLC

ISBN-13: 979-8-88865-204-6
Book version: P1.0—June, 2026

Contents

Acknowledgments xi

Preface xiii

1. **What's Programming?** 1
   Programs and Programming 2
   What's a Programming Language? 3
   What's a Bug? 4
   The Difference Between Brackets, Braces, and Parentheses 5
   Installing Python 5

2. **Hello, Python** 7
   How Does a Computer Run a Python Program? 7
   Expressions and Values: Arithmetic in Python 9
   What Is a Type? 12
   Variables and Computer Memory: Remembering Values 15
   How Python Tells You Something Went Wrong 23
   A Single Statement That Spans Multiple Lines 24
   Describing Code 26
   Making Code Readable 27
   The Object of This Chapter 28
   Exercises 29

3. **Designing and Using Functions** 31
   Functions That Python Provides 31
   Identities: How Python Keeps Track of Values 35
   Defining Custom Functions 36

Using Local Variables for Temporary Storage 39
Tracing Function Calls in the Memory Model 41
Designing New Functions: A Recipe 49
Writing and Running a Program 60
Omitting a return Statement: None 62
Dealing with Situations That Your Code Doesn't Handle 63
What Did You Call That? 64
Exercises 65

4. **Working with Text** 67
Creating Strings of Characters 67
Using Special Characters in Strings 71
Creating a Multiline String 72
Printing Information 73
Getting Information from the Keyboard 76
Formatted Strings 77
Quotes About Strings 80
Exercises 80

5. **Making Choices** 83
A Boolean Type 83
Choosing Which Statements to Execute 92
Nested if Statements 98
Memorizing Results of a Boolean Expression Evaluation 98
You Learned About Booleans: True or False? 100
Exercises 100

6. **A Modular Approach to Program Organization** 105
Importing Modules 105
Defining Your Modules 109
Testing Your Code Semiautomatically 116
Tips for Grouping Your Functions 118
Organizing Your Thoughts 118
Exercises 119

7. **Using Methods** **121**
Modules, Classes, and Methods 121
Calling Methods 122
Exploring String Methods 124
What Are Those Underscores? 128
A Methodical Review 130
Exercises 131

8. **Storing Collections of Data Using Lists** **133**
Storing and Accessing Data in Lists 133
Type Annotations for Lists 137
Modifying Lists 138
Operations on Lists 139
Slicing Lists 142
Aliasing: What's in a Name? 144
List Methods 145
Working with a List of Lists 147
Splitting Strings 149
A Summary List 150
Exercises 150

9. **Repeating Code Using Loops** **153**
Processing Items in a List 153
Processing Characters in Strings 155
Looping Over a Range of Numbers 156
Processing Lists Using Indices 158
Nesting Loops in Loops 161
Looping Until a Condition Is Reached 165
Repetition Based on User Input 167
Controlling Loops Using break and continue 168
Repeating What You've Learned 172
Exercises 173

10. **Reading and Writing Files** **177**
What Kinds of Files Are There? 177
Opening a File 179
Techniques for Reading Files 183

Files over the Internet 188
Writing Files 189
Writing Example Calls Using StringIO 191
Writing Algorithms That Use the File-Reading Techniques 193
Multiline Records 201
Looking Ahead 203
Notes to File Away 205
Exercises 206

11. Storing Data Using Other Collection Types 209
Storing Data Using Sets 209
Storing Data Using Tuples 215
Storing Data Using Dictionaries 220
Inverting a Dictionary 228
Using the in Operator on Tuples, Sets, and Dictionaries 229
Comparing Collections 229
Creating New Type Annotations 229
A Collection of New Information 232
Exercises 232

12. Designing and Benchmarking Algorithms 235
Searching for the Two Smallest Values 235
Timing the Functions 244
At a Minimum, You Saw This 246
Exercises 246

13. Searching and Sorting 249
Searching a List 249
Binary Search 256
Sorting 261
More Efficient Sorting Algorithms 271
Merge Sort: A Faster Sorting Algorithm 272
Sorting Out What You Learned 276
Exercises 277

14. **Object-Oriented Programming** **281**
Understanding a Problem Domain 282
Function isinstance, Class object, and Class Book 283
Writing a Method in Class Book 286
Plugging into Python Syntax: More Special Methods 292
A Little Bit of OO Theory 296
A Case Study: Molecules, Atoms, and PDB Files 300
Classifying What You've Learned 304
Exercises 305

15. **Testing and Debugging** **309**
Why Do You Need to Test? 309
Case Study: Testing above_freezing 310
Case Study: Testing running_sum 315
Choosing Test Cases 321
Hunting Bugs 323
Bugs We've Put in Your Ear 324
Exercises 324

16. **Mastering Iteration Tools** **327**
Core Idioms 327
Functional Programming 336
Built-In and Standard Library Helpers 342
Let's Reiterate 347
Exercises 348

17. **Handling Exceptions** **351**
Core Idioms 351
Accessing Exception Details 355
Common Built-in Exceptions 357
Raising and Chaining Exceptions 358
Defining Custom Exceptions 361
Exceptionally Important! 362
Exercises 363

Bibliography **365**
Index **367**

Acknowledgments

From Paul, Jennifer, and Jason:

This book would be confusing and riddled with errors if it weren't for a bunch of awesome people who patiently and carefully read our drafts.

We had a great team of people provide technical reviews for previous editions: in no particular order, Frank Ruiz, Stefan Turalski, Stephen Wolff, Peter W.A. Wood, Steve Wolfman, Adam Foster, Owen Nelson, Arturo Martínez Peguero, C. Keith Ray, Michael Szamosi, David Gries, Peter Beens, Edward Branley, Paul Holbrook, Kristie Jolliffe, Mike Riley, Sean Stickle, Tim Ottinger, Bill Dudney, Dan Zingaro, and Justin Stanley. We also appreciate all the people who reported errata; your feedback was invaluable.

Greg Wilson started us on this journey when he proposed that we write a textbook, and he was our guide and mentor as we worked together to create the first edition of this book.

We would like to thank Dmitry for bringing a fresh industry perspective and indulging our quirks. We think it's a stronger book, and the fourth edition would not have been possible without him. We also extend our thanks to Adaobi Obi Tulton for capably steering the project throughout, and Margaret Eldridge for her constant encouragement and support.

From Dmitry:

It was my unutterable pleasure to be invited as the *fourth* author of the *fourth* edition of this book. (Do all good things now come in *fours*?) From my first meeting with the Pragmatic team to delivering a thoroughly reworked and readable manuscript, the journey took me a record seven months.

This project would not have been possible without the unwavering support and encouragement of Paul, Jennifer, and Jason—the original "Gang of Three"; of my friends and colleagues, who persuaded me that a printed Python textbook is still very much a thing; of my family, including my geriatric cat, who patiently endured my typing marathons and occasional lamentations; and, above all, of my wonderful editor, Adaobi Obi Tulton, with whom I would gladly write another dozen books—if not in this life, then surely in the next.

Preface

This book uses the Python programming language to teach introductory computer science topics and a handful of useful applications. You'll certainly learn a fair amount of Python as you work through this book, but along the way you'll also learn about issues that every programmer needs to know: ways to approach a problem and break it down into parts, how and why to document your code, how to test your code to help ensure your program does what you want it to, and more.

We chose Python for several reasons:

- *It is free and well documented.* In fact, Python is one of the largest and best-organized open source projects going.
- *It runs everywhere.* The reference implementation, written in C, is used on everything from cell phones to supercomputers, and it's supported by professional-quality installers for Windows, macOS, and Linux.
- *It has a clean syntax.* Yes, every language makes this claim, but during the several years that we have been using it at the University of Toronto and at Suffolk University, we have found that students make noticeably fewer "punctuation" mistakes with Python than with C-like languages.
- *It is relevant.* Thousands of companies use it every day: it is one of the languages used at Google, Netflix, Facebook, Spotify, Dropbox, Amazon, Reddit, JPMorgan Chase, NASA, and Uber, to name a few. It is also widely used by academic research groups.
- *It is well supported by tools.* Legacy editors like vi and Emacs all have Python editing modes, and several professional-quality IDEs are available. (We use IDLE, the free development environment that usually comes with a standard Python installation.)

Our Approach

We have organized the book into two parts. The first covers fundamental programming ideas: how to store and manipulate information (numbers, text, lists, sets, dictionaries, and files), how to control the flow of execution (conditionals and loops), how to organize code (functions and modules), how to ensure your code works (testing and debugging), and how to plan your program (algorithms).

The second part of the book consists of more or less independent chapters on more advanced topics that assume all the basic material has been covered. The first of these chapters shows how to create and manage your own types of information. It introduces object-oriented concepts such as encapsulation, inheritance, and polymorphism. The other chapters cover testing and advanced topics, such as iteration tools and exception handling.

Further Reading

Lots of other good books on Python programming exist. Some are accessible to novices, such as *Automate the Boring Stuff with Python: Practical Programming for Total Beginners [Swe19]* and *Python Crash Course: A Hands-On, Project-Based Introduction to Programming [Mat23]*; others are for anyone with any previous programming experience (*How to Think Like a Computer Scientist: Learning with Python [DEM02]*, *Effective Python: 90 Specific Ways to Write Better Python [Sla19]*, *Fluent Python: Clear, Concise, and Effective Programming [Ram22]*). You may also want to take a look at "EDU-SIG: Python in Education," the special interest group for educators using Python,[1] and at Google's Python Class, a fully free course by Google, complete with written lessons, lecture videos, and in-browser code exercises.[2] Information about a variety of Python books and other resources is available at the Python Wiki.[3]

After you have a good grasp of programming in Python, we recommend that you learn a second programming language. There are many possibilities, such as well-known languages like C, C++, Java, and C#. Python is similar in concept to those languages. However, you will likely learn more *and become a better programmer* if you learn a programming language that requires a different mindset, such as *Rust [Wol25]*, *Erlang [Ost18]*, or *Haskell [Ski23]*. In any case, we strongly recommend learning a second programming language.

1. https://www.python.org/community/sigs/current/edu-sig/
2. https://developers.google.com/edu/python
3. https://wiki.python.org/moin/FrontPage

What You'll See

In this book, we'll do the following:

- We'll show you how to develop and use programs that solve real-world problems. Most of the examples will come from science and engineering, but the ideas can be applied to any domain.
- We'll start by teaching you the core features of Python. These features are included in most modern programming languages, so you can use what you learn no matter what you work on next.
- We'll also teach you how to think methodically about programming. In particular, we will show you how to break complex problems into simple ones and how to combine the solutions to those simpler problems to create complete applications.
- Finally, we'll introduce some tools that will help make your programming more productive, as well as some others that will help your applications cope with larger problems.

CHAPTER 1

What's Programming?

Before you learn what programming is, let's consider two real-world problems that seem very different, but inspire a similar solution.

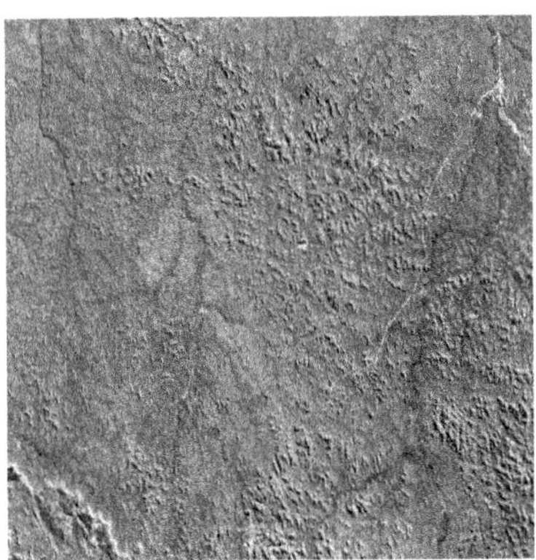

Take a look at the pictures above *(Photo credit: NASA/Goddard Space Flight Center Scientific Visualization Studio)*. The first one shows forest cover in the Amazon basin in 1975. The second one shows the same area twenty-six years later. Anyone can see that much of the rainforest has been destroyed, but how much is "much"?

Now look at this *(Photo credit: CDC)*:

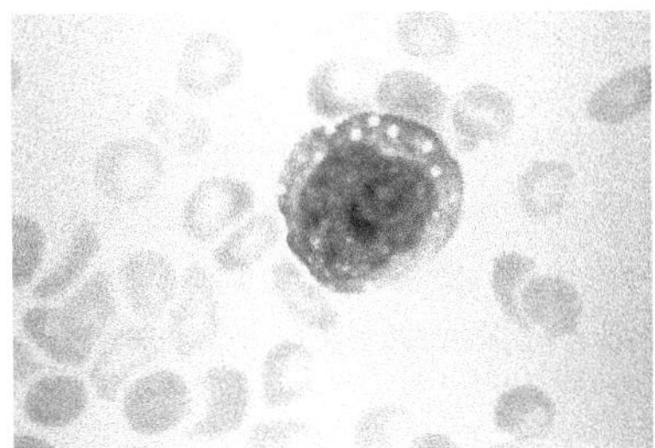

Are these blood cells healthy? Do any of them show signs of leukemia? It would take an expert doctor a few minutes to tell. Multiply those minutes by the number of people who need to be screened. There aren't enough human doctors in the world to check everyone.

That is where computers come in. Computer programs can measure the differences between two pictures and count the number of oddly shaped platelets in a blood sample. Geneticists use programs to analyze gene sequences; statisticians, to analyze the spread of diseases; geologists, to predict the effects of earthquakes; economists, to analyze fluctuations in the stock market; and climatologists, to study global warming. Increasingly, scientists are writing programs to assist them in their work. In turn, those programs are making entirely new kinds of science possible.

Of course, computers are suitable for a lot more than just science. We used computers to write this book. Your smartphone is a pretty powerful computer; you've probably used one today to scroll through TikTok or Instagram, join a Zoom study group, check your class schedule, order boba or tacos via a delivery app, or track your steps and sleep. Every day, someone discovers a new way to make a computer perform a task that has never been done before. Together, those "somethings" are changing the world.

This book will teach you how to make computers do what *you* want them to do. You may be planning to be a doctor, a linguist, or a physicist rather than a full-time programmer, but whatever you do, being able to program is as important as being able to write a letter or do basic arithmetic.

This chapter begins by explaining what programs and programming are. It then defines several key terms and provides helpful information for course instructors.

Programs and Programming

A *program* is a set of *commands* (also known as *instructions* or *operations*). When you write down directions to your house for a friend, you are writing a program. Your friend "executes" that program by following each instruction in turn.

Every program is written in terms of a few basic operations that its reader already understands. For example, the set of operations that your friend can understand might include the following: "Turn left at Darwin Street," "Go forward three blocks," and "If you get to the gas station, turn around—you've gone too far."

Computers, unlike your friends, have a different set of operations. Some operations are mathematical, like "Take the square root of a number," whereas others include "Read a line from the file named `data.txt`" and "Make a pixel blue."

You can "teach" a computer new operations by defining them in terms of old ones. For example, you can teach the computer that "Take the average" means "Add up the numbers in a sequence and divide by the sequence's size." You can then use the operations you have just defined to create still more operations, each layered on top of the ones that came before. It's a lot like creating life by assembling atoms to form proteins, then combining proteins to build cells, then combining cells to form organs, which ultimately combine to create a dog or a cat.

Defining new operations and combining them to do useful things is the heart and soul of programming. It is also a tremendously powerful way to think about other kinds of problems. According to *Jeannette Wing [Win06]*, computational thinking is about the following:

- *Conceptualizing, not programming.* Computer science isn't computer programming. Thinking like a computer scientist means more than being able to program a computer; it requires thinking at multiple levels of abstraction.
- *A way that humans, not computers, think.* Computational thinking is a way humans solve problems; it isn't trying to get humans to think like computers. Computers are dull and boring; humans are clever and imaginative. Humans make computers exciting. Equipped with computing devices, they use their ingenuity to tackle problems that you wouldn't have dared take on before the age of computing and build systems with functionality limited only by your imagination.
- *For everyone, everywhere.* Computational thinking will be a reality when it becomes so integral to human endeavors that it disappears as an explicit philosophy.

We hope that by the time you have finished reading this book, you will see the world in a slightly different way.

What's a Programming Language?

Directions to the nearest bus station can be given in English, Portuguese, Mandarin, Hindi, and many other languages. As long as the people you're talking to understand the language, they'll get to the bus station.

Similarly, there are many programming languages, and they all can add numbers, read information from files, and create user interfaces with windows, buttons, and scroll bars. The instructions appear differently, but they serve the same purpose. For example, in the Python programming language, here's how you add 3 and 4:

```
3 + 4
```

But here's how it's done in the Scheme programming language:

```
(+ 3 4)
```

They both convey the same idea—but they appear differently.

Every programming language has a way to write mathematical expressions, repeat a list of instructions several times, choose which of two instructions to do based on the current information you have, and much more. In this book, you'll learn how to do these things in the Python programming language. Once you understand Python, learning another programming language will be much easier.

What's a Bug?

Everyone has had a program crash. A standard story is that you were typing in a paper when, all of a sudden, your word processor crashed. You had forgotten to save, and you had to start all over again. Old versions of Microsoft Windows used to crash more often than they should have, showing the dreaded "blue screen of death." Usually, your computer shows some cryptic error message when a program crashes.

What happened in each case is that the people who wrote the program told the computer to do something it couldn't do: open a file that didn't exist, perhaps, or keep track of more information than the computer could handle, or maybe repeat a task with no way of stopping other than by rebooting the computer. (Programmers don't mean to make these kinds of mistakes; they are just part of the programming process.)

How Bugs Became "Bugs"

In 1947, engineers working on the *Harvard Mark II* computer found a moth stuck in a relay. They taped it into their logbook with the note: "First actual case of bug being found." The term *bug* had been used earlier in engineering, but this moment gave it a lasting place in computing lore.

Worse, some bugs don't cause a crash; instead, they give incorrect information. (This is worse because at least with a crash, you'll notice that there's a problem.) As a real-life example of this kind of bug, the calendar program used by one of the authors contains an entry for a friend who was born in 1978. That friend, according to the calendar program, had his 5,875,552nd birthday this past February. Bugs can be entertaining, but they can also be tremendously frustrating.

Every piece of software that you can buy has bugs in it. Part of your job as a programmer is to minimize the number of bugs and to reduce their severity. To find a bug, you must first identify where you provided incorrect instructions. Then, you need to determine the correct instructions and update the program without introducing additional bugs.

Every time you receive a software update for a program, it is for one of two reasons: new features have been added to the program, or bugs have been fixed. It's always a game of economics for the software company. Are there few enough bugs, and are they minor enough or infrequent enough for people to pay for the software?

In this book, we'll show you some fundamental techniques for finding and fixing bugs, as well as for preventing them in the first place.

The Difference Between Brackets, Braces, and Parentheses

One of the pieces of terminology that confuses beginner programmers is what to call certain characters. Several dictionaries use these names, so this book does too:

( ) Parentheses

[ ] Brackets

{ } Braces (Some people call these *curly brackets* or *curly braces*, but we'll stick to just *braces*.)

Installing Python

This book is written with Python 3.14, the most recent stable version at the time of writing, in mind. However, the book carefully avoids using advanced features of the language, which means any version at 3.8 and above will work just fine.

CHAPTER 2

Hello, Python

Programs are composed of commands that instruct the computer on what to do. These commands are called *statements*, which the computer executes. This chapter describes the simplest of Python's statements and shows how they can be used to do arithmetic, which is one of the most common tasks for computers and also a great place to start learning to program. It's also the basis of almost everything that follows.

How Does a Computer Run a Python Program?

To understand what happens when you're programming, it helps to have a mental model of how a computer executes a program.

A modern computer is built from several hardware components, including a *processor* (Central Processing Unit, a CPU) that runs programs and performs calculations, storage such as a *solid-state drive* (SSD) to hold data, and other essential parts, such as a touchscreen or monitor, keyboard, and Wi-Fi or cellular connectivity for getting online.

An operating system is a program that manages your computer's hardware

To manage all of these components, every computer runs an *operating system* (OS), such as Microsoft Windows, Linux, or macOS. An operating system is one of the few programs that has direct access to the hardware. When any other application (such as your browser, a spreadsheet program, or a game) wants to draw on the screen, find out what key was just pressed on the keyboard, or fetch data from storage, it sends a request to the OS. (See the diagram at the top of the next page.)

This arrangement may seem like a convoluted approach to getting things done, such as displaying images on the screen or responding to your actions. Yet, it means that only the people writing the OS have to worry about the

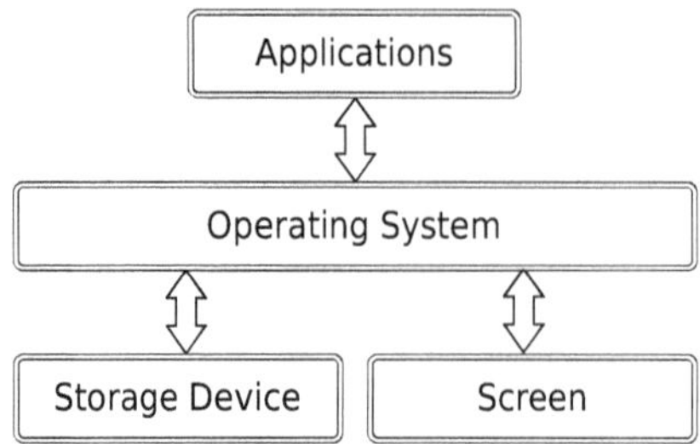

differences between one graphics card and another, as well as whether the computer is connected to a network via Ethernet or wireless. The rest of us, who are analyzing scientific data, creating mobile apps, editing videos, or exploring virtual worlds, only have to learn our way around the OS, and our programs will then run on thousands of different kinds of hardware.

Today, it's common to add another intermediary (a layer) between the programmer and the computer's hardware. When you write a program in Python, Java, or Visual Basic, the program doesn't run directly in contact with the OS. Instead, another program called an *interpreter* or *virtual machine* translates your program's commands into a language the OS understands. Command interpretation is easier, more secure, and more portable across operating systems than direct execution, although the latter is somewhat faster:

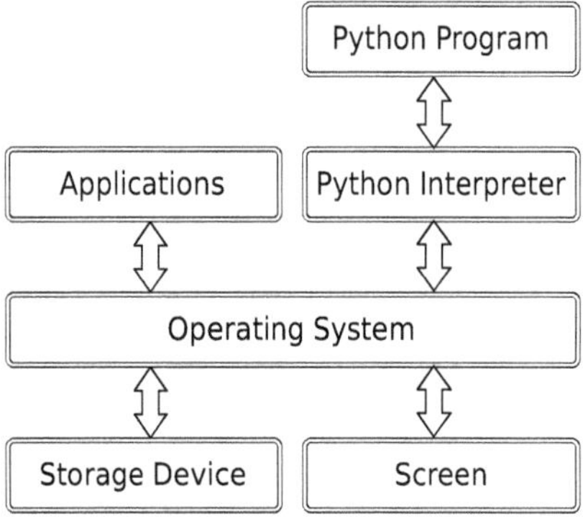

Programs are made up of statements

There are two ways to use the Python interpreter. One is to use a command to execute a Python program saved in a file with a .py extension. The other is to interact with the interpreter in a program called a *shell*, where you type statements one at a time. The interpreter will execute each statement when you type it, do what the statement says to do, and show any output as text, all in one window. You will explore Python in this chapter using a Python shell.

Install Python Now (If You Haven't Already)

If you haven't yet installed Python, please do so now. (Python 2 won't do; there are significant differences between it and Python 3, and this book uses Python 3.14.)

Programming requires practice: you won't learn how to program just by reading this book, much like you wouldn't know how to play guitar just by reading a book on how to play guitar.

Python comes with a program called IDLE, which you use to write Python programs. IDLE has a Python shell that communicates with the Python interpreter and also allows you to write and run programs that are saved in a file.

We *strongly* recommend that you open IDLE and follow along with the examples. Typing in the code in this book is the programming equivalent of repeating phrases back to an instructor as you're learning to speak a new language.

Why Is a CPU "Central"?

Older computers from the 1960s had more than one processing unit, including a central processing unit and peripheral processing units, also known as input/output processors. Modern computers also have more than one processing unit, the others usually being a graphics processing unit (GPU) or a digital signal processor (DSP).

Expressions and Values: Arithmetic in Python

You're familiar with mathematical expressions like `3 + 4` ("three plus four") and `2 - 3 / 5` ("two minus three divided by five"); each expression is built out of *values* like `2`, `3`, and `5` and *operators* like `+` and `-`, which combine their *operands* in different ways. In the expression `4 / 5`, the operator is "/" and the operands are `4` and `5`.

Expressions don't have to involve an operator: a number by itself is an expression. For example, `212` is an expression as well as a value.

Like any programming language, Python can *evaluate* basic mathematical expressions. For example, the following expression adds `4` and `13`:

```
>>> 4 + 13
17
```

The `>>>` symbol is called a *prompt*. When you start IDLE, the window should open with this symbol displayed; you don't type it. It is prompting you to type something. Type `4 + 13`, and then press the Return (or Enter) key to signal that you are done entering that *expression*. Python then evaluates the expression.

When an expression is evaluated, it produces a single value. In the previous expression, the evaluation of 4 + 13 produced the value 17. When you type the expression in the shell, Python shows the value that is produced.

Subtraction and multiplication are similarly unsurprising:

```
>>> 15 - 3
12
>>> 4 * 7
28
```

The following expression divides 5 by 2:

```
>>> 5 / 2
2.5
```

The result has a decimal point, even if it is a whole number:

```
>>> 4 / 2
2.0
```

Types

Every value in Python has a specific type

Every value in Python has a particular *type* (a *data type*, and the types of values determine how they behave when they're combined. Values like 4 and 17 have type int (short for *integer*), and values like 2.5 and 17.0 have type float. The word *float* is short for *floating point*, which refers to the decimal point that moves around between digits of a number.

An expression involving two floats produces a float:

```
>>> 17.0 - 10.0
7.0
```

When an expression's operands are an int and a float, Python automatically converts the int to a float. This conversion is why the following two expressions both return the same answer:

```
>>> 17.0 - 10
7.0
>>> 17 - 10.0
7.0
```

If you want, you can omit the zero after the decimal point when writing a floating-point number:

```
>>> 17 - 10.
7.0
>>> 17. - 10
7.0
```

However, this omission is considered bad *style* since it makes your programs harder to read; it's very easy to miss a dot on the screen and see 17 instead of 17. (with a period).

Integer Division, Modulo, and Exponentiation

Now and then, you want only the integer part of a division result. For example, you might want to know how many 24-hour days there are in 53 hours (which is two 24-hour days plus another 5 hours). To calculate the number of days, you can use *integer division*:

```
>>> 53 // 24
2
```

You can determine the number of hours remaining by using the *modulo* operator, which returns the remainder of the division:

```
>>> 53 % 24
5
```

Python doesn't round the result of integer division. Instead, it takes the *floor* of the result of the division (truncates the fractional part):

```
>>> 17 // 10
1
```

Be careful about using % and // with negative operands. Because Python takes the floor of the result of an integer division, the result is one smaller than you might expect if the result is negative:

```
>>> -17 // 10
-2
```

When using modulo, the sign of the result matches the sign of the divisor (the second operand):

```
>>> -17 % 10
3
>>> 17 % -10
-3
```

For the mathematically inclined, the relationship between // and % comes from this equation: for any two non-zero numbers a and b, (b * (a // b) + a % b) is equal to a.

For example, because -17 // 10 is -2, and -17 % 10 is 3; then 10 * (-17 // 10) + -17 % 10 is the same as 10 * -2 + 3, which is -17.

Floating-point numbers can also be operands for // and % operators. With //, division is performed, and the result is rounded down to the nearest whole number, although the type is a floating-point number:

```
>>> 3.3 // 1
3.0
>>> 3 // 1.0
3.0
>>> 3 // 1.1
2.0
>>> 3.5 // 1.1
3.0
>>> 3.5 // 1.3
2.0
```

The following expression calculates 3 raised to the power of 6:

```
>>> 3 ** 6
729
```

Operators that have two operands are referred to as *binary operators*. Negation is a *unary operator* because it applies to one operand:

```
>>> -5
-5
>>> --5
5
>>> ---5
-5
```

What Is a Type?

You've now seen two types of numbers (integers and floating-point numbers), so we ought to explain what we mean by a *type*. In Python, a type consists of two things:

- A set of values
- A set of operations that can be applied to those values

For example, in type int, the values are ..., -3, -2, -1, 0, 1, 2, 3, ..., and you have seen that these operators can be applied to those values: +, -, *, /, //, %, and **.

The values in type float are a subset of the real numbers, and it happens that the same set of operations can be applied to float values. You can observe the results of applying these to various values in the table below. If an operator behaves differently depending on the types of the operands, it is called an *overloaded operator*.

Symbol	Operator	Example	Result
-	Negation	-5	-5
+	Addition	11 + 3.1	14.1
-	Subtraction	5 - 19	-14
*	Multiplication	8.5 * 4	34.0
/	Division	11 / 2	5.5
//	Integer Division	11 // 2	5
%	Remainder	8.5 % 3.5	1.5
**	Exponentiation	2 ** 5	32

Table 1—Arithmetic Operators

Finite Precision

Floating-point numbers are not exactly the fractions you learned in grade school. For example, look at Python's version of the fractions $\frac{2}{3}$ and $\frac{5}{3}$:

```
>>> 2 / 3
0.6666666666666666
>>> 5 / 3
1.6666666666666667
```

The first value ends with a 6, and the second with a 7, which is unexpected: both should have an infinite number of 6s after the decimal point. The problem is that computers have a finite amount of memory, and to perform calculations quickly and efficiently, most programming languages limit the amount of information that can be stored for any single number. The number 0.6666666666666666 turns out to be the closest value to $\frac{2}{3}$ that the computer can store in its limited memory, and 1.6666666666666667 is as close as you can get to the real value of $\frac{5}{3}$.

In Programming, a + b ≠ b + a!

If you have to add up floating-point numbers, add them from smallest to largest to minimize the error.

Operator Precedence

Let's apply your knowledge of integers and floating-point numbers to convert Fahrenheit to Celsius. To do this, subtract 32 from the temperature in Fahrenheit and then multiply by $\frac{5}{9}$:

```
>>> 212 - 32 * 5 / 9
194.22222222222223
```

More on Numeric Precision

Integers (values of type int) in Python can be as large or as small as you like. However, float values are only *approximations* to real numbers. For example, ¼ can be stored exactly, but as you've already seen, ⅔ cannot. Using more memory won't solve the problem, though it will make the approximation closer to the real value, just as writing a larger number of 6s after the 0 in 0.666... doesn't make it exactly equal to ⅔.

The difference between ⅔ and 0.6666666666666666 may look tiny. However, if you use 0.6666666666666666 in a calculation, the error may be compounded. For example, if you add 1 to ⅔, the resulting value ends in ...6665, so in many programming languages, 1 + ⅔ is not equal to 5⁄3:

```
>>> 2 / 3 + 1
1.6666666666666665
>>> 5 / 3
1.6666666666666667
```

As you do more calculations, the rounding errors can get larger and larger, particularly if you're mixing very large and very small numbers. For example, suppose you add 10000000000 (10 billion) and 0.00000000001 (there are 10 zeros after the decimal point):

```
>>> 10000000000 + 0.00000000001
10000000000.0
```

The result ought to have twenty zeros between the first and last significant digit, but that's too many for the computer to store, so the result is just 10000000000—it's as if the addition never took place. Adding lots of small numbers to a large one can therefore have no effect at all, which is *not* what a bank wants when it totals up the values of its customers' savings accounts.

It's essential to be aware of the floating-point issue. There is no magic bullet to solve it because computers are limited in both memory and speed. *Numerical analysis*, the study of algorithms that approximate continuous mathematics, is a core subfield of applied mathematics and plays a crucial role in many areas of computer science, particularly in scientific computing and *machine learning*.

If you ever need to perform calculations where exact decimal representation matters, such as in financial applications, you can use Python's built-in *decimal* module.

Python claims the result is 194.22222222222223 degrees Celsius, when in fact it should be 100. The problem is that multiplication and division have higher *precedence* than subtraction; in other words, when an expression contains a mix of operators, the * and / are evaluated before the - and +. This means that what you calculated was 212 - ((32 * 5) / 9): the *subexpression* 32 * 5 is evaluated before the division is applied, and that division is evaluated before the subtraction occurs.

> Higher-precedence operators are applied before lower-precedence operators

You can alter the order of precedence by putting parentheses around subexpressions:

```
>>> (212 - 32) * 5 / 9
100.0
```

This table shows the order of precedence for arithmetic operators.

Precedence	Operator	Operation
Highest	**	Exponentiation
	-	Negation
	*, /, //, %	Multiplication, division, integer division, and remainder
Lowest	+, -	Addition and subtraction

Operators with higher precedence are applied before those with lower precedence. Here is an example that shows this:

```
>>> -2 ** 4
-16
>>> -(2 ** 4)
-16
>>> (-2) ** 4
16
```

Because exponentiation has higher precedence than negation, the subexpression 2 ** 4 is evaluated before negation is applied.

Operators on the same row of the table have equal precedence and are applied left to right, except for exponentiation, which is applied right to left. So, for example, because binary operators + and - are on the same row, 3 + 4 - 5 is equivalent to (3 + 4) - 5, and 3 - 4 + 5 is equivalent to (3 - 4) + 5.

It's a good rule to parenthesize complicated expressions even when you don't need to, since it helps the eye read things like 1 + 1.7 + 3.2 * 4.4 - 16 / 3. On the other hand, it's a good rule *not* to use parentheses in simple expressions such as 3.1 * 5.

Variables and Computer Memory: Remembering Values

Like mathematicians, programmers frequently assign names to values so that they can use them later. A name that refers to a value is called a *variable*. In Python, variable names can use letters, digits, and the underscore symbol (but they can't start with a digit). For example, X, species5618, and degrees_celsius are all allowed, but 777 isn't (it would be confused with a number), and neither is no-way! (it contains punctuation). Variable names are case-sensitive, so ph and pH are two different names.

New variable is created by *assigning* it a value:

```
>>> degrees_celsius = 26.0
```

This statement is called an *assignment statement*; we say that degrees_celsius is *assigned* the value 26.0. That makes degrees_celsius refer to the value 26.0. You can use variables anywhere you can use values. Whenever Python sees a variable in an expression, it substitutes the value to which the variable refers:

Variables are created by executing assignment statements

```
>>> degrees_celsius = 26.0
>>> degrees_celsius
26.0
>>> 9 / 5 * degrees_celsius + 32
78.80000000000001
>>> degrees_celsius / degrees_celsius
1.0
```

Variables are called *variables* because their values can vary as the program executes. You can assign a new value to a variable:

```
>>> degrees_celsius = 26.0
>>> 9 / 5 * degrees_celsius + 32
78.80000000000001
>>> degrees_celsius = 0.0
>>> 9 / 5 * degrees_celsius + 32
32.0
```

Assigning a value to a variable that already exists doesn't create a second variable. Instead, the existing variable is reused, which means that the variable no longer refers to its old value.

Equal Sign Is Not Equality in Python!

In mathematics, = means "the thing on the left is equal to the thing on the right." In Python, it means something quite different. An assignment is not symmetric: x = 12 assigns the value 12 to variable x, but 12 = x results in an error. Because of this, never describe the statement x = 12 as "x equals 12." Instead, read this as "x gets 12," "x becomes 12" or "x is assigned 12."

You can create other variables; this example calculates the difference between the boiling point of water and the temperature stored in degrees_celsius:

```
>>> degrees_celsius = 15.5
>>> difference = 100 - degrees_celsius
>>> difference
84.5
```

Values, Variables, and Computer Memory

We're going to develop a model of computer memory—a *memory model*—that will let you trace what happens when Python executes a Python program. This memory model will help you accurately predict and explain how Python executes code, a skill essential for becoming a proficient programmer.

Every location in the computer's memory has a *memory address*, much like a street address that uniquely identifies a house on the street. We're going to mark the memory addresses with an *id* prefix (short for *identifier*) so that they look different from integers: *id1*, *id2*, *id3*, and so on.

Here is how you draw the floating-point value 26.0 using the memory model:

id1:float
26.0

This image shows the value 26.0 at the memory address *id1*. We will always show the type of the value as well—in this case, float. We will refer to this box as an *object*: a value stored at a specific memory address with a defined type. During the execution of a program, every value that Python keeps track of is stored inside an object in computer memory.

In our memory model, a variable contains the memory address of the object it refers to. To make the image easier to interpret, draw arrows from variables to their corresponding objects.

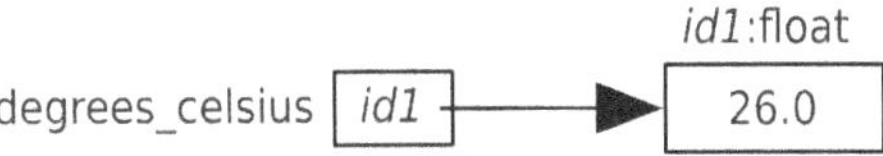

This is important, so let's repeat it:

- Python stores every value in memory as an object.
- Variables contain the memory addresses of values.

The Online Python Tutor

Philip Guo wrote a web-based memory visualizer that aligns well with our memory model.[a] It can trace both Python 3.6 and Python 3.14 code; make sure you select the correct version. The settings that most closely match our memory model are these:

- "Hide exited frames"
- "Render all objects on the heap"
- "Use text labels for pointers"

We strongly recommend using this visualizer whenever you want to trace the execution of a Python program.

a. http://pythontutor.com/visualize.html

We use the following terminology:

- Value 26.0 has the memory address *id1*.
- The object at the memory address *id1* has type float and the value 26.0.
- Variable degrees_celsius *contains* the memory address *id1*.
- Variable degrees_celsius *refers* to the value 26.0.

Whenever Python needs to know which value degrees_celsius refers to, it looks at the object at the memory address that degrees_celsius contains. In this example, that memory address is *id1*, so Python will use the value at the memory address *id1*, which is 26.0.

Assignment Statement

Here is the general form of an assignment statement:

```
«variable» = «expression»
```

The right side of the equal sign is called the *RHS* ("right-hand side"). The left side of the equal sign is called the *LHS* ("left-hand side"). The statement is executed as follows:

1. Evaluate the expression on the RHS to produce a value. This value has a memory address.
2. Store the memory address of the value in the variable on the LHS. Create a new variable if the name doesn't already exist; otherwise, reuse the existing variable, replacing the value at the memory address it contains.

Consider this example:

```
>>> degrees_celsius = 26.0 + 5
>>> degrees_celsius
31.0
```

Here is how Python executes the statement degrees_celsius = 26.0 + 5:

1. Evaluate the expression on the RHS: 26.0 + 5. The evaluation produces the value 31.0, which has a memory address. (Remember that Python stores all values in computer memory.)
2. Make the variable on the LHS, degrees_celsius, refer to 31.0 by storing the memory address of 31.0 in degrees_celsius.

Reassigning to Variables

Consider this code:

```
>>> difference = 20
>>> double = 2 * difference
>>> double
40
>>> difference = 5
>>> double
40
```

This demonstrates that assigning to a variable *does not change any other variable.* To trace this code, start by assigning the value 20 to the variable difference, and then assign the result of evaluating 2 * difference (40) to the variable double.

Next, assign the value 5 to the variable difference, but when you examine the value of double, it still refers to 40.

Here's how it works according to the rules. The first statement, difference = 20, is executed as follows:

1. Evaluate the expression on the RHS: 20. This produces the value 20, which you'll put at memory address *id1*.
2. Make the variable on the LHS, difference, refer to 20 by storing *id1* in difference.

Here is the current state of the memory model. (Variable double has not yet been created because you have not yet executed the assignment to it.)

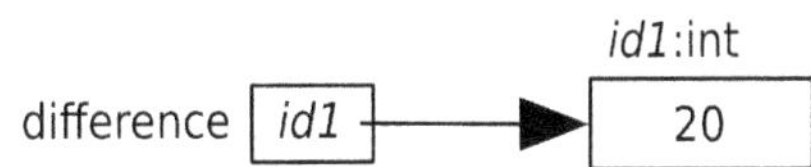

The second statement, double = 2 * difference, is executed as follows:

1. Evaluate the expression on the RHS: 2 * difference. As shown in the memory model, difference refers to the value 20, so this expression is equivalent to 2 * 20, which yields 40. Let's pick the memory address *id2* for the value 40.
2. Make the variable on the LHS, double, refer to 40 by storing *id2* in double.

Here is the current state of the memory model:

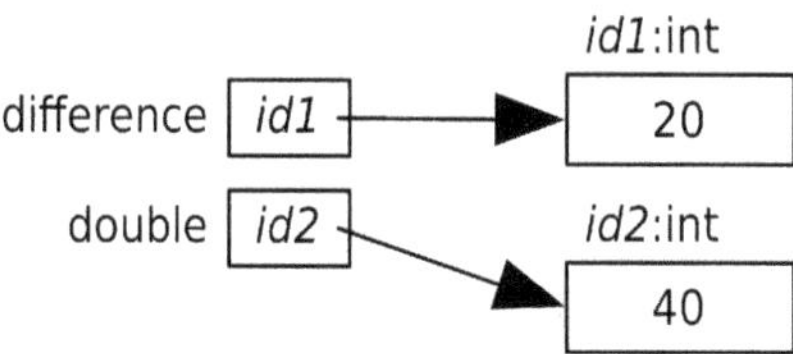

When Python executes the third statement, double, it merely looks up the value that double refers to (40) and displays it.

The fourth statement, difference = 5, is executed as follows:

1. Evaluate the expression on the RHS: 5. This produces the value 5, which we'll put at the memory address *id3*.
2. Make the variable on the LHS, difference, refer to 5 by storing *id3* in difference.

Here is the current state of the memory model:

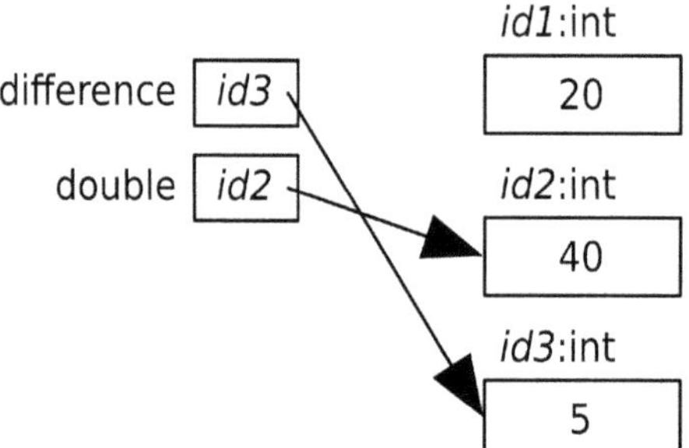

The variable double still contains *id2*, so it still refers to 40. Neither variable refers to 20 anymore.

The fifth and last statement, double, merely looks up the value that double refers to, which is still 40, and displays it.

You can even use a variable on both sides of an assignment statement:

```
>>> number = 3
>>> number
3
>>> number = 2 * number
>>> number
6
>>> number = number * number
>>> number
36
```

We'll now explain how Python executes this code, but won't explicitly mention memory addresses. Trace this on a piece of paper while we describe what happens; make up your memory addresses as you do this.

Python executes the first statement, `number = 3`, as follows:

1. Evaluate the expression on the RHS: `3`. This one is easy to evaluate: `3` is produced.
2. Make the variable on the LHS, `number`, refer to `3`.

Python executes the following statement, `number = 2 * number`, as follows:

1. Evaluate the expression on the RHS: `2 * number`. `number` currently refers to `3`, so this is equivalent to `2 * 3`, and `6` is produced.
2. Make the variable on the LHS, `number`, refer to `6`.

Python executes the third statement, `number = number * number`, as follows:

1. Evaluate the expression on the RHS: `number * number`. `number` currently refers to `6`, so this is equivalent to `6 * 6`, and `36` is produced.
2. Make the variable on the LHS, `number`, refer to `36`.

Augmented Assignment

In this example, the variable `score` appears on both sides of the assignment statement:

```
>>> score = 50
>>> score
50
>>> score = score + 20
>>> score
70
```

This pattern is so typical that Python provides a shorthand notation for this operation:

```
>>> score = 50
>>> score
50
>>> score += 20
>>> score
70
```

An *augmented assignment* combines an assignment statement with an operator to make the statement more concise. An augmented assignment statement is executed as follows:

1. Evaluate the expression on the RHS to produce a value.
2. Apply the operator attached to the equal sign to the variable on the LHS and the value that was produced, resulting in another value. Store the memory address of that value in the variable on the LHS.

Note that the operator is applied *after* the expression on the right is evaluated:

```
>>> d = 2
>>> d *= 3 + 4
>>> d
14
```

All the operators (except for negation) in Table 1, , on page 15, have shorthand versions. For example, you can square a number by multiplying it by itself:

```
>>> number = 10
>>> number *= number
>>> number
100
```

The code above is equivalent to the code below:

```
>>> number = 10
>>> number = number * number
>>> number
100
```

The table on the next page contains a summary of the augmented operators you've seen plus a few more based on arithmetic operators you learned about in Expressions and Values: Arithmetic in Python, on page 9.

Symbol	Example	Result
+=	`x = 7` `x += 2`	x refers to 9
-=	`x = 7` `x -= 2`	x refers to 5
*=	`x = 7` `x *= 2`	x refers to 14
/=	`x = 7` `x /= 2`	x refers to 3.5
//=	`x = 7` `x //= 2`	x refers to 3
%=	`x = 7` `x %= 2`	x refers to 1
**=	`x = 7` `x **= 2`	x refers to 49

Where Are the ++ and -- Operators?

After learning about augmented assignment like `x += 1`, you might expect Python to support `x++` (*increment*) or `x--` (*decrement*) operators like other languages do. But surprisingly, it doesn't!

Why not? Python avoids these increment and decrement shortcuts to keep the language explicit and readable: "In Python, readability matters more than shorthand."[1] Instead, you should always write `x += 1` or `x -= 1`, which makes it evident that you're updating a variable.

How Python Tells You Something Went Wrong

There are two kinds of errors in Python: *syntax errors*, which occur when you type something that isn't valid Python code, and *semantic errors*, which happen when you tell Python to do something that it just can't do, like dividing a number by zero or using a variable that doesn't exist.

Here is what happens when we use a variable that hasn't been created yet:

```
>>> 3 + moogah
Traceback (most recent call last):
  File "<python-input-0>", line 1, in <module>
    3 + moogah
        ^^^^^^
NameError: name 'moogah' is not defined
```

1. https://peps.python.org/pep-0020

The message is somewhat cryptic; Python error messages are intended for people who already know Python. (You'll get used to them and soon find them helpful.) The first two lines aren't much use right now, though they'll be indispensable when we start writing longer programs. The last line is the one that tells you what went wrong: the name moogah wasn't recognized—a NameError occurred.

Variables must be assigned values before they can be used

Here's another error message you may see:

```
>>> 2 +
  File "<python-input-0>", line 1
    2 +
       ^
SyntaxError: invalid syntax
```

The rules governing what is and isn't legal in a programming language are called its *syntax*. The message informs you that you violated Python's syntax rules—in this case, by attempting to add something to 2 without specifying what to add.

Earlier we claimed that 12 = x results in an error. Let's try it:

```
>>> 12 = x
  File "<python-input-1>", line 1
    12 = x
    ^^
SyntaxError: cannot assign to literal here. Maybe you meant '==' instead of '='?
```

A *literal* is any value, like 12 and 26.0. This error is a SyntaxError because when Python examines that assignment statement, it knows that you can't assign a value to a number even before it tries to execute it; you can't change the value of 12 to anything else. A 12 is just a 12. In other words, a value can't be on the LHS.

Incidentally, the Python interpreter is trying to be helpful and suggests that you may have used one equal sign instead of two. You will learn the difference later in Relational Operators, on page 85.

A Single Statement That Spans Multiple Lines

Sometimes statements get pretty intricate. The recommended Python style is to limit lines to 80 characters, including spaces, tabs, and other *whitespace* characters, and that's a suggested limit throughout the programming world. Here's what to do when lines get too long or when you want to split them up for clarity.

To split up a statement into more than one line, do one of two things:

1. Make sure your line break occurs within parentheses.
2. Use the line-continuation character, which is a backslash (\), at the end of the line.

Note that the line-continuation character is a backslash (\), not the division symbol (a forward slash, /). There must be no other characters on the line after the backslash, not even whitespace characters.

Here are examples of both:

```
>>> (2 +
... 3)
5
>>> 2 + \
... 3
5
```

Notice how you no longer get a SyntaxError. Each triple-dot prompt in the examples indicates that you are in the middle of entering an expression; we use them to align the code lines nicely. You do not type the dots any more than you type the greater-than signs in the usual >>> prompt, and if you are using IDLE, you won't see them at all.

Here is a more realistic (and tastier) example: let's say you're baking cookies. The authors live in countries that use the Celsius scale, but you own cookbooks that use the Fahrenheit scale. You are wondering how long it will take to preheat your oven. Here are your facts:

- The room temperature is 20 degrees Celsius.
- Your oven controls use the Celsius scale, and the oven heats up at 20 degrees per minute.
- Your cookbook uses the Fahrenheit scale, and it says to preheat the oven to 350 degrees.

You can convert tf degrees Fahrenheit to degrees Celsius as follows: (tf - 32) * 5 / 9. Let's use this information to try to solve your problem.

```
>>> room_temperature_c = 20
>>> cooking_temperature_f = 350
>>> oven_heating_rate_c = 20
>>> oven_heating_time = (
... ((cooking_temperature_f - 32) * 5 / 9) - room_temperature_c) / \
... oven_heating_rate_c
>>> oven_heating_time
7.833333333333333
```

Not bad—just under eight minutes to preheat.

The assignment statement to the variable oven_heating_time spans three lines. The first line ends with an open parenthesis, so you do not need a line-continuation character. The second ends *outside* the parentheses, so you need the line-continuation character. The third line completes the assignment statement.

That's still hard to read. Once you've continued an expression on the next line, you can indent (by pressing the spacebar multiple times or the Tab key) to your heart's content to make it more straightforward:

```
>>> oven_heating_time = (
...     ((cooking_temperature_f - 32) * 5 / 9) - room_temperature_c) / \
...     oven_heating_rate_c
```

Or even this—notice how the two subexpressions involved in the subtraction line up:

```
>>> oven_heating_time = (
...     ((cooking_temperature_f - 32) * 5 / 9) -
...      room_temperature_c) / \
...     oven_heating_rate_c
```

In the previous example, we clarified the expression by working with indentation. However, we could have made this process even clearer by converting the cooking temperature to the Celsius scale before calculating the heating time:

```
>>> room_temperature_c = 20
>>> cooking_temperature_f = 350
>>> cooking_temperature_c = (cooking_temperature_f - 32) * 5 / 9
>>> oven_heating_rate_c = 20
>>> oven_heating_time = (cooking_temperature_c - room_temperature_c) / \
...     oven_heating_rate_c
>>> oven_heating_time
7.833333333333333
```

The key takeaway here is that well-named temporary variables can significantly improve code clarity.

Describing Code

Programs can be quite complicated and are often thousands of lines long. It can be helpful to write a *comment* describing parts of the code so that when you or someone else reads it, the meaning is clear.

In Python, any time the # character is encountered, Python will ignore the rest of the line. Comments allow you to write English sentences (or, for that matter, sentences in any language):

```
>>> # Python ignores this sentence because of the # symbol.
```

The # symbol does not have to be the first character on the line; it can appear at the end of a statement:

```
>>> (212 - 32) * 5 / 9 # Convert 212 degrees Fahrenheit to Celsius.
100.0
```

Notice that the comment doesn't describe how Python works. It is meant for humans reading the code to help them understand why the code exists.

Making Code Readable

Much like there are spaces in English sentences to make the words easier to read, the use of spaces in Python code makes it easier to read. In particular, always put a space before and after every binary operator. For example, write `v = 4 + -2.5 / 3.6` instead of `v=4+-2.5/3.6`. There are situations where it may not make a difference, but that's a detail you don't want to fuss about, so always do it: it's rarely *harder* to read if there are spaces.

Psychologists have discovered that people can keep track of only a handful of things at any one time (*Forty Studies That Changed Psychology [Hoc04]*). Since programs can get quite complicated, choose names for your variables that will help you remember what they're for. Names `id1`, `X2`, and `foobar` won't remind you of anything when you come back to look at your program next week; use names like `celsius`, `average`, and `final_result` instead.

Other studies have shown that your brain automatically notices differences between things—in fact, there's no way to stop it from doing this. As a result, the more inconsistencies there are in a piece of text, the longer it takes to read. (JuSt thInK a bout how long It w o u l d tAKE you to rEa d this cHaPTer iF IT wAs fORmaTTeD like thIs.) It's therefore also important to use consistent names for variables. If you call something `maximum` in one place, don't call it `max_val` in another; if you use the name `max_val`, don't also use the name `maxVal`, and so on.

These rules are so crucial that many programming teams require members to follow a style guide for whatever language they're using, just as newspapers and book publishers specify how to capitalize headings and whether to use a comma before the last item in a list. In this book, we follow the PEP-8 Python style guide.[2]

You will also discover that lots of people have wasted many hours arguing over what the "best" style for code is. Some of your classmates (and your instructors) may have strong opinions about this as well. If they do, ask them what data they have to back up their beliefs. Strong opinions need strong evidence to be taken seriously.

The Object of This Chapter

In this chapter, you learned the following:

- An operating system is a program that manages your computer's hardware on behalf of other programs. An interpreter or virtual machine is a program that executes your code by translating it into instructions that the computer can understand and follow. The Python shell is an interpreter that reads your Python statements, executes them, and displays the results.
- Programs are made up of statements (instructions). These can be simple expressions like `3 + 4` and assignment statements like `celsius = 20` (which create new variables or change the values of existing ones). There are many other kinds of statements in Python, and we'll introduce them throughout the book.
- Every value in Python has a specific type, which determines what operations can be applied to it. The two types used to represent numbers are `int` and `float`. Floating-point numbers are approximations to real numbers.
- Python evaluates an expression by applying higher-precedence operators before lower-precedence operators. You can change that order by putting parentheses around subexpressions.
- Python stores every value in computer memory. A memory location containing a value is referred to as an object.
- Variables are created by executing assignment statements. If a variable already exists because of a previous assignment statement, Python will use that one instead of creating a new one.
- Variables contain memory addresses of values. We say that variables refer to values.
- Variables must be assigned values before they can be used in expressions.

---

2. https://peps.python.org/pep-0008/

Exercises

Here are some exercises for you to try on your own.

1. For each of the following expressions, what value will the expression give? Verify your answers by typing the expressions into Python.

   a. 9 - 3
   b. 8 * 2.5
   c. 9 / 2
   d. 9 / -2
   e. 9 // -2
   f. 9 % 2
   g. 9.0 % 2
   h. 9 % 2.0
   i. 9 % -2
   j. -9 % 2
   k. 9 / -2.0
   l. 4 + 3 * 5
   m. (4 + 3) * 5

2. Unary minus negates a number. Unary plus exists as well; for example, Python understands +5. If x has the value -17, what do you think +x should do? Should it leave the sign of the number alone? Should it act like absolute value, removing any negation? Use the Python shell to find out its behavior.

3. Write two assignment statements that do the following:

   a. Create a new variable, temp, and assign it the value 24.
   b. Convert the value in temp from Celsius to Fahrenheit by multiplying by 1.8 and adding 32; make temp refer to the resulting value.

   What is temp's new value?

4. For each of the following expressions, in which order are the subexpressions evaluated?

   a. 6 * 3 + 7 * 4
   b. 5 + 3 / 4
   c. 5 - 2 * 3 ** 4

5. a. Create a new variable x, and assign it the value 10.5.
   b. Create a new variable y, and assign it the value 4.
   c. Sum x and y, and make x refer to the resulting value. After this statement has been executed, what are the values of x and y?

6. Write a bullet list description of what happens when Python evaluates the statement `x += x - x` when `x` has the value `3`.
7. When a variable is used before it has been assigned a value, a `NameError` occurs. In the Python shell, write an expression that results in a `NameError`.
8. Which of the following expressions results in syntax errors?

   a. `6 * -----------8`
   b. `8 = people`
   c. `((((4 ** 3))))`
   d. `(-(-(-(-5))))`
   e. `4 += 7 / 2`

CHAPTER 3

Designing and Using Functions

People often perform the same kinds of tasks repeatedly, like converting temperatures or formatting text. To avoid duplicating code, programmers use *functions*: named chunks of code that can be reused whenever needed. Functions also help break complex code into smaller, more understandable pieces. In this chapter, you'll explore several *built-in* functions that come prepackaged with Python and learn how to define your own.

Functions That Python Provides

Python comes with many built-in functions that perform routine operations. One example is the abs function, which produces (*returns*) the absolute value of a number:

```
>>> abs
<built-in function abs>
>>> f = abs
>>> f
<built-in function abs>
>>> abs(-9)
9
>>> abs(3.3)
3.3
```

The first three statements demonstrate that abs (directly and via the variable f) is a function. The remaining two statements are a *function calls*.

Keep Your Shell Open

We recommend that you have IDLE (or any other Python IDE) open and try all the code under discussion; this is a good way to solidify your learning.

The general form of a function call is as follows:

«*function_name*»(«*arguments*»)

An *argument* is an expression that appears between the parentheses of a function call. In abs(-9), the argument is -9.

An argument is an expression that appears between the parentheses of a function call

Let's calculate the difference between the day and night temperatures, as might be seen on a weather report (a warm weather system moved in overnight):

```
>>> day_temperature = 3
>>> night_temperature = 10
>>> abs(day_temperature - night_temperature)
7
```

In this call of the function abs, the argument is day_temperature - night_temperature. Because day_temperature refers to 3 and night_temperature refers to 10, Python evaluates this expression to -7. This value is then *passed* to the abs function, which *returns* the value 7.

Here are the rules for executing a function call:

A function call is a command to execute a function

1. Evaluate each argument one at a time, working from left to right.
2. Pass the resulting values into the function.
3. Execute the function. When the function call finishes, it produces a value.

Because function calls produce values, they can be used in expressions:

```
>>> abs(-7) + abs(3.3)
10.3
```

You can also use function calls as arguments to other functions:

```
>>> pow(abs(-2), round(4.3))
16
```

Python sees the call on pow and starts by evaluating the arguments from left to right. The first argument is a call to the function abs, so Python executes it. The call abs(-2) produces 2, so that's the first value for the call on pow. Then Python executes round(4.3), which produces 4.

Now that the arguments to the pow function have been evaluated, Python finishes calling pow, passing in 2 and 4 as the argument values. That means that pow(abs(-2), round(4.3)) is equivalent to pow(2,4), and 2^4 is 16.

The diagram at the facing page shows the order in which Python evaluates the various pieces of this expression.

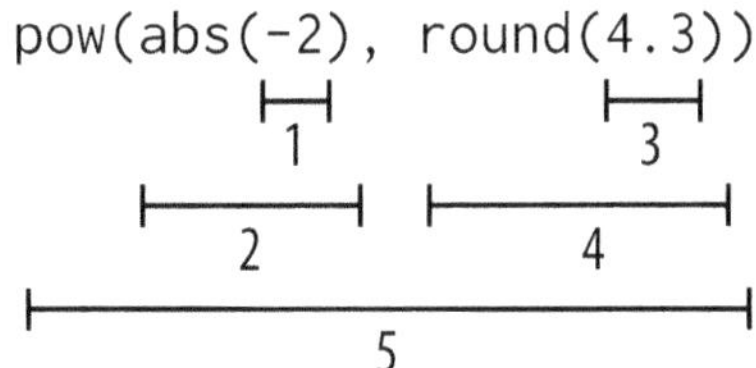

Each subexpression has been underlined and given a number to indicate when Python executes or evaluates that subexpression.

Some of the most useful built-in functions are used to convert between data types. Type names int and float can be used as functions:

```
>>> int(34.6)
34
>>> int(-4.3)
-4
>>> float(21)
21.0
```

In this example, you observe that when a floating-point number is converted to an integer, it is truncated, rather than rounded.

If you're not sure what a function does, try calling the built-in function help, which shows documentation for any function:

```
>>> help(abs)
Help on built-in function abs in module builtins:

abs(x, /)
    Return the absolute value of the argument.
```

The first line states which function is being described and to which *module* it belongs. Here, the module name is builtins. Modules are an organizational tool in Python and are discussed in Chapter 6, A Modular Approach, on page 105.

The rest of the output describes the function's functionality. The form of the function appears first: function abs expects one argument. (The / indicates that there are no more arguments.) After the form is an English description of what the function does when it is called.

Another built-in function is round, which rounds a floating-point number to the nearest integer:

```
>>> round(3.8)
4
>>> round(3.3)
3
```

```
>>> round(3.5)
4
>>> round(-3.3)
-3
>>> round(-3.5)
-4
```

What Is Banker's Rounding?

The built-in round function uses a method called banker's rounding. Instead of always rounding .5 up, it rounds to the nearest even number. For example:

```
>>> round(2.5)
2
>>> round(3.5)
4
```

Banker's rounding helps reduce rounding bias when you round lots of numbers. Always rounding .5 up would slightly inflate results over time, which matters in things like financial calculations and statistics.

The function round can be called with one or two arguments. If called with one, as you've been doing, it rounds to the nearest integer. If called with two, it rounds to a floating-point number, where the second argument indicates the precision:

```
>>> round(3.141592653, 2)
3.14
```

The documentation for round suggests that the second argument is optional, as indicated by its default value, None:

```
>>> help(round)
Help on built-in function round in module builtins:

round(number, ndigits=None)
    Round a number to a given precision in decimal digits.

    The return value is an integer if ndigits is omitted or None.  Otherwise
    the return value has the same type as the number. ndigits may be negative.
```

Let's explore the built-in function pow by starting with its help documentation:

```
>>> help(pow)
Help on built-in function pow in module builtins:

pow(base, exp, mod=None)
    Equivalent to base**exp with 2 arguments or base**exp % mod with 3 arguments

    Some types, such as ints, are able to use a more efficient algorithm when
    invoked using the three argument form.
```

The description demonstrates that the pow function can be called with either two or three arguments. The English description mentions that when called with two arguments, it is equivalent to x ** y, or x^y. Let's try it:

```
>>> pow(2, 4)
16
```

This call calculates 2^4. So far, so good. How about with three arguments?

```
>>> pow(2, 4, 3)
1
```

2^4 is 16, and evaluation of 16 % 3 produces 1.

Identities: How Python Keeps Track of Values

In Values, Variables, and Computer Memory, on page 17, you learned that Python stores each value in a separate object. Every object in Python is tracked by the system and can be distinguished from other objects, even if they hold the same value. This distinguishing feature is called the object's *identity*. An object's identity is usually related to its unique memory address, though it isn't guaranteed to be the actual address. You can find the identity of an object obj using the built-in function id:

```
>>> help(id)
Help on built-in function id in module builtins:

id(obj, /)
    Return the identity of an object.

    This is guaranteed to be unique among simultaneously existing objects.
    (CPython uses the object's memory address.)
```

How cool is that? Let's try it:

```
>>> id(-9)
140610723244688
>>> id(23.1)
140610725652592
>>> shoe_size = 8.5
>>> id(shoe_size)
140610727966896
>>> fahrenheit = 77.7
>>> id(fahrenheit)
140610725657616
```

The identities you get will likely be different from those listed here, as values are stored wherever there's free space available.

Functions (function objects) also have identities:

```
>>> id(abs)
139816718551376
>>> id(round)
139816718554336
```

Defining Custom Functions

The built-in functions are useful but generic. Often, there aren't built-in functions that do what you want, such as calculate mileage or play a game of cribbage. When you want functions to do these sorts of things, you have to write them yourself.

Because scientific work, international travel, and global communication often involve both Celsius and Fahrenheit temperature scales, it's helpful to have a quick way to convert between the two systems. Writing a conversion function makes these temperature conversions easier and more reliable, especially when they're needed repeatedly. It sure would be nice to be able to do this:

```
>>> convert_to_celsius(212)
100.0
>>> convert_to_celsius(78.8)
26.0
>>> convert_to_celsius(10.4)
-12.0
```

However, the function convert_to_celsius doesn't exist yet, so instead, you see this (focus only on the last line of the error message for now):

```
>>> convert_to_celsius(212)
Traceback (most recent call last):
  File "<python-input-0>", line 1, in <module>
    convert_to_celsius(212)
    ^^^^^^^^^^^^^^^^^^^^^^^
NameError: name 'convert_to_celsius' is not defined
```

To fix this, you have to write a *function definition* that tells Python what to do when the function is called.

You'll go over the syntax of function definitions soon, but let's start with an example:

```
>>> def convert_to_celsius(fahrenheit):
...     return (fahrenheit - 32) * 5 / 9
...
```

Python Reuses Small Numbers

Because small integers—up to about 250 or so, depending on the version of Python—are used so frequently, Python *interns* these values when it starts up: it creates them once and reuses the same objects whenever those values appear. Interning improves performance and reduces memory usage. The id function reveals this behavior by showing that repeated uses of the same small integer refer to the same object:

```
>>> i = 3
>>> j = 3
>>> k = 4 - 1
>>> id(i)
11576472
>>> id(j)
11576472
>>> id(k)
11576472
```

What that means is that variables i, j, and k refer to the same object. This phenomenon is called *aliasing*.

Larger integers and all floating-point values aren't necessarily interned:

```
>>> i = 30000000000
>>> j = 30000000000
>>> id(i)
139970772364592
>>> id(j)
39970772364496
>>> f = 0.0
>>> g = 0.0
>>> id(f)
139970777086128
>>> id(g)
139970774776848
```

Python decides for itself when to intern a value. The only reason you need to be aware of it is so that you aren't surprised when it happens; the output of your program is not affected by when Python decides to intern.

The *function body* is indented. Here, you indent four spaces, as the Python style guide recommends. If you forget to indent, you get an IndentationError:

```
>>> def convert_to_celsius(fahrenheit):
... return (fahrenheit - 32) * 5 / 9
...
  File "<python-input-1>", line 2
    return (fahrenheit - 32) * 5 / 9
    ^^^^^^
IndentationError: expected an indented block after function definition on line 1
```

Now that you've defined the function convert_to_celsius, your earlier function calls will work. You can even use the built-in function help on it:

```
>>> help(convert_to_celsius)
Help on function convert_to_celsius in module __main__:

convert_to_celsius(fahrenheit)
```

The output shows the first line of the function definition, which is referred to as the *function header*. (Later in this chapter, you'll see how to add more help documentation to a function.)

Here is a quick overview of how Python executes the following code:

```
>>> def convert_to_celsius(fahrenheit):
...     return (fahrenheit - 32) * 5 / 9
...
>>> convert_to_celsius(80)
26.666666666666668
```

1. Python executes the function definition, which creates the function object (but doesn't execute it yet).

2. Python creates a variable named convert_to_celsius whose value is the function definition.

A function definition introduces a new variable

3. Next, Python executes the function call convert_to_celsius(80). To do this, it assigns 80 to fahrenheit (which is a variable). For the duration of this function call, fahrenheit refers to 80.

4. Python now executes the return statement. The variable fahrenheit refers to 80, so the expression that appears after return is equivalent to (80 - 32) * 5 / 9. When Python evaluates that expression, 26.666666666666668 is produced. Use the word return to tell Python what value to produce as the result of the function call, so the result of calling convert_to_celsius(80) is 26.666666666666668.

The return statement determines the value produced as a result

5. Once Python has finished executing the function call, it returns to the place where the function was originally called.

Here is an image showing this sequence:

```
1 def convert_to_celsius(fahrenheit):
    3 return (fahrenheit - 32) * 5 / 9

2 convert_to_celsius(80)

4 (rest of program)
```

A function definition is a Python statement. The general form of a function definition is as follows:

```
def «function_name»(«parameters»):
    «body»
```

A parameter is a variable

The function header (that's the first line of the function definition) starts with def, followed by the name of the function, then a comma-separated list of *parameters* within parentheses, and then a colon. A parameter is a variable.

You can't have two functions with the same name in the same file; it isn't an error, but if you do it, the second function definition replaces the first one, much like assigning a value to a variable a second time replaces the first value.

Below the function header and indented (four spaces, as per Python's style guide) is a block of statements called the *function body*. The function body must contain at least one statement.

Most function definitions will include a return statement that, when executed, ends the function and produces a value. The general form of a return statement is as follows:

```
return «expression»
```

When Python executes a return statement, it evaluates the expression and then produces the result of that expression as the result of the function call.

Using Local Variables for Temporary Storage

Some computations are complex, and breaking them down into separate steps can lead to clearer code. In the following example, let's break down the evaluation of the quadratic polynomial $ax^2 + bx + c$ into several steps. Notice that all the statements inside the function are indented the same number of spaces to be aligned with each other. You can type this example into an editor first (without the leading >>> and ...) and then paste it into the Python shell. That makes fixing mistakes much easier:

```
>>> def quadratic(a, b, c, x):
...     first = a * x ** 2
...     second = b * x
...     third = c
...     return first + second + third
...
>>> quadratic(2, 3, 4, 0.5)
6.0
>>> quadratic(2, 3, 4, 1.5)
13.0
```

Keywords Are Words That Are Special to Python

Keywords are words that Python reserves for its use. You can't use them except as Python intends. Two of them are def and return. If you try to use them as either variable names or as function names (or anything else), Python produces an error:

```
>>> def = 3
  File "<python-input-0>", line 1
    def = 3
        ^
SyntaxError: invalid syntax
>>> def return(x):
  File "<python-input-1>", line 1
    def return(x):
        ^^^^^^
SyntaxError: invalid syntax
```

Here is a complete list of Python keywords (you'll see most of them in this book):

```
False     assert    continue  except    if        nonlocal    return
None      async     def       finally   import    not         try
True      await     del       for       in        or          while
and       break     elif      from      is        pass        with
as        class     else      global    lambda    raise       yield
```

A local variable is used within a function definition

Variables like first, second, and third that are created within a function are referred to as *local variables*. Local variables get created each time that function is called, and they are erased when the function returns. Because they only exist when the function is being executed, they can't be used outside of the function. Trying to access a local variable from outside the function is an error, just like trying to access a variable that has never been defined is an error:

```
>>> quadratic(2, 3, 4, 1.3)
11.280000000000001
>>> first
Traceback (most recent call last):
  File "<python-input-2>", line 1, in <module>
    first
NameError: name 'first' is not defined. Did you mean: 'list'?
```

A function's parameters are also local variables (assigned the argument values), so you get the same error if you try to use them outside of a function definition:

```
>>> a
Traceback (most recent call last):
  File "<python-input-3>", line 1, in <module>
    a
NameError: name 'a' is not defined
```

The part of a program in which a variable can be used is called the variable's *scope*. The scope of a local variable is from the line on which it is defined up until the end of the function.

As you might expect, if a function is defined to take a certain number of parameters, a call to that function must have the same number of arguments:

```
>>> quadratic(1, 2, 3)
Traceback (most recent call last):
  File "<python-input-1>", line 1, in <module>
    quadratic(1, 2, 3)
    ~~~~~~~~~^^^^^^^^^
TypeError: quadratic() missing 1 required positional argument: 'x'
```

A "positional argument" mentioned above is an argument that is referred to by its position on the list (such as "the first" or "the second"), as opposed to keyword arguments known by their names (see Printing Information, on page 73). Remember that you can use the built-in function help to find out information about a function's parameters.

Tracing Function Calls in the Memory Model

Read the following code. Can you predict what it will do when you run it?

```
>>> def f(x):
...     x = 2 * x
...     return x
...
>>> x = 1
>>> x = f(x + 1) + f(x + 2)
```

That code is confusing, mainly because the variable x is used repeatedly throughout the code. However, it *is* short and only uses Python features that you have seen so far: assignment statements, expressions, function definitions, and function calls. You're missing some information: Are all the x's the same variable? Does Python make a new x for each assignment? For each function call? For each function definition?

Here's the answer: whenever Python executes a function call, it creates a *namespace* (literally, a space for names) for the local variables for that call. You can think of a namespace as a scrap piece of paper; Python writes down the local variables on that piece of paper, keeps track of them as long as the function is being executed, and throws that paper away when the function returns.

Separately, Python keeps another namespace for the variables created in the shell. The variable x, which is a parameter of the function f, is a different variable from the x in the shell!

Let's refine your rules from Functions That Python Provides, on page 31, for executing a function call to include this namespace creation:

1. Evaluate the arguments left to right.
2. Create a namespace to hold the function call's local variables, including the parameters.
3. Pass the resulting argument values into the function by assigning them to the parameters.
4. Execute the function body. As before, when a return statement is executed, execution of the body terminates, and the value of the expression in the return statement is used as the value of the function call.

From now on, in the memory model, we will draw a separate box for each namespace to indicate that the variables inside it are in a separate area of computer memory. Programmers refer to this box as a *frame*. We separate the frames from the objects by a vertical dotted line:

Frames	**Objects**
Frames for namespaces go here	*Objects go here*

Using your newfound knowledge, let's trace that confusing code. Initially, no variables have been created; Python is about to execute the function definition. We have indicated this with an arrow:

```
➤ >>> def f(x):
  ...     x = 2 * x
  ...     return x
  ...
  >>> x = 1
  >>> x = f(x + 1) + f(x + 2)
```

As you've seen in this chapter, when Python executes that function definition, it creates a variable f in the frame for the shell's namespace plus a function object. (Python didn't execute the body of the function; that won't happen until the function is called.) Here is the result:

Reusing Variable Names Is Common

Using the same name for local variables in different functions is a common practice. For example, consider a program that handles distances—converting from meters to other units of distance, such as miles. In that program, there would be several functions that all deal with these distances, and it would be entirely reasonable to use meters as a parameter name in many different functions.

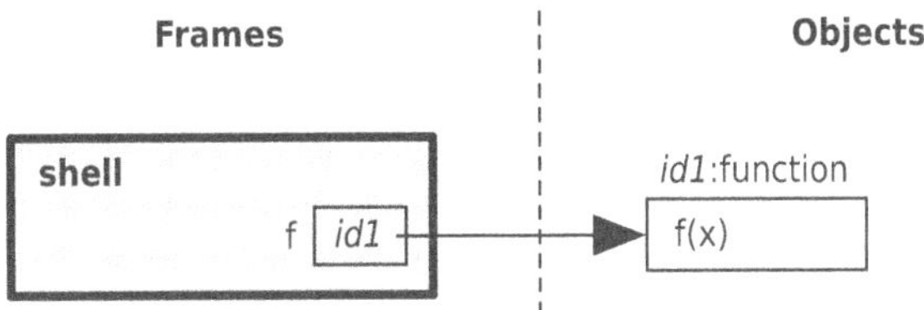

Now let's execute the first assignment to x in the shell.

```
>>> def f(x):
...     x = 2 * x
...     return x
...
>>> x = 1
>>> x = f(x + 1) + f(x + 2)
```

Once that assignment happens, both f and x are in the frame for the shell:

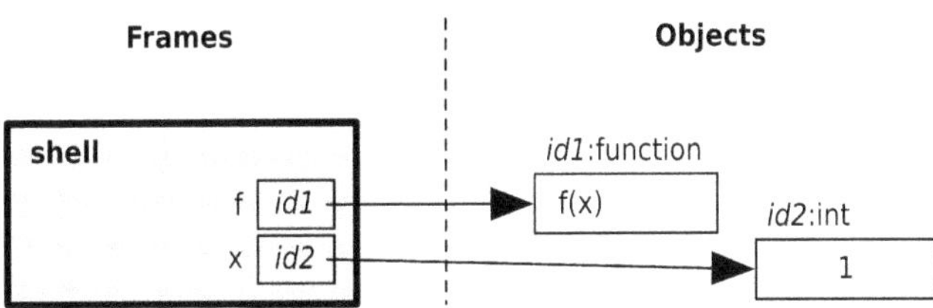

Now you are about to execute the second assignment to x in the shell:

```
>>> def f(x):
...     x = 2 * x
...     return x
...
>>> x = 1
>>> x = f(x + 1) + f(x + 2)
```

Following the rules for executing an assignment from Assignment Statement, on page 18, you first evaluate the expression on the RHS, which is f(x + 1) + f(x + 2). Python evaluates the left function call first: f(x+1).

Following the rules for executing a function call, Python evaluates the argument, x + 1. To find the value for x, Python looks in the current frame. The current frame is the frame for the shell, and its variable x refers to 1, so x + 1 evaluates to 2.

Now you have evaluated the argument to f. The next step is to create a namespace for the function call. We draw a frame, write in parameter x, and assign 2 to that parameter. This is shown in the diagram at the top of the next page.

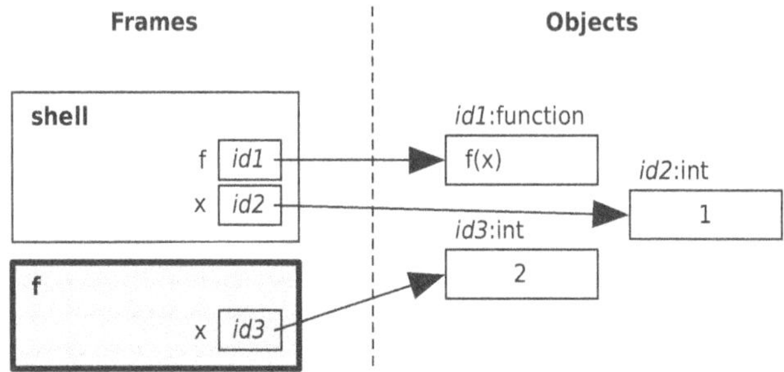

Notice that there are two variables called x, and they refer to different values. Python will always look in the current frame, which we will draw with a thicker border.

You are now about to execute the first statement of the function f:

```
>>> def f(x):
...     x = 2 * x
...     return x
...
>>> x = 1
>>> x = f(x + 1) + f(x + 2)
```

x = 2 * x is an assignment statement. The RHS is the expression 2 * x. Python looks up the value of x in the current frame and finds 2, so that the expression evaluates to 4. Python finishes executing that assignment statement by making x refer to that 4:

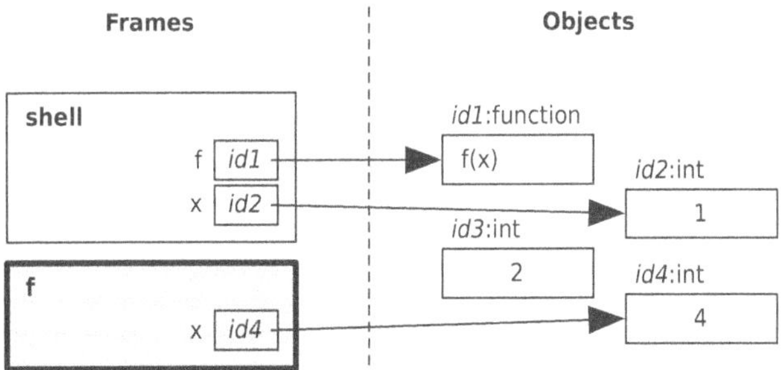

You are now about to execute the second statement of the function f, a return statement:

```
>>> def f(x):
...     x = 2 * x
...     return x
...
>>> x = 1
>>> x = f(x + 1) + f(x + 2)
```

You evaluate the expression, which is simply x. Python looks up the value for x in the current frame and finds 4, so that is the return value:

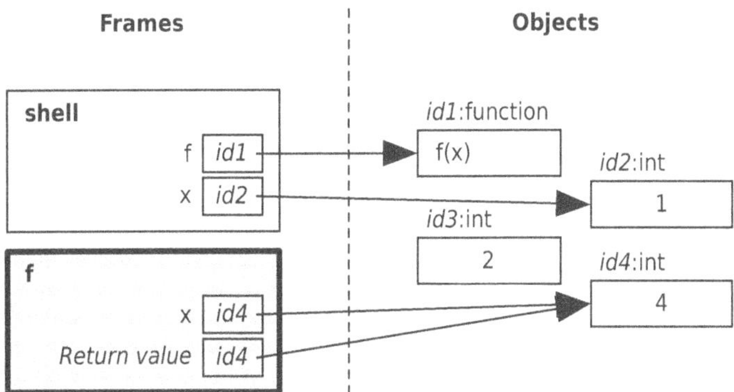

When the function returns, Python evaluates this expression: f(x + 1) + f(x + 2). Python just finished executing f(x + 1), which produced the value 4. It then executes the right function call: f(x + 2).

Following the rules for executing a function call, Python evaluates the argument, x + 2. To find the value for x, Python searches the current frame. The call to function f has returned, so that frame is erased. The only frame left is the frame for the shell, and its variable x still refers to 1; therefore, x + 2 evaluates to 3.

Now you have evaluated the argument to f. The next step is to create a namespace for the function call. We draw a frame, write in the parameter x, and assign 3 to that parameter:

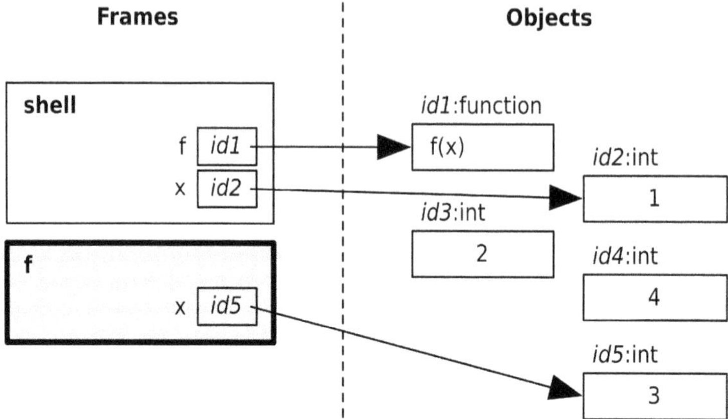

Again, you have two variables called x.

You are now about to execute the first statement of the function f:

```
>>> def f(x):
...     x = 2 * x
...     return x
...
>>> x = 1
>>> x = f(x + 1) + f(x + 2)
```

x = 2 * x is an assignment statement. The right side is the expression 2 * x. Python looks up the value of x in the current frame and finds 3, so that expression evaluates to 6. Python finished executing that assignment statement by assigning 6 to x:

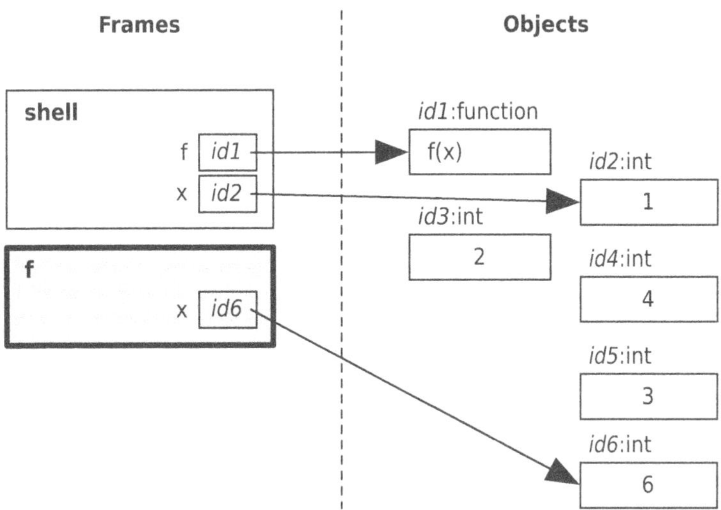

You are now about to execute the second statement of the function f, a return statement:

```
>>> def f(x):
...     x = 2 * x
...     return x
...
>>> x = 1
>>> x = f(x + 1) + f(x + 2)
```

You evaluate the expression, which is simply x. Python looks up the value for x in the current frame and finds 6, so that is the return value (as shown in the figure on page 48).

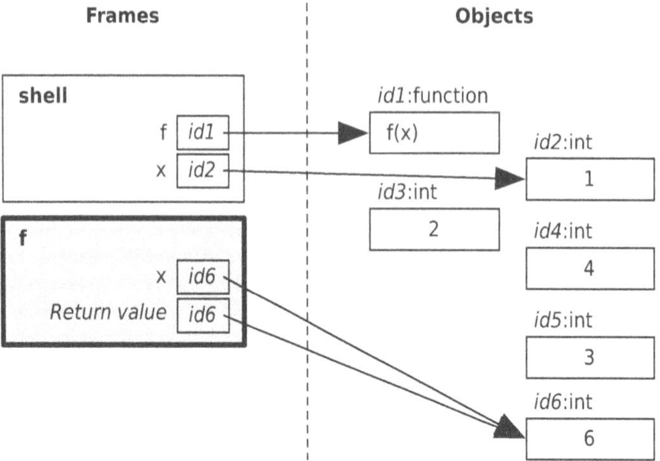

When the function returns, Python evaluates this expression: f(x + 1) + f(x + 2). Python just finished executing f(x + 2), which produced the value 6. Both function calls have been executed, so Python applies the + operator to 4 and 6, giving you 10.

You have now evaluated the right side of the assignment statement; Python completes it by making the variable on the LHS, x, refer to 10. You'll find the diagram at the top of the next page.

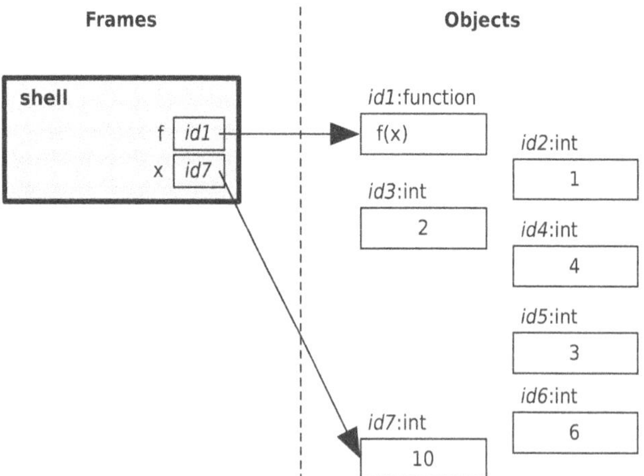

Phew! That's a lot to keep track of. Python does all that bookkeeping for you, but to become a good programmer, it's essential to understand each step.

Designing New Functions: A Recipe

Writing a good essay requires planning: deciding on a topic, learning the background material, writing an outline, and then filling in the outline until you're done.

Similarly, writing a good function also requires planning. You have an idea of what you want the function to do, but you need to decide on the details. *Every time you write a function, you need to figure out the answers to the following questions:*

- What do you name the function?
- What are the parameters, and what types of information do they refer to?
- What calculations are you doing with that information?
- What information does the function return?
- Does it work like you expect it to?

The function design recipe helps you find answers to all these questions.

This section describes a step-by-step recipe for designing and writing a function. Part of the outcome will be a working function, but equally importantal is the *documentation* for the function. Python uses three double quotation marks to start and end a special kind of note called a *docstring*, short for *documentation string*. A docstring must appear as the first unassigned object inside a function. It's meant for people reading the code, explaining what the function or component does. Python saves the docstring so it can be shown later using tools like help.

Here is an example of a completed function. We'll show you how we came up with this using a function design recipe (FDR), but it helps to see a completed example first:

```
>>> def days_difference(day1: int, day2: int) -> int:
...     """Return the number of days between day1 and day2, which are
...     both in the range 1-365 (thus indicating the day of the
...     year).
...
...     >>> days_difference(200, 224)
...     24
...     >>> days_difference(50, 50)
...     0
...     >>> days_difference(100, 99)
...     -1
...     """
...     return day2 - day1
...
```

Here are the parts of the function, including the docstring:

- The first line is the function header. We have annotated the parameters with the types of information that we expect to be passed to them (you expect both day1 and day2 to refer to values of type int), and the int after the -> is the type of value you expect the function to return. These *type annotations* are optional in Python, but will will use them throughout the book.
- The second line has three double quotes to start the docstring, which begins with a description of what the function will do when it is called. The description mentions both parameters and describes what the function returns.
- Next are some example calls and return values as you would expect to see in the Python shell. (We chose the first example because that made day1 smaller than day2, the second example because the two days are equal, and the third example because that made day1 bigger than day2.) The examples are still part of the docstring.
- Next are three double quotes to end the docstring.
- The last line is the body of the function.

There are five steps to the design recipe for functions. It may seem like much work at first, and you will often be able to write a function without rigidly following these steps, but this recipe can save you hours when you're working on more complicated functions.

1. *Examples.* The first step is to figure out what name you want to give to your function, what arguments it should require, and what information it will return. This name is often a short answer to the question, "What does your function do?" Type a couple of example calls and return values.

   Let's start with the examples because they're the easiest: before you write *anything*, you need to decide what information you have (the argument values) and what information you want the function to produce (the return value). Here are the examples from days_difference:

   ```
   ...     >>> days_difference(200, 224)
   ...     24
   ...     >>> days_difference(50, 50)
   ...     0
   ...     >>> days_difference(100, 99)
   ...     -1
   ```

2. *Header.* The second step is to decide on the parameter names, parameter types, and return type, and write the function header. Pick meaningful

parameter names to make it easy for other programmers to understand what information to give to your function. Include type annotations: Are you giving it integers? Floating-point numbers? Maybe both? You'll see a lot of other types in the upcoming chapters, so practicing this step now, while you have only a few choices, will help you later. If the answer is, "Both integers and floating-point numbers," then use float because integers are a subset of floating-point numbers.

Also, what type of value is returned? An integer, a floating-point number, or possibly either one of them?

The parameter types and return type form a *type contract* because the claim is that if you call this function with the correct types of values, you'll return the correct type of value. (We're not saying anything about what will happen if you get the *wrong* kind of values.)

Here is the header from days_difference:

```
>>> def days_difference(day1: int, day2: int) -> int:
```

3. *Description.* Write a short paragraph describing your function: this is what other programmers will read to understand what your function does, so it's essential to practice this! Mention every parameter in your description and describe the return value. Here is the description from days_difference:

```
...     """Return the number of days between day1 and day2, which are
...     both in the range 1-365 (thus indicating the day of the
...     year).
```

4. *Body.* By now, you should have a good idea of what you need to do to get your function to behave appropriately. It's time to write some code! Here is the body from days_difference:

```
...     return day2 - day1
```

5. *Test.* Run the examples to make sure your function body is correct. Add more example calls if you need. For days_difference, you copy and paste your examples into the shell and compare the results to what you expected:

```
>>> days_difference(200, 224)
24
>>> days_difference(50, 50)
0
>>> days_difference(100, 99)
-1
```

We will cover testing in detail in Chapter 15, Testing and Debugging, on page 309.

Designing Three Birthday-Related Functions

You'll now apply your function design recipe to solve this problem: Which day of the week will a birthday fall on, given what day of the week it is today and what day of the year the birthday is on? For example, if today is the third day of the year and it's a Thursday, and a birthday is on the 116th day of the year, what day of the week will it be on that birthday?

You'll design three functions that together will help you perform this calculation. You'll write them in the same file. Until you get to Chapter 6, A Modular Approach, on page 105, you'll need to put functions that you write in the same file if you want to be able to have them call one another.

Let's represent the day of the week using 1 for Sunday, 2 for Monday, and so on:

Day of the Week	Number	Day of the Week	Number
Sunday	1	Thursday	5
Monday	2	Friday	6
Tuesday	3	Saturday	7
Wednesday	4		

These numbers are used simply because you don't yet have the tools to easily convert between days of the week and their corresponding numbers. You'll have to do that translation in your head.

For the same reason, let's also ignore months and use the numbers 1 through 365 to indicate the day of the year. For example, you'll represent February 1st as 32, since it's the thirty-second day of the year.

How Many Days Difference?

You'll start by exploring how you arrived at the function days_difference. Here are the steps of the function design recipe. Try following along in the Python shell.

1. *Examples.* You want a clear name for the difference in days; let's use days_difference. In your examples, you want to call this function and state what it returns. If you want to know how many days there are between the 200th day of the year and the 224th day, you can hope that this will happen:

```
...     >>> days_difference(200, 224)
...     24
```

What are the special cases? For example, what if the two days are the same? How about if the second one is before the first?

```
...       >>> days_difference(50, 50)
...       0
...       >>> days_difference(100, 99)
...       -1
```

Now that you have a few examples, you can move on to the next step.

2. *Header.* You have a couple of example calls. The arguments in your function call examples are all integers, and the return values are integers as well, which provides you with the type contract. In the examples, both arguments represent a number of days, so you'll name them day1 and day2:

```
>>> def days_difference(day1: int, day2: int) -> int:
```

3. *Description.* You'll now describe what a call on the function will do. Because the documentation should thoroughly describe the function's behavior, you need to ensure that it's clear what the parameters mean:

```
...       """Return the number of days between day1 and day2, which are
...       both in the range 1-365 (thus indicating the day of the
...       year).
```

4. *Body.* You've laid everything out. Looking at the examples, you see that you can implement this using subtraction. Here is the whole function again, including the body:

```
>>> def days_difference(day1: int, day2: int) -> int:
...       """Return the number of days between day1 and day2, which are
...       both in the range 1-365 (thus indicating the day of the
...       year).
...
...       >>> days_difference(200, 224)
...       24
...       >>> days_difference(50, 50)
...       0
...       >>> days_difference(100, 99)
...       -1
...       """
...       return day2 - day1
...
```

5. *Test.* To test it, start the Python shell and copy and paste the calls into it, checking that you get back what you expect:

```
>>> days_difference(200, 224)
24
```

```
>>> days_difference(50, 50)
0
>>> days_difference(100, 99)
-1
```

Here's something cool. Now that you have a function with a docstring, you can use the help function to display its documentation:

```
>>> help(days_difference)
Help on function days_difference in module __main__:

days_difference(day1:int, day2:int) -> int
    Return the number of days between day1 and day2, which are both
    in the range 1-365 (thus indicating the day of the year).

    >>> days_difference(200, 224)
    24
    >>> days_difference(50, 50)
    0
    >>> days_difference(100, 99)
    -1
```

What Day Will It Be in the Future?

It will help your birthday calculations if you write a function to calculate its day of the week given the current weekday and the number of days ahead you're interested in. Remember that you're using the numbers 1 through 7 to represent Sunday through Saturday.

Again, follow the function design recipe:

1. *Examples.* You want a short name for calculating what weekday it'll be in the future. You could choose something like which_weekday or what_day; let's use get_weekday. There are lots of choices.

   Start with an example that asks what day it will be if today is Tuesday (day 3 of the week) and you want to know what tomorrow will be (1 day ahead):

   ```
   >>> get_weekday(3, 1)
   4
   ```

   Whenever you have a function that should return a value in a particular range, you should write example calls where you expect either end of that range as a result.

   What if it's Friday (day 6)? If you ask what day it will be tomorrow, you expect to get Saturday (day 7):

   ```
   >>> get_weekday(6, 1)
   7
   ```

What if it's Saturday (day 7)? If you ask what day it will be tomorrow, you expect to get Sunday (day 1):

```
>>> get_weekday(7, 1)
1
```

Also try asking about 0 days in the future, as well as a week ahead; both of these cases should return the day of the week you started with:

```
>>> get_weekday(1, 0)
1
>>> get_weekday(4, 7)
4
```

Let's also try 10 weeks and 2 days in the future, so you have a case where there are several intervening weeks:

```
>>> get_weekday(7, 72)
2
```

2. *Header.* In your example calls, the arguments are all integers, and the return values are integers as well, which provides your type contract.

   The first argument is the current day of the week, so name it current_weekday. The second argument is the number of days to calculate from the current date. Pick the name days_ahead, although days_from_now would also be fine:

   ```
   >>> def get_weekday(current_weekday: int, days_ahead: int) -> int:
   ```

3. *Description.* You need a comprehensive description of what this function will accomplish. Start with a sentence describing what the function does, and then explain the meaning of the parameters:

   ```
   ...     """Return which day of the week it will be days_ahead days
   ...     from current_weekday.
   ...
   ...     current_weekday is the current day of the week and is in
   ...     the range 1-7, indicating whether today is Sunday (1),
   ...     Monday (2), ..., Saturday (7).
   ...
   ...     days_ahead is the number of days after today.
   ```

   Notice that your first sentence uses both parameters and also describes what the function will return.

4. *Body.* Looking at the examples, you see that you can solve the first example by returning the current weekday plus the number of days ahead: return current_weekday + days_ahead. That, however, won't work for all of the examples; you need to wrap around from day 7 (Saturday) back to day 1 (Sunday). When you have this kind of wraparound, the

remainder operator (%) usually comes in handy. Notice that evaluation of (7 + 1) % 7 produces 1, (7 + 2) % 7 produces 2, and so on.

Let's try taking the remainder of the sum: return current_weekday + days_ahead % 7. Here is the entire function again, including the body:

```
>>> def get_weekday(current_weekday: int, days_ahead: int) -> int:
...     """Return which day of the week it will be days_ahead days from
...     current_weekday.
...
...     current_weekday is the current day of the week and is in the
...     range 1-7, indicating whether today is Sunday (1), Monday (2),
...     ..., Saturday (7).
...
...     days_ahead is the number of days after today.
...
...     >>> get_weekday(3, 1)
...     4
...     >>> get_weekday(6, 1)
...     7
...     >>> get_weekday(7, 1)
...     1
...     >>> get_weekday(1, 0)
...     1
...     >>> get_weekday(4, 7)
...     4
...     >>> get_weekday(7, 72)
...     2
...     """
...     return current_weekday + days_ahead % 7
...
```

5. *Test.* To test it, start the Python shell and copy and paste the calls into it, checking that you get back what you expect:

```
>>> get_weekday(3, 1)
4
>>> get_weekday(6, 1)
7
>>> get_weekday(7, 1)
8
```

Wait, that's not right. You expected a 1 in that third example, not an 8, because 8 isn't a valid number for a day of the week. You should have wrapped around to 1.

Taking another look at your function body, you see that because % has higher precedence than +, you need parentheses to ensure the correct evaluation:

```
>>> def get_weekday(current_weekday: int, days_ahead: int) -> int:
...     """Return which day of the week it will be days_ahead days
...     from current_weekday.
...
...     current_weekday is the current day of the week and is in
...     the range 1-7, indicating whether today is Sunday (1),
...     Monday (2), ..., Saturday (7).
...
...     days_ahead is the number of days after today.
...
...     >>> get_weekday(3, 1)
...     4
...     >>> get_weekday(6, 1)
...     7
...     >>> get_weekday(7, 1)
...     1
...     >>> get_weekday(1, 0)
...     1
...     >>> get_weekday(4, 7)
...     4
...     >>> get_weekday(7, 72)
...     2
...     """
...     return (current_weekday + days_ahead) % 7
...
```

Testing again, you know that you've fixed that bug in your code, but now you're getting the wrong answer for the second test!

```
>>> get_weekday(3, 1)
4
>>> get_weekday(6, 1)
0
>>> get_weekday(7, 1)
1
```

The problem here is that when `current_weekday + days_ahead` evaluates to a multiple of 7, then `(current_weekday + days_ahead) % 7` will evaluate to 0, not 7. All the other results work well; it's just that pesky 7.

Because you want a number in the range 1 through 7, but you're getting an answer in the range 0 through 6, and all the answers are correct except that you're seeing a 0 instead of a 7, you can use this trick:

a. Subtract 1 from the expression: `current_weekday + days_ahead - 1`.

b. Take the remainder.

c. Add 1 to the entire result: `(current_weekday + days_ahead - 1) % 7 + 1`.

Let's test it again:

```
>>> get_weekday(3, 1)
4
>>> get_weekday(6, 1)
7
>>> get_weekday(7, 1)
1
>>> get_weekday(1, 0)
1
>>> get_weekday(4, 7)
4
>>> get_weekday(7, 72)
2
```

You've passed all the tests, so you can now move on.

What Day Is My Birthday On?

You now have two functions related to day-of-year calculations. One of them calculates the difference between two days of the year. The other calculates the weekday for a future day given the weekday of the current day. You can use these two functions to determine the day of the week a birthday falls on, given the current day of the week, the current day of the year, and the day of the year the birthday occurs. Again, follow the function design recipe:

1. *Examples.* You want a name for what it means to calculate what weekday a birthday will fall on. Once more, there are lots of choices; use get_birthday_weekday.

   If today is a Thursday (day 5 of the week), and today is the third day of the year, what day will it be on the fourth day of the year? Hopefully Friday:

   ```
   >>> get_birthday_weekday(5, 3, 4)
   6
   ```

   What if it's the same day (Thursday, the 3rd day of the year), but the birthday is the 116th day of the year? For now, you can verify externally (looking at a calendar) that it turns out to be a Friday.

   ```
   >>> get_birthday_weekday(5, 3, 116)
   6
   ```

   What if today is Friday, April 26, the 116th day of the year, but the birthday you want is the 3rd day of the year? This scenario is interesting because the birthday is a couple of months before the current day:

   ```
   >>> get_birthday_weekday(6, 116, 3)
   5
   ```

2. *Header.* In your example calls, the arguments are all integers, and the return values are integers as well, which provides your type contract. If you're satisfied with the function name, stick with it.

   The first argument is the current day of the week, so use current_weekday, as you did for the previous function. (It's a good idea to be consistent with naming when possible.) The second argument is the current day of the year, which you'll use as current_day. The third argument is the day of the year the birthday falls on, and you'll use birthday_day:

```
>>> def get_birthday_weekday(current_weekday: int, current_day: int,
...                          birthday_day: int) -> int:
```

3. *Description.* You need a comprehensive description of what this function will accomplish. Start with a sentence describing what the function does, and then explain the meaning of the parameters:

```
...     """Return the day of the week it will be on birthday_day,
...     given that the day of the week is current_weekday and the
...     day of the year is current_day.
...
...     current_weekday is the current day of the week and is in
...     the range 1-7, indicating whether today is Sunday (1),
...     Monday (2), ..., Saturday (7).
...
...     current_day and birthday_day are both in the range 1-365.
```

   Again, notice that your first sentence uses all parameters and also describes what the function will return. If it gets more complicated, start writing multiple sentences to tell what the function does, but you managed to fit it in here.

4. *Body.* It's time to write the body of the function. You have a puzzle:

   a. Using days_difference, you can figure out how many days there are between two days.

      Using get_weekday, you can determine the day of the week it will be given the current day of the week and the number of days away.

   Start by figuring out how many days from now the birthday falls:

```
...     days_diff = days_difference(current_day, birthday_day)
```

   Now that you know this, you can use it to solve your problem: given the current weekday and the number of days ahead, you can call the function get_weekday to get your answer:

```
...     return get_weekday(current_weekday, days_diff)
```

Let's put it all together:

```
>>> def get_birthday_weekday(current_weekday: int, current_day: int,
...                          birthday_day: int) -> int:
...     """Return the day of the week it will be on birthday_day,
...     given that the day of the week is current_weekday and the
...     day of the year is current_day.
...
...     current_weekday is the current day of the week and is in
...     the range 1-7, indicating whether today is Sunday (1),
...     Monday (2), ..., Saturday (7).
...
...     current_day and birthday_day are both in the range 1-365.
...
...     >>> get_birthday_weekday(5, 3, 4)
...     6
...     >>> get_birthday_weekday(5, 3, 116)
...     6
...     >>> get_birthday_weekday(6, 116, 3)
...     5
...     """
...     days_diff = days_difference(current_day, birthday_day)
...     return get_weekday(current_weekday, days_diff)
...
```

5. *Test.* To test it, fire up the Python shell and copy and paste the calls into the shell, checking that you get back what you expect:

```
>>> get_birthday_weekday(5, 3, 4)
6
>>> get_birthday_weekday(5, 3, 116)
6
>>> get_birthday_weekday(6, 116, 3)
5
```

And you're done!

Writing and Running a Program

So far, you have used the shell to investigate Python. As you have seen, the shell displays the result of evaluating an expression:

```
>>> 3 + 5 / abs(-2)
5.5
```

In a program that is supposed to interact with a human, showing the result of every expression is probably not desirable behavior. (Imagine if your web browser showed you the result of every calculation it performed.)

How Does a Computer Run a Python Program?, on page 7, explained that to save code for later use, you can put it in a file with a .py extension. You can then tell the Python interpreter to run the code in that file rather than type commands in at the interactive prompt.

Here is a program that was written using IDLE and saved in a file called temperature.py. This program consists of a function definition for convert_to_celsius (from earlier in the chapter) and three calls to that function, which convert three different Fahrenheit temperatures to their Celsius equivalents.

```
def convert_to_celsius(fahrenheit: float) -> float:
    """Return the number of Celsius degrees equivalent to fahrenheit degrees.

    >>> convert_to_celsius(75)
    23.88888888888889
    """

    return (fahrenheit - 32.0) * 5.0 / 9.0

convert_to_celsius(80)
convert_to_celsius(78.8)
convert_to_celsius(10.4)
```

Notice that there is no >>> prompt. This never appears in a Python program; it is used exclusively in the shell.

To run the program in IDLE, select Run→Run Module. IDLE will open the Python shell and show the results of running the program. Here is the result. (The line containing RESTART is letting you know that the shell has restarted, wiping out any previous work done in the shell.)

```
Python 3.14.0b4 (main, Jul  9 2025, 09:00:21) [GCC 11.4.0] on linux
Enter "help" below or click "Help" above for more information.
>>>
===================== RESTART; /tmp/temperature_program.py ==================
>>>
```

Notice that no values are shown, unlike in Defining Custom Functions, on page 36, when you typed the equivalent code into the shell. To have a program print the value of an expression, use the built-in function print. Here is the same program, but with calls to the print function.

```
def convert_to_celsius(fahrenheit: float) -> float:
    """Return the number of Celsius degrees equivalent to fahrenheit
    degrees.

    >>> convert_to_celsius(75)
    23.88888888888889
    """

    return (fahrenheit - 32.0) * 5.0 / 9.0
```

```
print(convert_to_celsius(80))
print(convert_to_celsius(78.8))
print(convert_to_celsius(10.4))
```

And here is what happens when you run this program:

```
Python 3.14.0b4 (main, Jul  9 2025, 09:00:21) [GCC 11.4.0] on linux
Enter "help" below or click "Help" above for more information.
>>>
===================== RESTART; /tmp/temperature_program.py ===================
26.666666666666668
26.0
-12.0
>>>
```

Omitting a return Statement: None

If you don't have a return statement in a function, nothing is produced:

```
>>> def f(x):
...     x = 2 * x
...
>>> res = f(3)
>>> res
>>>
```

Wait, that can't be right—if res doesn't have a value, shouldn't you get a NameError? Let's investigate:

```
>>> print(res)
None
>>> id(res)
11330272
```

Variable res has a value: it's None! And None has an identity. If you don't have a return statement in your function, your function will return None. You can return None yourself if you like:

```
>>> def f(x):
...     x = 2 * x
...     return None
...
>>> print(f(3))
None
```

The value None is used to signal the absence of a value. You'll see some uses for it later in the book.

Dealing with Situations That Your Code Doesn't Handle

You'll often write a function that works only in some situations. For example, you might write a function that takes as a parameter the number of people who want to eat a pie and returns the percentage of the pie that each person gets to eat. If there are five people, each person gets 20% of the pie; if there are two people, each person gets 50%; if there is one person, that person gets 100%; but if there are zero people, what should the answer be?

Here is an implementation of this function:

```
def pie_percent(n: int) -> int:
    """Return the percentage of a pie that each person gets to eat if n
    people are sharing the pie.

    >>> pie_percent(5)
    20
    >>> pie_percent(2)
    50
    >>> pie_percent(1)
    100
    """

    return int(100 / n)
```

Reading the code, if someone calls pie_percent(0), then this will result in a ZeroDivisionError. There isn't anything that anyone can do about this situation; there isn't a sensible answer.

As a programmer, you warn other people about situations that your function isn't set up to handle by describing your assumptions in a *precondition*. Here is the same function with a precondition:

```
def pie_percent(n: int) -> int:
    """Assuming there are n people who want to eat a pie, return the
    percentage of the pie that each person gets to eat.

    Precondition: n > 0

    >>> pie_percent(5)
    20
    >>> pie_percent(2)
    50
    >>> pie_percent(1)
    100
    """

    return int(100 / n)
```

Whenever you write a function and you've assumed something about the parameter values, write a precondition that lets other programmers know your assumptions. If they ignore your warning and call it with invalid values, the fault does not lie with you!

If your function expects certain parameter values, add a precondition to warn others

Enforcing Preconditions Using Assertions

You can also use the assert statement to enforce preconditions during development. If the condition you provide is false, Python will stop the program and display an error message (AssertionError). Assertions are useful for catching mistakes early, especially when you want to make sure a function's input meets specific requirements. For example, you can write:

```
assert temperature >= 0
```

This statement ensures a value isn't below freezing. Assertions are mainly used during development and testing, not in code meant for everyday users, because they can be turned off when Python runs in optimized mode.

What Did You Call That?

- A function definition introduces a new variable that refers to a function object. The return statement describes the value that will be produced as a result of the function when the function is done being executed.
- A parameter is a variable that appears between the parentheses of a function header.
- A local variable is a variable that is used in a function definition to store an intermediate result to make code easier to write and read.
- A function call tells Python to execute a function.
- An argument is an expression that appears between the parentheses of a function call. The value that is produced when Python evaluates the expression is assigned to the corresponding parameter.
- If you made assumptions about the values of parameters, or you know that your function won't work with particular values, write a precondition to warn other programmers.

Exercises

Here are some exercises for you to try on your own.

1. Two of Python's built-in functions are `min` and `max`. In the Python shell, execute the following function calls:

   a. `min(2, 3, 4)`
   b. `max(2, -3, 4, 7, -5)`
   c. `max(2, -3, min(4, 7), -5)`

2. For the following function calls, in what order are the subexpressions evaluated?

   a. `min(max(3, 4), abs(-5))`
   b. `abs(min(4, 6, max(2, 8)))`
   c. `round(max(5.572, 3.258), abs(-2))`

3. Following the function design recipe, define a function that has one parameter, a number, and returns that number tripled.

4. Following the function design recipe, define a function that has two parameters, both of which are numbers, and returns the absolute value of the difference of the two. Hint: Call the built-in function `abs`.

5. Following the function design recipe, define a function that has one parameter, a distance in kilometers, and returns the distance in miles. (There are 1.6 kilometers per mile.)

6. Following the function design recipe, define a function that has three parameters, grades between 0 and 100 inclusive, and returns the average of those grades.

7. Following the function design recipe, define a function that has four parameters, all of them grades between 0 and 100 inclusive, and returns the average of the *best 3* of those grades. Hint: Call the function that you defined in the previous exercise.

8. Complete the examples in the docstring and then write the body of the following function:

```
def weeks_elapsed(day1, day2):
    """ (int, int) -> int

    Return the number of full weeks that have elapsed between day1 and
    day2, which are two days in the same year.

    >>> weeks_elapsed(3, 20)
    2
```

```
    >>> weeks_elapsed(20, 3)
    2
    >>> weeks_elapsed(8, 5)

    >>> weeks_elapsed(40, 61)

    """
```

9. Consider this code:

```
def square(num):
    """ (number) -> float

    Return the square of num.

    >>> square(3)
    9
    """
```

In the following table, fill in the Example column by writing square, num, square(3), and 3 next to the appropriate description.

Description	Example
Parameter	
Argument	
Function name	
Function call	

10. Write the body of the square function from the previous exercise.

CHAPTER 4

Working with Text

From email clients and web browsers to calendars and games, text plays a central role in computer programs. This chapter introduces a non-numeric data type that represents text, such as the words in this sentence or the sequence of bases in a strand of DNA. Along the way, you will learn how to make programs more interactive by printing messages to the users and gathering input from them.

Creating Strings of Characters

Computers may have been invented to do arithmetic, but these days, most of them spend a lot of their time processing text. Many programs create, store, search, and move text from one place to another.

Python uses type str to represent text as sequences of characters

In Python, text is represented as a *string*, which is a sequence of *characters* (letters, digits, and symbols). The type whose values are sequences of characters is str. The characters consist of those from the Latin alphabet found on most North American keyboards, as well as Chinese morphograms, chemical and musical symbols, and other types of characters.

Strings are created by placing pairs of quotes around the text

In Python, you indicate that a value is a string by enclosing it in either single or double quotes. As you will see in Using Special Characters in Strings, on page 71, single and double quotes are equivalent, except for strings that contain quotes. Use whichever you prefer. (For docstrings, the Python style guidelines say that double quotes are preferred.) Here are two examples:

```
>>> 'Aristotle'
'Aristotle'
>>> "Isaac Newton"
'Isaac Newton'
```

Note how Python always displays a string in single quotes, regardless of what quotes you used in the first place (unless the string contains a single quote *and* does not contain a double quote).

The opening and closing quotes must match:

```
>>> 'Charles Darwin"
  File "<python-input-0>", line 1
    'Charles Darwin"
    ^
SyntaxError: unterminated string literal (detected at line 1)
```

Python attempts to find the matching closing single quote but fails, resulting in an unterminated string.

Strings can contain any number of characters, limited only by computer memory. The shortest string is the *empty string*, containing no characters at all:

```
>>> ''
''
>>> ""
''
```

Operations on Strings

Python has a built-in function, len, that returns the number of characters between the opening and closing quotes:

```
>>> len('Albert Einstein')
15
>>> len('123!')
4
>>> len(' ')
1
>>> len('')
0
```

You can concatenate ("glue up") two strings using the + operator, which produces a new string containing the characters from both operands:

```
>>> 'Albert' + ' Einstein'
'Albert Einstein'
```

When + has two string operands, it is referred to as the *concatenation operator*. The + operator is one of the most frequently overloaded operators in Python. So far, you've applied it to integers, floating-point numbers, and strings, and you'll apply it to several more types in later chapters.

As the following example shows, adding an empty string to another string produces a new string that is just like the nonempty operand:

```
>>> "Alan Turing" + ''
'Alan Turing'
>>> "" + 'Grace Hopper'
'Grace Hopper'
```

Alan Turing and Grace Hopper

Alan Turing was a British pioneer who helped define the idea of a programmable computer in the 1930s. His theoretical *Turing machine* laid the groundwork for thinking about algorithms and computation.

Grace Hopper was an American computer scientist and naval officer who helped create one of the first programming languages. She popularized the idea that computers could use English-like commands, paving the way for modern languages.

Here is an interesting question: Can operator + be applied to a string and a numeric value? If so, would addition or concatenation occur? Let's give it a try:

```
>>> 'NH' + 3
Traceback (most recent call last):
  File "<python-input-0>", line 1, in <module>
    'NH' + 3
    ~~~~~^~~
TypeError: can only concatenate str (not "int") to str
```

This is the second time that you've seen a type error. The first time, in Using Local Variables for Temporary Storage, on page 39, you didn't pass the correct number of parameters to a function. Here, Python didn't like you combining values of different data types. Because the first operand was a string, Python expected the second operand also to be a string, but instead it was an integer. Now consider this example:

```
>>> 9 + ' planets'
Traceback (most recent call last):
  File "<python-input-0>", line 1, in <module>
    9 + ' planets'
    ~~^~~~~~~~~~~~
TypeError: unsupported operand type(s) for +: 'int' and 'str'
```

Here, because Python saw a 9 first, it expected the second operand also to be numeric. The order of the operands affects the error message that is displayed.

The concatenation operator must be applied to two strings. If you want to join a string with a number, apply the function str to the number to get its string representation, and then apply the concatenation:

```
>>> 'Four score and ' + str(7) + ' years ago'
'Four score and 7 years ago'
```

Function int can be applied to a string whose contents look like an integer, and float can be applied to a string whose contents are numeric:

```
>>> int('0')
0
>>> int("11")
11
>>> int('-324')
-324
>>> float('-324')
-324.0
>>> float("56.34")
56.34
```

It isn't always possible to get an integer or a floating-point representation of a string, and when an attempt to do so fails, an error occurs:

```
>>> int('a')
Traceback (most recent call last):
  File "<python-input-0>", line 1, in <module>
    int('a')
    ~~~^^^^^
ValueError: invalid literal for int() with base 10: 'a'
>>> float('b')
Traceback (most recent call last):
  File "<python-input-1>", line 1, in <module>
    float('b')
    ~~~~~^^^^^
ValueError: could not convert string to float: 'b'
```

In addition to +, len, int, and float, operator * can be applied to strings. A string can be repeated using the operator * and an integer, like this:

```
>>> 'AT' * 5
'ATATATATAT'
>>> 4 * '-'
'----'
```

If the integer is less than or equal to zero, the operator yields an empty string:

```
>>> 'GC' * 0
''
>>> 'TATATATA' * -3
''
```

Strings are values; you can assign a string to a variable. Also, operations on strings can be applied to those variables:

```
>>> sequence = 'ATTGTCCCCC'
>>> len(sequence)
10
>>> new_sequence = sequence + 'GGCCTCCTGC'
```

```
>>> new_sequence
'ATTGTCCCCCGGCCTCCTGC'
>>> new_sequence * 2
'ATTGTCCCCCGGCCTCCTGCATTGTCCCCCGGCCTCCTGC'
```

DNA, the Code of Life

Deoxyribonucleic acid (DNA) is the instruction manual for all living things. It's made up of long sequences of four chemical building blocks, represented by the letters A, T, C, and G (adenine, thymine, cytosine, and guanine). The order of these letters, called the DNA sequence, among other things, tells cells how to build proteins, which do most of the work in the body. In programming, we often use strings like 'ATCG' to represent and analyze DNA in digital form.

Using Special Characters in Strings

Suppose you want to put a single quote inside a string. If you write it directly, an error occurs:

```
>>> 'that's not going to work'
  File "<python-input-0>", line 1
    'that's not going to work'
                             ^
SyntaxError: unterminated string literal (detected at line 1)
```

When Python encounters the second quote—the one that is intended to be part of the string—it thinks the string is ended. It doesn't know what to do with the text that comes after the second quote.

A straightforward way to fix this error is to use double quotes around the string; you can also put single quotes around a string containing a double quote:

```
>>> "that's better"
"that's better"
>>> 'She said, "That is better."'
'She said, "That is better."'
```

If you need to put a double quote in a string, you can use single quotes around the string. But what if you want to put both kinds of quotes in one string? You could split the string into parts enclosed in different quotes and concatenate them:

```
>>> 'She said, "That' + "'" + 's hard to read."'
'She said, "That\'s hard to read."'
```

The result is a valid Python string. The backslash is called an *escape character*, and the combination of the backslash and the single quote is called an *escape sequence*. The name comes from the fact that you're "escaping" from Python's usual syntax rules for a moment. When Python sees a backslash inside a string, it means that the next character represents something that Python typically uses for other purposes, such as marking the end of a string.

The escape sequence \' is indicated using two symbols, but those two symbols represent a single character:

```
>>> len('\'')
1
>>> len('it\'s')
4
```

Python recognizes several escape sequences. Here are some common ones:

Escape Sequence	Description
\'	Single quote
\"	Double quote
\\	Backslash
\t	Tab
\n	Newline/Line feed (move down to the next line)
\r	Carriage return (move to the start of the same line)

Table 2—Escape Sequences

To demonstrate their use, let's introduce multiline strings and revisit the built-in print function.

Creating a Multiline String

If you create a string using single or double quotes, the whole string must fit onto a single line.

Here's what happens when you try to stretch a string across multiple lines:

```
>>> 'one
  File "<python-input-3>", line 1
    'one
    ^
SyntaxError: unterminated string literal (detected at line 1)
```

In this error report, Python indicates that it reached the end of the line before it encountered the end of the string.

To span multiple lines, put three single quotes or three double quotes around the string instead of one. The string can then span as many lines as you want:

Use triple quotes for multiline strings

```
>>> '''one
... two
... three'''
'one\ntwo\nthree'
```

Newline \n and tab \t are escape sequences

Notice that the string Python creates contains a \n escape sequence everywhere your input started a new line. Each newline is a character in the string.

Printing Information

Print values using the print function

In Writing and Running a Program, on page 60, the built-in function print was used to print values to the screen. You will use the print function to display messages to the program's users. Those messages may include the values that expressions produce and the values that the variables refer to. Here are two examples of printing:

```
>>> print(1 + 1)
2
>>> print("The Latin 'Oryctolagus cuniculus' means 'domestic rabbit'.")
The Latin 'Oryctolagus cuniculus' means 'domestic rabbit'.
```

Function print doesn't allow any styling of the output: no colors, no italics, no boldface. All output is plain text.

The first function call performs as expected, given the numeric examples you have seen previously. Still, the second does something slightly different from previous string examples: it strips off the quotes around the string. It shows you the string in a human-readable form, rather than its character representation. This example makes the difference between the two even clearer:

```
>>> print('In 1859, Charles Darwin revolutionized biology')
In 1859, Charles Darwin revolutionized biology
>>> print('and our understanding of ourselves')
and our understanding of ourselves
>>> print('by publishing "On the Origin of Species".')
by publishing "On the Origin of Species".
```

The following example demonstrates that when Python prints a string, any escape sequences are converted to a form that humans can easily interpret:

```
>>> print('one\ttwo\nthree\tfour')
one	two
three	four
```

The previous example illustrates how the tab character (\t) can be used to align values in columns.

Normalizing Line Endings

Different operating systems use different sets of characters to indicate the end of a line. This set of characters is called a *newline*. On Linux and macOS, a newline is represented by one \n character; on versions 9 and earlier of Mac OS, it is represented by one \r; and on Windows, the ends of lines are marked with both characters as \r\n.

Python always uses a single \n to indicate a newline, even on operating systems like Windows that do things other ways. This behavior is called *normalizing* the string; Python does this so that you can write the same program no matter what kind of machine you're running on.

In Creating a Multiline String, on page 72, you saw that \n indicates a new line in multiline strings. When a multiline string is printed, those \n sequences are displayed as new lines:

```
>>> numbers = '''one
... two
... three'''
>>> numbers
'one\ntwo\nthree'
>>> print(numbers)
one
two
three
```

Function print takes a comma-separated list of values and prints the values with a single space between them and a newline after the last value:

```
>>> print(1, 2, 3)
1 2 3
>>>
```

When called with no arguments, which is a comma-separated list of length zero, print ends the current line and advances to the next one:

```
>>> print()

>>>
```

Function print can print values of any type, and it can even print values of different types in the same function call:

```
>>> print(1, 'two', 'three', 4.0)
1 two three 4.0
```

As with other function calls, it is also possible to call print with an expression as an argument. It will print the value of that expression:

```
>>> radius = 5
>>> print("The diameter of the circle is", radius * 2, "cm.")
The diameter of the circle is 10 cm.
```

Function print has a few extra helpful features; here is the help documentation for it:

```
>>> help(print)
Help on built-in function print in module builtins:

print(*args, sep=' ', end='\n', file=None, flush=False)
    Prints the values to a stream, or to sys.stdout by default.

    sep
      string inserted between values, default a space.
    end
      string appended after the last value, default a newline.
    file
      a file-like object (stream); defaults to the current sys.stdout.
    flush
      whether to forcibly flush the stream.
```

The parameters sep, end, file, and flush have assignment statements in the function header! These are called *default parameter values*: by default, if you call the function print with a comma-separated list of values (known as positional arguments and denoted in the docstring as *args), the separator is a space; similarly, a newline character appears at the end of every printed string. (We won't discuss file and flush; they are beyond the scope of this text.)

You can supply different values by using *keyword arguments*. (In the Python documentation, these are often referred to explicitly as kwargs.) That's a fancy term for assigning a value to a parameter name in the function call. Here, you separate each value with a comma and a space instead of just a space by including sep=', ' as an argument:

```
>>> print('a', 'b', 'c')  # The separator is a space by default
a b c
>>> print('a', 'b', 'c', sep=', ')
a, b, c
```

Often, you'll want to print information without starting a new line. To do this, use the keyword argument end='' to tell Python to end with an empty string instead of a new line:

```
>>> print('a', 'b', 'c', sep=', ', end='')
a, b, c>>>
```

Notice how the last prompt appeared right after the 'c'. Typically, end='' is used only in programs, not in the shell. Here is a program that converts three temperatures from Fahrenheit to Celsius and prints using keyword arguments:

```
def convert_to_celsius(fahrenheit: float) -> float:
    """Return the number of Celsius degrees equivalent to fahrenheit degrees.

    >>> convert_to_celsius(75)
    23.88888888888889
    """

    return (fahrenheit - 32.0) * 5.0 / 9.0

print('80, 78.8, and 10.4 degrees Fahrenheit are equal to ', end='')
print(convert_to_celsius(80), end=', \n')
print(convert_to_celsius(78.8), end=', and ')
print(convert_to_celsius(10.4), end=' Celsius.\n')
```

Here's the output of running this program:

```
80, 78.8, and 10.4 degrees Fahrenheit are equal to 26.666666666666668,
26.0, and -12.0 Celsius.
```

Getting Information from the Keyboard

Provide input values using the input function

In Chapter 3, Designing and Using Functions, on page 31, you explored some built-in functions. Another built-in function is input, which reads a single line of text from the keyboard. It returns whatever the user enters as a string, even if it appears to be a number:

```
>>> species = input()
Homo sapiens
>>> species
'Homo sapiens'
>>> population = input()
8232458392
>>> population
'8232458392'
>>> type(population)
<class 'str'>
```

The second and sixth lines of that example, Homo sapiens and 8232458392, were typed in response to the calls to the function input.

If you are expecting the user to enter a number, you must use int or float to get an integer or a floating-point representation of the string:

```
>>> population = input()
8232458392
>>> population
```

```
'8232458392'
>>> population = int(population)
>>> population
8232458392
>>> population = population + 1
>>> population
8232458393
```

You don't actually need to stash the value that the call to input produces before converting it. This time, the function int is called on the result of the call to input and is equivalent to the previous code:

```
>>> population = int(input())
8232458392
>>> population = population + 1
8232458393
```

Finally, input can be given a string argument s, which is used to prompt the user for input (notice the space at the end of your prompt):

```
>>> species = input("Please enter a species: ")
Please enter a species: Python curtus
>>> print(species)
Python curtus
```

Since a Python program stops and waits for the user input when it encounters a call to input, it is fair to explain the reason for the pause to the users, especially when they are expected to enter more than one value.

Formatted Strings

It is common in text processing to construct a string using a template and specific values to fill into it. For example, you may have a generic birthday congratulations, such as "Happy AGEth birthday, NAME!", which you want to customize by specifying the congratulant's name and age.

Python historically provides four mechanisms for such customization, listed below in the order of recency and usability:

1. String concatenation
2. Substitution operator
3. str.format method
4. Formatted strings

Substitution Operator

The binary substitution operator (%) was used in older versions of Python to insert values into a string using placeholders. The operator requires a string with placeholders as the left operand and a parenthesized comma-separated collection (a *tuple*) of matching values as the second operand. A placeholder starts with a percent sign (%), immediately followed by the matching value's type code: `s` for a string, `d` or `i` for an integer, and `f` for a floating-point number (with six decimal places by default).

```
>>> name = 'Paul Newman'
>>> age = 100
>>> 'Happy %dth birthday, %s' % (age, name)
'Happy 100th birthday, Paul Newman'
```

F-strings are preferred over the substitution operator because they are clearer, safer, faster, and more powerful. The % operator is considered obsolete and is best avoided in new code.

Formatted strings (f-strings) are an efficient way to construct text

We'll examine only the formatted strings, which are the newest and generally the most concise and efficient way to format text in modern Python. A formatted string, also known as an f-string, is essentially a template string with additional marks denoting placeholders and indicating what and how to fill them in. An f-string starts with the letter `f` (or `F`) *before* the opening quotation mark. These f-strings without placeholders, once read by Python, are indistinguishable from "normal" strings:

```
>>> f'abc'
'abc'
>>> F"abc"
'abc'
```

A placeholder is any valid Python expression enclosed in braces. When a string is read, each placeholder is replaced with the value of the enclosed expression. If necessary, the value of the expression is automatically converted to a string.

```
>>> name = 'Paul Newman'
>>> age = 100
>>> f'Happy birthday, {name}!'
'Happy birthday, Paul Newman!'
>>> 'Happy birthday, {name}!' # Not an f-string!
'Happy birthday, {name}!'
>>> f'Happy {age}th birthday, {name}!'
'Happy 100th birthday, Paul Newman!'
```

Next year, you may update the variable `age` or compute the new age within the f-string (the *th* suffix requires special treatment, because it may become *st*, *nd*, or even *rd*):

```
>>> f'Happy {age+1}th birthday, {name}!'
'Happy 101th birthday, Paul Newman!'
```

If you want to use braces within an f-string, you must double each brace: `{{` and `}}`. Python will print them as { and }, and not treat them as placeholders:

```
>>> stuff = 'braces'
>>> f'stuff, {stuff}, and more {{stuff}}'
'stuff, braces, and more {stuff}'
```

In addition to the filler expression, a placeholder may contain a *format specifier*, which provides additional information about formatting the expression. A colon (:) separates the expression from the format specifier. A simple format specifier resembles a floating-point number, where the "integer" part defines the number of positions reserved for the result, and the decimal part, if present, determines the number of text symbols or decimal digits to display:

```
>>> f'Name: {name}.' # No format specifier
'Name: Paul Newman.'
>>> f'Name: {name:20}.'
'Name: Paul Newman         .'
>>> f'Name: {name:20.4}.' # Truncated
'Name: Paul                .'
>>> f'Age: {age}.'
'Age: 100.'
>>> f'Age: {age:20}.'
'Age:                  100.'
>>> f'Age: {age:20.2f}.'
'Age:               100.00.'
```

An extra `f` at the end of the format specifier indicates floating-point formatting.

You can insert various control symbols in front of the format specifier, such as *alignment*: < (left-align the result; default for strings), ^ (center the result), > (right-align the result; default for numbers).

```
>>> f'Name: {name:<20}.'
'Name: Paul Newman         .'
>>> f'Name: {name:^20}.'
'Name:     Paul Newman     .'
>>> f'Name: {name:>20}.'
'Name:          Paul Newman.'
```

Please explore more control symbols by reading Python documentation.

Quotes About Strings

In this chapter, you learned the following:

- Python uses type `str` to represent text as sequences of characters.
- Strings are created by placing pairs of single quotes `'` or double quotes `"` around the text.
- ```
  '''Should you want a string
  that crosses multiple lines,
  Use matched triple quotes.'''
  ```
- Special characters like newline (`\n`) and tab (`\t`) are represented using escape sequences that begin with a backslash. For example, `'this string\nspans\nthree lines'`.
- Values can be printed using the built-in function `print`, and input can be provided by the user via the built-in function `input`.
- Formatted strings (f-strings) are a modern, efficient way to construct text using embedded expressions and format specifiers.

Exercises

Here are some exercises for you to try on your own.

1. What value does each of the following expressions evaluate to? Verify your answers by typing the expressions into the Python shell.

    a. `'Computer' + ' Science'`
    b. `'Darwin\'s'`
    c. `'H2O' * 3`
    d. `'CO2' * 0`

2. Express each of the following phrases as Python strings using the appropriate type of quotation marks (single, double, or triple) and, if necessary, escape sequences. There is more than one correct answer for each of these phrases.

    a. They'll hibernate during the winter.
    b. "Absolutely not," he said.
    c. "He said, 'Absolutely not'," recalled Mel.
    d. hydrogen sulfide
    e. left\right

3. Rewrite the following string using single or double quotes instead of triple quotes:
  ```

```
'''A
B
C'''
```

4. Use built-in function len to find the length of the empty string.

5. Given variables x and y, which refer to values 3 and 12.5, respectively, use the function print to print the following messages. When numbers appear in the messages, variables x and y should be used.

   a. The rabbit is 3.
   b. The rabbit is 3 years old.
   c. 12.5 is average.
   d. 12.5 * 3
   e. 12.5 * 3 is 37.5.

6. Consider this code:

   ```
   >>> first = 'John'
   >>> last = 'Doe'
   >>> print(last + ', ' + first)
   ```

   What is printed by this code?

7. Use input to prompt the user for a number, store the number entered as a float in a variable named num, and then print the contents of num.

8. Given two pre-defined variables: name (a string) and score (a floating-point number), write an f-string that congratulates the person by name for achieving their score in a fictional game. The score must be shown with one decimal digit. Example output:

   ```
   Congratulations, Alex! You scored 92.5 points!
   ```

9. Complete the examples in the docstring and then write the body of the following function:

   ```
   def repeat(s: str, n: int) -> str:
       """Return s repeated n times; if n is negative, return the empty string.

       >>> repeat('yes', 4)
       'yesyesyesyes'
       >>> repeat('no', 0)

       >>> repeat('no', -2)

       >>> repeat('yesnomaybe', 3)

       """
   ```

(continued on next page...)

10. Complete the examples in the docstring and then write the body of the following function:

```
def total_length(s1: str, s2: str) -> int:
    """Return the sum of the lengths of s1 and s2.

    >>> total_length('yes', 'no')
    5
    >>> total_length('yes', '')

    >>> total_length('YES!!!!', 'Noooooo')

    """
```

CHAPTER 5

Making Choices

This chapter introduces another fundamental concept of programming: making choices. Choices are made whenever you want your program to behave differently depending on the data it's working with. For example, you might want to perform different actions depending on whether a solution is acidic or basic, or depending on whether a user types "yes" or "no" in response to a call to the built-in function input.

Let's introduce statements for making choices in this chapter called *control flow* statements (because they control the way the computer executes programs). These statements involve a Python type that represents truth and falsehood.

A Boolean Type

Python uses Boolean values to represent what is true and what isn't

Python has a type called bool (without an "e"). Unlike int and float, which have billions of possible values, bool has only two: True and False. True and False are values, just as much as the numbers 0 and -43.7.

Boolean Operators

There are only three basic Boolean operators: and, or, and not. not has the highest precedence, followed by and, followed by or.

not is a unary operator: it is applied to just one value, like the negation in the expression -(3 + 2). An expression involving not produces True if the original value is False, and it produces False if the original value is True:

```
>>> not True
False
>>> not False
True
```

George Boole and Claude Shannon

In the 1840s, the mathematician George Boole showed that the classical rules of logic could be expressed in purely mathematical form using only the two values *true* and *false*. A century later, Claude Shannon (the inventor of information theory) realized that Boole's work could be used to optimize the design of electromechanical telephone switches. His work directly led to the application of *Boolean logic* in the design of computer circuits.

In honor of Boole's work, most modern programming languages use a type named after him to keep track of what's true and what's not.

In the previous example, instead of not True, you could use False, and instead of not False, you could use True. Rather than apply not directly to a Boolean value, you would typically apply not to a Boolean variable or a more complex Boolean expression. The same goes for the following examples of the Boolean operators and and or, where we'll just use True and False. You'll see an example of how they are typically used at the end of this section.

and is a binary operator. It produces True only if *both* operands are True.

```
>>> True and True
True
>>> False and False
False
>>> True and False
False
>>> False and True
False
```

or is also a binary operator. It produces True if *either* operand is True, and it produces False only if both are False:

```
>>> True or True
True
>>> False or False
False
>>> True or False
True
>>> False or True
True
```

This definition is called *inclusive or*, as it allows for both possibilities, as well as either one of them. In English, the word *or* is also sometimes an *exclusive or*. For example, if someone says, 'You can have pizza or tandoori chicken,' they probably don't mean that you can have both. Unlike English (but like most programming languages), Python always interprets or as inclusive.

You can write an *exclusive or* expression using the “caret” (^) operator:

```
b1 ^ b2
```

Exclusive or means that one and only one of `b1` and `b2` has to be `True`. If `b1` is `True`, `b2` can’t be, and vice versa.

As mentioned earlier, Boolean operators are usually applied to Boolean expressions rather than Boolean constants. Suppose you want to express “It is not cold and windy” using two variables, `cold` and `windy`, that refer to Boolean values. You first have to decide what the ambiguous English expression means: is it not cold, but at the same time windy, or is it both not cold and not windy? A *truth table* for each alternative is shown in Table 3, Boolean Operators, on page 85, and the following code snippet illustrates what they look like when translated into Python:

```
>>> cold = True
>>> windy = False
>>> (not cold) and windy
False
>>> not (cold and windy)
True
```

cold	windy	cold and windy	cold or windy	(not cold) and windy	not (cold and windy)
True	**True**	True	True	False	False
True	**False**	False	True	False	True
False	**True**	False	True	True	True
False	**False**	False	False	False	True

Table 3—Boolean Operators

Boolean Operators in Other Languages

If you already know another language, such as C or Java, you might be used to && for `and`, || for `or`, and ! for `not`. These won’t work in Python, but the idea is the same.

Relational Operators

Relational operators compare values

As said earlier, `True` and `False` are values. Typically, those values are not written down directly in expressions but instead created in comparisons using a *relational operator*. For example, `3 < 5` is a comparison using the relational operator < that produces the value `True`, while `13 > 77` uses > and produces the value `False`.

As shown in the following table, Python has all the operators you're using. Some of them are represented using two characters instead of one, such as <= instead of ≤.

Symbol	Operation
>	Greater than
<	Less than
>=	Greater than or equal to
<=	Less than or equal to
==	Equal
!=	Not equal

The most crucial representation rule is that Python uses == for equality instead of just =, because = is used for assignment. Avoid typing `x = 3` when you mean to check whether variable `x` is equal to three: `x == 3`.

All relational operators are binary operators: they compare two values and produce `True` or `False` as appropriate. The greater-than (>) and less-than (<) operators work as follows:

```
>>> 45 > 34
True
>>> 45 > 79
False
>>> 45 < 79
True
>>> 45 < 34
False
```

You can compare integers to floating-point numbers with any of the relational operators. Integers are automatically converted to floating-point numbers when you perform this operation, just as they are when you add `14` to `23.3`:

```
>>> 23.1 >= 23
True
>>> 23.1 >= 23.1
True
>>> 23.1 <= 23.1
True
>>> 23.1 <= 23
False
```

The same holds for "equal" and "not equal":

```
>>> 67.3 == 87
False
>>> 67.3 == 67
```

```
False
>>> 67.0 == 67
True
>>> 67.0 != 67
False
>>> 67.0 != 23
True
```

Of course, it doesn't make much sense to compare two numbers that you know in advance, since you would also know the result of the comparison. Relational operators, therefore, almost always involve variables, like this:

```
>>> def is_positive(x: float) -> bool:
...     """Return True iff x is positive.
...
...     >>> is_positive(3)
...     True
...     >>> is_positive(-4.6)
...     False
...     """
...     return x > 0
...
>>> is_positive(3)
True
>>> is_positive(-4.6)
False
>>> is_positive(0)
False
```

In this docstring, let's use the abbreviation "iff," which stands for "if and only if." An equivalent phrase is "exactly when." The type contract states that the function will return a bool. The docstring describes the conditions under which True will be returned. It is implied that when those conditions aren't met, the function will return False.

Combining Comparisons

You have now seen three types of operators: arithmetic (+, -, and so on), Boolean (and, or, and not), and relational (<, ==, and so on).

Here are the rules for combining them:

- Arithmetic operators have higher precedence than relational operators. For example, + and / are evaluated before < or >.
- Relational operators have higher precedence than Boolean operators. For example, comparisons are evaluated before and, or, and not.
- All relational operators have the same precedence.

Remember, the order of precedence of operators is arithmetic (highest), relational, and then Boolean

These rules mean that the expression `1 + 3 > 7` is evaluated as `(1 + 3) > 7`, not as `1 + (3 > 7)`. These rules also mean that you can often skip the parentheses in complicated expressions:

```
>>> x = 2
>>> y = 5
>>> z = 7
>>> x < y and y < z
True
```

It's usually a good idea to put the parentheses in, though, since it helps the eye find the subexpressions and communicates the order to anyone reading your code:

```
>>> x = 5
>>> y = 10
>>> z = 20
>>> (x < y) and (y < z)
True
```

It's very common in mathematics to check whether a value lies in a particular range—in other words, that it is between two values. You can do this in Python by combining the comparisons with `and`:

```
>>> x = 3
>>> (1 < x) and (x <= 5)
True
>>> x = 7
>>> (1 < x) and (x <= 5)
False
```

This operation occurs so frequently that Python provides a clean and readable way to write it by *chaining* comparisons:

```
>>> x = 3
>>> 1 < x <= 5
True
```

Most combinations work as you would expect, but some cases may startle you:

```
>>> 3 < 5 != True
True
>>> 3 < 5 != False
True
```

It seems impossible for both of these expressions to be True. However, the first one is equivalent to this:

```
(3 < 5) and (5 != True)
```

while the second is equivalent to this:

```
(3 < 5) and (5 != False)
```

Since 5 is neither True nor False, the second half of each expression is True, so the expression as a whole is True as well. Using Numbers and Strings with Boolean Operators, on page 89, provides another cautionary example of mixing numbers and Boolean values.

This kind of expression is an example of something that's a bad idea, even though it's legal. It is strongly recommended that you only chain comparisons in ways that would seem natural to a mathematician—in other words, that you use < and <= together, or > and >= together, and nothing else. If you feel the impulse to do something else, resist. Use simple comparisons and combine them with and to keep your code readable. It's also a good idea to use parentheses whenever you think the expression you are writing may not be entirely clear.

Using Numbers and Strings with Boolean Operators

You have already seen that Python will convert an int to a float when the integer is used in an expression involving a floating-point number. Similarly, numbers and strings can coexist with Boolean operators. Python treats 0 and 0.0 as False and treats all other numbers as True:

```
>>> not 0
True
>>> not 1
False
>>> not 34.2
False
>>> not -87
False
```

An empty string is treated as False, and all other strings are treated as True:

```
>>> not ''
True
>>> not 'bad'
False
```

None is also treated as False. However, you are advised to use Boolean operators only with Boolean values.

Short-Circuit Evaluation

When Python evaluates an expression containing and or or, it does so from left to right. As soon as it knows enough to stop evaluating, it stops, even if some operands haven't been looked at yet. This feature is called *short-circuit evaluation.*

In an or expression, if the first operand is True, you know that the expression is True. Python knows this as well, so it doesn't even evaluate the second operand. Similarly, in an and expression, if the first operand is False, you know that the expression is False. Python is aware of this, and the second operand isn't evaluated.

To demonstrate this, let's use an expression that results in an error:

```
>>> 1 / 0
raceback (most recent call last):
  File "<python-input-0>", line 1, in <module>
    1 / 0
    ~~^~~
ZeroDivisionError: division by zero
```

Now, let's use that expression as the second operand to or:

```
>>> (2 < 3) or (1 / 0)
True
```

Since the first operand produces True, the second operand isn't evaluated, so the computer never actually tries to divide anything by zero.

Of course, if the first operand to an or is False, the second operand must be evaluated. The second operand also needs to be evaluated when the first operand to an and is True.

Comparing Strings

You can compare strings just as you would compare numbers. The characters in strings are represented by integers: a capital *A*, for example, is represented by 65, whereas a space is 32, and a lowercase *z* is 122. This encoding is called *ASCII,*[1] which stands for "American Standard Code for Information Interchange." One of its quirks is that all the uppercase letters come before all the lowercase letters, so a capital *Z* is less than a lowercase *a.*

One of the most common reasons for comparing two strings is to determine which one comes first alphabetically. The operation is referred to as *dictionary ordering* or *lexicographic ordering.* Python decides which string is greater than

1. https://en.wikipedia.org/wiki/ASCII.

Lexicographic Ordering and Code Points

Python's lexicographic ordering relies on the built-in function ord. The function returns the Unicode *code point* (the position of the character in the Unicode[a] encoding table) for a one-character string:

```
>>> ord('Z')
90
>>> ord('z')
122
>>> ord('Æ')
198
>>> ord('Щ') # One of the authors is Russian
1065
```

The sister built-in function chr, conversely, translates a code point expressed as an integer number into a one-character string:

```
>>> chr(90)
'Z'
>>> chr(677) # The initials of one of the authors!
'ʥ'
```

These functions are useful for working with characters at a more basic, individual-character level.

a. https://docs.python.org/3/howto/unicode.html

which by comparing corresponding characters from left to right. If the character from one string is greater than the character from the other, the first string is greater than the second. If all the characters are the same, the two strings are equal; if one string runs out of characters while the comparison is being done (in other words, is shorter than the other), then it is less. The following code fragment illustrates several comparisons in action:

```
>>> 'A' < 'a'
True
>>> 'A' > 'z'
False
>>> 'abc' < 'abd'
True
>>> 'abc' < 'abcd'
True
```

In addition to operators that compare strings lexicographically, Python provides a *membership* operator, in, that checks whether one string is a substring of another:

```
>>> 'Jan' in '01 Jan 1838'
True
```

```
>>> 'Feb' in '01 Jan 1838'
False
```

Using this idea, you can prompt the user for a date in this format and report whether that date is in January:

```
>>> date = input('Enter a date in the format DD MTH YYYY: ')
Enter a date in the format DD MTH YYYY: 24 Feb 2013
>>> 'Jan' in date
False
>>> date = input('Enter a date in the format DD MTH YYYY: ')
Enter a date in the format DD MTH YYYY: 03 Jan 2002
>>> 'Jan' in date
True
```

The in operator produces True exactly when the first string appears in the second string. The comparison is case sensitive:

```
>>> 'a' in 'abc'
True
>>> 'A' in 'abc'
False
```

An empty string is a substring of any string:

```
>>> '' in 'abc'
True
>>> '' in ''
True
```

The in operator also applies to other data types; you'll see examples of this in Chapter 8, Storing Collections of Data Using Lists, on page 133, and in Chapter 11, Storing Data Using Other Collection Types, on page 209.

Choosing Which Statements to Execute

An if statement allows you to modify your program's behavior based on a specific condition. The general form of an if statement is as follows:

```
if «condition»:
    «block»
```

The *condition* is an expression, such as color != "neon green" or x < y. (Note that this doesn't have to be a Boolean expression. As discussed in Using Numbers and Strings with Boolean Operators, on page 89, non-Boolean values are treated as True or False when required.)

If the condition is true, the statements in the block are executed; otherwise, they are not. As with functions, the block of statements must be indented to show that it belongs to

> The if statements control the flow of execution

the if statement. If you don't indent properly, Python will report an error, or worse, may execute the code that you wrote but do something you didn't intend because some statements were not appropriately indented. You'll briefly explore both problems in this chapter.

Here is a table of solution categories based on pH level (the measure of acidity or basicity of water-based solutions):

pH	0–4	5–6	7	8–9	10–14
Category	Strong acid	Weak acid	Neutral	Weak base	Strong base

You can use an if statement to print a message only when the pH level given by the program's user is acidic:

```
>>> ph = float(input('Enter the pH level: '))
Enter the pH level: 6.0
>>> if ph < 7.0:
...     print(ph, "is acidic.")
...
6.0 is acidic.
```

Recall from Getting Information from the Keyboard, on page 76, that you have to convert user input from a string to a floating-point number before doing the comparison. Additionally, you should provide a prompt for the user by passing a string to the function input; Python will display this string to inform the user of what information to type.

If the condition is false, the statements in the block aren't executed:

```
>>> ph = float(input('Enter the pH level: '))
Enter the pH level: 8.0
>>> if ph < 7.0:
...     print(ph, "is acidic.")
...
>>>
```

If you don't indent the block, Python lets you know:

```
>>> ph = float(input('Enter the pH level: '))
Enter the pH level: 6
>>> if ph < 7.0:
... print(ph, "is acidic.")
...
  File "<python-input-0>", line 2
    print(ph, "is acidic.")
    ^^^^^
IndentationError: expected an indented block after 'if' statement on line 1
```

Since you're using a block, you can have multiple statements that are executed only if the condition is true:

```
>>> ph = float(input('Enter the pH level: '))
Enter the pH level: 6.0
>>> if ph < 7.0:
...     print(ph, "is acidic.")
...     print("You should be careful with that!")
...
6.0 is acidic.
You should be careful with that!
```

When you indent the first line of the block, the Python interpreter changes its prompt to ... until the end of the block, which is signaled by a blank line:

```
>>> ph = float(input('Enter the pH level: '))
Enter the pH level: 8.0
>>> if ph < 7.0:
...     print(ph, "is acidic.")
...
>>> print("You should be careful with that!")
You should be careful with that!
```

Of course, sometimes you encounter situations where a single decision isn't sufficient. If multiple criteria need to be examined, you have several ways to handle it. One way is to use multiple `if` statements. For example, you might print different messages depending on whether a pH level is acidic or basic (if it's exactly 7, then it's neutral, and your code won't print anything):

```
>>> ph = float(input('Enter the pH level: '))
Enter the pH level: 8.5
>>> if ph < 7.0:
...     print(ph, "is acidic.")
...
>>> if ph > 7.0:
...     print(ph, "is basic.")
...
8.5 is basic.
>>>
```

The flowchart at the top of the facing page shows how Python executes the `if` statements. The diamonds are conditions, and the arrows indicate what path to take depending on the results of evaluating those conditions:

Notice that both conditions are evaluated, even though you know that only one of the blocks can be executed.

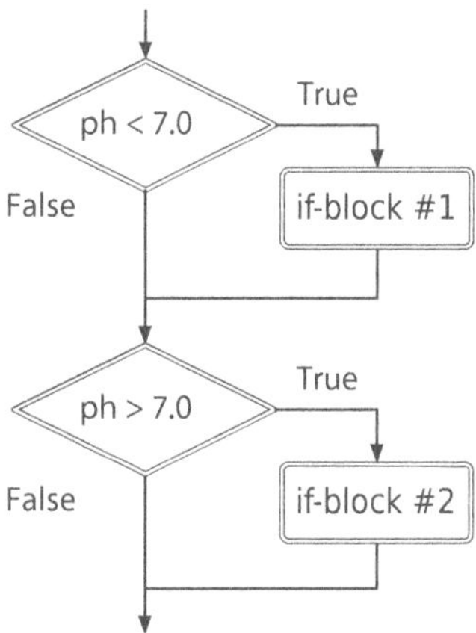

You can merge both cases by adding another condition/block pair using the elif keyword (which stands for "else if"); each condition/block pair is called a *clause*:

```
>>> ph = float(input('Enter the pH level: '))
Enter the pH level: 8.5
>>> if ph < 7.0:
...     print(ph, "is acidic.")
... elif ph > 7.0:
...     print(ph, "is basic.")
...
8.5 is basic.
>>>
```

The difference between the two is that elif is checked only when the if condition above it is evaluated to False. Here's a flowchart for this code:

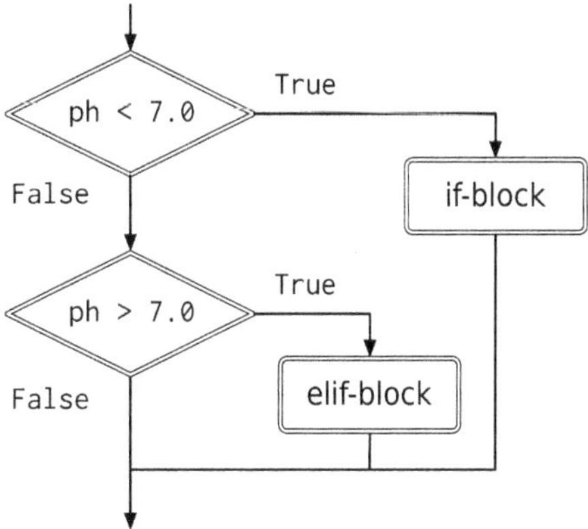

This flowchart shows that if the first condition evaluates to True, the second condition is skipped.

If the pH is exactly 7.0, neither clause matches, so nothing is printed:

```
>>> ph = float(input('Enter the pH level: '))
Enter the pH level: 7.0
>>> if ph < 7.0:
...     print(ph, "is acidic.")
... elif ph > 7.0:
...     print(ph, "is basic.")
...
>>>
```

With the ph example, you achieve the same result using two if statements as you did with an if/elif statement.

This substitution is not always valid; for example, if the body of the first if changes the value of a variable used in the second condition, they are not equivalent. Here is the version with two ifs:

```
>>> ph = float(input('Enter the pH level: '))
Enter the pH level: 6.0
>>> if ph < 7.0:
...     ph = 8.0
...
>>> if ph > 7.0:
...     print(ph, "is acidic.")
...
8.0 is acidic.
```

Here is the version with an if/elif:

```
>>> ph = float(input('Enter the pH level: '))
Enter the pH level: 6.0
>>> if ph < 7.0:
...     ph = 8.0
>>> elif ph > 7.0:
...     print(ph, "is acidic.")
...
>>>
```

As a rule of thumb, if two conditions are related, use if/elif instead of two ifs.

Multiple elif clauses can follow an if statement. This longer example translates a chemical formula into English:

```
>>> compound = input('Enter the compound: ')
Enter the compound: CH4
>>> if compound == "H2O":
...     print("Water")
```

```
... elif compound == "NH3":
...     print("Ammonia")
... elif compound == "CH4":
...     print("Methane")
...
Methane
>>>
```

As you saw in the code on page 96, if none of the conditions in a chain of if/elif statements are satisfied, Python does not execute any of the associated blocks. This isn't always what you'd like, though. In the translation example, you probably want your program to print something, even if it doesn't recognize the compound.

To do this, add an else clause at the end of the chain:

```
>>> compound = input('Enter the compound: ')
Enter the compound: H2SO4
>>> if compound == "H2O":
...     print("Water")
... elif compound == "NH3":
...     print("Ammonia")
... elif compound == "CH4":
...     print("Methane")
... else:
...     print("Unknown compound")
...
Unknown compound
>>>
```

An if statement can have at most one else clause, and it has to be the final clause in the statement. Notice that there is no condition associated with else:

```
if «condition»:
    «if_block»
else:
    «else_block»
```

Logically, that code is the same as this code (except that the condition is evaluated only once in the first form but twice in the second form):

```
if «condition»:
    «if_block»
if not «condition»:
    «else_block»
```

Nested if Statements

An if statement's block can contain any Python statement, which implies that it can include other if statements. An if statement inside another is called a *nested* if statement.

```
value = input('Enter the pH level: ')
if len(value) > 0:
    ph = float(value)
    if ph < 7.0:
        print(ph, "is acidic.")
    elif ph > 7.0:
        print(ph, "is basic.")
    else:
        print(ph, "is neutral.")
else:
    print("No pH value was given!")
```

In this case, you ask the user to provide a pH value, which you'll initially receive as a string. The first, or *outer*, if statement checks whether the user typed something, which determines whether you examine the value of pH with the *inner* if statement. (If the user didn't enter a number, then the function call float(value) will produce a ValueError.)

Nested if statements are sometimes necessary, but they can get complicated. To describe when a statement is executed, you have to combine conditions mentally; for example, the statement print(ph, "is acidic.") is executed only if the length of the string that value refers to is greater than 0 *and* pH < 7.0 also evaluates to True (assuming the user entered a number).

Memorizing Results of a Boolean Expression Evaluation

Take a look at the following line of code and guess what value is assigned to x:

```
>>> x = 15 > 5
```

If you said True, you were right: 15 is greater than 5, so the comparison produces True, and since that's a value like any other, it can be assigned to a variable.

The most common situation in which you would want to do this comes up when translating decision tables into software. For example, suppose you want to calculate someone's risk of heart disease using the following rules based on age and body mass index (BMI):

	Age<45	Age≥45
BMI<22	Low	Medium
BMI≥22	Medium	High

One way to implement this would be to use nested if statements:

```
if age < 45:
    if bmi < 22.0:
        risk = 'low'
    else:
        risk = 'medium'
else:
    if bmi < 22.0:
        risk = 'medium'
    else:
        risk = 'high'
```

The expression bmi < 22.0 is used multiple times. To simplify this code, you can evaluate each of the Boolean expressions once, create variables that refer to the values produced by those expressions, and use those variables multiple times:

```
young = age < 45
slim = bmi < 22.0
if young:
    if slim:
        risk = 'low'
    else:
        risk = 'medium'
else:
    if slim:
        risk = 'medium'
    else:
        risk = 'high'
```

You could also write this without nesting as follows:

```
young = age < 45
slim = bmi < 22.0
if young and slim:
    risk = 'low'
elif young and not slim:
    risk = 'medium'
elif not young and slim:
    risk = 'medium'
elif not young and not slim:
    risk = 'high'
```

Whether you use nesting or not, giving meaningful names to the Boolean variables (young and slim) helps make the code easier to understand.

You Learned About Booleans: True or False?

In this chapter, you learned the following:

- Python uses Boolean values, True and False, to represent what is true and what isn't. Programs can combine these values using three operators: not, and, and or.
- Boolean operators can also be applied to numeric values. 0, 0.0, the empty string, and None are treated as False; all other numeric values and strings are treated as True. It is best to avoid applying Boolean operators to non-Boolean values.
- Relational operators such as "equals" and "less than" compare values and produce a Boolean result.
- When different operators are combined in an expression, the order of precedence from highest to lowest is arithmetic, relational, and then Boolean.
- if statements control the flow of execution. As with function definitions, the bodies of if statements are indented, as are the bodies of elif and else clauses.

Exercises

Here are some exercises for you to try on your own.

1. What value does each expression produce? Verify your answers by typing the expressions into Python.

   a. True and not False
   b. True and not false (Notice the capitalization.)
   c. True or True and False
   d. not True or not False
   e. True and not 0
   f. 52 < 52.3
   g. 1 + 52 < 52.3
   h. 4 != 4.0

2. Variables x and y refer to Boolean values.

   a. Write an expression that produces True iff both variables are True.
   b. Write an expression that produces True iff x is False.
   c. Write an expression that produces True iff at least one of the variables is True.

3. Variables full and empty refer to Boolean values. Write an expression that produces True if and only if at most one of the variables is True.

4. You want an automatic wildlife camera to switch on if the light level is less than 0.01 lux or if the temperature is above freezing, but not if both conditions are true. (You should assume that function turn_camera_on has already been defined.)

   Your first attempt to write this is as follows:

```
if (light < 0.01) or (temperature > 0.0):
    if not ((light < 0.01) and (temperature > 0.0)):
        turn_camera_on()
```

   A friend says that this is an exclusive or and that you could write it more simply as follows:

```
if (light < 0.01) != (temperature > 0.0):
    turn_camera_on()
```

   Is your friend right? If so, explain why. If not, give values for light and temperature that will produce different results for the two fragments of code.

5. In Functions That Python Provides, on page 31, you saw the built-in function abs. Variable x refers to a number. Write an expression that evaluates to True if x and its absolute value are equal and evaluates to False otherwise. Assign the resulting value to a variable named result.

6. Write a function named different that has two parameters, a and b. The function should return True if a and b refer to different values, and False otherwise.

7. Variables population and land_area refer to floats.

   a. Write an if statement that will print the population if it is less than 10,000,000.

   b. Write an if statement that will print the population if it is between 10,000,000 and 35,000,000.

   c. Write an if statement that will print "Densely populated" if the land density (number of people per unit of area) is greater than 100.

   d. Write an if statement that will print "Densely populated" if the land density (number of people per unit of area) is greater than 100, and "Sparsely populated" otherwise.

8. Function convert_to_celsius from Defining Custom Functions, on page 36, converts from Fahrenheit to Celsius. Wikipedia, however, mentions eight

temperature scales:[2] Kelvin, Celsius, Fahrenheit, Rankine, Delisle, Newton, Rèaumur, and Rømer.

a. Write a convert_temperatures function to convert temperature t from source units to target units, where source and target are each one of "Kelvin", "Celsius", "Fahrenheit", "Rankine", "Delisle", "Newton", "Reaumur", and "Romer" units.

   Hint: On the Wikipedia page, there are eight tables, each with two columns and seven rows. That translates to an awful lot of if statements—at least 8 * 7—because each of the eight units can be converted to the seven other units. Possibly even worse, if you decided to add another temperature scale, you would need to add at least sixteen more if statements: eight to convert from your new scale to each of the current ones and eight to convert from the current ones to your new scale.

   A better approach is to choose one canonical scale, such as the Celsius scale. Your conversion function could work in two steps: convert from the source scale to Celsius and then from Celsius to the target scale.

b. Now, if you added a new temperature scale, how many if statements would you need to add?

9. Assume you want to print a strong warning message if the pH value is below 3.0 and otherwise just report on the acidity. Try this if statement:

```
>>> ph = 2
>>> if ph < 7.0:
...     print(ph, "is acidic.")
... elif ph < 3.0:
...     print(ph, "is VERY acidic! Be careful.")
...
2 is acidic.
```

   This code prints the wrong message when the pH of 2 is entered. What is the problem, and how can you fix it?

10. The following code displays a message(s) about the acidity of a solution:

```
ph = float(input("Enter the pH level: "))
if ph < 7.0:
    print("It's acidic!")
elif ph < 4.0:
    print("It's a strong acid!")
```

   a. What message(s) are displayed when the user enters 6.4?

---

2. http://en.wikipedia.org/wiki/Comparison_of_temperature_scales

b. What message(s) are displayed when the user enters 3.6?

c. Make a small change to one line of the code so that both messages are displayed when a value less than 4 is entered.

11. Why does the last example in Memorizing Results of a Boolean Expression Evaluation, on page 98, check to see whether someone is light (that is, that person's BMI is less than the threshold) rather than heavy? If you wanted to write the second assignment statement as `heavy = bmi >= 22.0`, what change(s) would you have to make to the code?

CHAPTER 6

A Modular Approach to Program Organization

It's rare for someone to write all of a program alone; it's much more common and productive to make use of the millions of lines of code that other programmers have written before and have packed into modules.

A module is a collection of functions and variables

A *module* is a collection of variables and functions that are grouped in a single file. The variables and functions in a module are usually related to one another in some way; for example, the math module contains the variable pi and mathematical functions such as cos (cosine) and sqrt (square root). This chapter shows you how to use some of the hundreds of modules that come with Python, as well as how to create your own modules.

Importing Modules

To gain access to the variables and functions from a module, you have to *import* it. To tell Python that you want to use functions in the module math, for example, use this import statement:

```
>>> import math
```

Importing a module creates a new variable with that name. That variable refers to an object whose type is module:

```
>>> type(math)
<class 'module'>
```

Once you have imported a module, you can use the built-in function help to see what it contains. Here is the first part of the help output:

```
>>> help(math)
Help on built-in module math:

NAME
    math

DESCRIPTION
    This module provides access to the mathematical functions
    defined by the C standard.

FUNCTIONS
    acos(x, /)
        Return the arc cosine (measured in radians) of x.

        The result is between 0 and pi.

    acosh(x, /)
        Return the inverse hyperbolic cosine of x.

    asin(x, /)
        Return the arc sine (measured in radians) of x.

        The result is between -pi/2 and pi/2.

[There are many other functions not shown here.]
```

The statement import math creates a variable called math that refers to a module object. In that object are all the names defined in that module. Some of them refer to function objects:

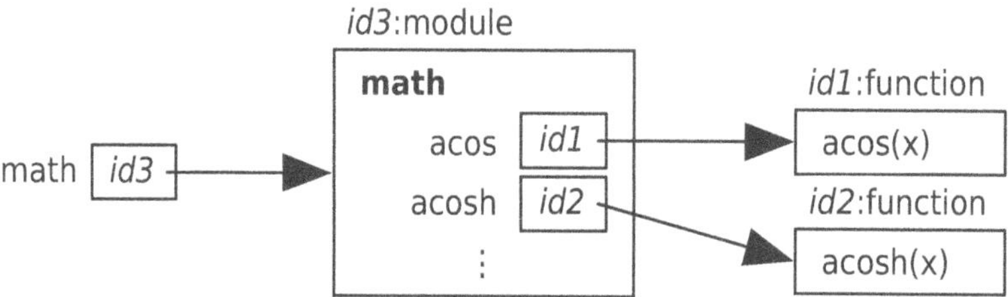

Great—your program can now use all the standard mathematical functions. When you attempt to calculate a square root, however, you encounter an error informing that Python is still unable to find the sqrt function:

```
>>> sqrt(9)
Traceback (most recent call last):
  File "<python-input-0>", line 1, in <module>
    sqrt(9)
    ^^^^
NameError: name 'sqrt' is not defined
```

The solution is to tell Python explicitly to look for the function in the module math by combining the module's name with the function's name using a dot:

```
>>> math.sqrt(9)
3.0
```

The dot is an operator, just like + and ** are operators. Its meaning is "look up the object that the variable to the left of the dot refers to and, in that object, find the name that occurs to the right of the dot." In math.sqrt(9), Python finds math in the current namespace, looks up the module object that math refers to, finds the function sqrt inside that module, and then executes the function call following the standard rules described in Tracing Function Calls in the Memory Model, on page 41.

Modules can contain more than just functions. The module math, for example, also defines some variables, such as pi. Once the module has been imported, you can use these variables like any others:

```
>>> import math
>>> math.pi
3.141592653589793
>>> radius = 5
>>> print('area is', math.pi * radius ** 2)
area is 78.53981633974483
```

You can even assign to variables imported from modules:

```
>>> import math
>>> math.pi = 3
>>> radius = 5
>>> print('area is', math.pi * radius ** 2)
area is 75
```

Don't do this! Changing the value of π isn't a good idea. It's such a bad idea that many languages allow programmers to define unchangeable *constants* as well as variables. As the name suggests, the value of a constant cannot be changed after it has been defined: π is always 3.14159 and a little bit, while SECONDS_PER_DAY is always 86,400. The fact that Python doesn't allow programmers to "freeze" values like this is one of the language's few significant flaws.

How Do You Mean, "this"?

Try *this* code:

```
>>> import this
```

(Don't worry, it's safe!) Enjoy the output!

Combining the module's name with the names of its contents is safe, but it isn't always convenient. For this reason, Python allows you to specify precisely what you want to import from a module, as shown here:

```
>>> from math import sqrt, pi
>>> sqrt(9)
3.0
>>> radius = 5
>>> print('circumference is', 2 * pi * radius)
circumference is 31.41592653589793
```

This statement doesn't introduce a variable called math. Instead, it creates the function sqrt and the variable pi in the current namespace, as if you had typed the function definition and variable assignment yourself. Restart your shell and try this:

```
>>> from math import sqrt, pi
>>> math.sqrt(9)
Traceback (most recent call last):
  File "<python-input-1>", line 1, in <module>
    math.sqrt(9)
    ^^^^
NameError: name 'math' is not defined. Did you forget to import 'math'?
>>> sqrt(9)
3.0
```

Here, you don't have a variable called math. Instead, you imported names sqrt and pi directly into the current namespace, as shown in this diagram:

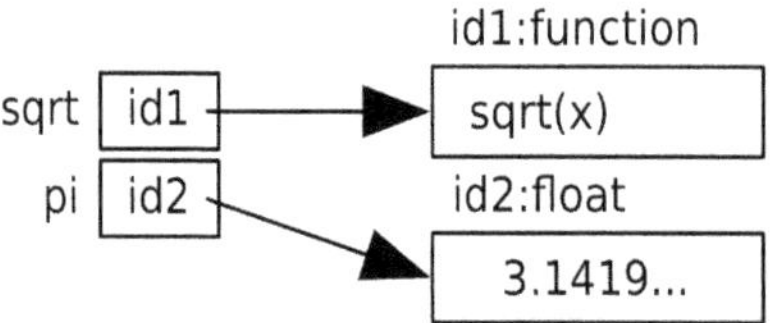

Direct importing of names can lead to problems when different modules provide functions that have the same name, causing a *name conflict*. If you import a function called spell from a module called magic (fictitious), and then you import another function called spell from the grammar module (also fictitious), the second replaces the first. It's exactly like assigning one value to a variable and then assigning another value: the most recent assignment or import wins.

Name conflicts are the reason why it's usually *not* a good idea to use import *, which brings in everything from the module at once:

```
>>> from math import *
>>> print(sqrt(8))
2.8284271247461903
```

Although import * saves some typing, you run the risk of your program accessing the incorrect function and not working correctly.

The standard Python library comprises several hundred modules that can perform a wide range of tasks, from determining the day of the week to fetching data from websites.[1] However, it's far too extensive to absorb in one sitting. Knowing how to use the library effectively is one of the key factors that distinguishes good programmers from those who are less skilled.

Defining Your Modules

Writing and Running a Program, on page 60, explained that to save code for later use, you can put it in a file with a .py extension, and demonstrated how to run that code. Chapter 3, Designing and Using Functions, on page 31, also included this function definition:

```
>>> def convert_to_celsius(fahrenheit: float) -> float:
...     """Return the number of Celsius degrees equivalent to fahrenheit
...     degrees.
...
...     >>> convert_to_celsius(75)
...     23.88888888888889
...     """
...     return (fahrenheit - 32.0) * 5.0 / 9.0
...
```

Put the function definition for convert_to_celsius from Defining Custom Functions, on page 36, in a file called temperature.py. You can save this file anywhere you like, although most programmers create a separate directory for each set of related files that they write. Add another function to temperature.py called above_freezing that returns True if and only if its parameter celsius is above freezing, as shown below:

modules/temperature.py

```
def convert_to_celsius(fahrenheit: float) -> float:
    """Return the number of Celsius degrees equivalent to fahrenheit
    degrees.

    >>> convert_to_celsius(75)
    23.88888888888889
    """
    return (fahrenheit - 32.0) * 5.0 / 9.0

def above_freezing(celsius: float) -> bool:
    """Return True iff temperature celsius degrees is above freezing.

    >>> above_freezing(5.2)
```

1. https://docs.python.org/3.14/library/

Module __builtins__

Python's built-in functions are actually in a module named __builtins__ (with two underscores before and after builtins). The double underscores before and after the name signal that it's part of Python; you'll see this convention used again later for other things. You can see what's in the module using help(__builtins__), or if you want to see what functions and variables are available, you can use the built-in function dir instead:

```
>>> dir(__builtins__)
['ArithmeticError', 'AssertionError', 'AttributeError', 'BaseException',
'BaseExceptionGroup', 'BlockingIOError', 'BrokenPipeError', 'BufferError',
'BytesWarning', 'ChildProcessError', 'ConnectionAbortedError',
'ConnectionError', 'ConnectionRefusedError', 'ConnectionResetError',
'DeprecationWarning', 'EOFError', 'Ellipsis', 'EncodingWarning',
'EnvironmentError', 'Exception', 'ExceptionGroup', 'False', 'FileExistsError',
'FileNotFoundError', 'FloatingPointError', 'FutureWarning', 'GeneratorExit',
'IOError', 'ImportError', 'ImportWarning', 'IndentationError', 'IndexError',
'InterruptedError', 'IsADirectoryError', 'KeyError', 'KeyboardInterrupt',
'LookupError', 'MemoryError', 'ModuleNotFoundError', 'NameError', 'None',
'NotADirectoryError', 'NotImplemented', 'NotImplementedError', 'OSError',
'OverflowError', 'PendingDeprecationWarning', 'PermissionError',
'ProcessLookupError', 'PythonFinalizationError', 'RecursionError',
'ReferenceError', 'ResourceWarning', 'RuntimeError', 'RuntimeWarning',
'StopAsyncIteration', 'StopIteration', 'SyntaxError', 'SyntaxWarning',
'SystemError', 'SystemExit', 'TabError', 'TimeoutError', 'True', 'TypeError',
'UnboundLocalError', 'UnicodeDecodeError', 'UnicodeEncodeError',
'UnicodeError', 'UnicodeTranslateError', 'UnicodeWarning', 'UserWarning',
'ValueError', 'Warning', 'ZeroDivisionError', '_IncompleteInputError',
'__build_class__', '__debug__', '__doc__', '__import__', '__loader__',
'__name__', '__package__', '__spec__', 'abs', 'aiter', 'all', 'anext', 'any',
'ascii', 'bin', 'bool', 'breakpoint', 'bytearray', 'bytes', 'callable', 'chr',
'classmethod', 'compile', 'complex', 'copyright', 'credits', 'delattr', 'dict',
'dir', 'divmod', 'enumerate', 'eval', 'exec', 'exit', 'filter', 'float',
'format', 'frozenset', 'getattr', 'globals', 'hasattr', 'hash', 'help', 'hex',
'id', 'input', 'int', 'isinstance', 'issubclass', 'iter', 'len', 'license',
'list', 'locals', 'map', 'max', 'memoryview', 'min', 'next', 'object', 'oct',
'open', 'ord', 'pow', 'print', 'property', 'quit', 'range', 'repr', 'reversed',
'round', 'set', 'setattr', 'slice', 'sorted', 'staticmethod', 'str', 'sum',
'super', 'tuple', 'type', 'vars', 'zip']
```

As of Python 3.14.0, 62 of the 160 items in __builtins__ are used to signal errors of particular kinds, such as SyntaxError and ZeroDivisionError. All errors, warnings, and exceptions are types similar to int, float, and function. Their names follow a naming convention in which the first letter of each word is uppercase.

We'll introduce some of this module's other members in later chapters.

```
True
>>> above_freezing(-2)
False
"""
return celsius > 0
```

Congratulations—you have created a module called temperature. Now that you've created this file, you can run it and import it like any other module:

```
>>> import temperature
>>> celsius = temperature.convert_to_celsius(33.3)
>>> temperature.above_freezing(celsius)
True
```

What Happens During Import

Let's try another experiment. Create a file called experiment.py with this one statement inside it:

```
print("The panda's scientific name is 'Ailuropoda melanoleuca'")
```

Run experiment.py and then import it:

```
>>> import experiment
The panda's scientific name is 'Ailuropoda melanoleuca'
```

What this shows is that *Python executes modules as it imports them.* You can do anything in a module that you would do in any other program, because as far as Python is concerned, it's just another bunch of statements to be run.

Let's try another experiment. Start a fresh Python session, run experiment.py, and try importing module experiment twice in a row:

```
>>> import experiment
The panda's scientific name is 'Ailuropoda melanoleuca'
>>> import experiment
>>>
```

Notice that the message wasn't printed the second time. That's because Python loads modules only the first time they're imported. Internally, Python keeps track of the modules it has already seen; when it is asked to load one that's already in that list, it just skips over it. Checking the previous imports saves time and will be particularly important when you start writing modules that import other modules, which in turn import other modules—if Python didn't keep track of what was already in memory, it could wind up loading commonly used modules like math dozens of times.

Even if you import a module, edit that module's file, and then reimport, the module won't be reloaded. Your edits won't have any effect until you restart the shell or import importlib and call importlib.reload. For example, after you've imported experiment, change the file contents to this:

```
print("The koala's scientific name is 'Phascolarctos cinereus'")
```

Restoring a Module

If you change the value of a variable or function from an imported module, you can restart the shell and reimport the module to restore it to its original value. In IDLE, you can restart the shell by choosing Shell→Restart Shell.

Without having to restart the shell, you can restore a user-defined module to its original state using the reload from the module importlib. For example, consider the module example, which contains a variable named x that refers to 2:

```
>>> import example
>>> example.x
2
>>> example.x = 7
>>> example.x
7
>>> import importlib
>>> example = importlib.reload(example)
>>> example.x
2
```

Function importlib.reload returns the module. This approach does not work the same way for built-in modules, such as math. Using the same approach with math.pi does not restore its value:

```
>>> import math
>>> math.pi
3.141592653589793
>>> math.pi = 3
>>> math.pi
3
>>> math = importlib.reload(math)
>>> math.pi
3
```

Let's now call importlib.reload to reload the module experiment:

```
>>> import experiment
The panda's scientific name is 'Ailuropoda melanoleuca'
>>> import experiment
>>> import importlib
>>> importlib.reload(experiment)
The koala's scientific name is 'Phascolarctos cinereus'
<module 'experiment' from '.../experiment.py'>
```

In this example, the call to importlib.reload returns the module that was imported.

Selecting Which Code Gets Run on Import: __main__

As you saw in Writing and Running a Program, on page 60, every Python module can be run directly (from the command line or by running it from an

IDE like IDLE), or, as you saw earlier in this section, it can be run indirectly (imported by another program). If a module is to be imported by another module, then the files containing the two modules should be saved in the same directory (an alternative approach would be to use absolute file paths, which are explained in Opening a File, on page 179).

Variable __name__ contains the current module's name

Sometimes you want to write code that should only be executed when the module is run directly, rather than when the module is imported. Python defines a special string variable called __name__ in every module to help you determine this. Suppose you put the following into echo.py:

```
print("__name__ is", __name__)
```

If you run this file, its output is as follows:

```
__name__ is __main__
```

As promised, Python has created a variable __name__. Its value is "__main__", meaning this module is the main program. But look at what happens when you import echo (instead of running it directly):

```
>>> import echo
__name__ is echo
```

The same thing happens if you write a program that does nothing but import your echoing module. Create a file import_echo.py with this code inside it:

```
import echo

print("After import, __name__ is", __name__,
      "and echo.__name__ is", echo.__name__)
```

When run from the command line, the code produces the following output:

```
__name__ is echo
After import, __name__ is __main__ and echo.__name__ is echo
```

When Python imports a module, it sets that module's __name__ variable to be the name of the module rather than the special string "__main__". That is how a module can tell whether it is the main program. Now, create a file named test_main.py with this code inside it:

```
if __name__ == "__main__":
    print("I am the main program.")
else:
    print("Another module is importing me.")
```

Try it. See what happens when you run test_main.py directly and when you import it.

Some of your modules contain not only function definitions but also programs. For example, create a new module temperature_program that contains the functions from temperature and the little program:

modules/temperature_program.py

```
def convert_to_celsius(fahrenheit: float) -> float:
    """Return the number of Celsius degrees equivalent to fahrenheit
    degrees.

    >>> convert_to_celsius(75)
    23.88888888888889
    """
    return (fahrenheit - 32.0) * 5.0 / 9.0

def above_freezing(celsius: float) -> bool:
    """Return True iff temperature celsius degrees is above freezing.

    >>> above_freezing(5.2)
    True
    >>> above_freezing(-2)
    False
    """
    return celsius > 0

fahrenheit = float(input('Enter the temperature in degrees Fahrenheit: '))
celsius = convert_to_celsius(fahrenheit)
if above_freezing(celsius):
    print('It is above freezing.')
else:
    print('It is below freezing.')
```

When that module is run, it prompts the user to enter a value and, depending on the value entered, prints one of two messages:

```
Python 3.14.0b4 (main, Jul  9 2025, 09:00:21) [GCC 11.4.0] on linux
Enter "help" below or click "Help" above for more information.
>>>
===================== RESTART; /tmp/temperature_program.py ==================
Enter the temperature in degrees Fahrenheit: 35
It is above freezing.
>>>
```

Let's create another module, baking.py, that uses the conversion function from the module temperature_program as shown below:

modules/baking.py

```
import temperature_program

def get_preheating_instructions(fahrenheit: float) -> str:
    """Return instructions for preheating the oven in fahreneheit degrees and
    Celsius degrees.

    >>> get_preheating_instructions(500)
```

```
    'Preheat oven to 500 degrees F (260.0 degrees C).'
    """

    cels = str(temperature_program.convert_to_celsius(fahrenheit))
    fahr = str(fahrenheit)
    return 'Preheat oven to ' + fahr + ' degrees F ('+ cels +' degrees C).'

fahr = float(input('Enter the baking temperature in degrees Fahrenheit: '))
print(get_preheating_instructions(fahr))
```

When baking.py is run, it imports temperature_program, causing the program at the bottom of temperature_program.py to be executed:

```
Python 3.14.0b4 (main, Jul  9 2025, 09:00:21) [GCC 11.4.0] on linux
Enter "help" below or click "Help" above for more information.
>>>
===================== RESTART; /tmp/baking.py ===================
Enter the temperature in degrees Fahrenheit: 15
It is below freezing.
Enter the baking temperature in degrees Fahrenheit: 500
Preheat oven to 500.0 degrees F (260.0 degrees C).
>>>
```

Since we don't care whether a temperature is above freezing when preheating your oven, when importing temperature_program.py, we can prevent that part of the code from executing by putting it in an if __name__ == '__main__' block as shown below:

modules/temperature_program_main.py

```
def convert_to_celsius(fahrenheit: float) -> float:
    """Return the number of Celsius degrees equivalent to fahrenheit
    degrees.

    >>> convert_to_celsius(75)
    23.88888888888889
    """
    return (fahrenheit - 32.0) * 5.0 / 9.0


def above_freezing(celsius: float) -> bool:
    """Return True iff temperature celsius degrees is above freezing.

    >>> above_freezing(5.2)
    True
    >>> above_freezing(-2)
    False
    """
    return celsius > 0

if __name__ == '__main__':
    fahrenheit = float(input('Enter the temperature in degrees Fahrenheit: '))
    celsius = convert_to_celsius(fahrenheit)
    if above_freezing(celsius):
```

```
        print('It is above freezing.')
    else:
        print('It is below freezing.')
```

Now when baking.py is run, only the code from temperature_program that is outside of the if __name__ == '__main__': block is executed:

```
Python 3.14.0b4 (main, Jul  9 2025, 09:00:21) [GCC 11.4.0] on linux
Enter "help" below or click "Help" above for more information.
>>>
==================== RESTART; /tmp/baking.py ==================
Enter the baking temperature in degrees Fahrenheit: 500
Preheat oven to 500.0 degrees F (260.0 degrees C).
>>>
```

You will see other uses of __name__ in the following sections and later chapters.

Testing Your Code Semiautomatically

In Designing New Functions: A Recipe, on page 49, we introduced the Function Design Recipe (FDR). Following the FDR, the docstrings that you write include example function calls.

The last step of the FDR involves testing the function. Up until now, you have been typing the function calls from the docstrings to the shell (or copying and pasting them) to run them and then comparing the results with what you expect to make sure they match.

Python has a module called *doctest* that allows you to run the tests included in docstrings all at once. It reports on whether the function calls return what you expect. You will use doctest to run the tests from the temperature_program module from Selecting Which Code Gets Run on Import: __main__, on page 112:

> Test your programs using the module doctest

```
Python 3.14.0b4 (main, Jul  9 2025, 09:00:21) [GCC 11.4.0] on linux
Enter "help" below or click "Help" above for more information.
>>>
==================== RESTART; /tmp/baking.py ==================
Enter the temperature in degrees Fahrenheit: 500
It is above freezing.
>>> import doctest
>>> doctest.testmod()
TestResults(failed=0, attempted=3)
>>>
```

That message indicates that three tests were conducted and none of them failed. That is, the three function calls in the docstrings were run, and they returned the same value that you expected and stated in the docstring.

Testing vs. Debugging

Testing is often confused with debugging, but they're not the same. Testing is the process of checking whether your code behaves as expected; it helps you find problems. Debugging comes afterward: it's the detective work of figuring out what went wrong and how to fix it. In short, testing asks, "Is there a bug?" and debugging answers, "Why is there a bug, and how do I fix it?"

Now let's see what happens when there is an error in your calculation. Instead of the calculation you've been using, `(fahrenheit - 32.0) * 5.0 / 9.0`, let's remove the parentheses: `fahrenheit - 32.0 * 5.0 / 9.0`.

Here is the result of running `doctest` on that module:

```
Python 3.14.0b4 (main, Jul  9 2025, 09:00:21) [GCC 11.4.0] on linux
Enter "help" below or click "Help" above for more information.
>>>
==================== RESTART; /tmp/baking.py =================
Enter the temperature in degrees Fahrenheit: 500
It is above freezing.
>>> import doctest
>>> doctest.testmod()
**********************************************************************
File "/tmp/temperature_program.py", line 5, in __main__.convert_to_celsius
Failed example:
    convert_to_celsius(75)
Expected:
    23.88888888888889
Got:
    57.22222222222222
**********************************************************************
1 item had failures:
   1 of   1 in __main__.convert_to_celsius
***Test Failed*** 1 failure.
TestResults(failed=1, attempted=3)
>>>
```

The failure message above indicates that the function call `convert_to_celsius(75)` was expected to return `23.88888888888889`, but it returned `57.22222222222222`. The other two tests ran and passed.

When a failure occurs, you need to review your code to identify the problem. You should also verify the expected return value listed in the docstring to ensure that it matches both the type contract and function's description.

Tips for Grouping Your Functions

Put functions and variables that logically belong together in the same module. If there isn't some logical connection—for example, if one of the functions calculates how much carbon monoxide different kinds of cars produce, while another figures out bone strength given the bone's diameter and density—then you shouldn't put them in one module just because you happen to be the author of both.

Of course, people often have different opinions about what is logical and what isn't. Take Python's `math` module, for example; should functions to multiply matrices go in there too, or should they go in a separate linear algebra module? What about basic statistical functions? Going back to the previous paragraph, should a function that calculates gas mileage go in the same module as one that calculates carbon monoxide emissions? You can always find a reason why two functions should *not* be in the same module, but a thousand modules with one function each are going to be hard for people (including you) to work with.

As a rule of thumb, if a module has less than a handful of things in it, it's probably too small, and if you can't sum up the contents and purpose of a module in a one- or two-sentence docstring, it's perhaps too large. These are just guidelines, though; in the end, you'll have to decide based on how more experienced programmers have organized modules, like the ones in the Python standard library, and eventually, on your sense of style.

Organizing Your Thoughts

In this chapter, you learned the following:

- A module is a collection of functions and variables grouped in a file. To use a module, you must first import it using `import «modulename»`. After it has been imported, you refer to its contents using `«modulename».«functionname»` or `«modulename».«variable»`.
- Variable `__name__` is created by Python and can be used to specify that some code should only run when the module is run directly and not when the module is imported.
- Programs have to do more than just run to be useful; they have to run correctly. One way to ensure that they do is to test them, which you can do in Python using the module `doctest`.

Exercises

Here are some exercises for you to try on your own.

1. Import module `math`, and use its functions to complete the following exercises. You can call `dir(math)` to get a listing of the items in `math`.
   a. Write an expression that produces the floor of `-2.8`.
   b. Write an expression that rounds the value of `-4.3` and then produces the absolute value of that result.
   c. Write an expression that produces the ceiling of the sine of `34.5`.
2. In the following exercises, you will work with Python's `calendar` module:
   a. Review the documentation on the module `calendar`.[2]
   b. Import module `calendar`.
   c. Using function `help`, read the description of function `isleap`.
   d. Use `isleap` to determine the next leap year.
   e. Use `dir` to get a list of what `calendar` contains.
   f. Find and use a function in module `calendar` to determine how many leap years there will be between the years 2000 and 2050, inclusive.
   g. Find and use a function in module `calendar` to determine which day of the week July 29, 2016, will be.
3. Create a file named `exercise.py` with this code inside it:

```
def average(num1: float, num2: float) -> float:
    """Return the average of num1 and num2.

    >>> average(10,20)
    15.0
    >>> average(2.5, 3.0)
    2.75
    """

    return num1 + num2 / 2
```

   a. Run `exercise.py`. Import `doctest` and run `doctest.testmod`.
   b. Both of the tests in the function `average`'s docstring fail. Fix the code and rerun the tests. Repeat this procedure until the tests pass.

2. https://docs.python.org/3.14/library/calendar.html

CHAPTER 7

Using Methods

So far, you've seen lots of functions: built-in functions, functions inside modules, and functions that you've defined. A *method* is another kind of function that is attached to a particular type. There are str methods, int methods, bool methods, and more—every type has its own set of methods. In this chapter, you'll explore how to use methods, and also how they differ from the rest of the functions that you've seen.

Modules, Classes, and Methods

Classes are like modules, but with methods

In Importing Modules, on page 105, you saw that a module is a kind of object, one that can contain functions and other variables. There is another kind of object that is similar to a module: a *class*. You've been using classes all along, probably without realizing it: a class is how Python represents a type.

You may have called built-in function help on int, float, bool, or str. Let's do that now with str (note that the first line indicates it's a class):

```
>>> help(str)
Help on class str in module builtins:

class str(object)
 |  str(object='') -> str
 |  str(bytes_or_buffer[, encoding[, errors]]) -> str
 |
 |  Create a new string object from the given object. If encoding or
 |  errors is specified, then the object must expose a data buffer
 |  that will be decoded using the given encoding and error handler.
 |  Otherwise, returns the result of object.__str__() (if defined)
 |  or repr(object).
 |  encoding defaults to 'utf-8'.
 |  errors defaults to 'strict'.
 |
 |  Methods defined here:
```

```
 |
 |  __add__(self, value, /)
 |      Return self+value.
 |
 |  __contains__(self, key, /)
 |      Return bool(key in self).
[Lots of other names with leading and trailing underscores not shown here.]
 |  capitalize(self, /)
 |      Return a capitalized version of the string.
 |
 |      More specifically, make the first character have upper case and the
 |      rest lower case.
 |
 |  casefold(self, /)
 |      Return a version of the string suitable for caseless comparisons.
 |
 |  center(self, width, fillchar=' ', /)
 |      Return a centered string of length width.
 |
 |      Padding is done using the specified fill character (default is a
 |      space).
 |
 |  count(self, sub[, start[, end]], /)
 |      Return the number of non-overlapping occurrences of substring sub
 |      in string S[start:end].
[There are many more of these as well.]
```

Near the top of this documentation is the description of the str function:

```
|  str(bytes_or_buffer[, encoding[, errors]]) -> str
|
|  Create a new string object from the given object.
```

It explains how to use str as a function: you can call it to create a string. For example, str(17) creates the string '17'.

Functions that create new objects are called *constructors*. Function str is a constructor for strings. Functions int, float, and bool are constructors for the namesake data types. You will learn more about constructors in Chapter 14, Object-Oriented Programming, on page 281.

Calling Methods

You can also use the name str to access methods defined in the str class, such as str.capitalize:

```
>>> str.capitalize
<method 'capitalize' of 'str' objects>
```

Methods are like functions, but the first argument is an object

Methods differ from regular functions in that they are tied to a specific object. Every method in class str requires a string as the first argument. Python provides a "dot" notation for calling a method where the object appears first, followed by the method call with any additional parameters:

```
>>> 'browning'.capitalize() # same as str.capitalize('browning')
'Browning'
>>> 'Sonnet 43'.center(26) # same as str.center('Sonnet 43', 26).
'        Sonnet 43         '
>>> 'How do I love thee? Let me count the ways.'.count('the')
2
```

When you call a string method like 'browning'.capitalize, the string 'browning' is automatically passed as the first parameter to the method. There's no need to pass it explicitly. More generally, methods in any class are always used with an object of that class, and that object is passed in automatically as the first parameter behind the scenes.

Here is the help for method lower in class str. Notice that you can get help for a single method by prefixing it with the class it belongs to.

```
>>> help(str.lower)
Help on method descriptor lower:

lower(self, /) unbound builtins.str method
    Return a copy of the string converted to lowercase.
```

Compare that documentation with the help for the sqrt function in the math module:

```
>>> import math
>>> help(math.sqrt)
Help on built-in function sqrt in module math:

sqrt(x, /)
    Return the square root of x.
```

In the help for str.lower, self refers to the string on which the method is being called (the object). The help for math.sqrt doesn't show any such object.

The general form of a method call is as follows:

```
«expression».«method_name»(«arguments»)
```

So far, every example you've seen has a single object as the expression, but any expression can be used as long as it evaluates to the correct type. Here's an example:

```
>>> ('TTA' + 'G' * 3).count('T')
2
```

Why Programming Languages Are Called *Object-Oriented*

The phrase *object-oriented* was introduced to describe a style of programming where objects are the primary focus: you tell objects to do things by calling their methods. This approach contrasts with *imperative* programming, where functions take the lead and objects are just inputs. The idea originated with the language *Simula* in the 1960s, which introduced the concept of programming with interacting objects. Python supports both styles, allowing you to choose the approach that best fits your problem.

The expression `('TTA' + 'G' * 3)` evaluates to the DNA sequence `'TTAGGG'`, and that is the object that is used in the call on string method `str.count`.

Here are the steps for executing a method call. These steps are similar to those for executing a function call in Tracing Function Calls in the Memory Model, on page 41.

1. Evaluate the `«expression»`, which may be something simple, like `'Elizabeth Barrett Browning'` (a poet from the 1800s), or more complicated, like `('TTA' + 'G' * 3)`. Either way, a single object is produced, and that will be the object you are interacting with during the method call.

2. Now that you have an object, evaluate the method arguments left to right. In our DNA example, the argument is `'T'`.

3. Pass the result of evaluating the initial expression as the first argument, and also pass the argument values from the previous step, into the method.

4. Execute the method.

When the method call finishes, it produces a value. In the DNA example, `'TTAGGG'.count('T')` returns the number of times `'T'` occurs in `'TTAGGG'`, which is `2`.

Exploring String Methods

Strings are central to programming; almost every program uses strings in some way. You'll explore some of the ways you can manipulate strings and, at the same time, firm up your understanding of methods.

Listed in Table 4, Common String Methods, on page 126 are the most commonly used string methods. You can find the complete list in Python's online documentation, or type `help(str)` into the shell.

If the optional parameters `start` and `end` are specified, a method operates on the substring only within that part of the string. The `start` parameter defines the position where the substring begins, with 0 being the start of the string, and the end parameter defines where the substring ends (the last character of the substring is at end-1). If not specified, the substring begins at the start of the string and goes to the end.

Notice that any method that appears to modify a string, such as str.upper or str.strip, instead returns a modified copy of the original string. Python strings are *immutable*: once created, they are "carved in stone" and cannot be modified.

Predicate Functions

A regular function (or a method) that returns a Boolean value (True or False) is called a *predicate* function. Historically, predicate function names start with the prefix is or is_, followed by the property that the function reports. So, the function str.isupper checks if a string *is* in the uppercase, while its sister function, str.upper, converts the string to uppercase.

Let's have a look at some examples. Let's call the method 'species'.startswith(prefix):

```
>>> 'species'.startswith('a')
False
>>> 'species'.startswith('spe')
True
```

The method takes a string argument and returns a bool indicating whether the object string whose method was called—the one to the left of the dot—starts with the string that is given as an argument. There is also an endswith method:

```
>>> 'species'.endswith('a')
False
>>> 'species'.endswith('es')
True
```

Sometimes strings have extra whitespace at the beginning and the end. The string methods lstrip, rstrip, and strip remove whitespace from the front, from the end, and from both ends, respectively. This example shows the result of applying these three methods to a string with leading and trailing whitespace:

```
>>> compound = '     \n  Methyl \n butanol    \n'
>>> compound.lstrip()
'Methyl \n butanol    \n'
>>> compound.rstrip()
'     \n  Methyl \n butanol'
>>> compound.strip()
'Methyl \n butanol'
```

Note that the other whitespace inside the string is unaffected; these methods only work from the front and end. Here is another example that uses string

Method	Description
str.capitalize	Returns a capitalized version of the string
str.count	Returns the number of nonoverlapping occurrences of substring sub in the string. This method is case-sensitive.
str.endswith	Returns True if the string ends with the specified suffix, False otherwise. This method is case-sensitive.
str.startswith	Returns True if the string starts with the specified prefix, False otherwise. This method is case-sensitive.
str.find	Return the smallest index in the string where substring sub is found. Returns -1 on failure. This method is case-sensitive.
str.islower	Returns True if all characters in the string are lowercase and there is at least one cased character in the string. Returns False otherwise
str.isupper	Returns True if all characters in the string are uppercase and there is at least one cased character in the string. Returns False otherwise
str.isnumeric	Returns True if all characters in the string are numeric and there is at least one character in the string, False otherwise
str.lower	Returns a copy of the string converted to lowercase
str.upper	Returns a copy of the string converted to uppercase
str.swapcase	Returns a copy of the string with all lowercase letters capitalized and all uppercase letters made lowercase
str.strip	Returns a copy of the string with leading and trailing whitespace removed. If chars is given and not None, remove characters in chars instead.
str.lstrip	Returns a copy of the string with leading whitespace removed. If chars is given and not None, remove characters in chars instead.
str.rstrip	Returns a copy of the string with trailing whitespace removed. If chars is given and not None, remove characters in chars instead.
str.replace	Returns a copy of the string with all occurrences of substring old replaced by new
str.split	Returns the whitespace-separated words in the string as a list. (You'll see the list type in Storing and Accessing Data in Lists, on page 133.)

Table 4—Common String Methods

method swapcase to change lowercase letters to uppercase and uppercase to lowercase:

```
>>> 'Computer Science'.swapcase()
'cOMPUTER sCIENCE'
```

Remember how a method call starts with an expression? Because 'Computer Science'.swapcase() is an expression, you can immediately call method endswith on the result of that expression to check whether that result has 'ENCE' as its last four characters:

```
>>> 'Computer Science'.swapcase().endswith('ENCE')
True
```

The next figure shows what happens when you do this:

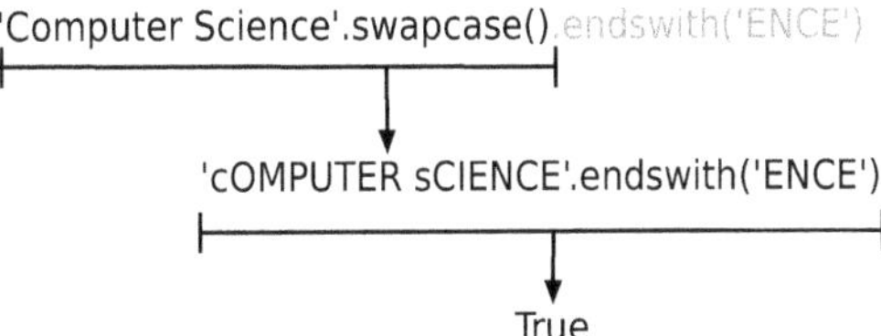

The call on method swapcase produces a new string, and that new string is used for the call on method endswith.

Both int and float are classes. It is possible to access the documentation for these either by calling help(int) or by calling help on an object of the class:

```
>>> help(0)
Help on int object:

class int(object)
 |  int([x]) -> integer
 |  int(x, base=10) -> integer
 |
 |  Convert a number or string to an integer, or return 0 if no arguments
 |  are given.  If x is a number, return x.__int__().  For floating-point
 |  numbers, this truncates towards zero.
 |
 |  If x is not a number or if base is given, then x must be a string,
 |  bytes, or bytearray instance representing an integer literal in the
 |  given base.  The literal can be preceded by '+' or '-' and be surrounded
 |  by whitespace.  The base defaults to 10.  Valid bases are 0 and 2-36.
 |  Base 0 means to interpret the base from the string as an integer literal.
 |  >>> int('0b100', base=0)
 |  4
 |
 |  Built-in subclasses:
 |      bool
```

```
 |
 |  Methods defined here:
 |
 |  __abs__(self, /)
 |      abs(self)
 |
 |  __add__(self, value, /)
 |      Return self+value.
 |
...
```

Most modern programming languages are structured this way: the "things" in the program are objects, and most of the code in the program consists of methods that use the data stored in those objects. Chapter 14, Object-Oriented Programming, on page 281, will show you how to create new kinds of objects; until then, you'll work with objects of types that are built into Python.

What Are Those Underscores?

Any method (or other name) beginning and ending with two underscores is considered special by Python. The help documentation for strings shows these methods, among many others:

Methods whose names begin and end with two underscores are special

```
 |  Methods defined here:
 |
 |  __add__(self, value, /)
 |      Return self+value.
```

These methods are typically connected with some other syntax in Python: use of that syntax will trigger a method call. For example, string method __add__ is called when anything is added to a string:

```
>>> 'TTA' + 'GGG'
'TTAGGG'
>>> 'TTA'.__add__('GGG')
'TTAGGG'
```

Programmers rarely call these special methods directly, but it is eye-opening to see this, which may help you understand how Python works.

Integers and floating-point numbers have similar features. Here is part of the help documentation for int:

```
>>> help(int)
Help on class int in module builtins:

class int(object)
...
 |  Methods defined here:
```

```
 |
 |  __abs__(self, /)
 |      abs(self)
 |
 |  __add__(self, value, /)
 |      Return self+value.
 |
...
 |  __gt__(self, value, /)
 |      Return self>value.
```

The documentation describes when these are called. Here, you can see both versions of getting the absolute value of a number:

```
>>> abs(-3)
3
>>> (-3).__abs__()
3
```

Put -3 in parentheses so that Python will call _abs_ after negating 3. Without the parentheses, _abs_ is called first, and the result is negated, which leads to an unexpected result:

```
>>> -3 .__abs__()
-3
```

This is functionally equivalent to:

```
>>> -(3 .__abs__())
-3
```

You need to put a space after 3 so that Python doesn't think you're making a floating-point number 3. (remember that you can leave off the trailing 0).

Let's add two integers using this trick:

```
>>> 3 + 5
8
>>> 3 .__add__(5)
8
```

And now let's compare two numbers to determine which is larger:

```
>>> 3 > 5
False
>>> 3 .__gt__(5)
False
>>> 5 > 3
True
>>> 5 .__gt__(3)
True
```

Dunders

The special methods, such as _init_, _len_, and _str_, are often called *dunder* (Double-*UNDER*score) methods.

Again, programmers don't typically call the underscore methods directly, but it's worth knowing that Python uses methods to handle all of these operators.

Function objects, like other objects, contain double-underscore variables. For example, the documentation for each function is stored in a variable called _doc_:

```
>>> import math
>>> math.sqrt.__doc__
'Return the square root of x.'
```

When you use built-in function print to print that _doc_ string, look what comes out! It looks just like the output from calling built-in function help on math.sqrt:

```
>>> print(math.sqrt.__doc__)
Return the square root of x.
>>> help(math.sqrt)
Help on built-in function sqrt in module math:

sqrt(x, /)
    Return the square root of x.
```

Every function object keeps track of its docstring in a special variable called _doc_.

A Methodical Review

In this chapter, you learned the following:

- Classes are like modules, except that classes contain methods and modules contain functions.
- Methods are like functions, except that the first argument must be an object of the class in which the method is defined.
- Methods whose names begin and end with two underscores are considered special by Python, and they are triggered by particular syntax.

Exercises

Here are some exercises for you to try on your own.

1. In the Python shell, execute the following method calls:

   a. 'hello'.upper()
   b. 'Happy Birthday!'.lower()
   c. 'WeeeEEEEeeeEEEEeee'.swapcase()
   d. 'ABC123'.isupper()
   e. 'aeiouAEIOU'.count('a')
   f. 'hello'.endswith('o')
   g. 'hello'.startswith('H')

2. Using string method count, write an expression that produces the number of o's in 'tomato'.

3. Using string method find, write an expression that produces the index of the first occurrence of o in 'tomato'.

4. Using string method find, write a *single* expression that produces the index of the *second* occurrence of o in 'tomato'. Hint: Call find twice.

5. Using your expression from the previous exercise, find the second o in 'avocado'. If you don't get the result you expect, revise the expression and try again.

6. Using string method replace, write an expression that produces a string based on 'runner' with the n's replaced by b's.

7. Variable s refers to ' yes '. When a string method is called with s as its argument, the string 'yes' is produced. Which string method was called?

8. Variable fruit refers to 'pineapple'. For the following function calls, in what order are the subexpressions evaluated?

   a. fruit.find('p', fruit.count('p'))
   b. fruit.count(fruit.upper().swapcase())
   c. fruit.replace(fruit.swapcase(), fruit.lower())

9. Using string methods, write expressions that produce the following:

   a. A copy of 'boolean' capitalized
   b. The first occurrence of '2' in 'CO2 H2O'
   c. The second occurrence of '2' in 'CO2 H2O'
   d. True if and only if 'Boolean' begins lowercase
   e. A copy of "MoNDaY" converted to lowercase and then capitalized
   f. A copy of " Monday" with the leading whitespace removed

10. Complete the examples in the docstring and then write the body of the following function:

```
def total_occurrences(s1: str, s2: str, ch: str) -> int:
    """Return the total number of times that ch occurs in s1 and s2.

    Precondition: len(ch) == 1

    >>> total_occurrences('color', 'yellow', 'l')
    3
    >>> total_occurrences('red', 'blue', 'l')

    >>> total_occurrences('green', 'purple', 'b')

    """
```

CHAPTER 8

Storing Collections of Data Using Lists

Lists can contain zero or more objects

Up to this point, you have seen numbers, Boolean values, strings, functions, and a few other types. Once one of these objects has been created, it is immutable: it can't be modified. In this chapter, you will learn how to use a Python data type named `list`. Lists may contain zero or more objects and are used to store ordered collections of data. Unlike the other types you've learned about, lists can be modified.

Storing and Accessing Data in Lists

This table shows the number of steps recorded each day over a continuous 14-day period by US adults in a *recent research study [MDWG12]*.

Day	Number of Steps	Day	Number of Steps
1	3124	8	2675
2	2980	9	2550
3	2567	10	2901
4	2754	11	3100
5	2890	12	3050
6	3012	13	2999
7	2805	14	2820

Based on what you have seen so far, you would need to create fourteen variables to store the number of steps counted each day, as shown in the code at the top of the next page.

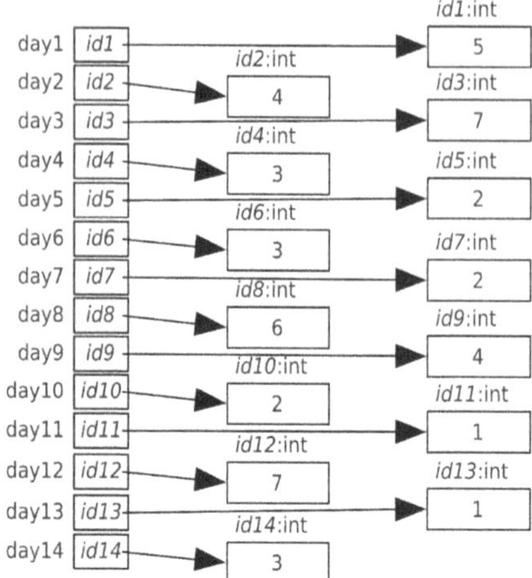

To track an entire year's worth of observations, you would need 365 variables (366 for a leap year).

Rather than dealing with this programming nightmare, you can use a *list* to record the 14 days of step counts. That is, you can use a list to record the 14 int objects that contain the counts:

```
>>> steps = [3124, 2980, 2567, 2754, 2890, 3012, 2805, 2675, 2550, 2901,
...          3100, 3050, 2999, 2820]
>>> steps
[3124, 2980, 2567, 2754, 2890, 3012, 2805, 2675, 2550, 2901, 3100, 3050,
 2999, 2820]
```

A list is an object; like any other object, it can be assigned to a variable. Here is what happens in the memory model:

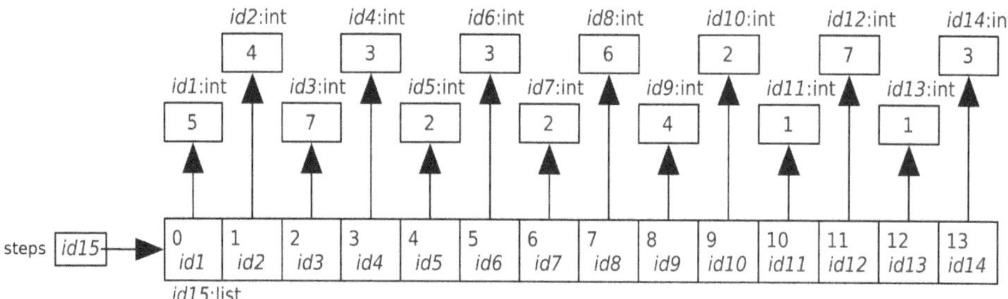

The general form of a list expression is as follows:

[«*expression1*», «*expression2*», ... , «*expressionN*»]

An empty list (a container without stored values) is expressed as [].

In the step count example, the variable steps refers to a list with fourteen items, also known as *elements*. The list itself is an object, but it also contains the memory addresses of fourteen other objects. The previous memory model shows steps after this assignment statement has been executed.

The items in a list are ordered, and each item has an *index* indicating its position in the list. The first item in a list is at index 0, the second at index 1, and so on. It would be more natural to use 1 as the first index, as human languages do. Python, however, follows the same convention as languages like C and Java, and starts counting at zero. To refer to a particular list item, put the index in brackets after a reference to the list (such as the name of a variable):

```
>>> steps = [3124, 2980, 2567, 2754, 2890, 3012, 2805, 2675, 2550, 2901,
...                3100, 3050, 2999, 2820]
>>> steps[0]
3124
>>> steps[1]
2980
>>> steps[12]
2999
>>> steps[13]
2820
```

Note that L[i] is often pronounced as "L sub i," following the mathematical convention of using subscripts to refer to elements in a vector or matrix.

1-Based Indexing

Several older programming languages, including Fortran, MATLAB, R, Lua, Julia, COBOL, Smalltalk, and Ada use 1 as the first index ("1-based indexing").

You can use only those indices that are in the range from zero up to one less than the length of the list, because the list index starts at 0, not at 1. In a fourteen-item list, the legal indices are 0, 1, 2, and so on, up to 13. Trying to use an out-of-range index results in an error:

```
>>> steps = [5, 4, 7, 3, 2, 3, 2, 6, 4, 2, 1, 7, 1, 3]
>>> steps[1001]
Traceback (most recent call last):
  File "<python-input-1>", line 1, in <module>
    steps[1001]
    ~~~~~^^^^^^
IndexError: list index out of range
```

Unlike most programming languages, Python also lets us index backward from the end of a list. The last item is at index -1, the one before it at index

-2, and so on. Negative indices provide a way to access the last item, second-to-last item, and so on, without having to figure out the size of the list:

```
>>> steps = [3124, 2980, 2567, 2754, 2890, 3012, 2805, 2675, 2550, 2901,
...                3100, 3050, 2999, 2820]
>>> steps[-1]
3
>>> steps[-2]
1
>>> steps[-14]
5
>>> steps[-15]
Traceback (most recent call last):
  File "<python-input-2>", line 1, in <module>
    steps[-15]
    ~~~~~^^^^^
IndexError: list index out of range
```

Since each item in a list is an object, the items can be assigned to other variables:

```
>>> steps = [3124, 2980, 2567, 2754, 2890, 3012, 2805, 2675, 2550, 2901,
...                3100, 3050, 2999, 2820]
>>> third = steps[2]
>>> print('Third day:', third)
Third day: 2567
```

In Aliasing: What's in a Name?, on page 144, you will learn that an entire list can be assigned to other variables. You will also discover what effect that has.

An Empty List

In Chapter 4, Working with Text, on page 67, you saw the empty string, which doesn't contain any characters. There is also an *empty list*. An empty list is a list with no items in it. As with all lists, an empty list is represented using brackets:

```
>>> steps = []
>>> steps
[]
```

Since an empty list has no items, attempting to index it results in an error:

```
>>> steps[0]
Traceback (most recent call last):
  File "<python-input-2>", line 1, in <module>
    steps[0]
    ~~~~~^^^
IndexError: list index out of range
>>> steps[-1]
Traceback (most recent call last):
```

```
  File "<python-input-3>", line 1, in <module>
    steps[-1]
    ~~~~~^^^^
IndexError: list index out of range
```

Lists Are Heterogeneous

Lists can contain any type of data, including integers, strings, and even other lists. Here is a list of information about the element krypton, including its name, symbol, melting point (in degrees Celsius), and boiling point (also in degrees Celsius):

```
>>> krypton = ['Krypton', 'Kr', -157.2, -153.4]
>>> krypton[1]
'Kr'
>>> krypton[2]
-157.2
```

A list is typically used to contain items of the same kind, such as temperatures, dates, or grades in a course. A list can be used to aggregate related information of different types, as you did with krypton; however, this "mix-and-match" approach is prone to error. Here, you need to remember which temperature comes first and whether the name or the symbol starts the list. Another common source of bugs is when you forget to include a piece of data in your list (or perhaps it was missing in your source of information). How, for example, would you keep track of similar information for iridium if you don't know the melting point? What information would you put at index 2? A more advanced approach to storing heterogeneous data is described in Chapter 14, Object-Oriented Programming, on page 281.

Type Annotations for Lists

Often, when writing type contracts for functions, you'll want to specify that the values in a list parameter are all of a particular type. For example, you might write a function to calculate the average of a list of floats:

```
>>> def average(L: list[float]) -> float:
...     """Return the average of the values in L.
...
...     >>> average([1.4, 1.6, 1.8, 2.0])
...     1.7
...     """
```

This trick doesn't prevent a programmer from calling the function with other kinds of data (even though this would often result in an error), but it does indicate what you expect when someone calls your function.

Modifying Lists

Suppose you're typing in a list of the noble gases and your fingers slip:

```
>>> nobles = ['helium', 'none', 'argon', 'krypton', 'xenon', 'radon']
```

Lists are mutable

The error here is that you typed 'none' instead of 'neon'. Here's the memory model that was created by that assignment statement:

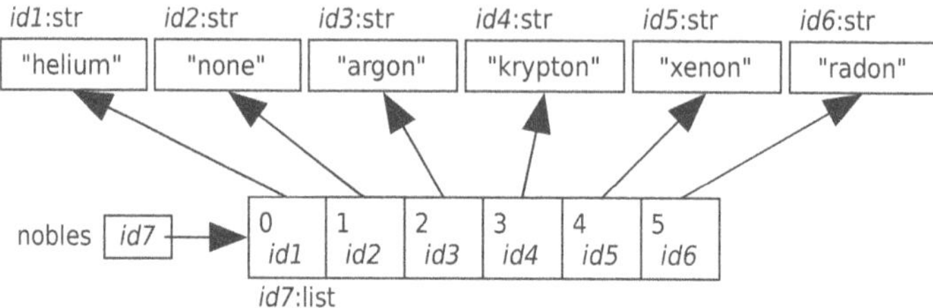

Rather than retyping the whole list, you can assign a new value to a specific element of the list:

```
>>> nobles[1] = 'neon'
>>> nobles
['helium', 'neon', 'argon', 'krypton', 'xenon', 'radon']
```

Here is the result after the assignment to nobles[1]:

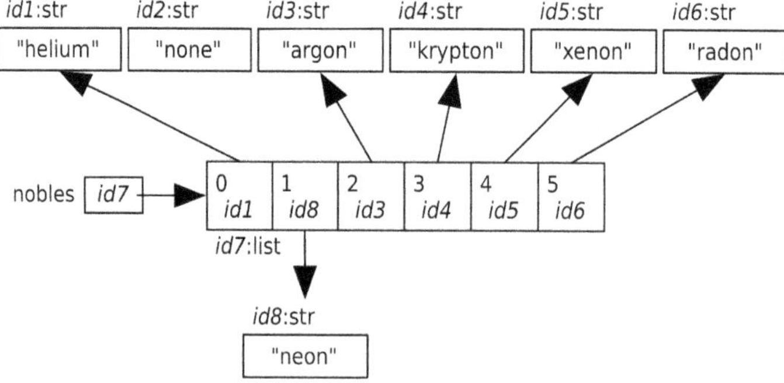

That memory model also shows that list objects are *mutable*. That is, the contents of a list can be *mutated*.

In the previous code, nobles[1] was used on the left side of the assignment operator. It can also be used on the right side. In general, an expression of the form L[i] (list L at index i) behaves just like a simple variable (see Variables and Computer Memory: Remembering Values, on page 15).

If L[i] is used in an expression (such as on the right of an assignment statement), it means "Get the value referred to by the memory address at index i of list L."

On the other hand, if L[i] is on the left of an assignment statement (as in nobles[1] = 'neon'), it means "Look up the memory address at index i of list L so it can be overwritten."

In contrast to lists, numbers and strings are immutable. You cannot, for example, change a letter in a string. Methods that appear to do that, like str.upper, actually create new strings:

```
>>> name = 'Darwin'
>>> print(name.upper())
DARWIN
>>> print(name)
Darwin
```

Because strings are immutable, it is only possible to use an expression of the form s[i] (string s at index i) on the RHS.

Operations on Lists

Functions That Python Provides, on page 31, and Operations on Strings, on page 68, introduced a few of Python's built-in functions. Some of these, such as len, can be applied to lists, as well as others you haven't seen before. (See the following table.)

Function	Description
len	Returns the number of items in list L
max	Returns the maximum value in list L
min	Returns the minimum value in list L
sum	Returns the sum of the values in list L
sorted	Returns a copy of list L where the items are in order from smallest to largest. This function does not modify L.

Table 5—List Operations

Here are some examples. The half-life of a radioactive substance is the time taken for half of it to decay. After this time has passed twice, three-quarters of the material will have decayed; after three times, seven-eighths will have decayed, and so on.

An *isotope* is a form of a chemical element. Plutonium has several isotopes, each with a different half-life. The code at the top of the following page shows some of the built-in functions in action, working on a list of the half-lives of plutonium isotopes Pu-238, Pu-239, Pu-240, Pu-241, and Pu-242.

```
>>> half_lives = [887.7, 24100.0, 6563.0, 14, 373300.0]
>>> len(half_lives)
5
>>> max(half_lives)
373300.0
>>> min(half_lives)
14
>>> sum(half_lives)
404864.7
>>> sorted(half_lives)
[14, 887.7, 6563.0, 24100.0, 373300.0]
>>> half_lives
[887.7, 24100.0, 6563.0, 14, 373300.0]
```

In addition to built-in functions, some of the operators that you have seen can also be applied to lists. Like strings, lists can be combined using the concatenation (+) operator:

```
>>> original = ['H', 'He', 'Li']
>>> final = original + ['Be']
>>> final
['H', 'He', 'Li', 'Be']
```

This code doesn't mutate either of the original list objects. Instead, it creates a new list whose entries refer to the items in the original lists.

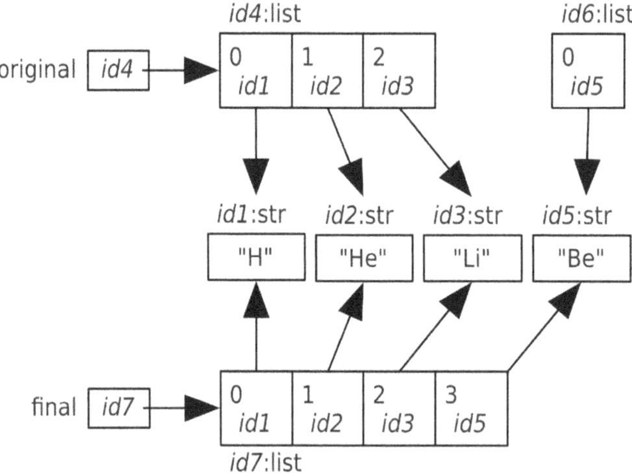

A list has a type, and Python complains if you misuse a value of some type. For example, an error occurs when the concatenation operator is applied to a list and a string:

```
>>> ['H', 'He', 'Li'] + 'Be'
Traceback (most recent call last):
  File "<python-input-10>", line 1, in <module>
    ['H', 'He', 'Li'] + 'Be'
    ~~~~~~~~~~~~~~~~~~^~~~~~
TypeError: can only concatenate list (not "str") to list
```

You can also multiply a list by an integer to get a new list containing the elements from the original list repeated that number of times:

```
>>> metals = ['Fe', 'Ni']
>>> metals * 3
['Fe', 'Ni', 'Fe', 'Ni', 'Fe', 'Ni']
```

As with concatenation, the original list isn't modified; instead, a new list is created.

One operator that does modify a list is del ("delete"). It can be used to remove an item from a list by position, as follows:

```
>>> metals = ['Fe', 'Ni']
>>> del metals[0]
>>> metals
['Ni']
```

The in Operator on Lists

The in operator can be applied to lists to check whether an object is a member of a list:

```
>>> nobles = ['helium', 'neon', 'argon', 'krypton', 'xenon', 'radon']
>>> gas = input('Enter a gas: ')
Enter a gas: argon
>>> if gas in nobles:
...     print(f'{gas.capitalize()} is noble.')
...
Argon is noble.
>>> gas = input('Enter a gas: ')
Enter a gas: nitrogen
>>> if gas in nobles:
...     print(f'{gas.capitalize()} is noble.')
...
>>>
```

Unlike with strings, when used with lists, the in operator checks only for a single item. This code checks whether the list [1, 2] is an item in the list [0, 1, 2, 3]:

```
>>> [1, 2] in [0, 1, 2, 3]
False
```

Slicing Lists

Slicing is used to create sublists

Geneticists describe *C. elegans* (nematodes, microscopic worms) phenotypes using three-letter short-form markers. Examples include *Emb* (embryonic lethality), *Him* (high incidence of males), *Unc* (uncoordinated), *Dpy* (dumpy: short and fat), *Sma* (small), and *Lon* (long). You can keep a list:

```
>>> celegans_phenotypes = ['Emb', 'Him', 'Unc', 'Lon', 'Dpy', 'Sma']
>>> celegans_phenotypes
['Emb', 'Him', 'Unc', 'Lon', 'Dpy', 'Sma']
```

It turns out that *Dpy* worms and *Sma* worms are difficult to distinguish from each other, so they aren't as easily differentiated in complex strains. You can produce a new list based on celegans_phenotypes, excluding *Dpy* and *Sma*, by slicing the original list:

```
>>> celegans_phenotypes = ['Emb', 'Him', 'Unc', 'Lon', 'Dpy', 'Sma']
>>> useful_markers = celegans_phenotypes[0:4]
```

This operation creates a *slice*: a new list consisting of only the four distinguishable markers, which are the first four items from the list that celegans_phenotypes refers to:

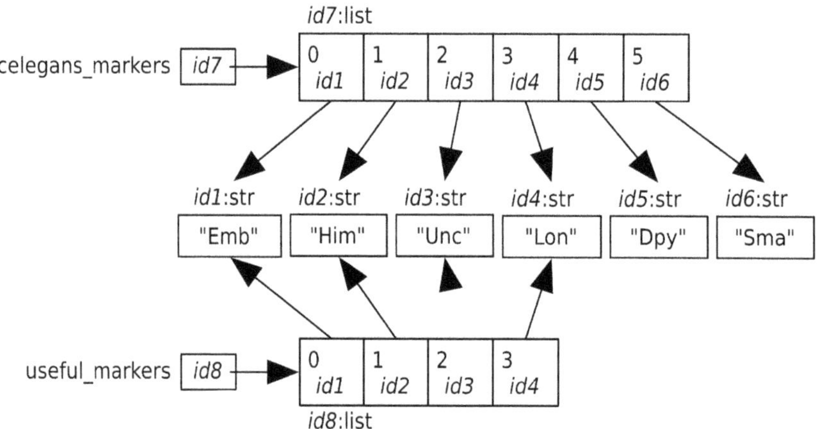

The first index in the slice is the starting point. The second index is *one more than* the index of the last item you want to include. For example, the last item you wanted to include, Lon, had an index of 3, so you used 4 for the second index. More rigorously, list[i:j] is a slice of the original list from index i (inclusive) up to, but not including, index j (exclusive). Python uses this convention to be consistent with the rule that the legal indices for a list go from 0 up to one less than the list's length.

The first index can be omitted if you want to slice from the beginning of the list, and the last index can be omitted if you want to slice to the end:

```
>>> celegans_phenotypes = ['Emb', 'Him', 'Unc', 'Lon', 'Dpy', 'Sma']
>>> celegans_phenotypes[:4]
['Emb', 'Him', 'Unc', 'Lon']
>>> celegans_phenotypes[4:]
['Dpy', 'Sma']
```

To create a copy of the entire list, omit both indices so that the "slice" runs from the start of the list to its end:

```
>>> celegans_phenotypes = ['Emb', 'Him', 'Unc', 'Lon', 'Dpy', 'Sma']
>>> celegans_copy = celegans_phenotypes[:]
>>> celegans_phenotypes[5] = 'Lvl'
>>> celegans_phenotypes
['Emb', 'Him', 'Unc', 'Lon', 'Dpy', 'Lvl']
>>> celegans_copy
['Emb', 'Him', 'Unc', 'Lon', 'Dpy', 'Sma']
>>> id(celegans_phenotypes)
140182369564096
>>> id(celegans_copy)
140182368052928
```

The list referred to by `celegans_copy` is a *clone* of the list referred to by `celegans_phenotypes`. The lists contain the same items, but the lists themselves are distinct objects with unique identities:

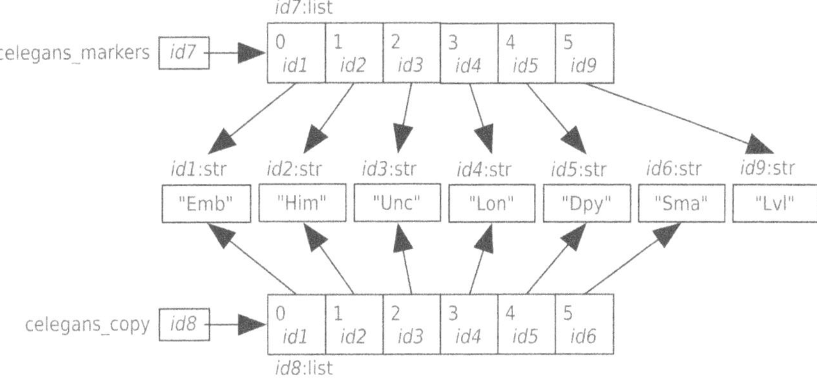

In List Methods, on page 145, you will learn about a list method that can be used to make a copy of a list.

Aliasing: What's in a Name?

An *alias* is an alternative name for an object. In Python, two variables are considered aliases when they have the same identity. For example, the following code creates two variables that both refer to the same list:

When two variables refer to the same object, they are called aliases

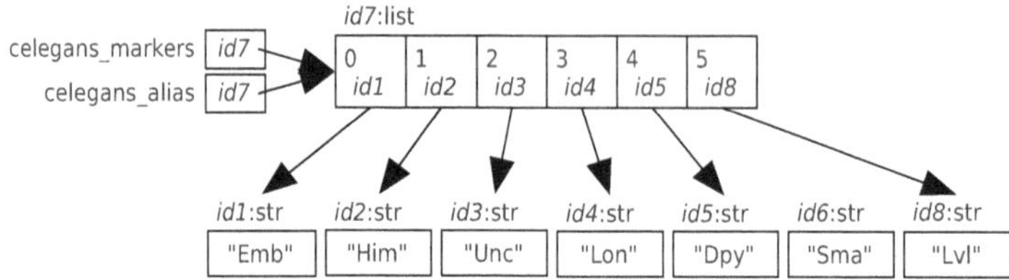

When you modify the list using one of the variables, references through the other variable also show the change:

```
>>> celegans_phenotypes = ['Emb', 'Him', 'Unc', 'Lon', 'Dpy', 'Sma']
>>> celegans_alias = celegans_phenotypes
>>> id(celegans_phenotypes)
140293381748160
>>> id(celegans_alias)
140293381748160
>>> id(celegans_phenotypes) == id(celegans_alias)
True
>>> celegans_phenotypes[5] = 'Lvl'
>>> celegans_phenotypes
['Emb', 'Him', 'Unc', 'Lon', 'Dpy', 'Lvl']
>>> celegans_alias
['Emb', 'Him', 'Unc', 'Lon', 'Dpy', 'Lvl']
```

Aliasing is one of the reasons why the notion of mutability is essential. For example, if x and y refer to the same list, then any changes you make to the list through x will be "seen" by y, and vice versa. Aliasing can lead to all sorts of hard-to-find errors in which a list's value changes as if by magic, even though your program doesn't appear to assign anything to it. Immutable values, such as strings, are immune to aliasing. Since a string can't be changed after it has been created, it's safe to have aliases for it.

Mutable Parameters

Aliasing occurs when you use list parameters, as parameters are variables. Here is a function that takes a list, removes its last item, and returns the list:

```
>>> def remove_last_item(L: list) -> list:
...     """Return list L with the last item removed.
...
```

```
...     Precondition: len(L) >= 0
...
...     >>> remove_last_item([1, 3, 2, 4])
...     [1, 3, 2]
...     """
...     del L[-1]
...     return L
...
>>>
```

In the code that follows, a list is created and stored in a variable; then that variable is passed as an argument to the remove_last_item function:

```
>>> celegans_markers = ['Emb', 'Him', 'Unc', 'Lon', 'Dpy', 'Lvl']
>>> remove_last_item(celegans_markers)
['Emb', 'Him', 'Unc', 'Lon', 'Dpy']
>>> celegans_markers
['Emb', 'Him', 'Unc', 'Lon', 'Dpy']
```

When the call on function remove_last_item is executed, parameter L is assigned the memory address that celegans_markers contains. That makes celegans_markers and L aliases. When the last item of the list that L refers to is removed, that change is "seen" by celegan_markers as well.

Since remove_last_item modifies the list parameter, the modified list doesn't need to be returned. You can remove the return statement:

```
>>> def remove_last_item(L: list) -> None:
...     """Remove the last item from L.
...
...     Precondition: len(L) >= 0
...
...     >>> remove_last_item([1, 3, 2, 4])
...     """
...     del L[-1]
...
>>> celegans_markers = ['Emb', 'Him', 'Unc', 'Lon', 'Dpy', 'Lvl']
>>> remove_last_item(celegans_markers)
>>> celegans_markers
['Emb', 'Him', 'Unc', 'Lon', 'Dpy']
```

As you'll see in List Methods, on page 145, several list methods modify a list and return None, like the second version of remove_last_item.

List Methods

Lists are objects and thus have methods. Table 6, List Methods, on page 146, gives some of the most commonly used list methods.

Method	Description
L.append	Appends value v to list L
L.clear	Removes all items from list L
L.count	Returns the number of occurrences of v in list L
L.extend	Appends the items in v to L
L.index	Returns the index of the first occurrence of v in the sublist L[start:stop]. An error is reported if v doesn't occur in the sublist.
L.insert	Inserts value v at index i in list L, shifting subsequent items to make room
L.pop	Removes and returns the last item of L (which must be nonempty)
L.remove	Removes the first occurrence of value v from list L
L.reverse	Reverses the order of the values in list L
L.sort	Sorts the values in list L in ascending order (numerical for numbers, alphabetical for strings). The reverse flag can be set to sort in descending order.

Table 6—List Methods

Here is a sample interaction that demonstrates how you can use list methods to create a list of various colors:

```
>>> colors = ['red', 'orange', 'green']
>>> colors.extend(['black', 'blue'])
>>> colors
['red', 'orange', 'green', 'black', 'blue']
>>> colors.append('purple')
>>> colors
['red', 'orange', 'green', 'black', 'blue', 'purple']
>>> colors.insert(2, 'yellow')
>>> colors
['red', 'orange', 'yellow', 'green', 'black', 'blue', 'purple']
>>> colors.remove('black')
>>> colors
['red', 'orange', 'yellow', 'green', 'blue', 'purple']
```

All the methods shown here modify the list instead of creating a new list. The same is true for the methods clear, reverse, sort, and pop. Of those methods, only pop returns a value other than None: specifically, the item that was removed from the list. The only method that returns a list is copy, which is equivalent to L[:].

Finally, a call to append isn't the same as using the plus sign (+). First, append appends a single value, while + expects two lists as operands. Second, append modifies the list rather than creating a new one.

Where Did My List Go?

Programmers occasionally forget that many list methods return None rather than creating and returning a new list. As a result, lists sometimes seem to disappear:

```
>>> colors = 'red orange yellow green blue purple'.split()
>>> colors
['red', 'orange', 'yellow', 'green', 'blue', 'purple']
>>> sorted_colors = colors.sort()
>>> print(sorted_colors)
None
```

In this example, colors.sort performed two actions: it sorted the items in the list and returned the value None. That's why variable sorted_colors refers to None. Variable colors, on the other hand, refers to the sorted list:

```
>>> colors
['blue', 'green', 'orange', 'purple', 'red', 'yellow']
```

Methods that mutate a collection, such as append and sort, return None; it's a typical error to expect that they'll return the resulting list. As discussed in Testing Your Code Semiautomatically, on page 116, mistakes like these can be caught by writing and running a few tests.

Working with a List of Lists

Lists can contain other lists

As stated in Lists Are Heterogeneous, on page 137, lists can contain items of any data type, including other lists. A list whose items are lists is called a *nested list*. For example, the following nested list describes life expectancies in different countries:

```
>>> life = [['Canada', 76.5], ['United States', 75.5], ['Mexico', 72.0]]
```

Here is the memory model that results from the execution of that assignment statement:

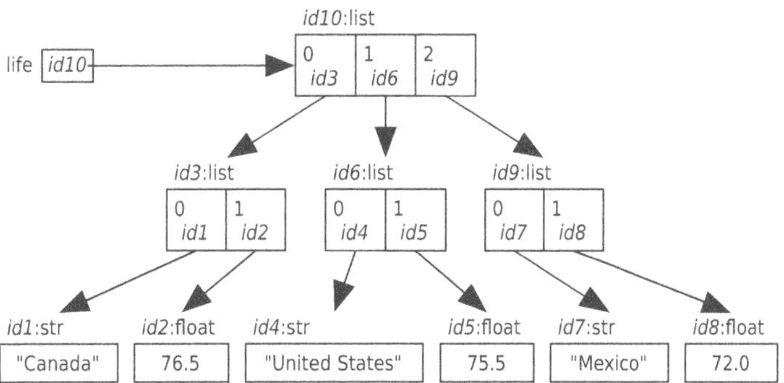

Notice that each item in the outer list is itself a list of two items. Use the standard indexing notation to access the items in the outer list:

```
>>> life = [['Canada', 76.5], ['United States', 75.5], ['Mexico', 72.0]]
>>> life[0]
['Canada', 76.5]
>>> life[1]
['United States', 75.5]
>>> life[2]
['Mexico', 72.0]
```

Since each of these items is also a list, you can index it again, just as you can chain together method calls or nest function calls:

```
>>> life = [['Canada', 76.5], ['United States', 75.5], ['Mexico', 72.0]]
>>> life[1]
['United States', 75.5]
>>> life[1][0]
'United States'
>>> life[1][1]
75.5
```

You can also assign inner lists to variables:

```
>>> life = [['Canada', 76.5], ['United States', 75.5], ['Mexico', 72.0]]
>>> canada = life[0]
>>> canada
['Canada', 76.5]
>>> canada[0]
'Canada'
>>> canada[1]
76.5
```

Assigning an inner list to a variable creates an alias for that list:

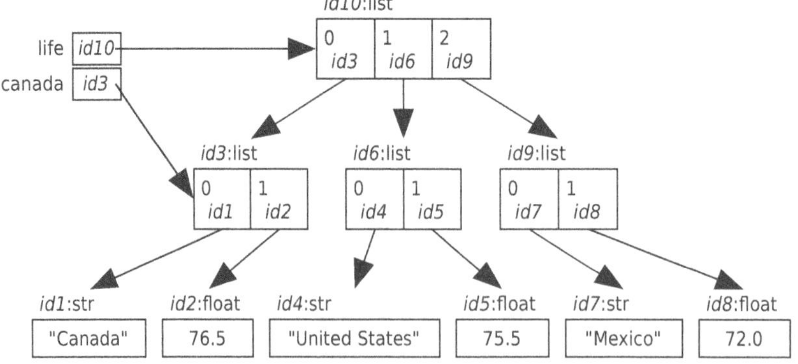

As before, any change you make through the inner list reference will be seen when you access the main list, and vice versa:

```
>>> life = [['Canada', 76.5], ['United States', 75.5], ['Mexico', 72.0]]
>>> canada = life[0]
>>> canada[1] = 80.0
>>> canada
['Canada', 80.0]
>>> life
[['Canada', 80.0], ['United States', 75.5], ['Mexico', 72.0]]
```

Splitting Strings

We introduced the method str.split in Exploring String Methods, on page 124 and promised to return to it later. The "later" is now.

The str.split method divides a string into parts

This method is a powerful, albeit imperfect, tool for text processing. It takes a string and splits it into fragments, essentially taking out whitespace characters. The fragments are returned as a new list and can be assigned to a variable. When the sep ("separator") argument is not set to None, the separator is used instead of whitespace.

In the example in Where Did My List Go?, on page 147, str.split converts a string of color names into a list of strings:

```
>>> colors = 'red orange yellow green blue purple'.split()
>>> colors
['red', 'orange', 'yellow', 'green', 'blue', 'purple']
```

Another frequent application of the method is to split a line from a *comma-separated values* (CSV) file. As the name suggests, CSV file columns are separated by commas and can be extracted using str.split(',') (or similar methods):

```
>>> colors = 'red,orange,yellow,green,blue,purple'
>>> colors.split() # Will not split
['red,orange,yellow,green,blue,purple']
>>> colors.split(',')
['red', 'orange', 'yellow', 'green', 'blue', 'purple']
```

Beware that if a column in a CSV file contains a comma (as in "Newman, Paul"), str.split(',') will split this column apart, as it is not aware of the structure of a CSV file. If you suspect that your CSV file has inner commas, use specialized modules (such as csv) to work with your data.

A Summary List

In this chapter, you learned the following:

- Lists are used to keep track of zero or more objects. The objects in a list are referred to as items or elements. Each item in the list has a position, referred to as an index, which ranges from zero to one less than the length of the list.
- Lists can contain any type of data, including other lists.
- Lists are mutable, which means that their contents can be modified.
- Slicing is used to create new lists that have the same values or a subset of the values of the originals.
- When two variables refer to the same object, they are called aliases.
- The str.split method divides a string into parts using whitespace or a specified separator, and returns the parts as a list.

Exercises

Here are some exercises for you to try on your own.

1. Variable kingdoms refers to the list ['Bacteria', 'Protozoa', 'Chromista', 'Plantae', 'Fungi', 'Animalia']. Using kingdoms and either slicing or indexing with positive indices, write expressions that produce the following:

   a. The first item of kingdoms
   b. The last item of kingdoms
   c. The list ['Bacteria', 'Protozoa', 'Chromista']
   d. The list ['Chromista', 'Plantae', 'Fungi']
   e. The list ['Fungi', 'Animalia']
   f. An empty list

2. Repeat the previous exercise using negative indices.

3. Variable appointments refers to the list ['9:00', '10:30', '14:00', '15:00', '15:30']. An appointment is scheduled for 16:30, so '16:30' needs to be added to the list.

   a. Using list method append, add '16:30' to the end of the list that appointments refers to.

   b. Instead of using append, use the + operator to add '16:30' to the end of the list that appointments refers to.

c. You used two approaches to add '16:30' to the list. Which approach modified the existing list and which approach created a new one?

4. Variable ids refers to the list [4353, 2314, 2956, 3382, 9362, 3900]. Using list methods, do the following:

   a. Remove 3382 from the list.
   b. Get the index of 9362.
   c. Insert 4499 in the list after 9362.
   d. Extend the list by adding [5566, 1830] to it.
   e. Reverse the list.
   f. Sort the list.

5. In this exercise, you'll create a list and then answer questions about that list.

   a. Assign a list that contains the atomic numbers of the six alkaline earth metals—beryllium (4), magnesium (12), calcium (20), strontium (38), barium (56), and radium (88)—to a variable called alkaline_earth_metals.
   b. Which index contains radium's atomic number? Write the answer in two ways, one using a positive index and one using a negative index.
   c. Which function tells you how many items there are in alkaline_earth_metals?
   d. Write code that returns the highest atomic number in alkaline_earth_metals. (Hint: Use one of the functions from Table 5, List Operations, on page 139.)

6. In this exercise, you'll create a list and then answer questions about that list.

   a. Create a list of temperatures in degrees Celsius with the values 25.2, 16.8, 31.4, 23.9, 28, 22.5, and 19.6, and assign it to a variable called temps.
   b. Using one of the list methods, sort temps in ascending order.
   c. Using slicing, create two new lists, cool_temps and warm_temps, which contain the temperatures below and above 20 degrees Celsius, respectively.
   d. Using list arithmetic, recombine cool_temps and warm_temps into a new list called temps_in_celsius.

7. Complete the examples in the docstring and then write the body of the following function:

```
def same_first_last(L: list) -> bool:
    """Return True if and only if first item of the list is the same as the
    last.

    Precondition: len(L) >= 2

    >>> same_first_last([3, 4, 2, 8, 3])
    True
```

```
    >>> same_first_last(['apple', 'banana', 'pear'])

    >>> same_first_last([4.0, 4.5])

    """
```

8. Complete the examples in the docstring and then write the body of the following function:

```
def is_longer(L1: list, L2: list) -> bool:
    """Return True if and only if the length of L1 is longer than the length
    of L2.

    >>> is_longer([1, 2, 3], [4, 5])
    True
    >>> is_longer(['abcdef'], ['ab', 'cd', 'ef'])

    >>> is_longer(['a', 'b', 'c'], [1, 2, 3]

    """
```

9. Draw a memory model showing the effect of the following statements:

```
values = [0, 1, 2]
values[1] = values
```

10. Variable units refers to the nested list [['km', 'miles', 'league'], ['kg', 'pound', 'stone']]. Using units and either slicing or indexing with positive indices, write expressions that produce the following:

    a. The first item of units (the first inner list)
    b. The last item of units (the last inner list)
    c. The string 'km'
    d. The string 'kg'
    e. The list ['miles', 'league']
    f. The list ['kg', 'pound']

11. Repeat the previous exercise using negative indices.

CHAPTER 9

Repeating Code Using Loops

Repeating a block of code is a fundamental way to control a program's behavior

This chapter introduces another fundamental kind of control flow: repetition. Up to now, to execute an instruction two hundred times, you would need to write that instruction two hundred times. Now, you'll see how to write the instruction once and use loops to repeat that code the desired number of times.

Processing Items in a List

With what you've learned so far, to print the items from a list of velocities of falling objects in metric and Imperial units, you would need to write a call to the print function for each velocity in the list:

```
>>> velocities = [0.0, 9.81, 19.62, 29.43]
>>> print(f'Metric: {velocities[0]} m/sec; ',
... f'Imperial: {velocities[0] * 3.28} ft/sec')
Metric: 0.0 m/sec; Imperial: 0.0 ft/sec
>>> print(f'Metric: {velocities[1]} m/sec; ',
... f'Imperial: {velocities[1] * 3.28} ft/sec')
Metric: 9.81 m/sec; Imperial: 32.1768 ft/sec
>>> print(f'Metric: {velocities[2]} m/sec; ',
... f'Imperial: {velocities[2] * 3.28} ft/sec')
Metric: 19.62 m/sec; Imperial: 64.3536 ft/sec
>>> print(f'Metric: {velocities[3]} m/sec; ',
... f'Imperial: {velocities[3] * 3.28} ft/sec')
Metric: 29.43 m/sec; Imperial: 96.5304 ft/sec
```

This code is used to process a list with just four values. Imagine processing a list with a thousand values. Lists were invented so that you wouldn't have to create a thousand variables to store a thousand values. For the same reason, Python has a *for loop* that lets you process each element in a list in turn without having to write one statement per element. You can use a for loop to print the velocities:

```
>>> velocities = [0.0, 9.81, 19.62, 29.43]
>>> for velocity in velocities:
...     print(f'Metric: {velocity} m/sec;',
...     f'Imperial: {velocity * 3.28} ft/sec')
...
Metric: 0.0 m/sec; Imperial: 0.0 ft/sec
Metric: 9.81 m/sec; Imperial: 32.1768 ft/sec
Metric: 19.62 m/sec; Imperial: 64.3536 ft/sec
Metric: 29.43 m/sec; Imperial: 96.5304 ft/sec
```

The general form of a for loop over a list is as follows:

```
for «variable» in «list»:
    «body»
```

A for loop is executed as follows:

- The loop variable is assigned the first item in the list, and the loop *body* is executed.
- The loop variable is then assigned the second item in the list, and the loop body is executed again.

  ...

- Finally, the loop variable is assigned the last item of the list, and the loop body is executed one last time.

As you saw in Defining Custom Functions, on page 36, a body is just a sequence of one or more statements. Each pass through the body is referred to as an *iteration*. At the start of each iteration, Python assigns the next item on the list to the loop variable. In the same vein as with function definitions and if statements, the statements in the loop body are indented.

In the previous code, before the first iteration, the variable velocity is assigned the value of velocities[0], and then the loop body is executed. Before the second iteration, velocity is assigned the value of velocities[1], and then the loop body is executed, and so on. In this way, the program can process each item sequentially. Table 7, Looping Over List Velocities, on page 155, contains the value of velocity at the start of each iteration, as well as the output printed during that iteration.

In the previous example, you created a new variable, velocity, to refer to the current item of the list inside the loop. You could have equally well used an existing variable.

Iteration	List Item Referred to at Start of Iteration	What Is Printed During This Iteration
1st	velocities[0]	Metric: 0.0 m/sec; Imperial: 0.0 ft/sec
2nd	velocities[1]	Metric: 9.81 m/sec; Imperial: 32.1768 ft/sec
3rd	velocities[2]	Metric: 19.62 m/sec; Imperial: 64.3536 ft/sec
4th	velocities[3]	Metric: 29.43 m/sec; Imperial: 96.5304 ft/sec

Table 7—Looping Over List Velocities

If you use an existing variable, the loop still starts with the variable referring to the first element of the list. The content of the variable before the loop is lost, precisely as if you had used an assignment statement to give a new value to that variable.

The variable is left holding its last value when the loop finishes:

```
>>> speed = 2
>>> velocities = [0.0, 9.81, 19.62, 29.43]
>>> for speed in velocities:
...     print('Metric:', speed, 'm/sec')
...
Metric: 0.0 m/sec
Metric: 9.81 m/sec
Metric: 19.62 m/sec
Metric: 29.43 m/sec
>>> print('Final:', speed)
Final: 29.43
```

Notice that the last print statement isn't indented, so it is not part of the for loop. It is executed only once, after the for loop execution has finished.

Processing Characters in Strings

It is also possible to loop over the characters of a string. The general form of a for loop over a string is as follows:

```
for «variable» in «str»:
    «body»
```

As with a for loop over a list, the loop variable gets assigned a new value at the beginning of each iteration. In the case of a loop over a string, the variable is assigned a single character at a time.

For example, you can loop over each character in a string, printing the uppercase letters. (The code is on the next page.)

```
>>> country = 'United States of America'
>>> for ch in country:
...     if ch.isupper():
...         print(ch)
...
U
S
A
```

In the previous code, variable ch is assigned country[0] before the first iteration, country[1] before the second, and so on. The loop iterates twenty-four times (once per character), and the if body is executed three times (once per uppercase letter).

Looping Over a Range of Numbers

You can also loop over a range of values to perform tasks a certain number of times and to process lists and strings more efficiently. To begin, you need to generate the range of numbers over which to iterate.

Generating Ranges of Numbers

Python's built-in function range produces an object that will generate a sequence of consecutive integers. When passed a single argument, as in range(stop), the sequence starts at 0 and continues up to but not including the integer stop:

```
>>> range(10)
range(0, 10)
>>> type(range(10))
<class 'range'>
```

The sequence belongs to Python's range data type. You can use a loop to access each number in the sequence one at a time:

```
>>> for num in range(10):
...     print(num)
...
0
1
2
3
4
5
6
7
8
9
```

To obtain the numbers from the sequence all at once, you can use the built-in list constructor to convert a range into a list:

```
>>> list(range(10))
[0, 1, 2, 3, 4, 5, 6, 7, 8, 9]
```

Here are some more examples:

```
>>> list(range(3))
[0, 1, 2]
>>> list(range(1))
[0]
>>> list(range(0))
[]
```

The sequence produced includes the start value and excludes the stop value, which is deliberately consistent with how sequence indexing works: the expression seq[0:5] takes a slice of seq up to, but not including, the value at index 5.

Notice that in the previous code, call list on the value produced by the call to range. The function range returns a range object, and creates a list based on its values to work with it using the set of list operations and methods with which you are already familiar.

The function range can also be passed two arguments, where the first is the start value and the second is the stop value:

```
>>> list(range(1, 5))
[1, 2, 3, 4]
>>> list(range(1, 10))
[1, 2, 3, 4, 5, 6, 7, 8, 9]
>>> list(range(5, 10))
[5, 6, 7, 8, 9]
```

By default, the function range generates numbers that increase successively by one, the increment referred to as its *step size*. You can specify a different step size for range with an optional third parameter.

Here we produce a list of leap years in the first half of this century:

```
>>> list(range(2000, 2050, 4))
[2000, 2004, 2008, 2012, 2016, 2020, 2024, 2028, 2032, 2036, 2040, 2044, 2048]
```

The step size can also be negative, which makes a descending sequence. When the step size is negative, the starting index should be *larger* than the stopping index:

```
>>> list(range(2050, 2000, -4))
[2050, 2046, 2042, 2038, 2034, 2030, 2026, 2022, 2018, 2014, 2010, 2006, 2002]
```

Otherwise, range's result will be empty:

```
>>> list(range(2000, 2050, -4))
[]
>>> list(range(2050, 2000, 4))
[]
```

It's possible to loop over the sequence produced by a call on range. For example, the following program calculates the sum of the integers from 1 to 100:

```
>>> total = 0
>>> for i in range(1, 101):
...     total = total + i
...
>>> total
5050
```

Notice that the upper bound passed to range is 101. It's one more than the greatest integer you want.

Processing Lists Using Indices

The loops over lists that you have written so far have been used to access list items. But what if you want to change the items in a list? For example, suppose you want to double all of the values in a list. The following doesn't work:

```
>>> values = [4, 10, 3, 8, -6]
>>> for num in values:
...     num = num * 2
...
>>> values
[4, 10, 3, 8, -6]
```

Each loop iteration assigned an item in the list values to variable num. Doubling that value inside the loop changes what num refers to, but it *doesn't* mutate the list object. For example, after one iteration of the loop, the list remains unchanged and num now refers to 8 (twice its original value). This is shown in the diagram at the top of the facing page.

Let's add a call to function print to show how the value that num refers to changes during each iteration:

```
>>> values = [4, 10, 3, 8, -6]
>>> for num in values:
...     num = num * 2
...     print(num)
...
8
20
6
```

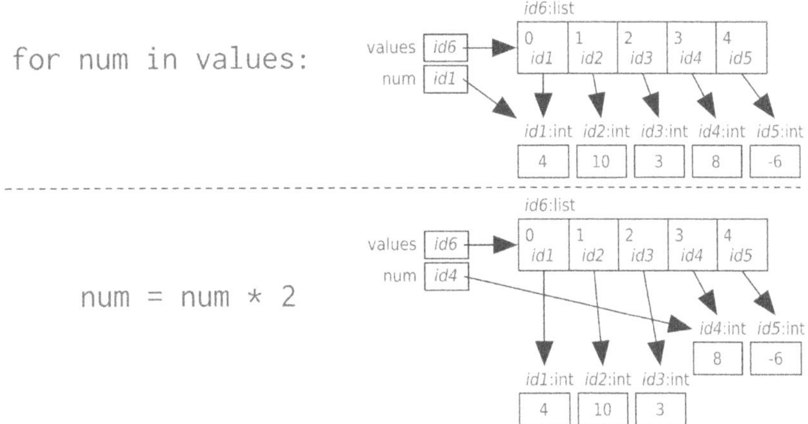


```
16
-12
>>> print(values)
[4, 10, 3, 8, -6]
```

The correct approach is to loop over the indices of the list. If variable values refers to a list, then len(values) is the number of items it contains, and the expression range(len(values)) produces a sequence containing exactly the indices for values:

```
>>> values = [4, 10, 3, 8, -6]
>>> len(values)
5
>>> list(range(5))
[0, 1, 2, 3, 4]
>>> list(range(len(values)))
[0, 1, 2, 3, 4]
```

The list that values refers to has five items, so its indices are 0, 1, 2, 3, and 4. Rather than looping over values, you can iterate over its indices, which are produced by range(len(values)):

```
>>> values = [4, 10, 3, 8, -6]
>>> for i in range(len(values)):
...     print(i)
...
0
1
2
3
4
```

Notice that the variable is named i, a convention that stands for *index*. You can use the value of the index to access the items on the list:

Why i, j, and k?

Ever wonder why loop indexes are so often named i, j, and k? The tradition comes from mathematics and the use of i, j, and k sub- and superscripts in algebra and physics. Early FORTRAN (*sic!*) programmers carried this habit into code. FORTRAN went as far as automatically treating variables whose names started with i through n as integers! Over time, i became the go-to name for the first loop variable, followed by j and k for nested loops.

```
>>> values = [4, 10, 3, 8, -6]
>>> for i in range(len(values)):
...     print(i, values[i])
...
0 4
1 10
2 3
3 8
4 -6
```

You can also use the index to modify list items:

```
>>> values = [4, 10, 3, 8, -6]
>>> for i in range(len(values)):
...     values[i] = values[i] * 2
...
>>> values
[8, 20, 6, 16, -12]
```

Evaluation of the expression on the right side of the assignment looks up the value at index i and multiplies it by two. Python then assigns that value to the item at index i in the list. When i refers to 1, for example, values[i] refers to 10, which is multiplied by 2 to produce 20. The list item values[1] is then assigned 20.

Processing Parallel Lists Using Indices

Sometimes, the data from one list corresponds to data from another. For example, consider these two lists:

```
>>> metals = ['Li', 'Na', 'K']
>>> weights = [6.941, 22.98976928, 39.0983]
```

The item at index 0 of metals has its atomic weight at index 0 of weights. The same is true for the items at index 1 in the two lists, and so on. These lists are *parallel lists*, because the item at index i of one list corresponds to the item at index i of the other list.

Suppose you want to print each metal and its weight. To do so, loop over each index of the lists, accessing the items at each index:

```
>>> metals = ['Li', 'Na', 'K']
>>> weights = [6.941, 22.98976928, 39.0983]
>>> for i in range(len(metals)):
...     print(metals[i], weights[i])
...
Li 6.941
Na 22.98976928
K 39.0983
```

This code works only when the length of weights is at least as long as the length of metals. If the length of weights is less than the length of metals, then an error would occur when trying to access an index of weights that doesn't exist. For example, if metals has three items and weights has only two, the first two print function calls would be executed. During the third function call, an error occurs when evaluating the second argument.

Beware of Parallel Loops!

Parallel loops can lead to bugs if the lists are not the same length or if one is accidentally modified independently of the other. A safer alternative is to use the built-in zip function, which pairs items from each list and stops when it exceeds the shortest one.

Nesting Loops in Loops

The body of a loop can contain another loop. In this code, the inner loop is executed once for each item in the outer list:

```
>>> outer = ['Li', 'Na', 'K']
>>> inner = ['F', 'Cl', 'Br']
>>> for metal in outer:
...     for halogen in inner:
...         print(metal + halogen)
...

LiF
LiCl
LiBr
NaF
NaCl
NaBr
KF
KCl
KBr
```

The number of times that function print is called is len(outer) * len(inner). The table at the top of the next page shows that for each iteration of the outer loop (in other words, for each item in outer), the inner loop executes three times (once for each item in inner).

Iteration of Outer Loop	What metal Refers To	Iteration of Inner Loop	What halogen Refers To	What Is Printed
1st	outer[0]	1st	inner[0]	LiF
		2nd	inner[1]	LiCl
		3rd	inner[2]	LiBr
2nd	outer[1]	1st	inner[0]	NaF
		2nd	inner[1]	NaCl
		3rd	inner[2]	NaBr
3rd	outer[2]	1st	inner[0]	KF
		2nd	inner[1]	KCl
		3rd	inner[2]	KBr

Sometimes an inner loop uses the same list as the outer loop. An example of this is shown in a function used to generate a multiplication table. After printing the header row, use a nested loop to print each row of the table in turn, using tabs (see Table 2, Escape Sequences, on page 72) to align the columns:

Loops and conditionals can be nested inside one another

```
def print_table(n: int) -> None:
    """Print the multiplication table for numbers 1 through n inclusive.

    >>> print_table(5)
        1       2       3       4       5
    1   1       2       3       4       5
    2   2       4       6       8       10
    3   3       6       9       12      15
    4   4       8       12      16      20
    5   5       10      15      20      25
    """
    # The numbers to include in the table.
    numbers = range(1, n + 1)

    # Print the header row.
    for i in numbers:
        print(f'\t{i}', end='')

    # End the header row.
    print()

    # Print each row number and the contents of each row.
1   for i in numbers:
2       print (i, end='')
3       for j in numbers:
4           print(f'\t{i * j}', end='')

        # End the current row.
5       print()
```

Each iteration of the outer loop prints a row. Each row consists of a row number, n tab-number pairs, and a newline. It's the inner loop's job to print the tabs and numbers part of the row. For print_table(5), let's take a closer look at what happens during the third iteration of the outer loop:

1. i is assigned 3, the third item of numbers.
2. The row number, 3, is printed.
3. This line of code is the inner loop header, and it will be executed five times. Before the first iteration of the inner loop, j is assigned 1; before the second iteration, it is assigned 2; and so on, until it is assigned 5 before the last iteration.
4. Five times this line is executed right after the previous line, using whatever value j was just assigned. The first time it prints a tab followed by 3, then a tab followed by 6, and so on until it prints a tab followed by 15.
5. Now that a row has been printed, the program prints a newline. This line of code is executed outside of the inner loop, ensuring it is executed only once per row.

Looping Over Nested Lists

In addition to looping over lists of numbers, strings, and Booleans, you can also loop over lists of lists. Here is an example of a loop over an outer list. The loop variable, which we've named inner_list, is assigned an item of nested list elements at the beginning of each iteration:

```
>>> elements = [['Li', 'Na', 'K'], ['F', 'Cl', 'Br']]
>>> for inner_list in elements:
...     print(inner_list)
...
['Li', 'Na', 'K']
['F', 'Cl', 'Br']
```

To access each string in the inner lists, you can loop over the outer list and then over each inner list using a nested loop. Here, Python prints every string in every inner list:

```
>>> elements = [['Li', 'Na', 'K'], ['F', 'Cl', 'Br']]
>>> for inner_list in elements:
...     for item in inner_list:
...         print(item)
...
Li
Na
K
F
Cl
Br
```

In the previous code, the outer loop variable, inner_list, refers to a list of strings, and the inner loop variable, item, refers to a string from that list.

When you have a nested list, and you want to do something with every item in the inner lists, you need to use a nested loop.

Looping Over Ragged Lists

Nothing says that nested lists have to be the same length:

```
>>> info = [['Isaac Newton', 1643, 1727],
...         ['Charles Darwin', 1809, 1882],
...         ['Alan Turing', 1912, 1954, 'alan@bletchley.uk']]
>>> for item in info:
...     print(len(item))
...
3
3
4
```

Nested lists with inner lists of varying lengths are referred to as *ragged lists*. Ragged lists can be challenging to process if the data isn't uniform; for example, trying to assemble a list of email addresses from data where some addresses are missing requires careful consideration.

Ragged data does arise normally. For instance, if a daily record is made of the time at which a person has a drink of water, each day will have a different number of entries:

```
>>> drinking_times_by_day = [["9:02", "10:17", "13:52", "18:23", "21:31"],
...                          ["8:45", "12:44", "14:52", "22:17"],
...                          ["8:55", "11:11", "12:34", "13:46",
...                           "15:52", "17:08", "21:15"],
...                          ["9:15", "11:44", "16:28"],
...                          ["10:01", "13:33", "16:45", "19:00"],
...                          ["9:01", "12:24", "18:51", "23:13"]]
>>> for day in drinking_times_by_day:
...     for drinking_time in day:
...         print(drinking_time, end=' ')
...     print()
...
9:02 10:17 13:52 18:23 21:31
8:45 12:44 14:52 22:17
8:55 11:11 12:34 13:46 15:52 17:08 21:15
9:15 11:44 16:28
10:01 13:33 16:45 19:00
9:01 12:24 18:51 23:13
```

The inner loop iterates over the items of day, and the length of that list varies.

Looping Until a Condition Is Reached

The most general kind of repetition is the while loop

for loops are applicable only if you know how many iterations of the loop you need. In some situations, it is not known in advance how many loop iterations to execute. In a game program, for example, you can't say in advance whether a player is going to want to play again or quit. In these situations, use a while loop. The general form of a while loop is as follows:

```
while «expression»:
    «body»
```

The while loop expression is sometimes referred to as the *loop condition*, and it is similar to condition of an if statement. When Python executes a while loop, it evaluates the loop condition. If that expression evaluates to False, that is the end of the execution of the loop. If the expression evaluates to True, on the other hand, Python executes the loop body once and then returns to the top of the loop to reevaluate the condition. If it still evaluates to True, the loop body is executed again. The process is repeated—expression, body, expression, body—until the expression evaluates to False, at which point Python stops executing the loop.

Here's an example:

```
>>> rabbits = 3
>>> while rabbits > 0:
...     print(rabbits)
...     rabbits = rabbits - 1
...
3
2
1
```

Notice that this loop did *not* print 0. When the number of rabbits reaches zero, the loop expression evaluates to False, so the body isn't executed. Here's a flowchart for this code:

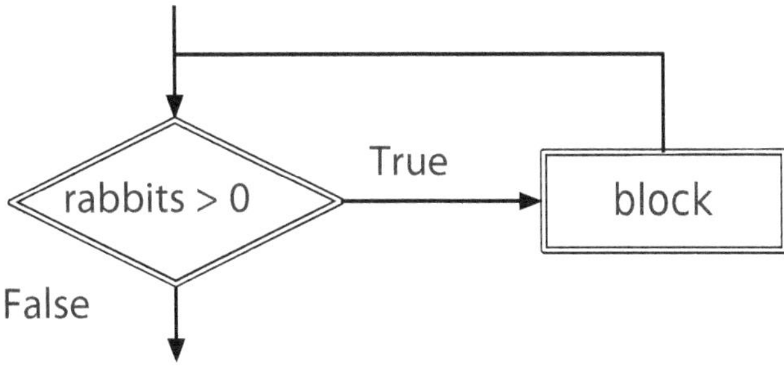

As a more useful example, you can calculate the growth of a bacterial colony using a simple exponential growth model, which is essentially a calculation of compound interest:

```
P(t + 1) = P(t) + r * P(t)
```

In this formula, P(t) is the population size at time t and r is the growth rate. Using this program, let's see how long it takes the bacteria to double their numbers:

```
time = 0
population = 1000   # 1000 bacteria to start with
growth_rate = 0.21  # 21% growth per minute
while population < 2000:
    population += (growth_rate * population)
    time += 1
    print(round(population))

print(f"It took {time} minutes for the bacteria to double.")
print(f"The final population was {round(population)} bacteria.")
```

Because variable time was updated in the body, its value after the loop was the time of the last iteration, which is exactly what you want. Running this program gives you the answer you were looking for:

```
1210
1464
1772
2144
It took 4 minutes for the bacteria to double.
The final population was 2144 bacteria.
```

Infinite Loops

The preceding example used population < 2000 as a loop condition so that the loop stopped when the population reached double its initial size *or more*. What would happen if you stopped only when the population was *exactly* double its initial size?

```
# Use multivalued assignment to set up controls
time, population, growth_rate = 0, 1000, 0.21

# Don't stop until we're exactly double the original size
while population != 2000:
    population += (growth_rate * population)
    time += 1
    print(round(population))

print("It took {time} minutes for the bacteria to double.")
```

Here is this program's output:

```
1210
1464
1772
2144
...3,680 lines or so later...
1696916047508032882540704952476272712571367324204883890954359318296
0543328315579176057807388835620019948480274142074026395598108551938
9894937237162662358663415284584196538765369142779491778980173371236
9299760706624049980700922383889131204039236535845638992662239517860
438573223789180194751476232890960712826888
Traceback (most recent call last):
  File "<python-input-0>", line 7, in <module>
    print(round(population))
          ~~~~~^^^^^^^^^^^^
OverflowError: cannot convert float infinity to integer
```

Whoops—since the population is never exactly two thousand bacteria, the loop theoretically never stops. The first set of dots represents more than three thousand values, each 21 percent larger than the one before. Eventually, these values are too large for the computer to represent, so the population becomes infinite—from Python's point of view. The built-in rounding function, round, fails to round and reports an OverflowError, implying that the number is too large, as explained in What Is a Type?, on page 12.

A loop like this one is called an *infinite loop*, because the computer will execute it forever (or until you kill your program, whichever comes first). In IDLE, you kill your program by selecting Shell→Restart Shell. Alternatively, from the command-line shell, you can kill it by pressing Ctrl - C. Infinite loops are a common kind of bug; the typical symptoms include printing the same value repeatedly or *hanging* (doing nothing at all).

Repetition Based on User Input

You can use function input in a loop to make the chemical formula translation example from Choosing Which Statements to Execute, on page 92, interactive. You will ask the user to enter a chemical formula, and your program, which is saved in a file named formulas.py, will print its name. The loop should continue until the user types quit:

```
text = ""
while text != "quit":
    text = input("Please enter a chemical formula (or 'quit' to exit): ")
    if text == "quit":
        print("…exiting program")
    elif text == "H2O":
        print("Water")
    elif text == "NH3":
```

```
        print("Ammonia")
    elif text == "CH4":
        print("Methane")
    else:
        print("Unknown compound")
```

Since the loop condition checks the value of the text, you must assign it a value before the loop begins. Now, you can run the program in formulas.py, and it will exit whenever the user types quit:

```
Please enter a chemical formula (or 'quit' to exit): CH4
Methane
Please enter a chemical formula (or 'quit' to exit): H2O
Water
Please enter a chemical formula (or 'quit' to exit): quit
…exiting program
```

The number of times that this loop executes will vary depending on user input, but it will iterate at least once.

Controlling Loops Using break and continue

As a rule, for and while loops execute all the statements in their body on each iteration; however, sometimes it is handy to break that rule. Python provides two ways to control the iteration of a loop: break, which terminates the loop's execution immediately, and continue, which skips ahead to the next iteration.

The break and continue statements can be used to change the way loops execute

The break Statement

In Repetition Based on User Input, on page 167, you saw a program that continually reads input from a user until the user types quit. Here is a program that accomplishes the same task, but this one uses the break statement to terminate the loop's execution when the user types quit:

```
while True:
    text = input("Please enter a chemical formula (or 'quit' to exit): ")
    if text == "quit":
        print("…exiting program")
        break
    elif text == "H2O":
        print("Water")
    elif text == "NH3":
        print("Ammonia")
    elif text == "CH4":
        print("Methane")
    else:
        print("Unknown compound")
```

The loop condition is unusual: it evaluates to True, so the loop appears to be infinite. However, when the user types quit, the first condition, text == "quit", evaluates to True. The print(...exiting program) statement is executed, and then the break statement, which causes the loop to terminate.

As a style point, you should be somewhat averse to loops that are written in such a manner. A loop with an explicit condition is easier to understand.

Sometimes a loop's task is finished before its final iteration. Using what you have seen so far, though, the loop still has to finish iterating. For example, let's write some code to find the index of the first digit in string 'C3H7'. The digit 3 is at index 1 in this string. Using a for loop, you would have to write something like this:

```
>>> s = 'C3H7'
>>> digit_index = -1 # This will be -1 until we find a digit.
>>> for i in range(len(s)):
...     # If we haven't found a digit, and s[i] is a digit
...     if digit_index == -1 and s[i].isdigit():
...         digit_index = i
...
>>> digit_index
1
```

Here we use variable digit_index to represent the index of the first digit in the string. It initially refers to -1, but when a digit is found, the digit's index, i, is assigned to digit_index. If the string doesn't contain any digits, then digit_index remains -1 throughout execution of the loop.

Once digit_index has been assigned a value, it is never again equal to -1, so the if condition will not evaluate to True. Even though the job of the loop is done, the loop continues to iterate until the end of the string is reached.

To fix this, you can terminate the loop early by using a break statement, which immediately leaves the loop body:

```
>>> s = 'C3H7'
>>> digit_index = -1 # This will be -1 until we find a digit.
>>> for i in range(len(s)):
...     # If we find a digit
...     if s[i].isdigit():
...         digit_index = i
...         break  # This exits the loop.
...
>>> digit_index
1
```

Notice that because the loop terminates early, you can simplify the if statement condition. As soon as digit_index is assigned a new value, the loop terminates, so it isn't necessary to check whether digit_index refers to -1. That check existed only to prevent digit_index from being assigned the index of a subsequent digit in the string.

Here's a flowchart for this code:

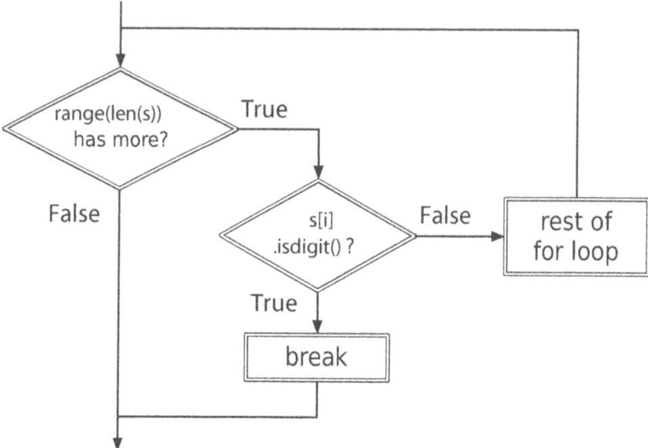

One more thing about break: it terminates only the *innermost* loop in which it's contained. In a nested loop, a break statement inside the inner loop will terminate only the inner loop, not both loops.

Böhm–Jacopini Theorem

The Böhm–Jacopini theorem (1966) states that any function can be implemented using only three control structures: sequences, conditionals, and while loops. Any for loop and any loop with break or continue can be rewritten as a simple while loop with explicit conditions.

The continue Statement

Another way to bend the rules for iteration is to use the continue statement, which causes Python to skip immediately ahead to the next iteration of a loop. Here, we add up all the digits in a string, and we also count how many digits there are. Whenever a nondigit is encountered, we use the continue statement to skip the rest of the loop body and return to the top of the loop in order to start the next iteration.

```
>>> s = 'C3H7'
>>> total = 0 # The sum of the digits seen so far.
>>> count = 0 # The number of digits seen so far.
>>> for char in s: # No need to know the position!
...     if not char.isdigit():
```

```
...         continue
...     total += int(char)
...     count += 1
...
>>> total
10
>>> count
2
```

When continue is executed, it *immediately* begins the next iteration of the loop. All statements in the loop body that appear after it are skipped, so the assignments to total and count are executed only when s[i] isn't a letter. Here's a flowchart for this code:

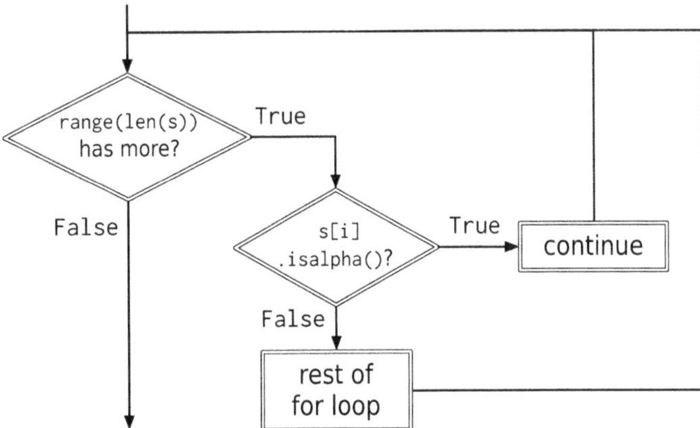

Using continue is one way to skip alphabetic characters, but this can also be accomplished by using if statements. In the previous code, continue prevents the variables from being modified; in other words, if the character isn't alphabetic, it should be processed.

The form of the previous sentence matches that of an if statement, and the updated code is as follows:

```
>>> s = 'C3H7'
>>> total = 0
>>> count = 0
>>> for char in s: # No need to know the position!
...     if char.isdigit():
...         total += int(char)
...         count += 1
...
>>> total
10
>>> count
2
```

This new version is easier to read than the first one. Most of the time, it is better to rewrite the code to avoid continue; almost always, the code ends up being more readable.

A Warning About break and continue

The break and continue statements have their place, but they should be used sparingly since they can make programs harder to understand. When people see while and for loops in programs, their first assumption is that the whole body will be executed every time—in other words, that the body can be treated as a single "super statement" when trying to understand the program. If the loop contains a break or continue statement, though, that assumption is false. Sometimes, only part of the body will be executed, which means the reader must keep two scenarios in mind.

There are always alternatives: well-chosen loop conditions (as in Repetition Based on User Input, on page 167) can replace break statements, and if statements can be used to skip statements instead of continue statements. It is up to the programmer to decide which option makes the program clearer and which makes it more complicated. As you saw in Describing Code, on page 26, programs are written for human beings; taking a few moments to make your code as straightforward as possible, or to make clarity a habit, will pay dividends for the lifetime of the program.

Now that code is getting pretty complicated, it's even more important to write comments describing the purpose of each tricky block of statements.

Repeating What You've Learned

In this chapter, you learned the following:

- Repeating a block of code is a fundamental way to control a program's behavior. A for loop can be used to iterate over the items of a list, the characters of a string, and a sequence of integers generated by the built-in function range.
- The most general kind of repetition is the while loop, which continues executing as long as some specified Boolean condition is true. However, the condition is tested only at the beginning of each iteration. If that condition is never false, the loop will be executed forever.
- The break and continue statements can be used to change the way loops execute.
- Control structures like loops and conditionals can be nested inside one another to any desired depth.

Exercises

Here are some exercises for you to try on your own.

1. Write a for loop to print all the values in the celegans_phenotypes list from Slicing Lists, on page 142, one per line. celegans_phenotypes refers to ['Emb', 'Him', 'Unc', 'Lon', 'Dpy', 'Sma'].

2. Write a for loop to print all the values in the half_lives list from Operations on Lists, on page 139, all on a single line. half_lives refers to [87.74, 24110.0, 6537.0, 14.4, 376000.0].

3. Write a for loop to add 1 to all the values from tracks from Storing and Accessing Data in Lists, on page 133, and store the converted values in a new list called more_tracks. The tracks list shouldn't be modified. tracks refers to [3124, 2980, 2567, 2754, 2890, 3012, 2805, 2675, 2550, 2901, 3100, 3050, 2999, 2820].

4. In this exercise, you'll create a nested list and then write code that performs operations on that list.

    a. Create a nested list where each element of the outer list contains the atomic number and atomic weight for an alkaline earth metal. The values are beryllium (4 and 9.012), magnesium (12 and 24.305), calcium (20 and 40.078), strontium (38 and 87.62), barium (56 and 137.327), and radium (88 and 226). Assign the list to variable alkaline_earth_metals.

    b. Write a for loop to print all the values in alkaline_earth_metals, with the atomic number and atomic weight for each alkaline earth metal on a different line.

    c. Write a for loop to create a new list called number_and_weight that contains the elements of alkaline_earth_metals in the same order but not nested.

5. The following function doesn't have a docstring, type annotations, or comments. Write enough of all three to make it easy for another programmer to understand what the function does and how. Compare your solution with those of at least two other people. How similar are they? Why do they differ?

```
def mystery_function(values):
    result = []
    for sublist in values:
        result.append([sublist[0]])
        for i in sublist[1:]:
            result[-1].insert(0, i)

    return result
```

6. In Repetition Based on User Input, on page 167, you saw a loop that prompted users until they typed quit. This code won't work if users type Quit, or QUIT, or any other version that isn't exactly quit. Modify that loop so that it terminates if a user types that word with any capitalization.

7. Consider the following statement, which creates a list of populations of countries in eastern Asia (China, DPR Korea, Hong Kong, Mongolia, Republic of Korea, and Taiwan) in millions: country_populations = [1295, 23, 7, 3, 47, 21]. Write a for loop that adds up all the values and stores them in variable total. (Hint: Give total an initial value of zero, and, inside the loop body, add the population of the current country to total.)

8. You are given two lists, rat_1 and rat_2, that contain the daily weights of two rats over a period of ten days. Assume the rats never have exactly the same weight. Write statements to do the following:

    a. If the weight of rat 1 is greater than that of rat 2 on day 1, print "Rat 1 weighed more than rat 2 on day 1."; otherwise, print "Rat 1 weighed less than rat 2 on day 1.".

    b. If rat 1 weighed more than rat 2 on day 1, and if rat 1 weighs more than rat 2 on the last day, print "Rat 1 remained heavier than Rat 2."; otherwise, print "Rat 2 became heavier than Rat 1."

    c. If your solution to the previous exercise used nested if statements, then do it without nesting, or vice versa.

9. Print the numbers in the range 33 to 49 (inclusive).

10. Print the numbers from 1 up to 10 in descending order, all on one line.

11. Using a loop, sum the numbers in the range 2 to 22 (inclusive), and then calculate the average.

12. Consider this code:

```
from typing import List

def remove_neg(num_list: List[float]) -> None:
    """Remove the negative numbers from the list num_list.

    >>> numbers = [-5, 1, -3, 2]
    >>> remove_neg(numbers)
    >>> numbers
    [1, 2]
    """

    for item in num_list:
        if item < 0:
            num_list.remove(item)
```

When remove_neg([1, 2, 3, -3, 6, -1, -3, 1]) is executed, it produces [1, 2, 3, 6, -3, 1]. The for loop traverses the elements of the list, and when a negative value (like -3 at position 3) is reached, it is removed, shifting the subsequent values one position earlier in the list (so 6 moves into position 3). The loop then continues on to process the next item, skipping over the value that moved into the removed item's position. If there are two negative numbers in a row (like -1 and -3), then the second one won't be removed.

Rewrite the code to avoid this problem.

13. Using nested for loops, print a right triangle of the character *T* on the screen where the triangle is one character wide at its narrowest point and seven characters wide at its widest point:

```
T
TT
TTT
TTTT
TTTTT
TTTTTT
TTTTTTT
```

14. Using nested for loops, print the triangle described in the previous exercise with its hypotenuse on the left side:

```
      T
     TT
    TTT
   TTTT
  TTTTT
 TTTTTT
TTTTTTT
```

15. Redo the previous two exercises using while loops instead of for loops.

16. Variables rat_1_weight and rat_2_weight contain the weights of two rats at the beginning of an experiment. Variables rat_1_rate and rat_2_rate are the rate that the rats' weights are expected to increase each week (for example, 4 percent per week).

    a. Using a while loop, calculate how many weeks it would take for the weight of the first rat to become 25 percent heavier than it was originally.

    b. Assume that the two rats have the same initial weight, but rat 1 is expected to gain weight at a faster rate than rat 2. Using a while loop, calculate how many weeks it would take for rat 1 to be 10 percent heavier than rat 2.

CHAPTER 10

Reading and Writing Files

A file is a *non-volatile* (durable) container for storing data. Its contents persist even after a program ends or the computer is shut down. Files are typically organized on *secondary storage* devices, such as hard disk drives (HDDs) or solid-state drives (SSDs). In contrast, variables are stored in *volatile memory* (RAM) and are lost when the program terminates or the system restarts. On the other hand, storing data in files and retrieving it is a relatively slow process compared to accessing data in variables. To summarize, files should be used for long-term storage when the benefit of non-volatility outweighs the cost of slow access.

In this chapter, you'll learn about different file formats, common ways to organize data, and how to read and write that data using Python. You'll first learn how to open and read information from files. After that, you'll learn about the different techniques for writing to files, and then you'll see several case studies that use the various techniques.

What Kinds of Files Are There?

Data files come in many different formats

There are many types of files, such as text files, audio files, video files, and various document formats used by word processors and presentation software. *Text files* contain only human-readable characters like letters, digits, and punctuation. Other file types often include binary data (*binary files*) or special formatting specific to their application. To work with such files, you need a program that understands the file's *format specification*.

Try opening an older Microsoft PowerPoint (`.ppt`) file in a text editor, such as Apple TextEdit, Microsoft Notepad, or one of the many Linux text editors (`vi`, `emacs`, `gedit`). Scroll through it; you'll see what looks like gibberish or random characters, as shown on the next page.

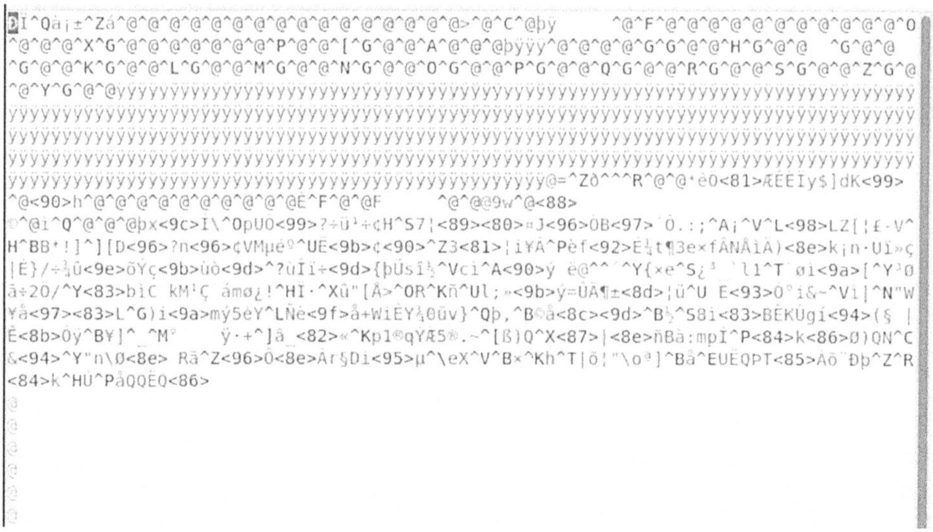

```
ÐÏ^Qà¡±^Zá^@^@^@^@^@^@^@^@^@^@^@^@^@^@^@^@>^@^C^@þÿ     ^@^F^@^@^@^@^@^@^@^@^@^@^O
^@^@^@^X^G^@^@^@^@^@^@^@^P^@^@^[^G^@^@^A^@^@^@þÿÿÿ^@^@^@^@^G^G^@^@^H^G^@^@  ^G^@^@
^G^@^@^K^G^@^@^L^G^@^@^M^G^@^@^N^G^@^@^O^G^@^@^P^G^@^@^Q^G^@^@^R^G^@^@^S^G^@^@^Z^G^@
^@^Y^G^@^@ÿÿÿÿÿÿÿÿÿÿÿÿÿÿÿÿÿÿÿÿÿÿÿÿÿÿÿÿÿÿÿÿÿÿÿÿÿÿÿÿÿÿÿÿÿÿÿÿÿÿÿÿÿÿÿÿÿÿÿÿÿÿÿ
ÿÿÿÿÿÿÿÿÿÿÿÿÿÿÿÿÿÿÿÿÿÿÿÿÿÿÿÿÿÿÿÿÿÿÿÿÿÿÿÿÿÿÿÿÿÿÿÿÿÿÿÿÿÿÿÿÿÿÿÿÿÿÿÿÿÿÿÿÿÿÿÿ
ÿÿÿÿÿÿÿÿÿÿÿÿÿÿÿÿÿÿÿÿÿÿÿÿÿÿÿÿÿÿÿÿÿÿÿÿÿÿÿÿÿÿÿÿÿÿÿÿÿÿÿÿÿÿÿÿÿÿÿÿÿÿÿÿÿÿÿÿÿÿÿÿ
ÿÿÿÿÿÿÿÿÿÿÿÿÿÿÿÿÿÿÿÿÿÿÿÿÿÿÿÿÿÿÿÿÿÿÿÿÿÿÿÿÿÿÿÿÿÿÿÿÿÿÿÿÿÿÿÿÿÿÿÿÿÿÿÿÿÿÿÿÿÿÿÿ
ÿÿÿÿÿÿÿÿÿÿÿÿÿÿÿÿÿÿÿÿÿÿÿÿÿÿÿÿÿÿÿÿÿÿÿÿÿÿÿÿÿÿÿÿÿÿ@=^Zð^^^R^@^@·è0<81>ÆÉEIy$]dK<99>
^@<90>h^@^@^@^@^@^@^@^@^@^@E^F^@^@F     ^@^@@9w^@<88>
©^@i^Q^@^@^@þx<9c>I\^OpUO<99>?÷ü¹÷¢H^S7¦<89><80>¤J<96>ÓB<97> Ó.:;^A¡^V^L<98>LZ[¦£-V^
H^BB*!]^][D<96>?n<96>¢VMµé°^UE<9b>¢<90>^Z3<81>¦i¥Ä^Pèf<92>E¼t¶3e×fÂNÅiÀ)<8e>k¡n·Uï»ç
|É}/÷¾û<9e>õÝç<9b>ùò<9d>^?ùÏï÷<9d>{þÛsî½^Vci^A<90>ý ë@^^ ^Y{×e^S¿³ `l1^T øi<9a>[^Y³Ø
ã÷2Ö/^Y<83>bìC kM¹Ç ámø¿!^HÌ·^Xû"[Å>^OR^Kñ^Ul;»<9b>ý=ÜÄ¶±<8d>¦ü^U E<93>Ó°i&~^Vi|^N"W
¥å<97><83>L^G)i<9a>mý5éY^LÑè<9f>å+WiÉY¼0ûv}^Qþ,^B©å<8c><9d>^B½^S8i<83>BÊKÚgí<94>(§ |
Ê<8b>Öÿ^B¥]^_^M°     ÿ·+^]ã_<82>«^Kp1®qYÆ5®.~^[ß)Q^X<87>|<8e>ñBà:mpÍ^P<84>k<86>Ø)QN^C
&<94>^Y"n\Ø<8e> Rã^Z<96>Ö<8e>Ár§Di<95>µ^\eX^V^B×^Kh^T|õ¦"\oª]^Bå^EUÉQPT<85>Áö Ðþ^Z^R
<84>k^HÚ^PåQQËQ<86>
@
@
@
@
@
@
```


What you're seeing is binary data and markup information not meant for human reading: internal formatting instructions, document structure, line art, embedded images, *metadata* (such as creation and modification dates, author, and edit history), and more. Without Microsoft PowerPoint or a compatible program, .ppt files cannot be adequately interpreted or displayed.

Away from Binary, Towards Text

Newer Microsoft Office files (.pptx, .docx, and .xlsx) use a format based on ZIP-compressed folders of *XML* files. While this format is more transparent than the older binary .ppt format, it's still difficult to interpret without knowing the internal structure. You'll still need PowerPoint (or a compatible app) to view the content as originally intended.

This transition reflects a broader trend in software toward using text-based formats (like XML and *JSON*), which are easier to inspect, edit, and process with other tools.

On the contrary, text files contain only human-readable characters. You can open a text file in any text editor and read and modify it.

Like any other container (a string or a list), a file can be empty, containing no data at all. Such a file typically has a size of 0 bytes. However, every file also has associated metadata maintained by the operating system, including information like its name, permissions, timestamps, and location on disk. This metadata exists even when the file's contents are empty.

The Python programs you have been writing are text files. By themselves, they are only characters in a file. Combined with a Python interpreter, these Python text files are robust; you can express a powerful algorithm following Python's syntax rules, and the interpreter will follow your instructions.

This power stems from applications that can process text files written in a specific syntax. Web browsers read and process HTML files, spreadsheets read and process comma-separated value files, calendar programs read and process calendar data files, and other programming language applications read and process files written with a particular programming language syntax.

In the next section, you'll learn how to write programs that print the contents of a text file.

Opening a File

When you want to write a program that opens and reads a file, that program needs to tell Python where that file is. By default, Python assumes that the file you want to read is in the same directory as the program that is doing the reading. If you're working in IDLE as you read this book, there's a little setup you should do:

1. Make a directory, perhaps called file_examples.

2. In IDLE, select File→New Window and type (or copy and paste) the following:

   ```
   First line of text
   Second line of text
   Third line of text
   ```

3. Save this file in your file_examples directory under the name file_example.txt.

4. In IDLE, select File→New Window and type (or copy and paste) this program:

   ```
   infile = open('file_example.txt', 'r')
   contents = infile.read()
   infile.close()
   print(contents)
   ```

5. Save this as file_reader.py in your file_examples directory.

When you run this program, this is what gets printed:

```
First line of text
Second line of text
Third line of text
```

You must save the two files in the same directory, as you'll see in the next section. Additionally, this approach will not work if you attempt to use the same commands from the Python shell.

The built-in function `open` opens a file (much like opening a book when you want to read it) and returns an object that knows how to retrieve information from the file, stored in the variable `infile`. This object also keeps track of how much you've read and which part of the file you're about to read next. The marker that keeps track of the current location in the file is called the *current [file] position* (also known as the *file cursor*) and acts much like a bookmark. The current position is initially set at the beginning of the file, but as you read or write data, it moves to the end of the data that you have just read or written.

Files can be read, written to, and added to

The first argument in the example call to the function `open('file_example.txt', 'r')` is the name of the file to open, and the second argument, `'r'`, indicates that you want to read the file; it is referred to as the file *mode*. Other options for the mode include `'w'` for writing and `'a'` for appending, which you'll see later in this chapter. If you call `open` with only the name of the file (omitting the mode), then the default is `'r'`.

The second statement, `contents = infile.read()`, tells Python that you want to read the contents of the entire file into a string, which you assign to a variable called `contents`, and the third statement, `infile.close`, releases all resources associated with the open file object.

The last statement prints the string.

When you run the program, you'll see that newline characters are treated just like every other character; it's just another character in the file.

The with Statement

Working with a file is a special case of a general programming pattern known as the *Acquire–Use–Release* pattern: obtain access to a resource, perform an action with the resource, and then clean up and release the resource. In the previous file example, you gained access to a file by calling the `open` function, then read the file contents, and finally tidied up by closing the file.

There's a catch: if a problem occurs and an error arises, your code may fail to execute the statement `infile.close`, and the associated resources are never released. Python provides a `with` statement for situations like this, where you always want to tidy up, regardless of whether an error occurs. For this reason, the `with` statement is frequently used for file access.

Here is the same example using a with statement:

```
with open('file_example.txt', 'r') as infile:
    contents = infile.read()

print(contents)
```

The general form of a with statement is as follows:

```
with «expression» as «variable»:
    «block»
```

How with Works

In What Are Those Underscores?, on page 128 you learned that names beginning and ending with two underscores are considered special by Python. The with statement uses two special methods, __enter__ and __exit__. Open file objects have these methods, which is why they can be used in a with statement.

The expression in a with statement evaluates to an object. This object's __enter__ method is then called. The result of this call is assigned to the variable.

After the block has been executed, Python calls the __exit__ method on the object even if the block causes an error. For file objects, the __exit__ method closes the file.

How Files Are Organized on Your Computer

A *file path* specifies the location of a file or folder in your computer's file system. It consists of a sequence of directory names leading from the *root directory* (or another starting point) to the target location, and it may optionally end with a file name.

Here is an example of the file path for file_example.txt:

```
/Users/pgries/Desktop/file_examples/file_example.txt
```

This file path is on a computer running Apple OS X. A file path in Linux would look similar. Both operating systems use a forward slash as the directory separator.

In Microsoft Windows, the path usually begins with a *drive letter*, such as C:. There is one drive letter per disk. Also, Microsoft Windows uses a backslash as the directory separator. (Before working with backslashes as directory separators, consider reviewing Using Special Characters in Strings, on page 71.)

Here is a path in Windows:

```
C:\Users\pgries\Desktop\file_examples\file_example.txt
```

Python's file-handling operations will automatically translate forward slashes to work in Windows, if needed, much like these operations automatically translate the two kinds of newlines that you learned about in Normalizing Line Endings, on page 74.

Specifying Which File You Want

Python maintains the *current working directory*, which is the directory it uses to locate files and folders. When you run a Python program, the current working directory is the directory where that program is started. For example, this may be the path of the file you have open in IDLE:

```
/home/pgries/Documents/py4book/Book/code/fileproc/program.py
```

Then this is the current working directory:

```
/home/pgries/Documents/py4book/Book/code/fileproc
```

When you call the open function, it searches for the specified file in the current working directory.

The default current working directory for the Python shell varies depending on the operating system. You can find out the current working directory using the getcwd function from the os module:

```
>>> import os
>>> os.getcwd()
'/home/pgries'
```

To open a file in a different directory, you must specify its location. You can do that with an *absolute path* or with a *relative path*. An absolute path (like all the previous examples) starts at the root of the file system, and a relative path is relative to the current working directory. Alternatively, you can change Python's current working directory to a different directory using the function chdir, short for "change directory":

```
>>> os.chdir('/home/pgries/Documents/py3book')
>>> os.getcwd()
'/home/pgries/Documents/py3book'
```

Let's say that you have a program called reader.py and a directory called data in the same directory as reader.py. Inside data, you might have files called data1.txt and data2.txt. Here is how you would open data1.txt:

```
open('data/data1.txt', 'r')
```

The string 'data/data1.txt' is a relative path.

To look in the *parent directory* (the directory *above* the current working directory), use two dots:

```
open('../data1.txt', 'r')
```

You can chain the dots to go up multiple directories. Here, Python looks for data1.txt three directories above the current working directory and then down into a data directory:

```
open('../../../data/data1.txt', 'r')
```

If you're still not clear on how directory paths work, try looking at this discussion on Wikipedia.[1]

Techniques for Reading Files

As mentioned at the beginning of the chapter, Python provides several techniques for reading files. You'll learn about them in this section.

All of these techniques work starting at the current position. That allows you to combine the techniques as needed.

The Read Technique

Use this technique when you want to read the contents of a file into a single string, or when you want to specify exactly how many characters to read. This technique was introduced in Opening a File, on page 179; here is the same example:

```
with open('file_example.txt', 'r') as infile:
    contents = infile.read()

print(contents)
```

When called with no arguments, the read method reads everything from the current position to the end of the file and advances the current position to the end of the file. When called with one integer argument, it reads that many characters and advances the current position after the characters that were just read. Here is a version of the same program in a file called file_reader_with_10.py; it reads ten characters and then the rest of the file:

```
with open('file_example.txt', 'r') as infile:
    first_ten_chars = infile.read(10)
    the_rest = infile.read()

print(f'The first 10 characters: {first_ten_chars}')
print(f'The rest of the file: {the_rest}')
```

1. http://en.wikipedia.org/wiki/Path_(computing)

Method call example_file.read(10) updates the current position, so the next call, example_file.read, reads everything from character 11 to the end of the file.

The Readlines Technique

Use this technique when you want to get a Python list of strings containing the individual lines from a file. Function readlines works much like function read, except that it splits up the lines into a list of strings. As with read, the current position is moved to the end of the file.

File contents are commonly stored in lists of strings

Reading at the End of a File

When the current file position is at the end of the file, methods read and readline return an empty string and readlines returns an empty list. To read the contents of a file a second time, you'll need to close and reopen the file.

This example reads the contents of a file into a list of strings and then prints that list:

```
with open('file_example.txt', 'r') as infile:
    lines = infile.readlines()

print(lines)
```

Here is the output:

```
['First line of text.\n', 'Second line of text.\n', 'Third line of text.\n']
```

Take a close look at that list: each line ends in a \n character. Python does not remove any characters from what is read; it only splits them into separate strings.

The last line of a file may or may not end with a newline character, as you learned in Exploring String Methods, on page 124.

Assume file planets.txt contains the following text:

```
Mercury
Venus
Earth
Mars
```

This example prints the lines in planets.txt backward, from the last line to the first (use the built-in function reversed, which returns the items in the list in reverse order):

```
>>> with open('planets.txt', 'r') as planets_file:
...     planets = planets_file.readlines()
```

```
...
>>> planets
['Mercury\n', 'Venus\n', 'Earth\n', 'Mars\n']
>>> for planet in reversed(planets):
...     print(planet.strip())
...
Mars
Earth
Venus
Mercury
```

You can use the Readlines technique to read the file, sort the lines, and print the planets alphabetically. Here, the built-in function sorted is used, which returns the items in the list in alphabetical order:

```
>>> with open('planets.txt', 'r') as planets_file:
...     planets = planets_file.readlines()
...
>>> planets
['Mercury\n', 'Venus\n', 'Earth\n', 'Mars\n']
>>> for planet in sorted(planets):
...     print(planet.strip())
...
Earth
Mars
Mercury
Venus
```

The "For Line in File" Technique

Use this technique when you want to do the same thing to every line from the current position to the end of a file. On each iteration, the current position is set at the beginning of the next line.

This code opens the file planets.txt and prints the length of each line in that file:

```
>>> with open('planets.txt', 'r') as data_file:
...     for line in data_file:
...         print(len(line))
...
8
6
6
5
```

Take a close look at the last line of output. There are only four characters in the word *Mars*, but the program reports that the line is five characters long. The reason for this is the same as for the readlines function: each line you read from the file has a newline character at the end. You can remove it using the string method str.strip, which returns a copy of a string with leading and trailing whitespace characters (spaces, tabs, and newlines) stripped away:

```
>>> with open('planets.txt', 'r') as data_file:
...     for line in data_file:
...         print(len(line.strip()))
...
7
5
5
4
```

The Readline Technique

This technique reads one line at a time, unlike the Readlines technique. Use this technique when you want to read only part of a file.

For example, you may treat lines differently depending on context; you may wish to process a file that has a *header* section followed by a series of records, either one record per line or with multiline records.

The following data, taken from the *Time Series Data Library [Hyn06]*, describes the number of colored fox fur pelts produced in Hopedale, Labrador, from 1834 to 1842. (The full data set has values for the years 1834–1925.)

```
Coloured fox fur production, HOPEDALE, Labrador, 1834-1842
#Source: C. Elton (1942) "Voles, Mice and Lemmings", Oxford Univ. Press
#Table 17, p.265--266
      22
      29
       2
      16
      12
      35
       8
      83
     166
```

The first line of a *Time Series Data Library* (*TSDL*) file contains a description of the data. The following two lines contain comments about the data, each of which begins with a # character. Each piece of actual data appears on a single line.

Let's use the Readline technique to skip the header, and then use the "For Line in File" technique to process the data in the file, counting how many fox fur pelts were produced.

```
with open('hopedale.txt', 'r') as hopedale_file:

    # Read and skip the description line.
    hopedale_file.readline()

    # Keep reading and skipping comment lines until we read the first piece
    # of data.
    data = hopedale_file.readline()
    while data.startswith('#'):
        data = hopedale_file.readline()

    # Now we have the first piece of data.  Accumulate the total number of
    # pelts.
    total_pelts = int(data)

    # Read the rest of the data.
    for data in hopedale_file:
        total_pelts += int(data)

print(f'Total number of pelts: {total_pelts}')
```

And here is the output:

```
Total number of pelts: 373
```

Each call to the readline method sets the current position to the beginning of the next line.

Sometimes the leading whitespace is important and you'll want to preserve it. In the Hopedale data, for example, the integers are right-justified to make them line up nicely. To preserve this alignment, you can use rstrip to remove the trailing newline. Here is a program that prints the data from that file, preserving the leading whitespace:

```
with open('hopedale.txt', 'r') as hopedale_file:

    # Read and skip the description line.
    hopedale_file.readline()

    # Keep reading and skipping comment lines until we read the first piece
    # of data.
    data = hopedale_file.readline()
    while data.startswith('#'):
        data = hopedale_file.readline()

    # Now we have the first piece of data.
    print(data.rstrip())

    # Read the rest of the data.
    for data in hopedale_file:
        print(data.rstrip())
```

And here is the output:

```
 22
 29
  2
 16
 12
 35
  8
 83
166
```

It's Unsafe to read

Calling read or readlines with no arguments is fine for small files, but risky for large or unknown-sized files. They may cause high memory usage, performance issues, and even crashes due to out-of-memory errors. Prefer line-by-line iteration or controlled chunk reading for safety and scalability.

Files over the Internet

The file containing the data you want could be located on a computer half a world away or even in the *cloud*. Provided the file is accessible over the Internet, though, you can read it just as you do a local file. For example, the Hopedale data not only exists on your computers, but it's also, at the time of writing, available online.[2]

The location of an object, such as a data file, on the Internet is specified by a *Uniform Resource Locator* (*URL*). A URL is a string that consists of the access protocol name (usually *https://* or *http://*), the remote computer name (for example, *robjhyndman.com*), and the file path at the remote computer (for example, */tsdldata/ecology1/hopedale.dat*). It informs your computer on how to request a remote resource, where to request it, and what exactly to request.

The urllib.request module contains a function called urlopen that opens a URL for reading. urlopen returns a file-like object that you can use as if you were reading a local file.

There's a hitch: because there are many kinds of files (images, music, videos, text, and more), the file-like object's read and readline methods both return a type you haven't yet encountered: bytes.

2. https://robjhyndman.com/tsdldata/ecology1/hopedale.dat

What's a Byte?

Computer hardware stores information as *bits*, *bi*nary digi*ts* representing ones and zeros. Bits are grouped into units of eight, referred to as *bytes*. All data, like text, sounds, and pixels, are ultimately encoded as sequences of bytes. Programming languages provide tools and abstractions that allow you to work with these bytes as higher-level data types, such as integers, characters, strings, images, and files.

Working With Bytes

When dealing with type bytes, such as a piece of information returned by a call to the urllib.urlrequest.read function, you need to decode it. To decode it, you need to know how it was encoded.

Common encoding schemes are described in the online Python documentation.[3] One of the most common encodings is UTF-8, a character encoding designed to represent Unicode.[4]

The Hopedale data on the web is encoded using UTF-8. This program reads the URL and uses the string method decode to decode the bytes object into a string:

```
from urllib.request import urlopen
url = 'https://robjhyndman.com/tsdldata/ecology1/hopedale.dat'
with urlopen(url) as doc:
    for line in doc:
        line = line.strip().decode('utf-8')
        print(line)
```

Writing Files

This program opens a file called topics.txt, writes the words Computer Science to the file, and then closes the file:

```
with open('topics.txt', 'w') as output_file:
    output_file.write('Computer Science')
```

In addition to writing characters to a file, the write method returns the number of characters written. For example, output_file.write('Computer Science') returns 16.

To create a new file or to replace the contents of an existing file, use write mode ('w'). If the file doesn't exist already, then a new file is created; otherwise,

3. https://docs.python.org/3/library/codecs.html#standard-encodings
4. https://docs.python.org/3/howto/unicode.html

HTTP Error 403: Forbidden

While attempting to connect to the remote computer, you may encounter an error message: urllib.error.HTTPError: HTTP Error 403: Forbidden. The error indicates that you don't have permission to access the requested resource. One common cause is an anti-scraping policy implemented by the server's administrators. You can try to bypass simple restrictions by adding a *User-Agent* header to your request, which makes your program appear to be a regular web browser (such as Chrome or Firefox):

```
from urllib.request import Request, urlopen
url = 'https://robjhyndman.com/tsdldata/ecology1/hopedale.dat'
req = Request(url, headers={'User-Agent':'Mozilla/5.0'})
with urlopen(req) as doc:
    for line in doc:
        line = line.strip().decode('utf-8')
        print(line)
```

the file contents are erased and replaced. Once opened for writing, you can use the write method to write a string to the file.

Rather than replacing the file contents, you can also add to a file using append mode ('a'). When you write to a file that is opened in append mode, the data you write is added to the end of the file, and the current file contents are not overwritten. For example, to add to your previous file topics.txt, you can append the words Software Engineering:

```
with open('topics.txt', 'a') as output_file:
    output_file.write('Software Engineering')
```

At this point, if you print the contents of topics.txt, you'd see the following:

```
Computer ScienceSoftware Engineering
```

Unlike the function print, the method write doesn't automatically append a newline; if you want a string to end in a newline, you have to include it manually using '\n'.

The next example (in a file called total.py) is more complex, and it involves both reading from and writing to a file. Notice that it uses typing.TextIO from the module typint as the type annotation for an open file. "IO" is short for "Input/Output." Your input file contains two numbers per line, separated by a space. The output file will contain three numbers per line: the two from the input file, followed by their sum (all separated by spaces).

```
from typing import TextIO

def sum_number_pairs(input_file: TextIO, output_file: TextIO) -> None:
    """Read the data from input_file, which contains two floats per line
    separated by a space. output_file for writing and, for each line in
```

```
    input_file, write a line to output_file that contains the two floats from
    the corresponding line of input_file plus a space and the sum of the two
    floats.
    """

    for number_pair in input_file:
        number_pair = number_pair.strip()
        operands = number_pair.split()
        total = float(operands[0]) + float(operands[1])
        new_line = f'{number_pair} {total}\n'
        output_file.write(new_line)

if __name__ == '__main__':
    with open('number_pairs.txt', 'r') as input_file, \
         open('number_pair_sums.txt', 'w') as output_file:
        sum_number_pairs(input_file, output_file)
```

File/URL reader is often opened outside the reading function

Notice that parameters are *open* files. That is why you don't need to call function open inside the function. Instead, that happens in the main program.

Assume that a file called number_pairs.txt exists with these contents:

```
1.3 3.4
2 4.2
-1 1
```

Then, this program creates a file named number_pair_sums.txt with the following contents:

```
1.3 3.4 4.7
2 4.2 6.2
-1 1 0.0
```

Writing Example Calls Using StringIO

To follow the function design recipe, you need to write example calls. Writing these calls using real files would involve creating test files for each of the situations you want to demonstrate. This approach is fragile because it means that you can't just give the program to someone—you need to remember to include the test files in case they want to try your function. It's also not optimal because anyone trying to understand the function needs to open the input and output files.

Python provides a class, StringIO, in the io module, that can be used as a *mock* open file. That means that you can read from it using the regular file-reading techniques as if it were a real file. StringIO objects can be used anywhere TextIO objects are expected.

Here, let's create a StringIO object containing the same information as file number_pairs.txt, and read the first line:

```
>>> from io import StringIO
>>> input_string = '1.3 3.4\n2 4.2\n-1 1\n'
>>> infile = StringIO(input_string)
>>> infile.readline()
'1.3 3.4\n'
```

You can also write to StringIO objects as if they were files, and retrieve their contents as a string using the method getvalue:

```
>>> from io import StringIO
>>> outfile = StringIO()
>>> outfile.write('1.3 3.4 4.7\n')
12
>>> outfile.write('2 4.2 6.2\n')
10
>>> outfile.write('-1 1 0.0\n')
9
>>> outfile.getvalue()
'1.3 3.4 4.7\n2 4.2 6.2\n-1 1 0.0\n'
```

You can now provide example calls in your sum_number_pairs function. Notice that you need two backslashes inside the examples because they are part of the docstring (see Using Special Characters in Strings, on page 71):

```
from typing import TextIO
from io import StringIO

def sum_number_pairs(input_file: TextIO, output_file: TextIO) -> None:
    """Read the data from input_file, which contains two floats per line
    separated by a space. output_file for writing and, for each line in
    input_file, write a line to output_file that contains the two floats from
    the corresponding line of input_file plus a space and the sum of the two
    floats.

    >>> infile = StringIO('1.3 3.4\\n2 4.2\\n-1 1\\n')
    >>> outfile = StringIO()
    >>> sum_number_pairs(infile, outfile)
    >>> outfile.getvalue()
    '1.3 3.4 4.7\\n2 4.2 6.2\\n-1 1 0.0\\n'
    """

    for number_pair in input_file:
        number_pair = number_pair.strip()
        operands = number_pair.split()
        total = float(operands[0]) + float(operands[1])
        new_line = f'{number_pair} {total}\n'
        output_file.write(new_line)
```

```
if __name__ == '__main__':
    with open('number_pairs.txt', 'r') as input_file, \
          open('number_pair_sums.txt', 'w') as output_file:
        sum_number_pairs(input_file, output_file)
```

Writing Algorithms That Use the File-Reading Techniques

There are several common methods for organizing information in files. The remainder of this chapter will demonstrate how to apply various file-reading techniques to these situations and how to develop algorithms to assist with this process.

Skipping the Header

Many data files begin with a header. As described in The Readline Technique, on page 186, TSDL files begin with a one-line description, followed by comments in lines starting with a #. The Readline technique can be used to skip this header. The method ends when you read the first real piece of data, which will be the first line after the description that doesn't start with a #.

In English, you might try this algorithm to process this kind of a file:

```
Skip the first line in the file
Skip over the comment lines in the file
For each of the remaining lines in the file:
    Process the data on that line
```

Data processing programs often consist of input, processing, and output stages

The problem with this approach is that you can't tell whether a line is a comment line until you've read it, but you can read a line from a file only once—there's no simple way to "back up" in the file. An alternative approach is to read the line, skip it if it's a comment, and process it if it's not. Once you've processed the first line of data, you process the rest. Written in English, this looks something like:

```
Skip the first line in the file
Find and process the first line of data in the file
For each of the remaining lines:
    Process the data on that line
```

The key aspect to note about this algorithm is that it processes lines in two places: once when it encounters the first "interesting" line in the file, and again when it handles all subsequent lines. The code is shown on the following page.

```
from typing import TextIO
from io import StringIO

def skip_header(reader: TextIO) -> str:
    """Skip the header in reader and return the first real piece of data.

    >>> infile = StringIO('Example\\n# Comment\\n# Comment\\nData line\\n')
    >>> skip_header(infile)
    'Data line\\n'
    """

    # Read the description line
    line = reader.readline()

    # Find the first non-comment line
    line = reader.readline()
    while line.startswith('#'):
        line = reader.readline()

    # Now line contains the first real piece of data
    return line

def process_file(reader: TextIO) -> None:
    """Read and print the data from reader, which must start with a single
    description line, then a sequence of lines beginning with '#', then a
    sequence of data.

    >>> infile = StringIO('Example\\n# Comment\\nLine 1\\nLine 2\\n')
    >>> process_file(infile)
    Line 1
    Line 2
    """

    # Find and print the first piece of data
    line = skip_header(reader).strip()
    print(line)

    # Read the rest of the data
    for line in reader:
        line = line.strip()
        print(line)

if __name__ == '__main__':
    with open('hopedale.txt', 'r') as input_file:
        process_file(input_file)
```

In skip_header, you return the first line of read data because once you've found it, you can't reread it (you can go forward but not backward). You'll want to use skip_header in all of the file-processing functions in this section. Rather than copying the code each time you want to use it, you can put the function in a file called time_series.py (because of the *Time Series Data Library*) and use it in other programs using import time_series, as shown in the next example. This arrangement allows you to reuse the skip_header code, and if it needs to be modified, then there is only one copy of the function to edit.

This program processes the Hopedale data set to find the smallest number of fox pelts produced in any year. As you progress through the file, you keep the smallest value seen so far in a variable called smallest. That variable is initially set to the value on the first line, since it's the smallest (and only) value seen so far:

```
from typing import TextIO
import time_series

def smallest_value(reader: TextIO) -> int:
    """Read and process reader and return the smallest value after the
    time_series header.

    >>> infile = StringIO('Example\\n1\\n2\\n3\\n')
    >>> smallest_value(infile)
    1
    >>> infile = StringIO('Example\\n3\\n1\\n2\\n')
    >>> smallest_value(infile)
    1
    """

    line = time_series.skip_header(reader)

    # Now line contains the first data value; this is also the smallest value
    # found so far, because it is the only one we have seen.
    smallest = int(line)

    for line in reader:
        value = int(line)

        # If we find a smaller value, remember it.
        if value < smallest:
            smallest = value

    return smallest

if __name__ == '__main__':
    with open('hopedale.txt', 'r') as input_file:
        print(smallest_value(input_file))
```

As with any algorithm, there are alternative ways to write this code; for example, you can replace the if statement with a call to the built-in min function:

```
smallest = min(smallest, value)
```

Dealing with Missing Values in Data

We also have data for colored fox fur production in Hebron, Labrador:

```
Coloured fox fur production, Hebron, Labrador, 1834-1839
#Source: C. Elton (1942) "Voles, Mice and Lemmings", Oxford Univ. Press
#Table 17, p.265--266
#remark: missing value for 1836
    55
```

```
262
-
102
178
```

The hyphen indicates that data for the year 1836 is missing. Unfortunately, calling read_smallest on the Hebron data produces this error:

```
>>> import read_smallest
>>> read_smallest.smallest_value(open('hebron.txt', 'r'))
Traceback (most recent call last):
  File "<python-input-1>", line 1, in <module>
    read_smallest.smallest_value(open('hebron.txt', 'r'))
    ~~~~~~~~~~~~~~~~~~~~~~~~~~~~^^^^^^^^^^^^^^^^^^^^^^^^^
  File "./read_smallest.py", line 23, in smallest_value
    value = int(line)
ValueError: invalid literal for int() with base 10: '    -    \n'
```

The problem is that '-' isn't an integer, so calling int('-') fails. Missing values aren't an isolated problem. In general, you will often need to skip blank lines, comments, or lines containing other "nonvalues" in your data. Real data sets often contain omissions or contradictions; dealing with them is just a fact of scientific life.

For the development of this algorithm, assume that the first value is an integer, because otherwise the time series would start at the second value.

To fix your code, you must add a check inside the loop that processes a line only if it contains a real value. Let's assume that the first value is never a hyphen because in the TSDL data sets, missing entries are always marked with hyphens. So, you need to check for that before trying to convert the string you have read to an integer:

```
from typing import TextIO
from io import StringIO
import time_series

def smallest_value_skip(reader: TextIO) -> int:
    """Read and process reader, which must start with a time_series header.
    Return the smallest value after the header.  Skip missing values, which
    are indicated with a hyphen.

    >>> infile = StringIO('Example\\n1\\n-\\n3\\n')
    >>> smallest_value_skip(infile)
    1
    """

    line = time_series.skip_header(reader)
    # Now line contains the first data value; this is also the smallest value
    # found so far, because it is the only one we have seen.
    smallest = int(line)
```

```
    for line in reader:
        if line.strip().isdigit():
            value = int(line)
            smallest = min(smallest, value)

    return smallest

if __name__ == '__main__':
    with open('hebron.txt', 'r') as input_file:
        print(smallest_value_skip(input_file))
```

Notice that the update to smallest is nested inside the check for non-numeric values.

Processing Whitespace-Delimited Data

Another TSDL file, lynx.dat,[5] (*Time Series Data Library [Hyn06]*), contains information about lynx pelts from the years 1821 to 1934. All data values are integers. Each line contains many values separated by whitespace. For reasons best known to the file's author, each value ends with a period. (Note that author M. J. Campbell's name below is misspelled in the original file.)

```
Annual Number of Lynx Trapped, MacKenzie River, 1821-1934
#Original Source: Elton, C. and Nicholson, M. (1942)
#"The ten year cycle in numbers of Canadian lynx",
#J. Animal Ecology, Vol. 11, 215--244.
#This is the famous data set which has been listed before in
#various publications:
#Cambell, M.J. and Walker, A.M. (1977) "A survey of statistical work on
#the MacKenzie River series of annual Canadian lynx trappings for the years
#1821-1934 with a new analysis", J.Roy.Statistical Soc. A 140, 432--436.
  269.  321.  585.  871. 1475. 2821. 3928. 5943. 4950. 2577.  523.   98.
  184.  279.  409. 2285. 2685. 3409. 1824.  409.  151.   45.   68.  213.
  546. 1033. 2129. 2536.  957.  361.  377.  225.  360.  731. 1638. 2725.
  . . .
 6313. 3794. 1836.  345.  382.  808. 1388. 2713. 3800. 3091. 2985. 3790.
  674.   81.   80.  108.  229.  399. 1132. 2432. 3574. 2935. 1537.  529.
  485.  662. 1000. 1590. 2657. 3396.
```

Now let's develop a program to find the largest value. To process the file, let's break each line into pieces and strip off the periods. Your algorithm remains the same as it was for the fox pelt data: find and process the first line of data in the file, and then process each subsequent line. However, the notion of "processing a line" needs to be examined further because each line contains many values. Your refined algorithm, shown on the next page, uses nested loops to handle the concept of "for each line and for each value on that line."

5. http://robjhyndman.com/tsdldata/ecology1/lynx.dat

```
Find the first line containing real data after the header
For each piece of data in the current line:
    Process that piece

For each of the remaining lines of data:
    For each piece of data in the current line:
        Process that piece
```

Once again, you are processing lines in two different places. That is a strong hint that you should write a helper function to avoid duplicate code. Rewriting your algorithm to make it specific to the problem of finding the largest value clarifies this further:

```
Find the first line of real data after the header
Find the largest value in that line

For each of the remaining lines of data:
    Find the largest value in that line
    If that value is larger than the previous largest, remember it
```

The *helper function* find_largest finds the largest value in a line and must split the line accordingly. The string method str.split will split around the whitespace, but you still have to remove the periods at the ends of the values.

You can also simplify your code by initializing largest to -1, since that value is guaranteed to be smaller than any of the (positive) values in the file. That way, no matter what the first value is, it'll be larger than the "previous" value (your -1) and replace it.

```
from typing import TextIO
from io import StringIO
import time_series

def find_largest(line: str) -> int:
    """Return the largest value in line, which is a whitespace-delimited
    string of integers that each end with a '.'.

    >>> find_largest('1. 3. 2. 5. 2.')
    5
    """
    # The largest value seen so far.
    largest = -1
    for value in line.split():
        # Remove the trailing period and spaces, if any
        v = int(value.rstrip(". "))
        # If we find a larger value, remember it.
        if v > largest:
            largest = v

    return largest
```

You now face the same choice as with skip_header: you can put find_largest in a module (possibly time_series), or you can include it in the same file as the rest of the code. Let's choose the latter this time because the code is specific to this particular dataset and problem:

```
from typing import TextIO
from io import StringIO
import time_series

def find_largest(line: str) -> int:
    """Return the largest value in line, which is a whitespace-delimited
    string of integers that each end with a '.'.

    >>> find_largest('1. 3. 2. 5. 2.')
    5
    """
    # The largest value seen so far.
    largest = -1
    for value in line.split():
        # Remove the trailing period and spaces, if any
        v = int(value.rstrip(". "))
        # If we find a larger value, remember it.
        if v > largest:
            largest = v

    return largest

def process_file(reader: TextIO) -> int:
    """Read and process reader, which must start with a time_series header.
    Return the largest value after the header. There may be multiple pieces
    of data on each line.

    >>> infile = StringIO('Example\\n 20. 3.\\n 100. 17. 15.\\n')
    >>> process_file(infile)
    100
    """

    line = time_series.skip_header(reader).strip()
    # The largest value so far is the largest on this first line of data.
    largest = find_largest(line)

    # Check the rest of the lines for larger values.
    for line in reader:
        large = find_largest(line)
        if large > largest:
            largest = large
    return largest

if __name__ == '__main__':
    with open('lynx.txt', 'r') as input_file:
        print(process_file(input_file))
```

Notice how simple the code in process_file looks, because we decided to write helper functions! To illustrate the clarity, here is the same code without using time_series.skip_header and find_largest as helper methods:

```
from typing import TextIO
from io import StringIO

def process_file(reader: TextIO) -> int:
    """Read and process reader, which must start with a time_series header.
    Return the largest value after the header.  There may be multiple pieces
    of data on each line.

    >>> infile = StringIO('Example\\n 20. 3.\\n')
    >>> process_file(infile)
    20
    >>> infile = StringIO('Example\\n 20. 3.\\n 100. 17. 15.\\n')
    >>> process_file(infile)
    100
    """

    # Read the description line
    line = reader.readline()

    # Find the first non-comment line
    line = reader.readline()
    while line.startswith('#'):
        line = reader.readline()

    # Now line contains the first real piece of data

    # The largest value seen so far in the current line
    largest = -1

    for value in line.split():

        # Remove the trailing period
        v = int(value.rstrip(". "))
        # If we find a larger value, remember it
        if v > largest:
            largest = v

    # Check the rest of the lines for larger values
    for line in reader:

        # The largest value seen so far in the current line
        largest_in_line = -1

        for value in line.split():

            # Remove the trailing period
            v = int(value.rstrip(". "))
            # If we find a larger value, remember it
```

```
            if v > largest_in_line:
                largest_in_line = v

        if largest_in_line > largest:
            largest = largest_in_line
    return largest

if __name__ == '__main__':
    with open('lynx.txt', 'r') as input_file:
        print(process_file(input_file))
```

Multiline Records

Not every data record will fit onto a single line. Here is a file in simplified Protein Data Bank (PDB) format that describes the arrangements of atoms in ammonia:

```
COMPND      AMMONIA
ATOM      1  N  0.257  -0.363   0.000
ATOM      2  H  0.257   0.727   0.000
ATOM      3  H  0.771  -0.727   0.890
ATOM      4  H  0.771  -0.727  -0.890
END
```

The first line is the name of the molecule. All subsequent lines down to the one containing `END` specify the ID, type, and *XYZ* coordinates of one of the atoms in the molecule.

Reading this file is straightforward using the techniques you have developed in this chapter. But what if the file contained two or more molecules, like this?

```
COMPND      AMMONIA
ATOM      1  N  0.257  -0.363   0.000
ATOM      2  H  0.257   0.727   0.000
ATOM      3  H  0.771  -0.727   0.890
ATOM      4  H  0.771  -0.727  -0.890
END
COMPND      METHANOL
ATOM      1  C  -0.748  -0.015   0.024
ATOM      2  O  0.558   0.420  -0.278
ATOM      3  H  -1.293  -0.202  -0.901
ATOM      4  H  -1.263   0.754   0.600
ATOM      5  H  -0.699  -0.934   0.609
ATOM      6  H  0.716   1.404   0.137
END
```

As always, tackle this problem by dividing it into smaller ones and solving each of those in turn. Your first algorithm is as follows:

```
While there are more molecules in the file:
    Read a molecule from the file
    Append it to the list of molecules read so far
```

Simple, except the only way to tell whether there is another molecule left in the file is to try to read it. Your modified algorithm is as follows:

```
reading = True
while reading:
    Try to read a molecule from the file
    If there is one:
        Append it to the list of molecules read so far
    else:  # nothing left
        reading = False
```

In Python, this is as follows:

```
from typing import TextIO
from io import StringIO

def read_molecule(reader: TextIO) -> list:
    """Read a single molecule from reader and return it, or return None to
    signal end of file.  The first item in the result is the name of the
    compound; each list contains an atom type and the X, Y, and Z coordinates
    of that atom.

    >>> instring = ('COMPND TEST\\nATOM 1 N 0.1 0.2 0.3\\n' +
    'ATOM 2 N 0.2 0.1 0.0\\nEND\\n')
    >>> infile = StringIO(instring)
    >>> read_molecule(infile)
    ['TEST', ['N', '0.1', '0.2', '0.3'], ['N', '0.2', '0.1', '0.0']]
    """

    # If there isn't another line, we're at the end of the file.
    line = reader.readline()
    if not line:
        return None

    # Name of the molecule: "COMPND   name"
    parts = line.split()
    name = parts[1]

    # Other lines are either "END" or "ATOM num atom_type x y z"
    molecule = [name]

    line = reader.readline()
    while not line.startswith('END'):
        parts = line.split()
        molecule.append(parts[2:])
        line = reader.readline()
    return molecule

def read_all_molecules(reader: TextIO) -> list:
    """Read zero or more molecules from reader, returning a list of the
    molecule information.
```

```
    >>> cmpnd1 = ('COMPND T1\\nATOM 1 N 0.1 0.2 0.3\\n' +
    'ATOM 2 N 0.2 0.1 0.0\\nEND\\n')
    >>> cmpnd2 = ('COMPND T2\\nATOM 1 A 0.1 0.2 0.3\\n' +
    'ATOM 2 A 0.2 0.1 0.0\\nEND\\n')
    >>> infile = StringIO(cmpnd1 + cmpnd2)
    >>> result = read_all_molecules(infile)
    >>> result[0]
    ['T1', ['N', '0.1', '0.2', '0.3'], ['N', '0.2', '0.1', '0.0']]
    >>> result[1]
    ['T2', ['A', '0.1', '0.2', '0.3'], ['A', '0.2', '0.1', '0.0']]
    """

    # The list of molecule information.
    result = []

    molecule = read_molecule(reader)
    while molecule:  # None is treated as False in a while loop
        result.append(molecule)
        molecule = read_molecule(reader)
    return result

if __name__ == '__main__':
    with open('multimol.pdb', 'r') as molecule_file:
        molecules = read_all_molecules(molecule_file)
    print(molecules)
```

The work of actually reading a single molecule has been put into a function of its own that must return some false value (such as None) if it can't find another molecule in the file. This function checks the first line it attempts to read to determine whether any unread data remains in the file. If not, it returns immediately to tell read_all_molecules that the end of the file has been reached. Otherwise, it pulls the name of the molecule out of the first line and then reads the molecule's atoms one at a time down to the END line.

Notice that read_molecule uses the same trick to spot the END that marks the end of a single molecule as read_all_molecules uses to spot the end of the file.

Looking Ahead

Let's add one final complication. Suppose that molecules didn't have END markers but instead just a COMPND line followed by one or more ATOM lines. How would you read multiple molecules from a single file in that case?

```
COMPND      AMMONIA
ATOM      1  N  0.257  -0.363   0.000
ATOM      2  H  0.257   0.727   0.000
ATOM      3  H  0.771  -0.727   0.890
ATOM      4  H  0.771  -0.727  -0.890
COMPND      METHANOL
ATOM      1  C  -0.748  -0.015   0.024
```

```
ATOM      2  O  0.558   0.420  -0.278
ATOM      3  H  -1.293  -0.202  -0.901
ATOM      4  H  -1.263   0.754   0.600
ATOM      5  H  -0.699  -0.934   0.609
ATOM      6  H  0.716   1.404   0.137
```

At first glance, it doesn't seem much different from the problem you just solved: read_molecule could extract the molecule's name from the COMPND line and then read ATOM lines until it got either an empty string signaling the end of the file or another COMPND line signaling the start of the next molecule. However, once it has read the COMPND line, the line is no longer available for the next call to read_molecule, so how can you obtain the name of the second molecule (and all the ones following it)?

To solve this problem, your functions must always "look ahead" one line at a time. Let's start with the function that reads multiple molecules:

```
from typing import TextIO

def read_all_molecules(reader: TextIO) -> list:
    """Read zero or more molecules from reader and
    return a list of the molecules read.
    """

    result = []
    line = reader.readline()
    while line:
        molecule, line = read_molecule(reader, line)
        result.append(molecule)

    return result
```

This function begins by reading the first line of the file. Provided that line is not the empty string (that is, the file being read is not empty), it passes both the opened file to read from and the line into read_molecule, which is supposed to return two things: the next molecule in the file and the first line immediately after the end of that molecule (or an empty string if the end of the file has been reached).

This simple description is enough to get you started writing the read_molecule function. First it needs to verify that line indeed marks the start of a molecule. It then reads lines from reader one at a time, looking for one of three situations:

- The end of the file, which signals the end of both the current molecule and the file
- Another COMPND line, which signals the end of this molecule and the start of the next one
- An ATOM, which is to be added to the current molecule

The most important thing is that when this function returns, it returns both the molecule *and* the next line so that its caller can keep processing. The result is probably the most complicated function you have seen so far, but understanding the idea behind it will help you know how it works:

```
from typing import TextIO

def read_molecule(reader: TextIO, line: str) -> list:
    """Read a molecule from reader, where line refers to the first line of
    the molecule to be read. Return the molecule and the first line after
    it (or the empty string if the end of file has been reached).
    """

    fields = line.split()
    molecule = [fields[1]]

    line = reader.readline()
    while line and not line.startswith('COMPND'):
        fields = line.split()
        if fields[0] == 'ATOM':
            key, num, atom_type, x, y, z = fields
            molecule.append([atom_type, x, y, z])
        line = reader.readline()

    return molecule, line
```

Finally, the line highlighted in the code fragment on page 205 demonstrates an *unpacking* operation, where the list elements are simultaneously assigned to the variables key, num, atom_type, x, y, and z in a single statement. For such an assignment to work, the number of variables on the LHS must equal the number of elements in the list on the RHS. See Assigning to Multiple Variables Using Tuples, on page 219, for more information on simultaneous assignments.

Incidentally, the highlighted lines in the code fragments on page 204 and on page 205 utilize *tuples* ("immutable lists"). You'll learn more about them in Storing Data Using Tuples, on page 215.

Notes to File Away

In this chapter, you learned the following:

- When files are opened and read, their contents are commonly stored in lists of strings.
- Data stored in files is usually formatted in one of a small number of ways, from one value per line to multiline records with explicit end-of-record markers. Each format can be processed stereotypically.
- Data processing programs should be broken into input, processing, and output stages so that each can be reused independently.

- Files can be read (content retrieved), written to (content replaced), and added to (new content appended). When a file is opened in writing mode and it doesn't exist, a new file is created.
- Data files come in many different formats, so custom code is often required, but you can reuse as much as possible by writing helper functions.
- To make the functions usable by different types of readers, the reader (for a file or URL) is opened outside the function, passed as an argument to the function, and then closed outside the function.
- typing.TextIO is used in type annotations to indicate an open file.

Exercises

Here are some exercises for you to try on your own.

1. Write a program that makes a backup of a file. Your program should prompt the user for the name of the file to copy and then create a new file with the same contents but with the .bak file extension.
2. Suppose the file alkaline_metals.txt contains the name, atomic number, and atomic weight of the alkaline earth metals:

   ```
   beryllium 4 9.012
   magnesium 12 24.305
   calcium 20 20.078
   strontium 38 87.62
   barium 56 137.327
   radium 88 226
   ```

   Write a for loop to read the contents of alkaline_metals.txt and store it in a list of lists, with each inner list containing the name, atomic number, and atomic weight for an element. (Hint: Use str.split.)
3. All of the file-reading functions you have seen in this chapter read forward through the file from the first character or line to the last. How could you write a function that would read backward through a file?
4. In Processing Whitespace-Delimited Data, on page 197, you used the "For Line in File" technique to process data line by line, breaking it into pieces using the string method str.split. Rewrite the function process_file to skip the header as usual, but then use the Read technique to read all the data at once.
5. Modify the file reader in read_smallest_skip.py of Skipping the Header, on page 193, so that it can handle files with no data after the header.

6. Modify the file reader in read_smallest_skip.py of Skipping the Header, on page 193, so that it uses a continue statement inside the loop instead of an if statement. Which form do you find easier to read?

7. Modify the PDB file reader of Multiline Records, on page 201, so that it ignores blank lines and comment lines in PDB files. A blank line contains only space and tab characters (that is, one that looks empty when viewed). A comment is any line beginning with the keyword CMNT.

8. Modify the PDB file reader to check that the serial numbers on atoms start at 1 and increase by 1. What should the modified function do if it finds a file that doesn't obey this rule?

CHAPTER 11

Storing Data Using Other Collection Types

In Chapter 8, Storing Collections of Data Using Lists, on page 133, you learned how to store collections of data using lists. Strings are collections of characters, too. In this chapter, you will learn about three other kinds of collections: sets, tuples, and dictionaries. With four different options for storing your data collections, you can choose the one that best suits your needs to keep your code clean and efficient.

Storing Data Using Sets

Sets are used to store unordered collections of unique values

A *set* is an unordered collection of distinct items. *Unordered* means that items aren't stored in any particular order. Something is either in the set or it's not, but there's no notion of it being the first, second, or last item. *Distinct* means that any item appears in a set at most once; there are no duplicates.

Python has a type called set that allows you to store mutable collections of unordered, distinct items. (Remember that a *mutable* object is one that you can modify.) Let's create a set containing the vowels:

```
>>> vowels = {'a', 'e', 'i', 'o', 'u'}
>>> vowels
{'a', 'u', 'o', 'i', 'e'}
```

Searching through sets and dictionaries is very fast

It resembles a list, except that sets use braces ({}) instead of brackets ([]). Notice that, when displayed in the shell, the set is shown in an unordered manner. Python does some mathematical tricks behind the scenes to make accessing the items very fast, and one of the side effects of this is that the items aren't in any particular order.

Let's show that each item is distinct; duplicates are ignored:

```
>>> vowels = {'a', 'e', 'a', 'a', 'i', 'o', 'u', 'u'}
>>> vowels
{'u', 'o', 'i', 'e', 'a'}
```

Even though there were three 'a's and two 'u's when you created the set, only one of each was kept. Python considers the two sets to be equal:

```
>>> {'a', 'e', 'i', 'o', 'u'} == {'a', 'e', 'a', 'a', 'i', 'o', 'u', 'u'}
True
```

The reason they are equal is that they contain the same items. Again, order doesn't matter, and only one of each element is kept.

Variable vowels refers to an object of type set:

```
>>> type(vowels)
<class 'set'>
>>> type({1, 2, 3})
<class 'set'>
```

In Storing Data Using Dictionaries, on page 220, you'll learn about a type that also uses the notation {}, which prevents you from using that notation to represent an empty set. Instead, to create an empty set, you need to call the function set with no arguments:

```
>>> set()
set()
>>> type(set())
<class 'set'>
```

The function set is a constructor. It expects either no arguments (to create an empty set) or a single argument that is a collection of values. For example, let's create a set from a list:

```
>>> set([2, 3, 2, 5])
{2, 3, 5}
```

Because duplicates aren't allowed, only one of the 2s appears in the set, shown in the diagram on the facing page.

The function set expects at most one argument. You can't pass several values as separate arguments:

```
>>> set(2, 3, 5)
Traceback (most recent call last):
  File "<python-input-0>", line 1, in <module>
    set(2, 3, 5)
    ~~~^^^^^^^^^
TypeError: set expected at most 1 argument, got 3
```

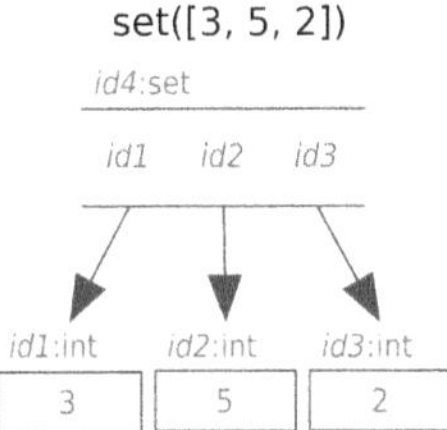

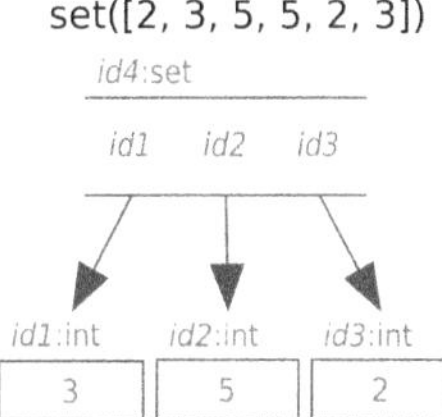

In addition to lists, there are a couple of other types that can be used as arguments to the function set. One is a set:

```
>>> vowels = {'a', 'e', 'a', 'a', 'i', 'o', 'u', 'u'}
>>> vowels
{'i', 'a', 'u', 'e', 'o'}
>>> set(vowels)
{'i', 'a', 'u', 'e', 'o'}
>>> set({5, 3, 1})
{1, 3, 5}
```

Another such type is range from Generating Ranges of Numbers, on page 156. In the following code, a set is created with the values 0 to 4 inclusive:

```
>>> set(range(5))
{0, 1, 2, 3, 4}
```

In Storing Data Using Tuples, on page 215, you will learn about the tuple type, another type of sequence, that can also be used as an argument to the function set.

Set Operations

In mathematics, set operations include union, intersection, add, and remove. In Python, these are implemented as methods:

Method	Description
S.add	Adds item v to a set S—this has no effect if v is already in S
S.clear	Removes all items from set S
S.difference	Returns a set with items that occur in set S but not in set other
S.intersection	Returns a set with items that occur both in sets S and other
S.issubset	Returns True if and only if all of set S's items are also in set other
S.issuperset	Returns True if and only if set S contains all of set other's items
S.remove	Removes item v from set S
S.symmetric_difference	Returns a set with items that are in exactly one of sets S and other—any items that are in both sets are *not* included in the result
S.union	Returns a set with items that are either in set S or other (or in both)

Sets are mutable. The methods add, remove, and clear all modify a set. The letter *y* is sometimes considered to be a vowel; let's add it to the set of vowels:

```
>>> vowels = {'a', 'e', 'i', 'o', 'u'}
>>> vowels
{'o', 'u', 'a', 'e', 'i'}
>>> vowels.add('y')
>>> vowels
{'u', 'y', 'e', 'a', 'o', 'i'}
```

Other methods, such as intersection and union, return new sets based on their arguments.

In the following code, you'll see all of these methods in action:

```
>>> ten = set(range(10))
>>> lows = {0, 1, 2, 3, 4}
>>> odds = {1, 3, 5, 7, 9}
>>> lows.add(9)
>>> lows
{0, 1, 2, 3, 4, 9}
>>> lows.difference(odds)
{0, 2, 4}
>>> lows.intersection(odds)
{1, 3, 9}
>>> lows.issubset(ten)
True
>>> lows.issuperset(odds)
False
>>> lows.remove(0)
>>> lows
{1, 2, 3, 4, 9}
>>> lows.symmetric_difference(odds)
{2, 4, 5, 7}
>>> lows.union(odds)
{1, 2, 3, 4, 5, 7, 9}
>>> lows.clear()
>>> lows
set()
```

Many of the tasks performed by methods can also be accomplished using operators. If acids and bases are two sets, for example, then acids | bases creates a new set containing their union (that is, all the elements from both acids and bases). In contrast, acids <= bases tests whether acids is a subset of bases—that is, that all the values in acids are also in bases. Some of the operators that sets support are listed in the following table.

Method Call	Operator
some_set.difference	some_set - other_set
some_set.intersection	some_set & other_set
some_set.issubset	some_set <= other_set
some_set.issuperset	some_set >= other_set
some_set.union	some_set | other_set
some_set.symmetric_difference	some_set ^ other_set

The following code shows the set operations in action.

```
>>> lows = set([0, 1, 2, 3, 4])
>>> odds = set([1, 3, 5, 7, 9])
>>> lows - odds           # Equivalent to lows.difference(odds)
{0, 2, 4}
>>> lows & odds           # Equivalent to lows.intersection(odds)
{1, 3}
>>> lows <= odds          # Equivalent to lows.issubset(odds)
False
>>> lows >= odds          # Equivalent to lows.issuperset(odds)
False
>>> lows | odds           # Equivalent to lows.union(odds)
{0, 1, 2, 3, 4, 5, 7, 9}
>>> lows ^ odds           # Equivalent to lows.symmetric_difference(odds)
{0, 2, 4, 5, 7, 9}
```

Set Example: Arctic Birds

Suppose you have a file used to record observations of birds in the Canadian Arctic, and you want to know which species have been observed. The observations file, observations.txt, has one species per line:

```
canada goose
canada goose
long-tailed jaeger
canada goose
snow goose
canada goose
long-tailed jaeger
canada goose
northern fulmar
```

The program on the next page reads each line of the file, strips off the leading and trailing whitespace, and adds the species on that line to the set. Notice the type annotation specifying that the function returns a set of strings.

```
from typing import Set, TextIO
from io import StringIO

def observe_birds(observations_file: TextIO) -> Set[str]:
    """Return a set of the bird species listed in observations_file, which has
    one bird species per line.

    >>> infile = StringIO('bird 1\\nbird 2\\nbird 1\\n')
    >>> birds = observe_birds(infile)
    >>> birds == {'bird 1', 'bird 2'}
    True
    """
    birds_observed = set()
    for line in observations_file:
        bird = line.strip()
        birds_observed.add(bird)

    return birds_observed

if __name__ == '__main__':
    with open('observations.txt') as observations_file:
        print(observe_birds(observations_file))
```

The resulting set contains four species. Since sets don't include duplicates, calling the method `add` with a species already in the set had no effect.

You can loop over the values in a set. In the following code, a `for` loop is used to print each species:

```
>>> for species in birds_observed:
...     print(species)
...
long-tailed jaeger
canada goose
northern fulmar
snow goose
```

Looping over a set works precisely like a loop over a list, except that the order in which items are encountered is arbitrary; there is no guarantee that they will come out in the order in which they were added, in alphabetical order, in order by length, or any other order.

Set Contents Must Be Immutable

Sets employ a mathematical technique called *hashing*, which relies on immutable set values. Mutable values, such as lists, cannot be added to sets because mutable values in general are unhashable.

```
>>> S = set()
>>> L = [1, 2, 3]
>>> S.add(L)
Traceback (most recent call last):
  File "<python-input-2>", line 1, in <module>
    S.add(L)
    ~~~~~^^^
TypeError: cannot use 'list' as a set element (unhashable type: 'list')
```

This restriction means that you can't store a set of sets. Sets themselves can't be immutable, since you need to add and remove values, so a set can't contain another one. To solve this problem, Python has another data type called a *frozen set*. As the name implies, frozen sets are sets that cannot be mutated. An empty frozen set is created using the frozenset constructor; to create a frozen set that contains some values, use frozenset(values), where values is a list, tuple, set, or other collection.

In the next section, you will learn about tuples, which can also be used as items in sets.

Storing Data Using Tuples

Tuples are immutable ordered sequences similar to lists

Lists aren't the only kind of ordered sequence in Python. You've already learned about one of the others: strings (see Chapter 4, Working with Text, on page 67). Formally, a string is an immutable sequence of characters. The characters in a string are ordered, and a string can be indexed and sliced like a list to create new strings:

```
>>> rock = 'anthracite'
>>> rock[9]
'e'
>>> rock[0:3]
'ant'
>>> rock[-5:]
'acite'
>>> for character in rock[:5]:
...     print(character)
...

a
n
t
h
r
```

Python also has an immutable sequence type called a *tuple*. Tuples are written using parentheses instead of brackets; like strings and lists, they can be subscripted, sliced, and looped over:

```
>>> bases = ('A', 'C', 'G', 'T')
>>> for base in bases:
...     print(base)
...
A
C
G
T
```

There's one small catch: although () represents the empty tuple, a tuple with one element is *not* written as (x) but as (x,) (with a trailing comma) to avoid ambiguity. If the trailing comma weren't required, (5 + 3) could mean either 8 (under the rules of arithmetic) or the tuple containing only the value 8:

```
>>> (8)
8
>>> type((8))
<class 'int'>
>>> (8,)
(8,)
>>> type((8,))
<class 'tuple'>
>>> (5 + 3)
8
>>> (5 + 3,)
(8,)
```

Unlike lists, once a tuple is created, it cannot be mutated:

```
>>> life = (['Canada', 76.5], ['United States', 75.5], ['Mexico', 72.0])
>>> life[0] = life[1]
Traceback (most recent call last):
  File "<python-input-1>", line 1, in <module>
    life[0] = life[1]
    ~~~~^^^
TypeError: 'tuple' object does not support item assignment
```

However, the objects inside tuples *can* still be mutated:

```
>>> life = (['Canada', 76.5], ['United States', 75.5], ['Mexico', 72.0])
>>> life[0][1] = 80.0
>>> life
(['Canada', 80.0], ['United States', 75.5], ['Mexico', 72.0])
```

Here is an example that explores what is mutable and what isn't. Let's build the same tuple as in the previous example, but let's do it in steps. First, let's create three lists:

```
>>> canada = ['Canada', 76.5]
>>> usa = ['United States', 75.5]
>>> mexico = ['Mexico', 72.0]
```

That builds this memory model:

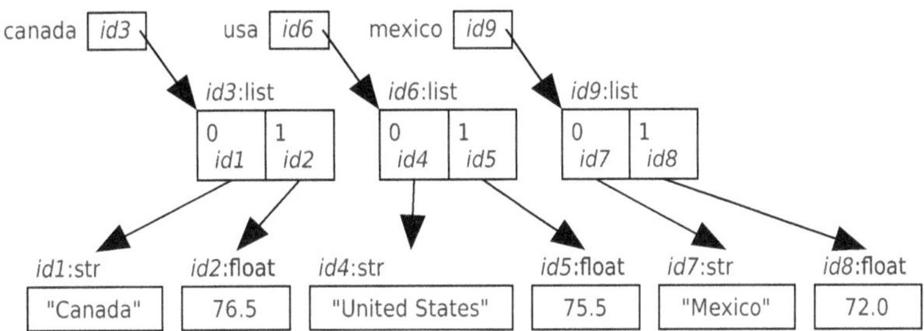

Let's create a tuple using those variables:

```
>>> life = (canada, usa, mexico)
```

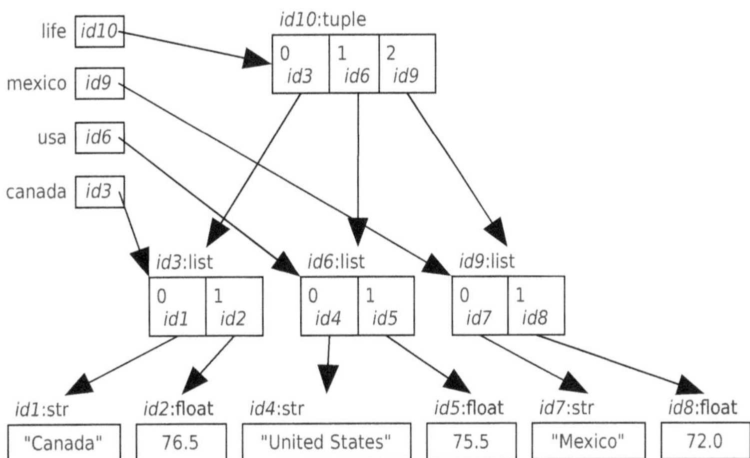

Notice that none of the four variables know about the others, and that the tuple object contains three references, one for each of the country lists.

Now, let's change what variable mexico refers to:

```
>>> mexico = ['Mexico', 72.5]
>>> life
(['Canada', 76.5], ['United States', 75.5], ['Mexico', 72.0])
```

Notice that the tuple that the variable life refers to hasn't changed. The new picture is on the next page.

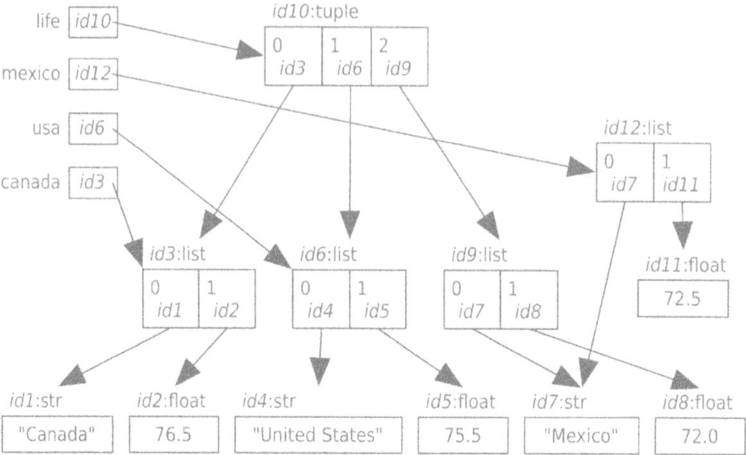

life[0] will always refer to the same list object—we can't change the memory address stored in life[0]—but we can mutate that list object. And because variable canada also refers to that list, it sees the mutation:

```
>>> life[0][1] = 80.0
>>> canada
['Canada', 80.0]
```

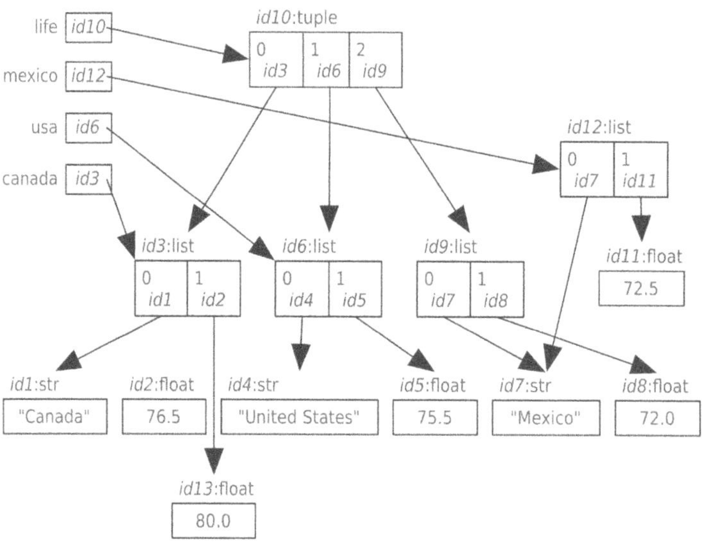

We hope it is clear how essential it is to thoroughly understand variables and references, as well as how collections contain references to objects, not variables.

Assigning to Multiple Variables Using Tuples

You can assign to multiple variables in the same assignment statement:

```
>>> (x, y) = (10, 20)
>>> x
10
>>> y
20
```

As with a normal assignment statement (see Assignment Statement, on page 18), Python first evaluates all expressions on the right side of the = symbol, and then it assigns those values to the variables on the left side.

Python uses the comma as a tuple constructor, allowing you to omit the parentheses:

```
>>> 10, 20
(10, 20)
>>> x, y = 10, 20
>>> x
10
>>> y
20
```

Multiple assignment also works with lists and sets. Python will happily unpack information from any collection:

```
>>> [[w, x], [[y], z]] = [{10, 20}, [(30,), 40]]
>>> w
10
>>> x
20
>>> y
30
>>> z
40
```

Any depth of nesting will work as long as the structure on the right can be translated into the structure on the left.

One of the most common uses of multiple assignment is to swap the values of two variables:

```
>>> s1 = 'first'
>>> s2 = 'second'
>>> s1, s2 = s2, s1
>>> s1
'second'
>>> s2
'first'
```

The assignment works because the expressions on the RHS are evaluated before being assigned to the variables on the LHS. We will revisit multiple assignments in Packing and Unpacking, on page 334.

Storing Data Using Dictionaries

Here is the same bird-watching observation file that you saw in Set Example: Arctic Birds, on page 213:

```
canada goose
canada goose
long-tailed jaeger
canada goose
snow goose
canada goose
long-tailed jaeger
canada goose
northern fulmar
```

Suppose you want to count how often each species is observed. Your first attempt uses a list of lists, where each inner list contains two items. The item at index 0 of the inner list represents the species, and the item at index 1 represents the number of times it has been seen so far. To build this list, iterate over the lines of the observations file. For each line, search the outer list for the species listed on that line. If you find that the species is listed, increment the number of times it has been observed; if you do not find it, add a new entry for the species:

Dictionaries store unordered collections of pairs of immutable keys and mutable values

```
from typing import TextIO
from io import StringIO

def count_birds(observations_file: TextIO) -> list[list]:
    """Return a set of the bird species listed in observations_file, which has
    one bird species per line.

    >>> infile = StringIO('bird 1\\nbird 2\\nbird 1\\n')
    >>> count_birds(infile)
    [['bird 1', 2], ['bird 2', 1]]
    """
    bird_counts = []
    for line in observations_file:
        bird = line.strip()
        found = False
        # Find bird in the list of bird counts.
        for entry in bird_counts:
            if entry[0] == bird:
                entry[1] = entry[1] + 1
                found = True
                break
        if not found:
```

```
            bird_counts.append([bird, 1])

    return bird_counts

if __name__ == '__main__':
    with open('observations.txt') as observations_file:
        bird_counts = count_birds(observations_file)

        # Print each bird and the number of times it was seen
        for entry in bird_counts:
            print(entry[0], entry[1])
```

Here is the output:

```
canada goose 5
long-tailed jaeger 2
snow goose 1
northern fulmar 1
```

This code uses a Boolean variable, found. Once a species is read from the file, found is assigned False. The program then iterates over the list, searching for the specified species at index 0 of one of the inner lists. If the species occurs in an inner list, found is assigned True. At the end of the loop over the list, if found still refers to False, it means that this species is not yet present in the list, and so it is added, along with the number of observations of it, which is currently 1.

The code works, but there are two things wrong with it. The first is that it is complex. The more nested loops a program contains, the harder it is to understand, fix, and extend. The second is that it is inefficient. Suppose you were interested in beetles instead of birds and that you had millions of observations of tens of thousands of species. Scanning the list of names each time you want to add a new observation would take a long time, even on a fast computer (a topic we will return to in Chapter 13, Searching and Sorting, on page 249).

Can you use a set to solve both problems at once? Sets can look up values in a single step; why not combine each bird's name and the number of times it has been seen into a two-valued tuple and put those tuples in a set?

The problem with this idea is that you can look for values only if you know what those values are. In this case, you won't. You will know only the name of the species, but not how many times it has been seen previously.

The right approach is to use another data structure called a *dictionary*. Also known as a *map*, a dictionary is an unordered, mutable collection of key-value pairs. In plain English, Python's dictionaries are like dictionaries that map words to definitions. They associate a key (like a word) with a value (such as a definition). The keys form a set: any particular key can appear once at most in a dictionary. Like the elements in sets, keys must be immutable (though the values associated with them don't have to be).

Dictionaries are created by putting key-value pairs inside braces (each key is followed by a colon and then by its value):

```
>>> bird_to_observations = {'canada goose': 3, 'northern fulmar': 1}
>>> bird_to_observations
{'canada goose': 3, 'northern fulmar': 1}
```

We chose the variable name bird_to_observations since this variable refers to a dictionary where each key is a bird, and each value is the number of observations of that bird. In other words, the dictionary maps birds to observations. Here is a picture of the resulting dictionary:

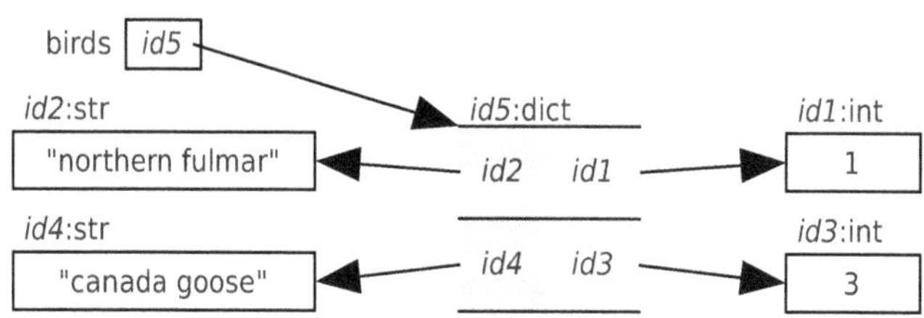

To get the value associated with a key, put the key in square brackets, much like indexing into a list:

```
>>> bird_to_observations['northern fulmar']
1
```

Indexing a dictionary with a key that it doesn't contain produces an error, just like an out-of-range index for a list does:

```
>>> bird_to_observations['canada goose']
3
>>> bird_to_observations['long-tailed jaeger']
Traceback (most recent call last):
  File "<python-input-1>", line 1, in <module>
    bird_to_observations['long-tailed jaeger']
    ~~~~~~~~~~~~~~~~~~~~^^^^^^^^^^^^^^^^^^^^^^
KeyError: 'long-tailed jaeger'
```

An empty dictionary is denoted by an empty set of braces {}. (This is why you can't use this notation for the empty set.) It doesn't contain any key-value pairs, so indexing into it always results in an error.

As with sets, dictionaries are unordered:

```
>>> dict1 = {'canada goose': 3, 'northern fulmar': 1}
>>> dict2 = {'northern fulmar': 1, 'canada goose': 3}
>>> dict1 == dict2
True
```

Updating and Checking Membership

To update the value associated with a key, you use the same notation as for lists, except you use a key instead of an index. If the key is already in the dictionary, this assignment statement changes the value associated with it. If the key isn't present, the key-value pair is added to the dictionary:

```
>>> bird_to_observations = {}
>>>
>>> # Add a new key/value pair, 'snow goose': 33.
>>> bird_to_observations['snow goose'] = 33
>>>
>>> # Add a new key/value pair, 'eagle': 999.
>>> bird_to_observations['eagle'] = 999
>>> bird_to_observations
{'eagle': 999, 'snow goose': 33}
>>>
>>> # Change the value associated with key 'eagle' to 9.
>>> bird_to_observations['eagle'] = 9
>>> bird_to_observations
{'eagle': 9, 'snow goose': 33}
```

To remove an entry from a dictionary, use del d[k], where d is the dictionary and k is the key being removed. Only entries that are present can be removed; trying to remove one that isn't there results in an error:

```
>>> bird_to_observations = {'snow goose': 33, 'eagle': 9}
>>> del bird_to_observations['snow goose']
>>> bird_to_observations
{'eagle': 9}
>>> del bird_to_observations['gannet']
Traceback (most recent call last):
  File "<python-input-1>", line 1, in <module>
    del bird_to_observations['gannet']
        ~~~~~~~~~~~~~~~~~~~~^^^^^^^^^^
KeyError: 'gannet'
```

To test whether a key is in a dictionary, you can use the in operator:

```
>>> bird_to_observations = {'eagle': 999, 'snow goose': 33}
>>> 'eagle' in bird_to_observations
True
>>> if 'eagle' in bird_to_observations:
...     print('eagles have been seen')
...
eagles have been seen
```

```
>>> del bird_to_observations['eagle']
>>> 'eagle' in bird_to_observations
False
>>> if 'eagle' in bird_to_observations:
...   print('eagles have been seen')
...
>>>
```

The in operator only checks the keys of a dictionary. In this example, 33 in birds evaluates to False, since 33 is a value, not a key.

Looping over Dictionaries

Like the other collections you've seen, you can loop over dictionaries. The general form of a for loop over a dictionary is as follows:

```
for «variable» in «dictionary»:
    «block»
```

For dictionaries, the loop variable is assigned each key from the dictionary in turn:

```
>>> bird_to_observations = {'canada goose': 183, 'long-tailed jaeger': 71,
... 'snow goose': 63, 'northern fulmar': 1}
>>> for bird in bird_to_observations:
...     print(bird, bird_to_observations[bird])
...
canada goose 183
long-tailed jaeger 71
snow goose 63
northern fulmar 1
```

When Python loops over a dictionary, it assigns each key to the loop variable. (It's a lot easier to go from a dictionary key to the associated value than it is to take the value and find the associated key, which may not even be unique.)

Dictionary Operations

Like lists, tuples, and sets, dictionaries are objects. Their methods are described in Table 8, Dictionary Methods, on page 225. The following code shows how the methods can be used:

```
>>> scientist_to_birthdate = {'Newton' : 1642, 'Darwin' : 1809,
...                           'Turing' : 1912}
>>> scientist_to_birthdate.keys()
dict_keys(['Darwin', 'Newton', 'Turing'])
>>> scientist_to_birthdate.values()
dict_values([1809, 1642, 1912])
>>> scientist_to_birthdate.items()
dict_items([('Darwin', 1809), ('Newton', 1642), ('Turing', 1912)])
>>> scientist_to_birthdate.get('Newton')
```

```
1642
>>> scientist_to_birthdate.get('Curie', 1867)
1867
>>> scientist_to_birthdate
{'Darwin': 1809, 'Newton': 1642, 'Turing': 1912}
>>> researcher_to_birthdate = {'Curie' : 1867, 'Hopper' : 1906,
...                            'Franklin' : 1920}
>>> scientist_to_birthdate.update(researcher_to_birthdate)
>>> scientist_to_birthdate
{'Hopper': 1906, 'Darwin': 1809, 'Turing': 1912, 'Newton': 1642,
 'Franklin': 1920, 'Curie': 1867}
>>> researcher_to_birthdate
{'Franklin': 1920, 'Hopper': 1906, 'Curie': 1867}
>>> researcher_to_birthdate.clear()
>>> researcher_to_birthdate
{}
```

Method	Description
D.clear	Removes all key-value pairs from dictionary D
D.get	Returns the value associated with key k, or None if the key isn't present. (Usually you'll want to use D[k] instead.)
D.get	Returns the value associated with key k, or a default value v if the key isn't present
D.keys	Returns dictionary D's keys as a set-like object—entries are guaranteed to be unique
D.items	Returns dictionary D's (key, value) pairs as set-like objects
D.pop	Removes key k from dictionary D and returns the value that was associated with k; if k isn't in D, an error is raised.
D.pop	Removes key k from dictionary D and returns the value that was associated with k; if k isn't in D , returns v.
D.setdefault	Returns the value associated with key k in D; if k isn't a key in D, adds the key k with the value v to D and returns v.
D.values	Returns dictionary D's values as a list-like object—entries may or may not be unique
D.update	Updates dictionary D with the contents of dictionary other; for each key in other, if it is also a key in D, replaces that key in D's value with the value from other; for each key in other, if that key isn't in D, adds that key-value pair to D. You can use the operator | to the same effect: D | other.

Table 8—Dictionary Methods

As you can see from this output, the keys and values methods return the dictionary's keys and values, respectively, while items returns the (key, value) pairs. Similar to the range object you learned about previously, these are virtual sequences over which you can loop. Similarly, the constructor function list can be applied to them to create lists of key-value tuples.

Because dictionaries usually map values from one concept (scientists, in your example) to another (birthdays), it's common to use variable names that express this relationship—hence the name scientist_to_birthdate.

One common use of items is to loop over the keys and values in a dictionary together:

```
for key, value in dictionary.items():
    # Do something with the key and value
```

For example, the same format can be used to loop over the scientists and their birth years:

```
>>> scientist_to_birthdate = {'Newton' : 1642, 'Darwin' : 1809,
...                           'Turing' : 1912}
>>> for scientist, birthdate in scientist_to_birthdate.items():
...     print(scientist, 'was born in', birthdate)
...
Turing was born in 1912
Darwin was born in 1809
Newton was born in 1642
```

Instead of a single loop variable, there are two. The two parts of each of the two-item tuples returned by the method items are associated with a variable. Variable scientist refers to the first item in the tuple, which is the key, and birthdate refers to the second item, which is the value.

Dictionaries and Key Order

The way Python stores dictionaries has a side effect: the keys are always returned in the same order as they were added. The language designers have warned that you should not rely on this, although it may become a guaranteed feature in future versions.

In keeping with this advice, none of the examples in this book rely on dictionary key order.

Dictionary Example

Back to bird-watching once again. Like before, let's count the number of times each species has been seen. To do this, create an initially empty dictionary. Each time you read an observation from a file, check to see whether you have encountered that bird before—that is, whether the bird is already a key in your dictionary. If it is, add 1 to the value associated with it. If it isn't, add the bird as a key to the dictionary with the value 1. Here is the program that performs this task. Notice the type annotation for dictionaries:

```
from typing import TextIO
from io import StringIO

def count_birds(observations_file: TextIO) -> dict[str, int]:
    """Return a set of the bird species listed in observations_file, which has
    one bird species per line.

    >>> infile = StringIO('bird 1\\nbird 2\\nbird 1\\n')
    >>> count_birds(infile)
    {'bird 1': 2, 'bird 2': 1}
    """
    bird_to_observations = {}
    for line in observations_file:
        bird = line.strip()
        if bird in bird_to_observations:
            bird_to_observations[bird] += 1
        else:
            bird_to_observations[bird] = 1

    return bird_to_observations

if __name__ == '__main__':
    with open('observations.txt') as observations_file:
        bird_to_observations = count_birds(observations_file)
        for bird, observations in bird_to_observations.items():
            print(bird, observations)
```

The function body can be shortened by using the method dict.get, which saves three lines:

```
def count_birds(observations_file: TextIO) -> dict[str, int]:
    """Return a set of the bird species listed in observations_file, which has
    one bird species per line.

    >>> infile = StringIO('bird 1\\nbird 2\\nbird 1\\n')
    >>> count_birds(infile)
    {'bird 1': 2, 'bird 2': 1}
    """
    bird_to_observations = {}
    for line in observations_file:
        bird = line.strip()
        bird_to_observations[bird] = bird_to_observations.get(bird, 0) + 1

    return bird_to_observations
```

Using the get method makes the program shorter, but some programmers find it harder to understand at a glance. If the first argument to get is not a key in the dictionary, it returns 0; otherwise, it returns the value associated with that key. After that, 1 is added to that value. The dictionary is updated to associate that sum with the key that bird refers to.

Inverting a Dictionary

You might want to print the birds in another order—in order of the number of observations, for example. To do this, you need to *invert* the dictionary; that is, create a new dictionary in which you use the values as keys and the keys as values. This task is a little trickier than it first appears. There's no guarantee that the values are unique, so you have to handle what are called *collisions*. For example, if you invert the dictionary {'a': 1, 'b': 1, 'c': 1}, a key would be 1, but it's not clear what the value associated with it would be.

Since you'd like to keep all of the data from the original dictionary, you may need to use a collection, such as a set, to keep track of the values associated with a key. If you go this route, the inverse of the dictionary shown earlier would be {1: {'a', 'b', 'c'}}. Here's a program to invert the dictionary of birds to observations to the dictionary of observations to birds:

```
>>> bird_to_observations
{'canada goose': 5, 'northern fulmar': 1, 'long-tailed jaeger': 2,
'snow goose': 1}
>>>
>>> # Invert the dictionary
>>> observations_to_birds_list = {}
>>> for bird, counts in bird_to_observations.items():
...     if counts not in observations_to_birds_list:
...         observations_to_birds_list[counts] = set()
...     observations_to_birds_list[counts].add(bird)
...
>>> observations_to_birds_list
{5: {'canada goose'}, 1: {'snow goose', 'northern fulmar'},
 2: {'long-tailed jaeger'}}
```

This program loops over each key-value pair in the original dictionary, bird_to_observations. If that value is not yet a key in the inverted dictionary, observations_to_birds_list, it is added as a key and its value is an empty set. After that, the key associated with it in the original dictionary is appended to its set of values.

Now that the dictionary is inverted, you can print each key and all of the items in its value list:

```
>>> # Print the inverted dictionary
... counts_sorted = sorted(observations_to_birds_list.keys())
>>> for count in counts_sorted:
...     birds = ", ".join(observations_to_birds_list[count])
...     print(f'{count} : {birds}')
...
1 : snow goose, northern fulmar
```

```
2 : long-tailed jaeger
5 : canada goose
```

The loop passes over each key in the inverted dictionary. The items in the set associated with each key are combined into one comma-and-space-separated string using the str.join method that takes a list of strings and combines them into one string using its object (str) as the "glue."

Using the in Operator on Tuples, Sets, and Dictionaries

As with lists, the in operator can be applied to tuples and sets to check whether an item is a member of the collection:

```
>>> odds = set([1, 3, 5, 7, 9])
>>> 9 in odds
True
>>> 8 in odds
False
>>> '9' in odds
False
>>> evens = (0, 2, 4, 6, 8)
>>> 4 in evens
True
>>> 11 in evens
False
```

When used on a dictionary, in checks whether a value is a key in the dictionary:

```
>>> bird_to_observations = {'canada goose': 183, 'long-tailed jaeger': 71,
...     'snow goose': 63, 'northern fulmar': 1}
>>> 'snow goose' in bird_to_observations
True
>>> 183 in bird_to_observations
False
```

Note that the values in the dictionary are ignored; the in operator only checks the keys.

Comparing Collections

You've now seen strings, lists, sets, tuples, and dictionaries. They all have their uses. The table on the next page compares them.

Creating New Type Annotations

For each built-in type annotation such as int str, list, set, tuple, and dict you can specify the kind of thing it contains. To explore this, let's revisit atoms and molecules from Multiline Records, on page 201, using dictionaries and tuples in addition to lists.

Collection	Mutable?	Ordered?	Use When…
str	No	Yes	You want to keep track of text.
list	Yes	Yes	You want to keep track of an ordered sequence that you want to update.
tuple	No	Yes	You want to build an ordered sequence that you know won't change or that you want to use as a key in a dictionary or as a value in a set.
set	Yes	No	You want to keep track of values, but order doesn't matter, and you don't want to keep duplicates. The values must be immutable.
dictionary	Yes	No	You want to keep a mapping of keys to values. The keys must be immutable.

Hash Tables and Why They Matter

Hash tables are one of the most important data structures in computer science. They allow programs to store and retrieve data in constant time on average, regardless of the amount of data. This speed is made possible by a process called *hashing*, which converts a key (like a string or number) into an index that tells the computer where to find the corresponding value in memory.

Python dictionary is a data type that uses a hash table under the hood. When you write `my_dict['name'] = 'Alice'`, Python hashes the key `'name'` to determine where to store `'Alice'`. Later, it uses the same hash to retrieve the value quickly. Thanks to hash tables, Python dictionaries are incredibly fast for operations like lookups, insertions, and deletions, making them a go-to tool for many programming tasks.

Recall functions `read_molecule` and `read_all_molecules`; here are the headers and docstrings:

```
def read_molecule(reader: TextIO) -> list:
    """Read a single molecule from reader and return it, or return None to
    signal end of file.  The first item in the result is the name of the
    compound; each list contains an atom type and the X, Y, and Z coordinates
    of that atom.

    >>> instring = ('COMPND TEST\\nATOM 1 N 0.1 0.2 0.3\\n' +
    'ATOM 2 N 0.2 0.1 0.0\\nEND\\n')
    >>> infile = StringIO(instring)
    >>> read_molecule(infile)
    ['TEST', ['N', '0.1', '0.2', '0.3'], ['N', '0.2', '0.1', '0.0']]
    """
```

```
def read_all_molecules(reader: TextIO) -> list:
    """Read zero or more molecules from reader, returning a list of the
    molecule information.

    >>> cmpnd1 = ('COMPND T1\\nATOM 1 N 0.1 0.2 0.3\\n' +
    'ATOM 2 N 0.2 0.1 0.0\\nEND\\n')
    >>> cmpnd2 = ('COMPND T2\\nATOM 1 A 0.1 0.2 0.3\\n' +
    'ATOM 2 A 0.2 0.1 0.0\\nEND\\n')
    >>> infile = StringIO(cmpnd1 + cmpnd2)
    >>> result = read_all_molecules(infile)
    >>> result[0]
    ['T1', ['N', '0.1', '0.2', '0.3'], ['N', '0.2', '0.1', '0.0']]
    >>> result[1]
    ['T2', ['A', '0.1', '0.2', '0.3'], ['A', '0.2', '0.1', '0.0']]
    """
```

Assuming that molecules have unique names, it would make sense for read_all_molecules to return a dictionary where the keys are the names of compounds and the values are the atoms.

Additionally, instead of using a four-item list for atoms, each atom will be represented as a tuple where the first item is the type of the atom and the second item is a tuple of three coordinates.

You can introduce new names for these compound types (pun unintended). Here, let's define two new types: Atom and CompoundDict:

```
Atom = tuple[str, tuple[str, str, str]]
CompoundDict = dict[str, Atom]
```

They lead to the new function specifications:

```
def read_molecule(reader: TextIO) -> CompoundDict:
    """Read a single molecule from reader and return it, or return None to
    signal end of file.  The returned dictionary has one key/value pair where
    the key is the name of the compound and the value is a list of Atoms.

    >>> instring = 'COMPND TEST\\nATOM 1 N 0.1 0.2 0.3\\n'+\
'ATOM 2 N 0.2 0.1 0.0\\nEND\\n'
    >>> infile = StringIO(instring)
    >>> read_molecule(infile)
    {'TEST': [('N', ('0.1', '0.2', '0.3')), ('N', ('0.2', '0.1', '0.0'))]}
    """

def read_all_molecules(reader: TextIO) -> CompoundDict:
    """Read zero or more molecules from reader, returning a list of the
    molecule information.

    >>> cmpnd1 = 'COMPND T1\\nATOM 1 N 0.1 0.2 0.3\\n'+\
'ATOM 2 N 0.2 0.1 0.0\\nEND\\n'
    >>> cmpnd2 = 'COMPND T2\\nATOM 1 A 0.1 0.2 0.3\\n'+\
'ATOM 2 A 0.2 0.1 0.0\\nEND\\n'
    >>> infile = StringIO(cmpnd1 + cmpnd2)
```

```
>>> result = read_all_molecules(infile)
>>> result['T1']
[('N', ('0.1', '0.2', '0.3')), ('N', ('0.2', '0.1', '0.0'))]
>>> result['T2']
[('A', ('0.1', '0.2', '0.3')), ('A', ('0.2', '0.1', '0.0'))]
"""
```

A Collection of New Information

In this chapter, you learned the following:

- Sets are used in Python to store unordered collections of unique values. They support the same operations as sets in mathematics.
- Tuples are another kind of Python sequence. Tuples are ordered sequences, similar to lists, except they are immutable.
- Dictionaries are used to store unordered collections of key-value pairs. The keys must be immutable, but the values do not need to be.
- Looking things up in sets and dictionaries is much faster than searching through lists. If you have a program that is doing the latter, consider changing your choice of data structures.

Exercises

Here are some exercises for you to try on your own.

1. Write a function called find_dups that takes a list of integers as its input argument and returns a set of those integers occurring two or more times in the list.
2. Write the bodies of the new versions of functions read_molecule and read_all_molecules from Creating New Type Annotations, on page 229.
3. Python's set objects have a method called pop that removes and returns an arbitrary element from the set. If the set gerbils contains five cuddly little animals, for example, calling gerbils.pop five times will return those animals one by one, leaving the set empty at the end. Use this information to write a function called mating_pairs that takes two equal-sized sets, males and females, as input and returns a set of pairs; each pair must be a tuple containing one male and one female. (The elements of males and females may be strings containing gerbil names or gerbil ID numbers—your function must work with both.)
4. The PDB file format is often used to store information about molecules. A PDB file may contain zero or more lines that begin with the word AUTHOR (which may be in uppercase, lowercase, or mixed case), followed by spaces or tabs, followed by the name of the person who created the file. Write a function that

takes a list of filenames as an input argument and returns the set of all author names found in those files.

5. The keys in a dictionary are guaranteed to be unique, but the values are not necessarily unique. Write a function called count_values that takes a single dictionary as an argument and returns the number of distinct values it contains. Given the input {'red': 1, 'green': 1, 'blue': 2}, for example, it should return 2.

6. After doing a series of experiments, you have compiled a dictionary showing the probability of detecting certain kinds of subatomic particles. The particles' names are the dictionary's keys, and the probabilities are the values: {'neutron': 0.55, 'proton': 0.21, 'meson': 0.03, 'muon': 0.07, 'neutrino': 0.14}. Write a function that takes a single dictionary of this kind as input and returns the particle that is least likely to be observed. Given the dictionary shown earlier, for example, the function would return 'meson'.

7. Write a function called count_duplicates that takes a dictionary as an argument and returns the number of values that appear two or more times.

8. A *balanced color* is one whose red, green, and blue values add up to 1.0. Write a function called is_balanced that takes a dictionary whose keys are 'R', 'G', and 'B' and whose values are between 0 and 1 as input and that returns True if they represent a balanced color.

9. Write a function called dict_intersect that takes two dictionaries as arguments and returns a dictionary that contains only the key-value pairs found in both of the original dictionaries.

10. Programmers sometimes use a dictionary of dictionaries as a simple database. For example, to keep track of information about famous scientists, you might have a dictionary where the keys are strings and the values are dictionaries, as shown here:

```
{
  'jgoodall'  : {'surname'  : 'Goodall',
                 'forename' : 'Jane',
                 'born'     : 1934,
                 'died'     : None,
                 'notes'    : 'primate researcher',
                 'author'   : ['In the Shadow of Man',
                               'The Chimpanzees of Gombe']},
  'rfranklin' : {'surname'  : 'Franklin',
                 'forename' : 'Rosalind',
                 'born'     : 1920,
                 'died'     : 1957,
                 'notes'    : 'contributed to discovery of DNA'},

   'rcarson'  : {'surname'  : 'Carson',
                 'forename' : 'Rachel',
```

```
                    'born'      : 1907,
                    'died'      : 1964,
                    'notes'     : 'raised awareness of effects of DDT',
                    'author'    : ['Silent Spring']}
}
```

Write a function called db_headings that returns the set of keys used in *any* of the inner dictionaries. In this example, the function should return set('author', 'forename', 'surname', 'notes', 'born', 'died').

11. Write another function called db_consistent that takes a dictionary of dictionaries in the format described in the previous question and returns True if and only if every one of the inner dictionaries has precisely the same keys. (This function would return False for the previous example, since Rosalind Franklin's entry doesn't contain the 'author' key.)

12. A *sparse vector* is a vector whose entries are almost all zero, like [1, 0, 0, 0, 0, 0, 3, 0, 0, 0]. Storing all those zeros in a list wastes memory, so programmers often use dictionaries instead to keep track of just the nonzero entries. For example, the vector shown earlier would be represented as {0:1, 6:3}, because the vector it is meant to represent has the value 1 at index 0 and the value 3 at index 6.

    a. The sum of two vectors is just the element-wise sum of their elements. For example, the sum of [1, 2, 3] and [4, 5, 6] is [5, 7, 9]. Write a function called sparse_add that takes two sparse vectors stored as dictionaries and returns a new dictionary representing their sum.

    b. The dot product of two vectors is the sum of the products of corresponding elements. For example, the dot product of [1, 2, 3] and [4, 5, 6] is 4+10+18, or 32. Write another function called sparse_dot that calculates the dot product of two sparse vectors.

    c. Your boss has asked you to write a function called sparse_len that will return the length of a sparse vector (just as Python's len returns the length of a list). What do you need to ask her before you can start writing it?

CHAPTER 12

Designing and Benchmarking Algorithms

Algorithms and Khwarizmi

The word "algorithm" comes from the name of the 9th-century Persian mathematician al-Khwarizmi, who lived in the region of Khwarazm (now part of Uzbekistan). His work on arithmetic and algebra was foundational in medieval mathematics, and his name was Latinized as "Algoritmi," eventually giving rise to the modern term "algorithm."

An *algorithm* is a set of steps that accomplishes a task, such as the steps involved in synthesizing caffeine. Each function in a program, as well as the program itself, is an algorithm that is written in a programming language like Python. Writing a program directly in Python, without careful planning, can waste hours, days, or even weeks of effort. Instead, programmers often write algorithms in a combination of English and mathematics and then translate them into Python.

The most effective way to design algorithms is to use top-down design

In this chapter, you'll learn an algorithm-writing technique called *top-down design*. You start by describing your solution in English and then mark the phrases that correspond directly to Python statements. Those that don't correspond are then rewritten in more detail in English until everything in your description can be written in Python.

Searching for the Two Smallest Values

This section will explore how to find the index of the two smallest items in an unsorted list using three quite different algorithms. You'll go through a top-down design using each approach. A natural assumption is that a list has at least two items.

Looking Ahead: Testing Your Algorithms

Top-down design is easy to describe, but practicing it is not trivial. Often, parts of an algorithm written in English can be tricky to translate into Python; in fact, an implementation may *look* reasonable but still contain bugs, which is a common issue in many fields. In mathematics, for example, the first versions of "proofs" often handle common cases well but fail for odd cases (*Proofs and Refutations* [Lak76]). Mathematicians address this by seeking counterexamples, and programmers (good programmers, at least) handle it by testing their code as they write it.

In this chapter, we have omitted a discussion of how we tested the presented algorithms. The first versions we wrote had minor bugs, and we discovered them only through thorough testing. We will discuss testing further in Chapter 15, Testing and Debugging, on page 309.

To begin, suppose you have data showing the number of humpback whales sighted off the coast of British Columbia over the past decade:

809	834	477	478	307	122	96	102	324	476

The first value, 809, represents the number of sightings ten years ago; the last one, 476, represents the number of sightings last year.

Let's start with a simpler problem: what is the smallest value during those years? This code tells you just that:

```
>>> counts = [809, 834, 477, 478, 307, 122, 96, 102, 324, 476]
>>> min(counts)
96
```

To determine the year when the population bottomed out, you can use list.index to find the index of the smallest value:

```
>>> counts = [809, 834, 477, 478, 307, 122, 96, 102, 324, 476]
>>> low = min(counts)
>>> counts.index(low)
6
```

Or, more succinctly:

```
>>> counts = [809, 834, 477, 478, 307, 122, 96, 102, 324, 476]
>>> counts.index(min(counts))
6
```

Now, what if you want to find the indices of the *two* smallest values? Lists don't have a direct method to do this, so you'll need to design an algorithm yourself and then translate it into a Python function. Here is the header for a function that performs this task:

```
def find_two_smallest(L: list[float]) -> tuple[int, int]:
    """Return a tuple of the indices of the two smallest values in list L.

    >>> items = [809, 834, 477, 478, 307, 122, 96, 102, 324, 476]
    >>> find_two_smallest(items)
    (6, 7)
    >>> items == [809, 834, 477, 478, 307, 122, 96, 102, 324, 476]
    True
    """
```

As you may recall from Designing New Functions: A Recipe, on page 49, the next step in the function design recipe is to write the function body.

There are at least three distinct algorithms, each of which will be subjected to top-down design. Let's start by giving a high-level description of each. Each of these descriptions is the first step in doing a top-down design for that approach.

- *Find, remove, find.* Find the index of the minimum, remove it from the list, and find the index of the new minimum item in the list. After you have the second index, you need to put back the value you removed and, if necessary, adjust the second index to account for that removal and reinsertion.
- *Sort, identify minimums, get indices.* Sort the list, get the two smallest numbers, and then find their indices in the original list.
- *Walk through the list.* Examine each value in the list in order, keep track of the two smallest values found so far, and update these values when a new smaller value is found.

The first two algorithms mutate the list, either by removing an item or by sorting the list. Your algorithms must restore the mutated lists back to their original state, or the people who call your functions will be annoyed with you. The last two lines of the docstring check that the list isn't mutated.

While you are investigating these algorithms in the next few pages, consider this question: *Which one is the fastest?*

Find, Remove, Find

Here is the algorithm again, rewritten with one instruction per line and explicitly discussing the parameter L:

```
def find_two_smallest(L: list[float]) -> tuple[int, int]:
    """Return a tuple of the indices of the two smallest values in list L.

    >>> items = [809, 834, 477, 478, 307, 122, 96, 102, 324, 476]
    >>> find_two_smallest(items)
    (6, 7)
    >>> items == [809, 834, 477, 478, 307, 122, 96, 102, 324, 476]
    True
```

```
    """
    # Find the index of the minimum item in L
    # Remove that item from the list
    # Find the index of the new minimum item in the list
    # Put the smallest item back in the list
    # If necessary, adjust the second index
    # Return the two indices
```

To address the first step, find the index of the minimum item in *L*, skim the output produced by calling help(list) and find that there are no methods that do exactly that. Let's refine it:

```
def find_two_smallest(L: list[float]) -> tuple[int, int]:
    """ (see above) """

    # Get the minimum item in L             <-- This line is new
    # Find the index of that minimum item   <-- This line is new
    # Remove that item from the list
    # Find the index of the new minimum item in the list
    # Put the smallest item back in the list
    # If necessary, adjust the second index
    # Return the two indices
```

Those first two statements match Python functions and methods: min does the first, and list.index does the second. (There are other ways; for example, you could have written a loop to perform the search.)

You can see that list.remove implements the third statement, and the refinement of "Find the index of the new minimum item in the list" is also straightforward.

Notice that some of the English statements are left in as comments, which makes it easier to understand the problem that each chunk of code solves:

```
def find_two_smallest(L: list[float]) -> tuple[int, int]:
    """ (see above) """

    # Find the index of the minimum and remove that item
    smallest = min(L)
    min1 = L.index(smallest)
    L.remove(smallest)

    # Find the index of the new minimum
    next_smallest = min(L)
    min2 = L.index(next_smallest)

    # Put the smallest item back in the list
    # If necessary, adjust the second index
    # Return the two indices
```

Since you removed the smallest item, you need to put it back where it was. Because removing a value affects the indices of the following values, you might need to add 1 to min2 if the smallest item came before the second-smallest item:

```
def find_two_smallest(L: list[float]) -> tuple[int, int]:
    """ (see above) """

    # Find the index of the minimum and remove that item
    smallest = min(L)
    min1 = L.index(smallest)
    L.remove(smallest)

    # Find the index of the new minimum
    next_smallest = min(L)
    min2 = L.index(next_smallest)

    # Put smallest back into L
    # Fix min2 in case it was affected by the removal and reinsertion:
    # If min1 comes before min2, add 1 to min2
    # Return the two indices
```

That's enough refinement (finally!) to do it all in Python:

```
def find_two_smallest(L: list[float]) -> tuple[int, int]:
    """Return a tuple of the indices of the two smallest values in list L.

    >>> items = [809, 834, 477, 478, 307, 122, 96, 102, 324, 476]
    >>> find_two_smallest(items)
    (6, 7)
    >>> items == [809, 834, 477, 478, 307, 122, 96, 102, 324, 476]
    True
    """

    # Find the index of the minimum and remove that item
    smallest = min(L)
    min1 = L.index(smallest)
    L.remove(smallest)

    # Find the index of the new minimum
    next_smallest = min(L)
    min2 = L.index(next_smallest)

    # Put smallest back into L
    L.insert(min1, smallest)

    # Fix min2 in case it was affected by the removal and reinsertion:
    if min1 <= min2:
        min2 += 1

    return (min1, min2)
```

That seems like a lot of thought and care, and it is. However, even if you go right to code, you'll have to think through all those steps. By writing them down first, you have a better chance of getting it right with minimal effort.

Sort, Identify Minimums, Get Indices

Here is the second algorithm rewritten with one instruction per line:

```
def find_two_smallest(L: list[float]) -> tuple[int, int]:
    """Return a tuple of the indices of the two smallest values in list L.

    >>> items = [809, 834, 477, 478, 307, 122, 96, 102, 324, 476]
    >>> find_two_smallest(items)
    (6, 7)
    >>> items == [809, 834, 477, 478, 307, 122, 96, 102, 324, 476]
    True
    """

    # Sort a copy of L
    # Get the two smallest numbers
    # Find their indices in the original list L
    # Return the two indices
```

That looks straightforward; you can use the built-in function `sorted`, which returns a copy of the list with the items in order from smallest to largest. You could have used the `list.sort` method to sort `L`, but that breaks a fundamental rule: never mutate the contents of parameters unless the docstring explicitly states to do so.

```
def find_two_smallest(L: list[float]) -> tuple[int, int]:
    """ (see above) """

    # Get a sorted copy of the list so that the two smallest items are at the
    # front
    temp_list = sorted(L)
    smallest = temp_list[0]
    next_smallest = temp_list[1]

    # Find their indices in the original list L
    # Return the two indices
```

Now, you can find the indices and return them the same way you did in find-remove-find:

```
def find_two_smallest(L: list[float]) -> tuple[int, int]:
    """Return a tuple of the indices of the two smallest values in list L.

    >>> items = [809, 834, 477, 478, 307, 122, 96, 102, 324, 476]
    >>> find_two_smallest(items)
    (6, 7)
    >>> items == [809, 834, 477, 478, 307, 122, 96, 102, 324, 476]
    True
    """

    # Get a sorted copy of the list so that the two smallest items are at the
    # front
    temp_list = sorted(L)
    smallest = temp_list[0]
    next_smallest = temp_list[1]
```

```
    # Find the indices in the original list L
    min1 = L.index(smallest)
    min2 = L.index(next_smallest)

    return (min1, min2)
```

Walk Through the List

Your last algorithm begins in the same way as the first two:

```
from typing import List, Tuple

def find_two_smallest(L: List[float]) -> Tuple[int, int]:
    """Return a tuple of the indices of the two smallest values in list L.

    >>> items = [809, 834, 477, 478, 307, 122, 96, 102, 324, 476]
    >>> find_two_smallest(items)
    (6, 7)
    >>> items == [809, 834, 477, 478, 307, 122, 96, 102, 324, 476]
    True
    """

    # Examine each value in the list in order
    # Keep track of the indices of the two smallest values found so far
    # Update the indices when a new smaller value is found
    # Return the two indices
```

Let's move the second line before the first one because it describes the whole process; it isn't a single step. Also, when you see phrases like *each value*, think of iteration; the third line is part of that iteration, so let's indent it:

```
def find_two_smallest(L):
    """ (see above) """

    # Keep track of the indices of the two smallest values found so far
    # Examine each value in the list in order
    #     Update the indices when a new smaller value is found
    # Return the two indices
```

Every loop has three parts: an initialization section to set up the variables you'll need, a loop condition, and a loop body. Here, the initialization will set up `min1` and `min2`, which will be the indices of the smallest two items encountered so far. A natural choice is to set them to the first two items of the list:

```
def find_two_smallest(L):
    """ (see above) """

    # Set min1 and min2 to the indices of the smallest and next-smallest
    # values at the beginning of L
    # Examine each value in the list in order
    #     Update the indices when a new smaller value is found
    # Return the two indices
```

You can turn that first line into a couple of lines of code; let's leave the English version as a comment:

```
def find_two_smallest(L):
    """ (see above) """

    # Set min1 and min2 to the indices of the smallest and next-smallest
    # Values at the beginning of L
    if L[0] < L[1]:
        min1, min2 = 0, 1
    else:
        min1, min2 = 1, 0

    # Examine each value in the list in order
    #     Update the indices when a new smaller value is found
    # Return the two indices
```

You now have a couple of choices. You can iterate with a for loop over the values, a for loop over the indices, or a while loop over the indices. Since you're trying to find indices and you want to look at all of the items in the list, let's use a for loop over the indices—and you'll start at index 2 because you've examined the first two values already. At the same time, let's refine the statement in the body of the loop to mention min1 and min2.

```
def find_two_smallest(L):
    """ (see above) """

    # Set min1 and min2 to the indices of the smallest and next-smallest
    # values at the beginning of L
    if L[0] < L[1]:
        min1, min2 = 0, 1
    else:
        min1, min2 = 1, 0

    # Examine each value in the list in order
    for i in range(2, len(values)):
    #     Update min1 and/or min2 when a new smaller value is found
    # Return the two indices
```

Now for the body of the loop. Let's pick apart "update min1 and/or min2 when a new smaller value is found." Here are the possibilities:

- If L[i] is smaller than both min1 and min2, then you have a new smallest item; so min1 currently holds the second smallest, and min2 currently holds the third smallest. You need to update both of them.
- If L[i] is larger than min1 and smaller than min2, you have a new second smallest.
- If L[i] is larger than both, skip it.

```
def find_two_smallest(L):
    """ (see above) """

    # Set min1 and min2 to the indices of the smallest and next-smallest
    # values at the beginning of L
    if L[0] < L[1]:
        min1, min2 = 0, 1
    else:
        min1, min2 = 1, 0

    # Examine each value in the list in order
    for i in range(2, len(L)):
    #     L[i] is smaller than both min1 and min2, in between, or
    #     larger than both:
    #     If L[i] is smaller than min1 and min2, update them both
    #     If L[i] is in between, update min2
    #     If L[i] is larger than both min1 and min2, skip it
    return (min1, min2)
```

All of those are easily translated to Python; in fact, you don't even need code for the "larger than both" case:

```
from typing import List, Tuple

def find_two_smallest(L: List[float]) -> Tuple[int, int]:
    """Return a tuple of the indices of the two smallest values in list L.

    >>> items = [809, 834, 477, 478, 307, 122, 96, 102, 324, 476]
    >>> find_two_smallest(items)
    (6, 7)
    >>> items == [809, 834, 477, 478, 307, 122, 96, 102, 324, 476]
    True
    """

    # Set min1 and min2 to the indices of the smallest and next-smallest
    # values at the beginning of L
    if L[0] < L[1]:
        min1, min2 = 0, 1
    else:
        min1, min2 = 1, 0

    # Examine each value in the list in order
    for i in range(2, len(L)):
        # L[i] is smaller than both min1 and min2, in between, or
        # larger than both

        # New smallest?
        if L[i] < L[min1]:
            min2 = min1
            min1 = i
        # New second smallest?
        elif L[i] < L[min2]:
            min2 = i

    return (min1, min2)
```

Timing the Functions

Benchmarking a program means measuring how long it takes to run. The timing is fundamental to the theoretical study of algorithms. It is also important from a pragmatic perspective: fast programs are more useful than slow ones.

This section introduces one method for measuring the time it takes for code to run. You'll see how to run the three functions you developed to find the two lowest values in a list of 1,400 monthly air pressure readings in Darwin, Australia, from 1882 to 1998.[1]

The module time contains functions related to time. One of these functions is perf_counter, which returns a time in seconds. You can call it before and after the code you want to time and take the difference to find out how many seconds elapsed. Multiply by 1000 to convert from seconds to milliseconds:

The performance of a program can be characterized by how much time it takes to run

```
import time

t1 = time.perf_counter()

# Code to time goes here

t2 = time.perf_counter()
print(f'The code took {(t2 - t1) * 1000:.2f}ms.')
```

Let's time all three of your find_two_smallest functions. Rather than copying and pasting the timing code three times, let's write a function that takes another function as a parameter, as well as the list to search in. Use the type annotation typing.Callable from module typing for this parameter:

```
Callable[list[«parameter types»], «return type»]
```

Since you're not interested in what this function parameter returns, use typing.Any as the return type (it matches any specific type). This timing function will return how many milliseconds it takes to execute a call on the function. After the timing function is the main program that reads the file of sea level pressures and then calls the timing function with each of the find_two_smallest functions:

```
import time
import find_remove_find5
import sort_then_find3
import walk_through7

from typing import Callable, Any

def time_find_two_smallest(find_func: Callable[list[list[float]], Any],
```

1. http://www.stat.duke.edu/~mw/ts_data_sets.html

```
                          lst: list[float]) -> float:
    """Return how many seconds find_func(lst) took to execute.
    """

    t1 = time.perf_counter()
    find_func(lst)
    t2 = time.perf_counter()
    return (t2 - t1) * 1000.0

if __name__ == '__main__':
    # Gather the sea level pressures
    sea_levels = []
    with open('sea_levels.txt', 'r') as sea_levels_file:
        for line in sea_levels_file:
            sea_levels.append(float(line))

    # Time each of the approaches
    find_remove_find_time = time_find_two_smallest(
        find_remove_find5.find_two_smallest, sea_levels)

    sort_get_minimums_time = time_find_two_smallest(
        sort_then_find3.find_two_smallest, sea_levels)

    walk_through_time = time_find_two_smallest(
        walk_through7.find_two_smallest, sea_levels)

    print(f'"Find, remove, find" took {find_remove_find_time:.2f}ms.')
    print(f'"Sort, get minimums" took {sort_get_minimums_time:.2f}ms.')
    print(f'"Walk through the list" took {walk_through_time:.2f}ms.')
```

The execution times were as follows (note that they may vary depending on the computer; you'll probably see different times):

Algorithm	Running Time (ms)
Find, remove, find	0.05ms
Sort, identify, index	0.12ms
Walk through the list	0.07ms

Notice how small these times are. No human being can notice the difference between values that are less than a millisecond. If this code never has to process lists with more than 1,400 values, you would be justified in choosing an implementation based on simplicity or clarity rather than on speed.

But what if you wanted to process millions of values? Find-remove-find outperforms the other two algorithms on 1,400 values, but how much does that tell you about how each will perform on data sets that are a thousand times larger? That will be covered in Chapter 13, Searching and Sorting, on page 249.

Benchmarking with timeit

To accurately measure the performance of a Python function or code fragment, use the built-in timeit module instead of writing custom code to measure it. It minimizes interference from background processes and averages the result over many runs.

Here's how to use it in a script:

```
import timeit
from find_remove_find5 import find_two_smallest
sea_levels = ...

# Run find_func(lst) 1000 times
execution_time = timeit.timeit("find_two_smallest(sea_levels)", number=1000)

print(f"Average time: {execution_time / 1000:.2f} seconds")
```

The timeit call executes the code multiple times and reports the total time it takes to complete the code execution. Divide by the number of runs to get an average.

At a Minimum, You Saw This

In this chapter, you learned the following:

- The most effective way to design algorithms is to use top-down design, in which goals are broken down into subgoals until the steps are small enough to be translated directly into a programming language.
- Almost all problems have more than one correct solution. Choosing between them often involves a trade-off between simplicity and performance.
- The performance of a program can be characterized by how much time it uses. The elapsed time can be determined experimentally by benchmarking its execution. One way to profile time is to use the function perf_counter from the time module.

Exercises

Here are some exercises for you to try on your own.

1. A DNA sequence is a string made up of the letters *A*, *T*, *G*, and *C*. To find the complement of a DNA sequence, *A*s are replaced by *T*s, *T*s by *A*s, *G*s by *C*s, and *C*s by *G*s. For example, the complement of AATTGCCGT is TTAACGGCA.

    a. Write an outline in English of the algorithm you would use to find the complement.

b. Review your algorithm. Will any characters be changed to their complement and then changed back to their original value? If so, rewrite your outline. Hint: Convert one character at a time, rather than all of the *As*, *Ts*, *Gs*, or *Cs* at once.

c. Using the algorithm that you have developed, write a function named `complement` that takes a DNA sequence (a `str`) and returns its complement.

2. In this exercise, you'll develop a function that finds the minimum or maximum value in a list, depending on the caller's request.

   a. Write a loop (including initialization) to find both the minimum value in a list and that value's index in one pass through the list.

   b. Write a function named `min_index` that takes one parameter (a `list`) and returns a tuple containing the minimum value in the list and that value's index in the list.

   c. You might also want to find the maximum value and its index. Write a function named `min_or_max_index` that has two parameters: a `list` and a `bool`. If the Boolean parameter refers to `True`, the function returns a tuple containing the minimum and its index; if it refers to `False`, it returns a tuple containing the maximum and its index.

3. In The Readline Technique, on page 186, you learned how to read some files from the Time Series Data Library. In particular, you learned about the Hopedale data set, which describes the number of colored fox fur pelts produced from 1834 to 1842. This file contains one value per year per line.

   a. Write an outline in English of the algorithm you would use to read the values from this data set to compute the average number of pelts produced per year.

   b. Translate your algorithm into Python by writing a function named `hopedale_average` that takes a filename as a parameter and returns the average number of pelts produced per year.

4. Write a set of doctests for the find-two-smallest functions. Think about what kinds of data are interesting, long lists or short lists, and what order the items are in. Here is one list to test with: `[1, 2]`. What other interesting ones are there?

5. What happens if the functions to find the two smallest values in a list are passed a list of length one? What should happen, and why? How about length zero? Modify one of the docstrings to describe what happens.

6. One or more of the three functions to find the two smallest values don't work if there are duplicate values and particularly if the two smallest

values are the same. Write doctests to demonstrate the problem, run them, and fix the algorithms that exhibit this bug.

7. This one is a fun challenge.

   Edsger Dijkstra is known for his work on programming languages. He came up with a neat problem that he called the Dutch National Flag problem: given a list of strings, each of which is either 'red', 'green', or 'blue' (each is repeated several times in the list), rearrange the list so that the strings are in the order of the Dutch national flag—all the 'red' strings first, then all the 'green' strings, then all the 'blue' strings.

   Write a function called dutch_flag that takes a list and solves this problem.

CHAPTER 13

Searching and Sorting

A huge part of computer science involves studying how to organize, store, and retrieve data. There are many ways to manage and process data, and it is essential to develop an understanding of how to evaluate the effectiveness of each approach. This chapter introduces you to some tools and concepts that you can use to tell whether a particular approach is faster or slower than another.

> Almost all problems have more than one correct solution

As you know, there are many solutions to each programming problem. If a problem involves a large amount of data, a slow algorithm will mean the problem can't be solved in a reasonable amount of time, even with a potent computer. This chapter includes several examples of both slower and faster algorithms. Try running them yourself; experiencing just how slow (or fast) something is has a much more profound effect on your understanding than the data included in this chapter.

Searching and sorting data are fundamental parts of programming. In this chapter, you'll see several algorithms for searching and sorting lists, and then you'll use them to explore what it means for one algorithm to be faster than another. As a bonus, this approach will give you another set of examples of how there are many solutions to any problem, and that the approach you take to solving a problem will dictate which solution you come up with.

Searching a List

As you have already seen in Table 6, List Methods, on page 146, Python lists have a method called `index` that searches for a particular item:

```
index(value, start=0, stop=9223372036854775807, /) method of builtins.list
        instance
    Return first index of value.

    Raises ValueError if the value is not present.
```

List method index starts at the front of the list and examines each item in turn. For reasons that will soon become clear, this technique is called *linear search*. Linear search is used to find an item in an *unsorted* list. If there are duplicate values, the algorithm will find the leftmost one:

Linear search is the simplest way to find a value in a list

```
>>> ['d', 'a', 'b', 'a'].index('a')
1
```

You'll write several versions of linear search to demonstrate how to compare different algorithms that all solve the same problem.

After you perform this analysis, you will see that you can search a *sorted* list much faster than an unsorted list.

An Overview of Linear Search

Linear search starts at index 0 and examines each item sequentially. At each index, ask this question: is the value you are looking for at the current index? You'll see three variations of this. All of them use a loop of some kind, and they are all implementations of this function:

```
from typing import Any

def linear_search(lst: list, value: Any) -> int:
    """Return the index of the first occurrence of value in lst, or return
    -1 if value is not in lst.

    >>> linear_search([2, 5, 1, -3], 5)
    1
    >>> linear_search([2, 4, 2], 2)
    0
    >>> linear_search([2, 5, 1, -3], 4)
    -1
    >>> linear_search([], 5)
    -1
    """

    # examine the items at each index i in lst, starting at index 0:
    #    is lst[i] the value we are looking for?  if so, stop searching.
```

The algorithm in the function body describes what every variation will do to look for the value.

It is helpful to have a visual representation of how linear search works. (These pictures will be used throughout this chapter for both searching and sorting.)

Because these versions examine index 0 first, then index 1, then index 2, and so on, this means that partway through your searching process you encounter this situation (note that len(lst) is the index of the first item *not* on the list):

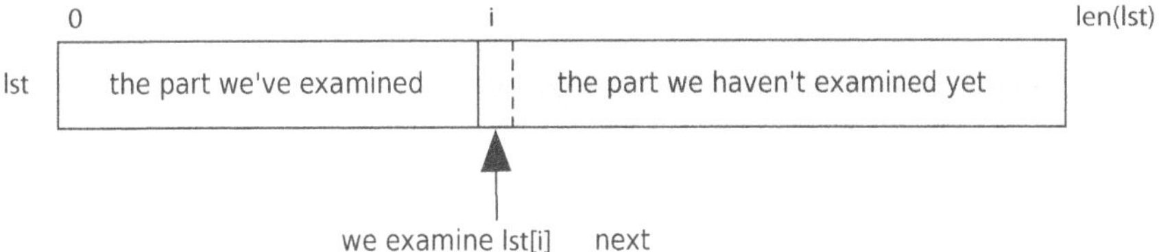

There is a part of the list that has been examined and another part that remains to be examined. Let's use variable i to mark the current index.

Here's a concrete example of searching for a value in a list that starts like this: [2, -3, 5, 9, 8, -6, 4, 15, ...]. You don't know how long the list is, but let's say that after six iterations, you have examined items at indices 0, 1, 2, 3, 4, and 5. Index 6 is the index of the next item to examine:

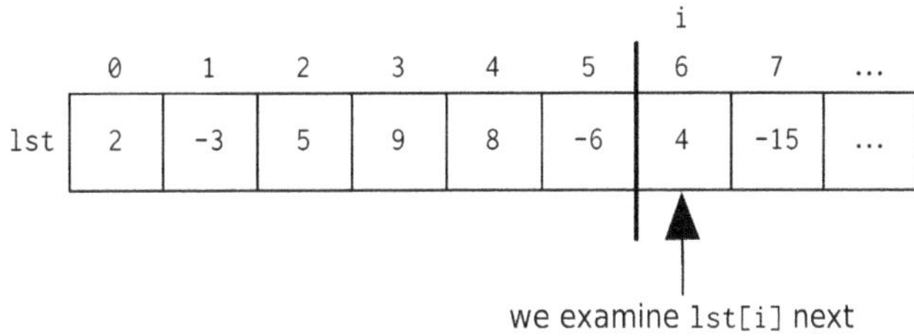

That vertical line divides the list into two: the part you have examined and the part you haven't. Because you stop when you find the value, you know that the value isn't in the first part:

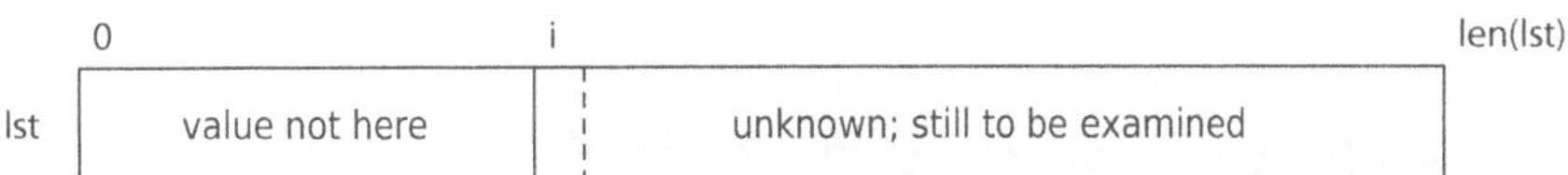

An invariant describes the data being used in a loop

This picture is sometimes referred to as an *invariant* of linear search. An invariant is something that remains unchanged throughout a process. But variable i is changing—how can that picture be an invariant? Here is a text version of the picture:

```
lst[0:i] doesn't contain value, and 0 <= i <= len(lst)
```

This word version states that you know the value wasn't found before index i and that i is somewhere between 0 and the length of the list. If your code matches that word version, that word version is an invariant of the code, and so is the picture version.

You can use invariants to come up with the initial values of your variables. For example, with linear search, at the very beginning the entire list is unknown—you haven't examined anything:

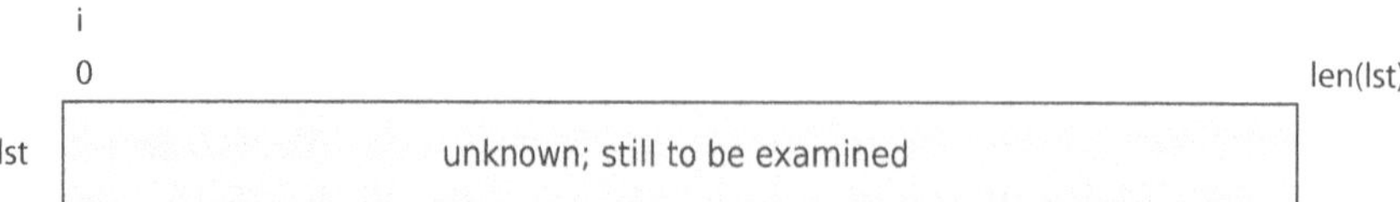

Variable i refers to 0 at the beginning, because then the section with the label value not here is empty; further, lst[0:0] is an empty list, which is precisely what you want according to the word version of the invariant. So, the initial value of i should be 0 in all of your versions of linear search.

The while Loop Version of Linear Search

Let's develop your first version of linear search. You need to refine your comments to bring them closer to Python norms:

```
Examine every index i in lst, starting at index 0:
    Is lst[i] the value you are looking for?  if so, stop searching
```

Here's a refinement:

```
i = 0  # The index of the next item in lst to examine

While the unknown section isn't empty, and lst[i] isn't
the value you are looking for:
    add 1 to i
```

That's easier to translate. The unknown section is empty when i == len(lst), so it isn't empty as long as i != len(lst). Here is the code:

```
from typing import Any

def linear_search(lst: list, value: Any) -> int:
    """Return the index of the first occurrence of value in lst, or return
    -1 if value is not in lst.

    >>> linear_search([2, 5, 1, -3], 5)
    1
    >>> linear_search([2, 4, 2], 2)
    0
    >>> linear_search([2, 5, 1, -3], 4)
    -1
    >>> linear_search([], 5)
    -1
    """

    i = 0  # The index of the next item in lst to examine.
```

```
    # Keep going until we reach the end of lst or until we find value.
    while i != len(lst) and lst[i] != value:
        i = i + 1

    # If we fell off the end of the list, we didn't find value.
    if i == len(lst):
        return -1
    else:
        return i
```

This version uses variable i as the current index and marches through the values in lst, stopping in one of two situations: when you have run out of values to examine, or when you find the value you are looking for.

The first check in the loop condition, i != len(lst), makes sure that you still have values to look at; if you were to omit that check, then if value isn't in lst, you would end up trying to access lst[len(lst)], which would result in an IndexError.

The second check, lst[i] != value, causes the loop to exit when value is found. The loop body increments i; enter the loop when you haven't reached the end of lst, and when lst[i] isn't the value you are looking for.

After the loop terminates, if i == len(lst), then value wasn't in lst, so you return -1. Otherwise, the loop terminated because value was found at index i.

The for Loop Version of Linear Search

The first version evaluates two Boolean subexpressions each time the loop is executed. But the first check, i != len(lst), is almost unnecessary; it evaluates to True nearly every time through the loop, so the only effect it has is to make sure you don't attempt to index past the end of the list. You can instead exit the function as soon as you find the value:

```
i = 0  # The index of the next item in lst to examine

For each index i in lst:
    If lst[i] is the value you are looking for:
        return i

If you get here, value was not in lst, so you return -1
```

In this version, let's use Python's for loop to examine each index.

```
from typing import Any

def linear_search(lst: list, value: Any) -> int:
    # Same docstring as before
    for i in range(len(lst)):
        if lst[i] == value:
            return i

    return -1
```

With this version, you no longer need the first check because the for loop controls the number of iterations. This for loop version is significantly faster than your first version; you'll see how much faster it is shortly.

Sentinel Search

The last linear search you will study is called the *sentinel search*. (A sentinel is a guard whose job it is to stand watch.) One problem with the while loop linear search is that you check i != len(lst) every time through the loop, even though it can never evaluate to False except when value is not in lst. So, let's play a trick: add value to the end of lst before the search. That way, you are guaranteed to find it! You also need to remove it before the function exits so that the list looks unchanged to whoever called this function:

```
Set up the sentinel: append value to the end of lst

i = 0  # The index of the next item in lst to examine

While lst[i] is not the value you are looking for:
    Add 1 to i

Remove the sentinel

return i
```

Let's translate that to Python:

```
from typing import Any

def linear_search(lst: list, value: Any) -> int:
    # Same docstring as before

    # Add the sentinel.
    lst.append(value)

    i = 0

    # Keep going until we find value.
    while lst[i] != value:
        i += 1

    # Remove the sentinel.
    lst.pop()

    # If we reached the end of the list we didn't find value.
    if i == len(lst):
        return -1
    return i
```

All three of your linear search functions are correct. Which one you prefer is essentially a matter of taste: some programmers dislike returning in the middle of a loop—they won't like the second version. Others dislike modifying parameters in any way—they won't like the third version. Still, others may dislike the extra check that occurs in the first version.

Timing the Searches

Here is a program that you can use to time the three searches on a list with about ten million values:

```
import time
import linear_search_1
import linear_search_2
import linear_search_3

from typing import Callable, Any

def time_it(search: Callable[list[list, Any]], L: list, v: Any) -> float:
    """Time how long it takes to run function search to find
    value v in list L.
    """

    t1 = time.perf_counter()
    search(L, v)
    t2 = time.perf_counter()
    return (t2 - t1) * 1000.0

def print_times(v: Any, L: list) -> None:
    """Print the number of milliseconds it takes for linear_search(v, L)
    to run for list.index, the while loop linear search, the for loop
    linear search, and sentinel search.
    """

    # Get list.index's running time.
    t1 = time.perf_counter()
    L.index(v)
    t2 = time.perf_counter()
    index_time = (t2 - t1) * 1000.0

    # Get the other three running times.
    while_time = time_it(linear_search_1.linear_search, L, v)
    for_time = time_it(linear_search_2.linear_search, L, v)
    sentinel_time = time_it(linear_search_3.linear_search, L, v)

    print("{0}\t{1:.2f}\t{2:.2f}\t{3:.2f}\t{4:.2f}".format(
            v, while_time, for_time, sentinel_time, index_time))

L = list(range(10000001))  # A list with just over ten million values

print_times(10, L)  # How fast is it to search near the beginning?
print_times(5000000, L)  # How fast is it to search near the middle?
print_times(10000000, L)  # How fast is it to search near the end?
```

This program uses the function perf_counter in the built-in module time. The function time_it will call whichever search function it's given on v and L and returns the time it took for that search. The function print_times calls time_it with the various linear search functions you have been exploring and prints the corresponding search times.

Linear Search Running Time

The running times of the three linear searches are compared with those of Python's list.index in Table 9, Running Times for Linear Search (in milliseconds), on page 256.

This comparison used a list of 10,000,001 items and three test cases: an item near the front, an item roughly in the middle, and the last item. Except for the first case, where the speeds differ by very little, your while loop linear search takes about six times as long as the one built into Python. The for loop search and sentinel search take about three and three and a half times longer, respectively.

Case	while	for	sentinel	list.index
First	0.01	0.00	0.00	0.01
Middle	262.31	131.36	153.95	44.19
Last	525.36	262.34	307.87	88.17

Table 9—Running Times for Linear Search (in milliseconds)

What is more interesting is the way the *running times* of these functions increase with the number of items they have to examine. Roughly speaking, when they have to look through twice as much data, every one of them takes twice as long. This observation is reasonable because indexing a list, adding 1 to an integer, and evaluating the loop control expression require the computer to do a fixed amount of work. Doubling the number of times the loop has to be executed, therefore, doubles the total number of operations, which in turn should double the total running time. That is why this kind of search is called *linear*: the time required to perform it grows linearly with the amount of data being processed.

Binary Search

Consider a list of 1 million *sorted* values. Linear search starts at the beginning of the list and asks, "Is this value what I'm looking for?" If it isn't, the same is asked about the second value, and then the third. Up to 1 million questions are asked. This algorithm doesn't take advantage of the list being sorted.

Binary search is much faster than linear search, but requires a sorted list

Here's a new algorithm, called *binary search*, that relies on the list being sorted. Look at the middle value and ask, "Is this value bigger than or smaller than the one I'm looking for?" With that one question, you can eliminate 500,000 values! That leaves a list of 500,000 values to search. Let's do it again: look at the middle value, ask the same question, and eliminate another 250,000 values. *You have eliminated 3/4 of the list with only two questions!* Asking only 20 questions, you can locate a particular value in a list of 1 million sorted values.

Logarithms

The *logarithm* of a number is the number of times that number can be divided by another number, called the *base*, until the result is 1. For binary search, let's use base 2, because you divide the list in half each iteration.

The logarithm base 2 of 1, which is written as $\log_2 1$, is 0: you don't need to divide 1 at all to reach 1.

$\log_2 2$ is 1, because $2/2$ is 1.

$\log_2 4$ is 2: $4/2$ is 2, and $2/2$ is 1, so we divided by 2 twice to reach 1.

$\log_2 8$ is 3: $8/2$ is 4, $4/2$ is 2, and $2/2$ is 1. Every time you double the number, the logarithm base 2 increases by 1.

Here's a table of base 2 logarithms:

N (the # of items)	N as a power of 2	$\log_2 N$
1	2^0	0
2	2^1	1
4	2^2	2
8	2^3	3
16	2^4	4
32	2^5	5
64	2^6	6
128	2^7	7
256	2^8	8
512	2^9	9
1024	2^{10}	10

Table 10—Logarithmic Growth

To determine how fast it is, let's consider the size of a list that can be searched with a certain number of questions. With only one question, you can determine whether a list of length 1 contains a value. With two questions, you can search a list of length 2. With three questions, you can search a list of length 4. Four questions, length 8. Five questions, length 16. Every time you ask another question, you can search a list twice as large.

Using logarithmic notation, `N` sorted values can be searched in `ceil(log₂N)` steps, where `ceil` is the ceiling function that rounds a value up to the nearest integer.

As shown in Table 11, Logarithmic Growth, on page 258, this increase is significantly slower than the time required for linear search.

Searching N Items	Worst Case—Linear Search	Worst Case—Binary Search
100	100	7
1000	1000	10
10,000	10,000	14
100,000	100,000	17
1,000,000	1,000,000	20
10,000,000	10,000,000	24

Table 11—Logarithmic Growth

The key to binary search is to keep track of three parts of the list: the left part, which contains values that are smaller than the value you are searching for; the right part, which contains values that are equal to or larger than the value you are searching for; and the middle part, which contains values that you haven't yet examined—the unknown section. If there are duplicate values, you will return the index of the leftmost one, which is why the "equal to" section belongs on the right.

Let's use two variables to keep track of the boundaries: i will mark the index of the first unknown value, and j will mark the index of the last unknown value:

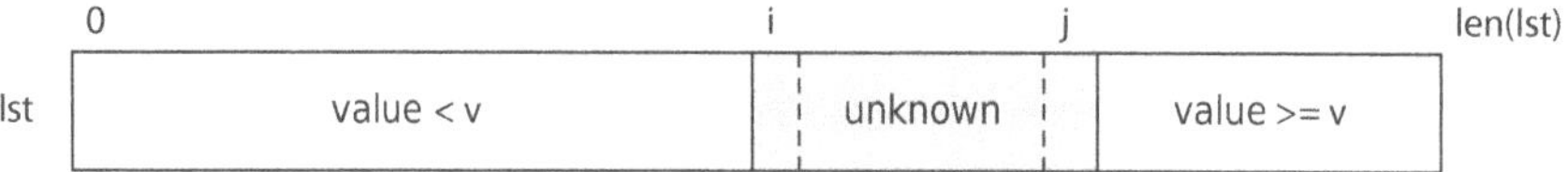

At the beginning of the algorithm, the unknown section comprises the entire list, so set i to 0 and j to the length of the list minus one:

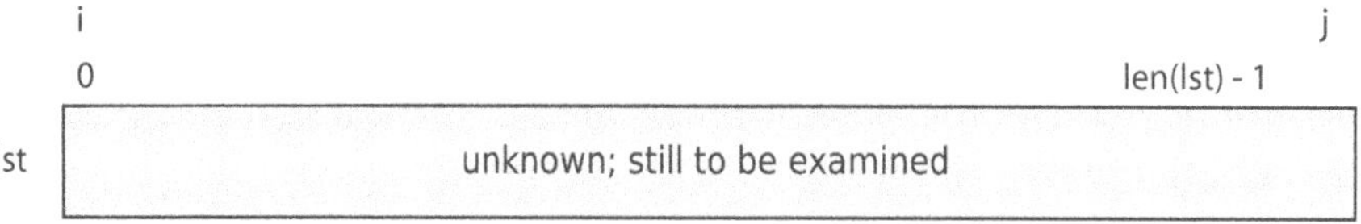

You are done when that unknown section is empty—when you've examined every item in the list, which happens when i == j + 1—when the values *cross*. (When i == j, there is still one item left in the unknown section.) Here is a picture of what the values are when the unknown section is empty:

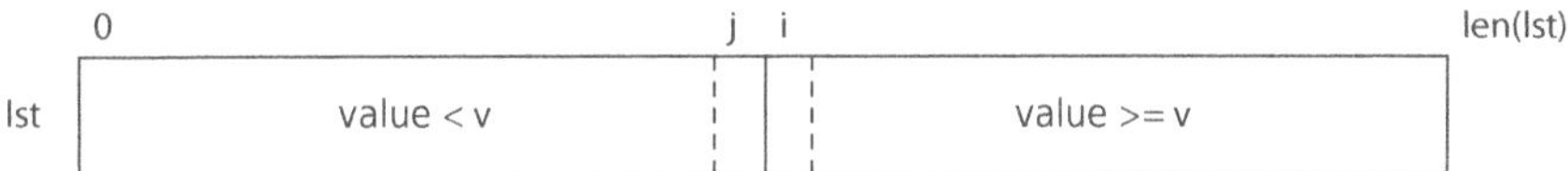

To make progress, set either i or j to near the middle of the range between them. Let's call this index m, which is at (i + j) // 2. (Notice the use of integer division: you are calculating an index, so you need an integer.)

Think for a moment about the value at m. If it is less than v, you need to move i up, while if it is greater than v, you should move j down. But where exactly do you move them?

When you move i up, you don't want to set it to the midpoint exactly, because L[m] isn't included in the range; instead, set it to one past the middle—in other words, to m + 1.

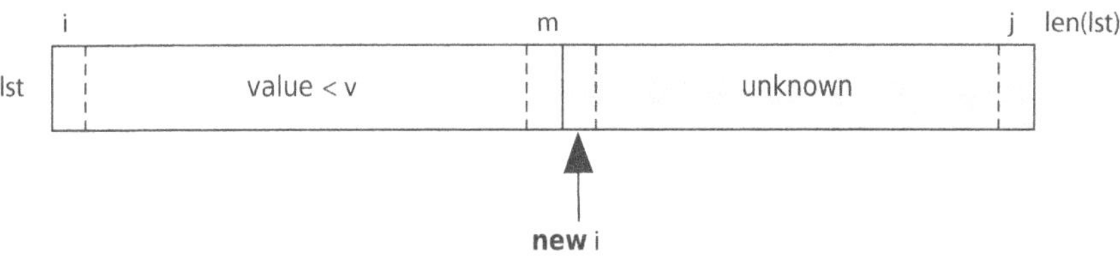

Similarly, when you move j down, move it to m - 1:

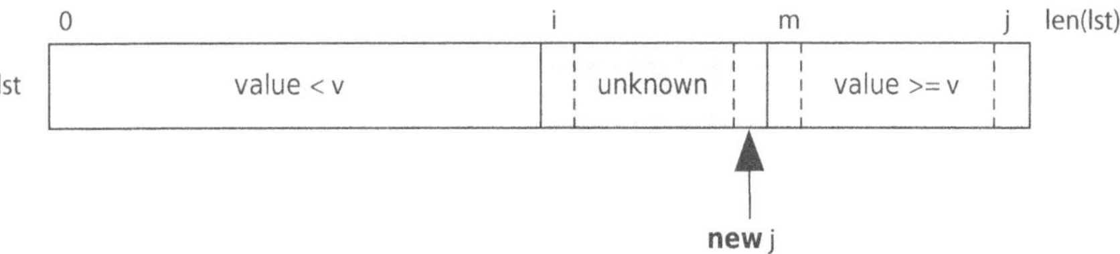

The completed function is as follows:

```
from typing import Any

def binary_search(L: list, v: Any) -> int:
    """Return the index of the first occurrence of value in L, or return
    -1 if value is not in L.

    >>> binary_search([1, 3, 4, 4, 5, 7, 9, 10], 1)
    0
    >>> binary_search([1, 3, 4, 4, 5, 7, 9, 10], 4)
    2
    >>> binary_search([1, 3, 4, 4, 5, 7, 9, 10], 5)
    4
```

```
    >>> binary_search([1, 3, 4, 4, 5, 7, 9, 10], 10)
    7
    >>> binary_search([1, 3, 4, 4, 5, 7, 9, 10], -3)
    -1
    >>> binary_search([1, 3, 4, 4, 5, 7, 9, 10], 11)
    -1
    >>> binary_search([1, 3, 4, 4, 5, 7, 9, 10], 2)
    -1
    >>> binary_search([], -3)
    -1
    >>> binary_search([1], 1)
    0
    """

    # Mark the left and right indices of the unknown section.
    i = 0
    j = len(L) - 1

    while i != j + 1:
        m = (i + j) // 2 # Find the middle
        if L[m] < v:
            i = m + 1
        else:
            j = m - 1

    if 0 <= i < len(L) and L[i] == v:
        return i
    return -1

if __name__ == '__main__':
    import doctest
    doctest.testmod()
```

There are many tests because the algorithm is quite complicated, and it must be tested pretty thoroughly. These tests cover these cases:

- The value is the first item.
- The value occurs twice. You want the index of the first one.
- The value is in the middle of the list.
- The value is the last item.
- The value is smaller than everything in the list.
- The value is larger than everything in the list.
- The value isn't in the list, but it is larger than some and smaller than others.
- The list has no items.
- The list has one item.

In Chapter 15, Testing and Debugging, on page 309, you'll learn a different testing framework that allows you to write tests in a separate Python file (thus making docstrings shorter and easier to read; only a couple of examples are necessary), and you'll learn strategies for coming up with your own test cases.

Binary Search Running Time

Binary search is *much* more complicated to write and understand than linear search. Is it fast enough to make the extra effort worthwhile? To find out, you can compare it to list.index. As before, search for the first, middle, and last items in a list with about ten million elements, as shown in Table 12, Running Times for Binary Search, on page 261.

Case	list.index	binary_search	Ratio
First	0.0080	0.0132	0.60
Middle	45.0905	0.0086	5239.77
Last	91.0210	0.0087	10503.28

Table 12—Running Times for Binary Search

The results are impressive. Binary search is *several thousand times faster* than its linear counterpart when searching through ten million items. Most importantly, if you double the number of items, binary search requires only one more iteration, whereas the time for list.index nearly doubles.

Note also that although the time taken for linear search grows in step with the index of the item found, there is no such pattern for binary search. Regardless of the item's location, it takes the same number of steps.

Built-In Binary Search

The Python standard library's bisect module includes binary search functions that are slightly faster than your binary search. The function bisect_left returns the index where an item should be inserted in a list to keep it in sorted order, assuming it is sorted to begin with. The function insort_left does the insertion.

The word *left* in the name signals that these functions find the leftmost (lowest index) position where they can perform their jobs; the complementary functions bisect_right and insort_right find the rightmost position.

There is one minor drawback to binary search: the algorithm assumes that the list is sorted, but sorting is time- and memory-intensive. You'll see that next.

Sorting

Now, let's look at a slightly more complex problem. The following table[1] shows the number of acres burned in forest fires in Canada from 1918 to 1987. What were the worst years?

1. http://robjhyndman.com/tsdldata/annual/canfire.dat

563	7590	1708	2142	3323	6197	1985	1316	1824	472
1346	6029	2670	2094	2464	1009	1475	856	3027	4271
3126	1115	2691	4253	1838	828	2403	742	1017	613
3185	2599	2227	896	975	1358	264	1375	2016	452
3292	538	1471	9313	864	470	2993	521	1144	2212
2212	2331	2616	2445	1927	808	1963	898	2764	2073
500	1740	8592	10856	2818	2284	1419	1328	1329	1479

Table 13—Acres Lost to Forest Fires in Canada (in thousands), 1918–1987

One way to find out how much forest was destroyed in the N worst years is to sort the list and then take the last N values, as shown in the following code:

```
def find_largest(n: int, L: list) -> list:
    """Return the n largest values in L in order from smallest to largest.

    >>> L = [3, 4, 7, -1, 2, 5]
    >>> find_largest(3, L)
    [4, 5, 7]
    """

    copy = sorted(L)
    return copy[-n:]
```

This algorithm is short, clean, and easy to understand, but it relies on a bit of black magic. How *do* the function sorted and the method list.sort work? And how efficient are they?

It turns out that many sorting algorithms have been developed over the years, each with its strengths and weaknesses. They can be divided into two categories: those that are simple but inefficient, and those that are efficient but more difficult to understand and implement. Let's examine two of the former kind. The rest rely on more advanced techniques; you'll see one of these, rewritten to use only the material seen so far.

Looking at how an algorithm's running time grows with the input's size is the standard way to analyze and compare efficiency

Both of the simple sorting algorithms keep track of two sections in the list being sorted. The section at the front contains values that are now in sorted order; the section at the back contains values that have yet to be sorted. Here is the main part of the invariant that you can use for your two simple sorts:

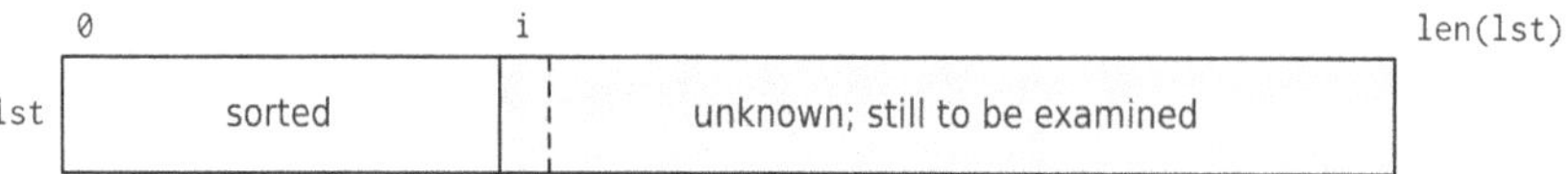

One of the two algorithms has an additional property in its invariant: the items in the sorted section must be smaller than all the items in the unknown section.

Both of these sorting algorithms will work their way through the list, making the sorted section one item longer on each iteration. You'll see that there are two ways to do this. Here is an outline for your code:

```
i = 0  # The index of the first unknown item in lst; lst[:i] is sorted
while i != len(L):
    # Do something to incorporate L[i] into the sorted section

    i += 1
```

Most Python programmers would probably write the loop header as for i in range(len(L)) rather than incrementing i explicitly in the loop body. Let's do the latter here to explicitly initialize i (to set up the loop invariant) and to show the increment separately from the work this particular algorithm is doing. The "do something..." part is where the two simple sorting algorithms will differ.

Selection Sort

Selection sort works by searching the unknown section for the smallest item and moving it to the index i. Here is your algorithm:

```
i = 0  # The index of the first unknown item in lst

# lst[:i] is sorted and those items are smaller than those in list[i:]
while i != len(L):
    # Find the index of the smallest item in lst[i:]
    # Swap that smallest item with the item at index i
    i += i
```

As you can probably guess from this description, selection sort works by repeatedly selecting the smallest item in the unsorted section and placing it just after the sorted section. This method works because the items are selected in order. In the first iteration, i is 0, and lst[0:] refers to the entire list. That means that in the first iteration, select the smallest item and move it to the front. In the second iteration, select the second-smallest item and move it to the second spot, and so on. This is shown in the diagram at the top of the next page.

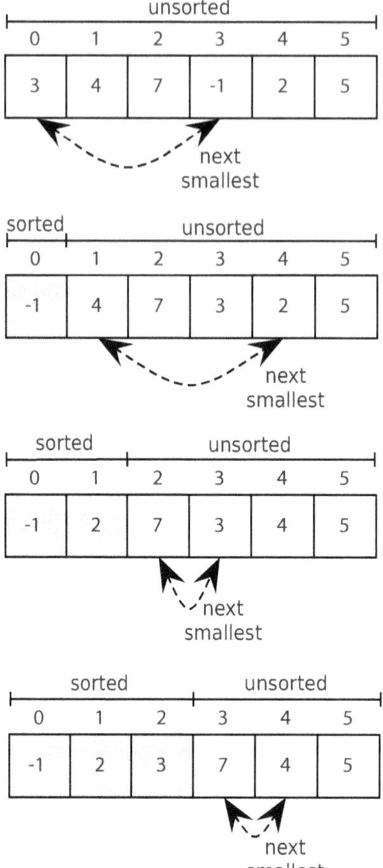

The file named sorts.py contains a selection sort function, partially in English, as shown in the following code:

```
def selection_sort(L: list) -> None:
    """Reorder the items in L from smallest to largest.

    >>> L = [3, 4, 7, -1, 2, 5]
    >>> selection_sort(L)
    >>> L
    [-1, 2, 3, 4, 5, 7]
    """

    i = 0
    while i != len(L):
        # Find the index of the smallest item in L[i:]
        # Swap that smallest item with L[i]
        i += 1
```

You can replace the second comment with a single line of code.

```
def selection_sort(L: list) -> None:
    """Reorder the items in L from smallest to largest.

    >>> L = [3, 4, 7, -1, 2, 5]
    >>> selection_sort(L)
    >>> L
    [-1, 2, 3, 4, 5, 7]
    """

    i = 0
    while i != len(L):
        # Find the index of the smallest item in L[i:]
        L[i], L[smallest] = L[smallest], L[i]
        i += 1
```

Now, all that's left is finding the index of the smallest item in `L[i:]`. This is complex enough that it's worth making it a function:

```
def find_min(L: list, b: int) -> int:
    """Return the index of the smallest value in L[b:].

    Precondition: L[b:] is not empty.

    >>> find_min([3, -1, 7, 5], 0)
    1
    >>> find_min([3, -1, 7, 5], 1)
    1
    >>> find_min([3, -1, 7, 5], 2)
    3
    """

    smallest = b  # The index of the smallest so far.
    i = b + 1
    while i != len(L):
        if L[i] < L[smallest]:
            # We found a smaller item at L[i].
            smallest = i

        i += 1

    return smallest

def selection_sort(L: list) -> None:
    """Reorder the items in L from smallest to largest.

    >>> L = [3, 4, 7, -1, 2, 5]
    >>> selection_sort(L)
    >>> L
    [-1, 2, 3, 4, 5, 7]
    """

    i = 0
    while i != len(L):
        smallest = find_min(L, i)
        L[i], L[smallest] = L[smallest], L[i]
        i += 1
```

The function find_min examines each item in L[b:], keeping track of the index of the minimum item so far in variable smallest. Whenever it finds a smaller item, it updates smallest. Because it is returning the index of the smallest value, it won't work if L[b:] is empty; hence the precondition.

This operation is complicated enough that a couple of doctests may not be sufficient to test it thoroughly. Here's a list of test cases for sorting:

- An empty list
- A list of length 1
- A list of length 2 (this is the shortest case where items can move)
- An already-sorted list
- A list with all the same values
- A list with duplicates

Here are your expanded doctests:

```
def selection_sort(L: list) -> None:
    """Reorder the items in L from smallest to largest.

    >>> L = [3, 4, 7, -1, 2, 5]
    >>> selection_sort(L)
    >>> L
    [-1, 2, 3, 4, 5, 7]
    >>> L = []
    >>> selection_sort(L)
    >>> L
    []
    >>> L = [1]
    >>> selection_sort(L)
    >>> L
    [1]
    >>> L = [2, 1]
    >>> selection_sort(L)
    >>> L
    [1, 2]
    >>> L = [1, 2]
    >>> selection_sort(L)
    >>> L
    [1, 2]
    >>> L = [3, 3, 3]
    >>> selection_sort(L)
    >>> L
    [3, 3, 3]
    >>> L = [-5, 3, 0, 3, -6, 2, 1, 1]
    >>> selection_sort(L)
    >>> L
    [-6, -5, 0, 1, 1, 2, 3, 3]
    """
```

```
    i = 0

    while i != len(L):
        smallest = find_min(L, i)
        L[i], L[smallest] = L[smallest], L[i]
        i += 1
```

As with binary search, the doctest is so long that, as documentation for the function, it obscures rather than helps clarify. Again, you'll see how to fix this in Chapter 15, Testing and Debugging, on page 309.

Insertion Sort

Like selection sort, *insertion sort* keeps a sorted section at the beginning of the list. Rather than scan all of the unsorted section for the next smallest item, though, it takes the next item from the unsorted section—the one at index i—and inserts it where it belongs in the sorted section, increasing the size of the sorted section by one.

```
i = 0  # The index of the first unknown item in lst; lst[:i] is sorted

while i != len(L):
    # Move the item at index i to where it belongs in lst[:i + 1]

    i += 1
```

The reason you should use lst[i + 1] is that the item at index i may be larger than all the items in the sorted section. If that is the case, then the current item won't move:

```
def insertion_sort(L: list) -> None:
    """Reorder the items in L from smallest to largest.

    >>> L = [3, 4, 7, -1, 2, 5]
    >>> insertion_sort(L)
    >>> L
    [-1, 2, 3, 4, 5, 7]
    """

    i = 0
    while i != len(L):
        # Insert L[i] where it belongs in L[0:i+1].
        i += 1
```

The approach is the same as in selection sort; the difference lies in the comment within the loop. Like you did with selection sort, let's write a helper function to do the work:

```
def insert(L: list, b: int) -> None:
    """Precondition: L[0:b] is already sorted.
    Insert L[b] where it belongs in L[0:b + 1].
```

```
    >>> L = [3, 4, -1, 7, 2, 5]
    >>> insert(L, 2)
    >>> L
    [-1, 3, 4, 7, 2, 5]
    >>> insert(L, 4)
    >>> L
    [-1, 2, 3, 4, 7, 5]
    """

    # Find where to insert L[b] by searching backwards from L[b]
    # for a smaller item.
    i = b
    while i != 0 and L[i - 1] >= L[b]:
        i -= 1

    # Move L[b] to index i, shifting the following values to the right.
    value = L[b]
    del L[b]
    L.insert(i, value)

def insertion_sort(L: list) -> None:
    """Reorder the items in L from smallest to largest.

    >>> L = [3, 4, 7, -1, 2, 5]
    >>> insertion_sort(L)
    >>> L
    [-1, 2, 3, 4, 5, 7]
    """

    i = 0

    while i != len(L):
        insert(L, i)
        i += 1
```

How does insert work? It works by finding out where L[b] belongs and then relocating it. Where does it belong? It belongs after every value less than or equal to it and before every value that is greater than it. You need the check i != 0 in case L[b] is smaller than every value in L[0:b], which will place the current item at the beginning of the list. This code passes all the tests written earlier for selection sort. The diagram on the facing page illustrates the process.

Selection sort and insertion sort differ only by how they make progress

Performance

You now have two sorting algorithms. Which should you use? Because neither is too difficult to understand, it's reasonable to decide based on how fast they are.

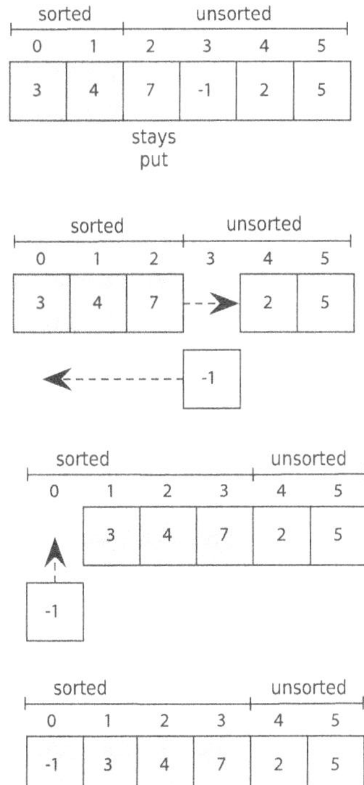

It's easy enough to write a program to compare their running times, along with that for list.sort:

```
import time
import random
from sorts import selection_sort
from sorts import insertion_sort

def built_in(L: list) -> None:
    """Call list.sort --- we need our own function to do this so that we can
    treat it as we treat our own sorts.
    """

    L.sort()

def print_times(L: list) -> None:
    """Print the number of milliseconds it takes for selection sort, insertion
    sort, and list.sort to run.
    """

    print(len(L), end='\t')
    for func in (selection_sort, insertion_sort, built_in):
        if func in (selection_sort, insertion_sort) and len(L) > 10000:
            continue
```

```
        L_copy = L[:]
        t1 = time.perf_counter()
        func(L_copy)
        t2 = time.perf_counter()
        print("{0:7.1f}".format((t2 - t1) * 1000.), end='\t')
    print()  # Print a newline.

for list_size in [10, 1000, 2000, 3000, 4000, 5000, 10000]:
    L = list(range(list_size))
    random.shuffle(L)
    print_times(L)
```

Here are the results:

List Length	Selection Sort	Insertion Sort	list.sort
1000	29	14	0.1
2000	117	59	0.2
3000	264	135	0.3
4000	471	239	0.4
5000	730	362	0.5
10000	2979	1477	1.3

Something is clearly wrong, as your sorting functions are thousands of times slower than the built-in function. What's more, the time required by your routines is growing faster than the size of the data. On a thousand items, for example, selection sort takes about 0.03 milliseconds per item, but on ten thousand items, it needs about 3 milliseconds per item—far more than a tenfold increase! What is going on?

To answer this, examine what happens in the inner loops of your two algorithms. In the first iteration of selection sort, the inner loop examines *every* element to find the smallest one. In the second iteration, it examines all but one; in the third, it examines all but two, and so on.

> The average running time of simple sorting algorithms is proportional to N*N

If there are N items in the list, then the number of iterations of the inner loop, in total, is roughly N + (N - 1) + (N - 2) + ... + 1, or N*(N + 1)/2. Putting it another way, the number of steps required to sort N items is roughly proportional to N^2 + N. For large values of N, you can ignore the second term and say that the time needed by selection sort grows as the square of the number of values being sorted. Indeed, examining the timing data further reveals that doubling the list size increases the running time by a factor of four.

The same analysis can be applied to insertion sort, as it also examines one element on the first iteration, two on the second, and so on. (It's just examining the already sorted values rather than the unsorted values.)

So why is insertion sort slightly faster? The reason is that, on average, only half of the values need to be scanned to find the location in which to insert the new value. In contrast, with selection sort, *every* value in the unsorted section needs to be examined to select the smallest one. But, wow, list.sort is *significantly* faster!

More Efficient Sorting Algorithms

Still, why is list.sort so much more efficient? The answer is the same as it was for binary search: t takes advantage of the fact that some values are already sorted.

A First Attempt

Consider the following function:

```
import bisect

def bin_sort(values: list) -> list:
    """Return a sorted version of values.  (This does not mutate values.)

    >>> L = [3, 4, 7, -1, 2, 5]
    >>> bin_sort(L)
    [-1, 2, 3, 4, 5, 7]
    """

    result = []
    for v in values:
        bisect.insort_left(result, v)

    return result
```

The average running time of more complex sorting algorithms is proportional to N $\log_2$N

This code uses bisect.insort_left to determine where to insert each value from the original list into a new list that is kept in sorted order. As you have already seen, doing this takes time proportional to $\log_2$N, where N is the length of the list. Since N values need to be inserted, the overall running time should be N $\log_2$N. As shown in the following table, this growth rate is significantly slower than N^2 with the list length.

N	N^2	N $\log_2$N
10	100	33
100	10,000	664
1000	1,000,000	9965

Unfortunately, there's a flaw in this analysis. It's correct to say that bisect.insort_left requires only $\log_2 N$ time to determine where to insert a value, but inserting it takes additional time. To create an empty slot in the list, you must move all the values above that slot up one position. On average, this means copying half of the list's values, so the cost of insertion is proportional to N. Since there are N values to insert, your total time is $N*(N + \log_2 N)$. For large values of N, this is once again roughly proportional to N^2.

Merge Sort: A Faster Sorting Algorithm

There are several well-known, fast sorting algorithms; merge sort, quick sort, and heap sort are the ones you are most likely to encounter in a future computer science course. Most of them involve techniques that you haven't learned yet, but merge sort can be written in a more accessible way. Merge sort is built around the idea that taking two sorted lists and merging them is proportional to the number of items in both lists. The running time for merge sort is $N \log_2 N$.

Start with tiny lists and keep merging them until you have a single sorted list.

Merging Two Sorted Lists

Given two sorted lists L1 and L2, you can produce a new sorted list by iterating through L1 and L2 and comparing pairs of elements. (You'll see how to make these two sorted lists in a bit.)

Here is the code for merge:

```
def merge(L1: list, L2: list) -> list:
    """Merge sorted lists L1 and L2 into a new list and return that new list.

    >>> merge([1, 3, 4, 6], [1, 2, 5, 7])
    [1, 1, 2, 3, 4, 5, 6, 7]
    """

    newL = []
    i1 = 0
    i2 = 0

    # For each pair of items L1[i1] and L2[i2], copy the smaller into newL.
    while i1 != len(L1) and i2 != len(L2):
        if L1[i1] <= L2[i2]:
            newL.append(L1[i1])
            i1 += 1
        else:
            newL.append(L2[i2])
            i2 += 1
```

```
    # Gather any leftover items from the two sections.
    # Note that one of them will be empty because of the loop condition.
    newL.extend(L1[i1:])
    newL.extend(L2[i2:])
    return newL
```

i1 and i2 are the indices into L1 and L2, respectively; in each iteration, compare L1[i1] to L2[i2] and copy the smaller item to the resulting list. At the end of the loop, you have run out of items in one of the two lists, and the two extend calls will append the rest of the items to the result.

Merge Sort

Here is the header for mergesort:

```
def mergesort(L: list) -> None:
    """Reorder the items in L from smallest to largest.

    >>> L = [3, 4, 7, -1, 2, 5]
    >>> mergesort(L)
    >>> L
    [-1, 2, 3, 4, 5, 7]
    """
```

The mergesort function uses the merge operation to perform the bulk of the work. Here is the algorithm, which creates and keeps track of a list of lists:

- Take list L and make a list of one-item lists from it.
- As long as there are two lists left to merge, merge them, and append the new list to the list of lists.

The first step is straightforward:

```
# Make a list of 1-item lists so that we can start merging.
workspace = []
for i in range(len(L)):
    workspace.append([L[i]])
```

The second step is trickier. If you remove the two lists, then you'll run into the same problem that you ran into in bin_sort: all the following lists will need to shift over, which takes time proportional to the number of lists.

Instead, keep track of the index of the next two lists to merge. Initially, they will be at indices 0 and 1, and then 2 and 3, and so on The diagram on the next page shows this.

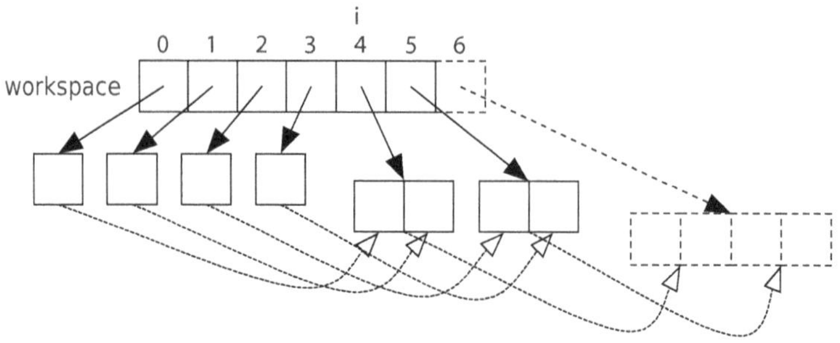

Here is your refined algorithm:

- Take list L and make a list of one-item lists from it.
- Start index i off at 0.
- As long as there are two lists (at indices i and i + 1), merge them, append the new list to the list of lists, and increment i by 2.

With that, you can go straight to code:

```
def mergesort(L: list) -> None:
    """Reorder the items in L from smallest to largest.

    >>> L = [3, 4, 7, -1, 2, 5]
    >>> mergesort(L)
    >>> L
    [-1, 2, 3, 4, 5, 7]
    """

    # Make a list of 1-item lists so that we can start merging.
    workspace = []
    for i in range(len(L)):
        workspace.append([L[i]])

    # The next two lists to merge are workspace[i] and workspace[i + 1].
    i = 0
    # As long as there are at least two more lists to merge, merge them.
    while i < len(workspace) - 1:
        L1 = workspace[i]
        L2 = workspace[i + 1]
        newL = merge(L1, L2)
        workspace.append(newL)
        i += 2

    # Copy the result back into L.
    if len(workspace) != 0:
        L[:] = workspace[-1][:]
```

Notice that since you're constantly making new lists, you need to copy the last of the merged lists back into the parameter L.

Merge Sort Analysis

Merge sort's performance turns out to be N $\log_2$N, where N is the number of items in L. The following diagram illustrates how the one-item lists are merged into two-item lists, then four-item lists, and so on, until a single N-item list is formed:

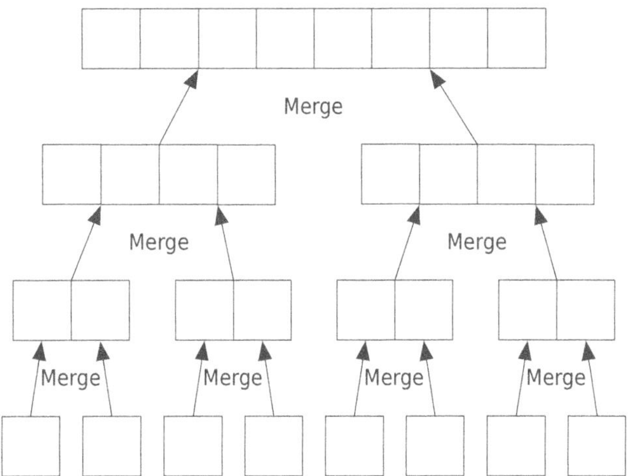

The first part of the function, which creates a list of one-item lists, takes N iterations, one for each item.

The second loop, where you continually merge lists, requires careful analysis. Start with the last iteration, in which you merge two lists with approximately N/2 items. As you've seen, the function merge copies each element into its result exactly once, so with these two lists, this merge step takes roughly N steps.

In the previous iteration, there were four lists of size N/4 to be merged into two lists of size N/2. Each of these two merges takes roughly N/2 steps, so the two merges together take roughly N steps total.

In the iteration before that, there were a total of eight lists of size N/8 to merge into the four lists of size N/4. Four merges of this size together also take roughly N steps.

You can subdivide a list with N items a total of $\log_2$ N times using an analysis similar to the one used for binary search. Since at each "level" there are a total of N items to be merged, each of these $\log_2$ N levels takes roughly N steps. Hence, merge sort takes time proportional to N $\log_2$ N.

That's an awful lot of code to sort a list! There are shorter and clearer versions but, again, they rely on techniques that hasn't been yet introduced.

Despite the extensive code and the somewhat messy approach (which creates a *numerous* sublists), merge sort proves to be significantly faster than selection sort and insertion sort. More importantly, it grows at the same rate as the built-in sort (all times in ms):

List Length	Selection Sort	Insertion Sort	Merge Sort	list.sort
1000	29	14	1.5	0.1
2000	117	58	3.1	0.2
3000	265	135	4.5	0.3
4000	466	237	6.2	0.4
5000	732	370	8.1	0.5
10000	3001	1494	17.9	1.2

Sorting Out What You Learned

In this chapter, you learned the following:

- An invariant describes the data being used in a loop. The initial values for the variables used in the loop establish the invariant, and the work done inside the loop makes progress toward the solution. When the loop terminates, the invariant remains true, and the solution has been reached.
- Linear search is the simplest way to find a value in a list, but on average, the time required is directly proportional to the length of the list.
- Binary search is much faster—the average time is proportional to the logarithm of the list's length—but it works only if the list is in sorted order.
- Similarly, the average running time of simple sorting algorithms, such as selection sort, is proportional to the square of the input size N. In contrast, the running time of more complex sorting algorithms grows as $N \log_2 N$.
- Looking at how the running time of an algorithm grows as a function of the size of its inputs is the standard way to analyze and compare the algorithm's efficiency.
- Selection sort and insertion sort have almost the same invariant; the only difference is that with selection sort, the sorted section contains values that are smaller than all the values in the unsorted section. The two algorithms differ by how they make progress: selection sort selects the next-smallest item to put at the end of the sorted section, whereas insertion sort inserts the next item into the sorted section.

Big-Oh and All That

This method of analyzing the performance of searching and sorting algorithms may seem like hand-waving, but a well-developed mathematical theory underpins it. If f and g are functions, then the expression f(x) = O(g(x)) is read "f is big-oh of g" and means that for sufficiently large values of x, f(x) is bounded above by some constant multiple of g(x), or equivalently that function g gives you an upper bound on the values of function f. Computer scientists use this to group algorithms into families, such as those sorting functions that perform in N^2 time and those that execute in $N \log_2 N$ time.

These distinctions have critical practical applications. In particular, one of the biggest puzzles in theoretical computer science today is whether two families of algorithms (called P and NP for reasons that we won't go into here) are the same or not. Almost everyone thinks they aren't, but no one has been able to prove it (despite the offer of a million-dollar prize for the first correct proof). If it turns out that they *are* the same, then many of the algorithms used to encrypt data in banking and military applications (as well as on the web) will be much more vulnerable to attack than expected.

Exercises

Here are some exercises for you to try on your own.

1. All three versions of linear search start at index 0. Rewrite all to search from the end of the list instead of from the beginning. Make sure you test them.

2. For the new versions of linear search: if there are duplicate values, which do they find?

3. Binary search is significantly faster than the built-in search, but requires that the list be sorted. As you know, the running time for the best sorting algorithm is on the order of $N \log_2 N$, where N is the length of the list. If you search multiple times on the same list of data, it makes sense to sort it once before performing the searches. Roughly how many times do you need to search to make sorting and then searching faster than using the built-in search?

4. Given the unsorted list [6, 5, 4, 3, 7, 1, 2], show what the contents of the list would be after each iteration of the loop as it is sorted using the following:

   a. Selection sort
   b. Insertion sort

5. Another sorting algorithm is *bubble sort*. Bubble sort involves keeping a sorted section at the end of the list. The list is traversed, pairs of elements are compared, and larger elements are swapped into the higher position. The operation is repeated until all elements are sorted.

   a. Using the English description of bubble sort, write an outline of the bubble sort algorithm in English.

   b. Continue using top-down design until you have a Python algorithm.

   c. Turn it into a function called `bubble_sort`.

   d. Try it out on the test cases from `selection_sort`.

6. In the description of bubble sort in the previous exercise, the sorted section of the list was at the end of the list. In this exercise, bubble sort will maintain the sorted section at the beginning of the list. Ensure that you are still implementing bubble sort!

   a. Rewrite the English description of bubble sort from the previous exercise with the necessary changes so that the sorted elements are at the beginning of the list instead of at the end.

   b. Using your English description of bubble sort, write an outline of the bubble sort algorithm in English.

   c. Write the function `bubble_sort_2`.

   d. Try it out on the test cases from `selection_sort`.

7. Modify the timing program to compare bubble sort with insertion and selection sort. Explain the results.

8. The analysis of `bin_sort` said, “Since N values have to be inserted, the overall running time is $N \log_2 N$.” Point out a flaw in this reasoning, and explain whether it affects the overall conclusion.

9. There are at least two ways determine with loop conditions. One of them is to answer the question, “When is the work done?” and then negate it. In function `merge` in Merging Two Sorted Lists, on page 272, the answer is, “When you run out of items in one of the two lists,” which is described by this expression: `i1 == len(L1) or i2 == len(L2)`. Negating this leads to the condition `i1 != len(L1) and i2 != len(L2)`.

   Another way to come up with a loop condition is to ask, “What are the valid values of the loop index?” In the function `merge`, the answer to this is `0 <= i1 < len(L1) and 0 <= i2 < len(L2)`; since `i1` and `i2` start at zero, you can drop the comparisons with zero, giving you `i1 < len(L1) and i2 < len(L2)`.

   Is there another way to do it? Have you tried both approaches? Which do you prefer?

10. In the function `mergesort` in Merge Sort, on page 273, there are two calls to `extend`. They are there because when the preceding loop ends, one of the two lists still has items in it that haven't been processed. Rewrite that loop so that these `extend` calls aren't needed.

CHAPTER 14

Object-Oriented Programming

Imagine you've been hired to help write a program to keep track of books in a bookstore. Every record about a book would likely include the title, authors, publisher, price, and ISBN, which stands for International Standard Book Number—a unique identifier for a book.

Read this code and try to guess what it prints:

```
python_book = Book(
    'Practical Programming',
    ['Campbell', 'Gries', 'Montojo'],
    'Pragmatic Bookshelf',
    '978-1-6805026-8-8',
    25.0)

survival_book = Book(
    "New Programmer's Survival Manual",
    ['Carter'],
    'Pragmatic Bookshelf',
    '978-1-93435-681-4',
    19.0)

print(f'{python_book.title} was written by {python_book.num_authors()} '
      'authors and costs ${python_book.price}')

print(f'{survival_book.title} was written by {survival_book.num_authors()} '
      'authors and costs ${survival_book.price}')
```

You might guess that this code creates two book objects, one called *Practical Programming* and one called *New Programmer's Survival Manual*. You might even guess the output:

```
Practical Programming was written by 3 authors and costs $25.0
New Programmer's Survival Manual was written by 1 authors and costs $19.0
```

There's a problem, though: this code doesn't run. Python doesn't have a `Book` type. And that is what this chapter is about: how to define and use your own types.

Understanding a Problem Domain

In the book example, we wrote the code based on what we *wanted* to do with books. The concept of a Book type originates from the *problem domain*: managing books in a bookstore. We considered this problem domain and identified the key features of a book that mattered to us.

You might have decided to keep track of the number of pages, the date it was published, and much more; what you choose to keep track of depends exactly on what your program is supposed to do.

It's common to define multiple related types. For example, if this code was part of an online store, you might also have an Inventory type, perhaps a ShoppingCart type, and much more.

Object-oriented programming revolves around defining and using new types. As you learned in Modules, Classes, and Methods, on page 121, a class is how Python represents a type. Object-oriented programming involves at least these phases:

> In object-oriented languages, new types are defined by creating classes

1. *Understanding the problem domain.* This step is crucial: you need to know what your customer wants before you can write a program that does what the customer wants.

2. *Figuring out what type(s) you might want.* A good starting point is to read the description of the problem domain and look for the main nouns and noun phrases.

3. *Figuring out what features you want your type to have.* Here you should write some code that *uses* the type you're thinking about, much like we did with the Book code at the beginning of this chapter. This step is a lot like the "Examples" step in the function design recipe, where you decide what the code that you're about to write should do.

4. *Writing a class that represents this type.* You now need to tell Python about your type. To do this, you will write a class, including a set of methods inside that class. (You will use the function design recipe as you design and implement each of your methods.)

5. *Testing your code.* Your methods will have been tested separately as you followed the function design recipe, but it's essential to think about how the various methods will interact.

Function isinstance, Class object, and Class Book

The function isinstance reports whether an object is an *instance* of a class—that is, whether an object has a particular type:

```
>>> isinstance('abc', str)
True
>>> isinstance(55.2, str)
False
```

'abc' is an instance of str, but 55.2 is not.

Python has a class called object. Every other class is based on it:

```
>>> help(object)
Help on class object in module builtins:

class object
 |  The base class of the class hierarchy.
```

The function isinstance reports that both 'abc' and 55.2 are instances of the class object:

```
>>> isinstance(55.2, object)
True
>>> isinstance('abc', object)
True
```

Even classes and functions are instances of object:

```
>>> isinstance(str, object)
True
>>> isinstance(max, object)
True
```

What's happening here is that every class in Python is *derived* from class object, and so every instance of every class is an object.

Using object-oriented terminology, we say that class object is the *superclass* of class str, and class str is a *subclass* of class object. The superclass information is available in the help documentation for a type. For example, the following shows that the superclass of class int is object:

```
>>> help(int)
Help on class int in module builtins:

class int(object)
```

Here, you see that the class SyntaxError is a subclass of the class Exception (you will read more about them in Chapter 17, Handling Exceptions, on page 351):

```
>>> help(SyntaxError)
Help on class SyntaxError in module builtins:

class SyntaxError(Exception)
```

Class object has the following *attributes* (attributes are variables inside a class that refer to methods, functions, variables, or even other classes):

```
>>> dir(object)
['__class__', '__delattr__', '__dir__', '__doc__', '__eq__', '__format__',
'__ge__', '__getattribute__', '__gt__', '__hash__', '__init__',
'__init_subclass__', '__le__', '__lt__', '__ne__', '__new__', '__reduce__',
'__reduce_ex__', '__repr__', '__setattr__', '__sizeof__', '__str__',
'__subclasshook__']
```

Every class in Python, including ones that you define, automatically *inherits* these attributes from class object. More generally, every subclass inherits the features of its superclass. Inheritance is a powerful tool; it helps avoid much duplicate code and makes interactions between related types consistent.

Let's try this out. Here is the simplest class that you can write:

```
>>> class Book:
...     """Information about a book."""
...
```

Just as keyword def tells Python that you're defining a new function, keyword class signals that you're defining a new type.

Much like str is a type, Book is a type:

```
>>> type(str)
<class 'type'>
>>> type(Book)
<class 'type'>
```

Your Book class isn't empty, either, because it has inherited all the attributes of class object:

```
>>> dir(Book)
['__class__', '__delattr__', '__dict__', '__dir__', '__doc__', '__eq__',
'__firstlineno__', '__format__', '__ge__', '__getattribute__', '__getstate__',
'__gt__', '__hash__', '__init__', '__init_subclass__', '__le__', '__lt__',
'__module__', '__ne__', '__new__', '__reduce__', '__reduce_ex__', '__repr__',
'__setattr__', '__sizeof__', '__static_attributes__', '__str__',
'__subclasshook__', '__weakref__']
```

If you look carefully, you'll see that this list is nearly identical to the output for dir(object). There are three additional attributes in the class Book; every subclass of the class object automatically has these attributes in addition to the inherited ones:

```
>>> set(dir(Book)) - set(dir(object))
{'__weakref__', '__module__', '__firstlineno__', '__dict__',
 '__static_attributes__'}
```

You'll get to those attributes later on in this chapter. First, let's create a Book object and give that Book a title and a list of authors:

```
>>> ruby_book = Book()
>>> ruby_book.title = 'Programming Ruby'
>>> ruby_book.authors = ['Thomas', 'Fowler', 'Hunt']
```

The first assignment statement creates a Book object and then assigns that object to the variable ruby_book. The second assignment statement creates a title variable *inside* the Book object; that variable refers to the string 'Programming Ruby'. The third assignment statement creates a variable authors, also inside the Book object, which refers to the list of strings ['Thomas', 'Fowler', 'Hunt'].

The variables title and authors are called *instance variables* because they are variables inside an instance of a class. You can access these instance variables through the variable ruby_book:

```
>>> ruby_book.title
'Programming Ruby'
>>> ruby_book.authors
['Thomas', 'Fowler', 'Hunt']
```

In the expression ruby_book.title, Python finds variable ruby_book, then sees the dot and goes to the memory location of the Book object, and then looks for variable title. Here is a model of computer memory for this situation:

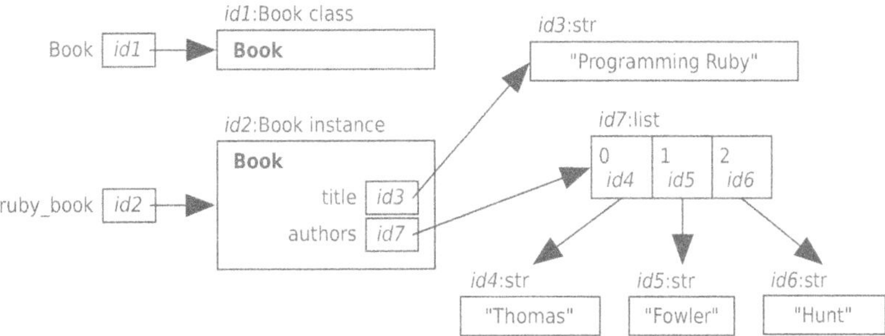

You can even get help on your Book class:

```
>>> help(Book)
Help on class Book in module __main__:

class Book(builtins.object)
 |  Information about a book.
 |
 |  Data descriptors defined here:
 |
 |  __dict__
 |      dictionary for instance variables
 |
 |  __weakref__
 |      list of weak references to the object
```

The first line tells you that you asked for help on the class Book. After that is the header for class Book; the (builtins.object) part tells you that Book is a subclass of class object. The next line shows the Book docstring. The last section is titled "Data descriptors." The descriptors are special pieces of information that Python stores with every user-defined class.

Writing a Method in Class Book

As you saw in Chapter 7, Using Methods, on page 121, there are two ways to call a method. One way is to access the method through the class, and the other is to use object-oriented syntax. These two calls are equivalent:

```
>>> str.capitalize('browning')
'Browning'
>>> 'browning'.capitalize()
'Browning'
```

You'd probably like to be able to write similar code involving the class Book. For example, you might want to ask how many authors a Book has:

```
>>> Book.num_authors(ruby_book)
3
>>> ruby_book.num_authors()
3
```

To get this to work, define a method called num_authors inside Book. Here it is:

```
class Book:
    """Information about a book."""

    def num_authors(self) -> int:
        """Return the number of authors of this book.
        """

        return len(self.authors)
```

The first argument of a method must be the object the method is being called on

The Book method num_authors resembles a function except that it has a parameter called self, which refers to a Book object. Assuming this class is defined in the file book.py, you can import it, create a Book object, and call num_authors:

```
>>> import book
>>> ruby_book = book.Book()
>>> ruby_book.title = 'Programming Ruby'
>>> ruby_book.authors = ['Thomas', 'Fowler', 'Hunt']
>>> ruby_book.num_authors()
3
```

No Magic in self

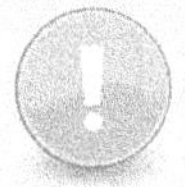

In Python, self is not a keyword (unlike this, which performs a similar function in Java and C++). You can use any other valid name for this parameter, even this:

```
def num_authors(this) -> int:
    return len(this.authors)
```

However, breaking the naming convention is strongly discouraged because it may confuse other Python programmers. Additionally, many software development tools expect a self.

The call lists the object first; think of it as asking the book how many authors it has. Thinking of method calls this way helps to develop an object-oriented mentality.

In the ruby_book example, the title and list of authors were assigned after the Book object was created. That approach isn't scalable; you don't want to have to type those extra assignment statements every time you create a Book. Instead, write a special *initializer* dunder (double underscore) method called __init__ that does this for you as you create the Book. Also, include the publisher, ISBN, and price as parameters of the __init__ method:

```
from typing import Any

class Book:
    """Information about a book, including title, list of authors,
    publisher, ISBN, and price.
    """

    def __init__(self, title: str, authors: list[str], publisher: str,
                 isbn: str, price: float) -> None:
        """Initialize a new book entitled title, written by the people in
        authors, published by publisher, with ISBN isbn and costing
        price dollars.

        >>> python_book = Book( \
                'Practical Programming', \
```

"Procedural" Method Calls Are Un-Pythonic

The method call in the code fragment on page 287 can be re-written in a "procedural" manner, rather than an object-oriented one:

```
>>> book.Book.num_authors(ruby_book)
3
```

This notation, while valid, is rarely needed in everyday OOP and should be avoided. The OOP approach is cleaner, more idiomatic, and easier for others to read and maintain.

```
                ['Campbell', 'Gries', 'Montojo'], \
                'Pragmatic Bookshelf', \
                '978-1-6805026-8-8', \
                25.0)
        >>> python_book.title
        'Practical Programming'
        >>> python_book.authors
        ['Campbell', 'Gries', 'Montojo']
        >>> python_book.publisher
        'Pragmatic Bookshelf'
        >>> python_book.ISBN
        '978-1-6805026-8-8'
        >>> python_book.price
        25.0

        """

        self.title = title
        # Copy the authors list in case the caller modifies that list later.
        self.authors = authors.copy()
        self.publisher = publisher
        self.ISBN = isbn
        self.price = price

    def num_authors(self) -> int:
        """Return the number of authors of this book.

        >>> python_book = Book( \
                'Practical Programming', \
                ['Campbell', 'Gries', 'Montojo'], \
                'Pragmatic Bookshelf', \
                '978-1-6805026-8-8', \
                25.0)
        >>> python_book.num_authors()
        3
        """

        return len(self.authors)
```

Notice that you can include doctests for methods just as you do for functions. Notice also that you should not specify the type of the first parameter of a method, since its type is always the class in which it is defined.

Also notice the call to the list.copy on line 35. Without this call, the variable self.authors becomes an alias to authors and will change at will if the authors variable is mutated.

This module contains a single (complicated) statement: the class definition. When Python executes this module, it creates a class object and assigns it to the variable Book:

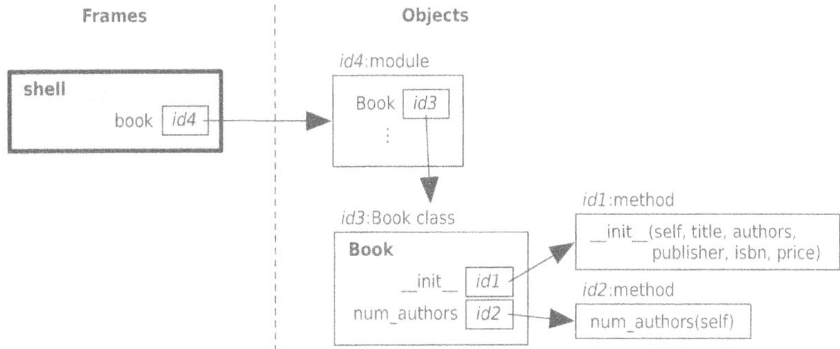

Method __init__ is called whenever a Book object is created. Its purpose is to initialize the new object. Here are the steps that Python follows when creating an object:

1. It creates an object at a particular memory address.
2. It calls method __init__, passing in the new object into the parameter self.
3. It produces that object's memory address.

Initializer ≠ Constructor

The __init__ method is sometimes referred to as a constructor—but, strictly speaking, it is not. The __new__ method creates and returns a new object, while the __init__ method initializes the new instance after it has been created.

Let's try it out in the shell:

```
>>> import book
>>> python_book = book.Book(
...         'Practical Programming',
...         ['Campbell', 'Gries', 'Montojo'],
...         'Pragmatic Bookshelf',
...         '978-1-6805026-8-8',
...         25.0)
>>> python_book.title
'Practical Programming'
>>> python_book.authors
```

```
['Campbell', 'Gries', 'Montojo']
>>> python_book.publisher
'Pragmatic Bookshelf'
>>> python_book.ISBN
'978-1-6805026-8-8'
>>> python_book.price
25.0
```

Classes vs. Instances

Methods belong to classes. Instance variables belong to objects. If you attempt to access an instance variable in the same way as a method, you get an error:

```
>>> import book
>>> book.Book.title
Traceback (most recent call last):
  File "<python-input-1>", line 1, in <module>
    book.Book.title
AttributeError: type object 'Book' has no attribute 'title'
>>> dir(book.Book)
['__class__', '__delattr__', '__dict__', '__dir__', '__doc__', '__eq__',
 '__firstlineno__', '__format__', '__ge__', '__getattribute__', '__getstate__',
 '__gt__', '__hash__', '__init__', '__init_subclass__', '__le__', '__lt__',
 '__module__', '__ne__', '__new__', '__reduce__', '__reduce_ex__', '__repr__',
 '__setattr__', '__sizeof__', '__static_attributes__', '__str__',
 '__subclasshook__', '__weakref__', 'num_authors']
```

Instances of the the class Book contain instance variables and have access to the methods defined in the Book class:

```
>>> python_book = book.Book(
...         'Practical Programming',
...         ['Campbell', 'Gries', 'Montojo'],
...         'Pragmatic Bookshelf',
...         '978-1-6805026-8-8',
...         25.0)
>>> dir(python_book)
['ISBN', '__class__', '__delattr__', '__dict__', '__dir__', '__doc__',
 '__eq__', '__firstlineno__', '__format__', '__ge__', '__getattribute__',
 '__getstate__', '__gt__', '__hash__', '__init__', '__init_subclass__',
 '__le__', '__lt__', '__module__', '__ne__', '__new__', '__reduce__',
 '__reduce_ex__', '__repr__', '__setattr__', '__sizeof__',
 '__static_attributes__', '__str__', '__subclasshook__', '__weakref__',
 'authors', 'num_authors', 'price', 'publisher', 'title']
>>> python_book.title
'Practical Programming'
```

Notice that ISBN, authors, price, publisher, and title are all available in the object as instance variables in addition to the contents of the class Book.

The following image illustrates the memory model generated by this code:

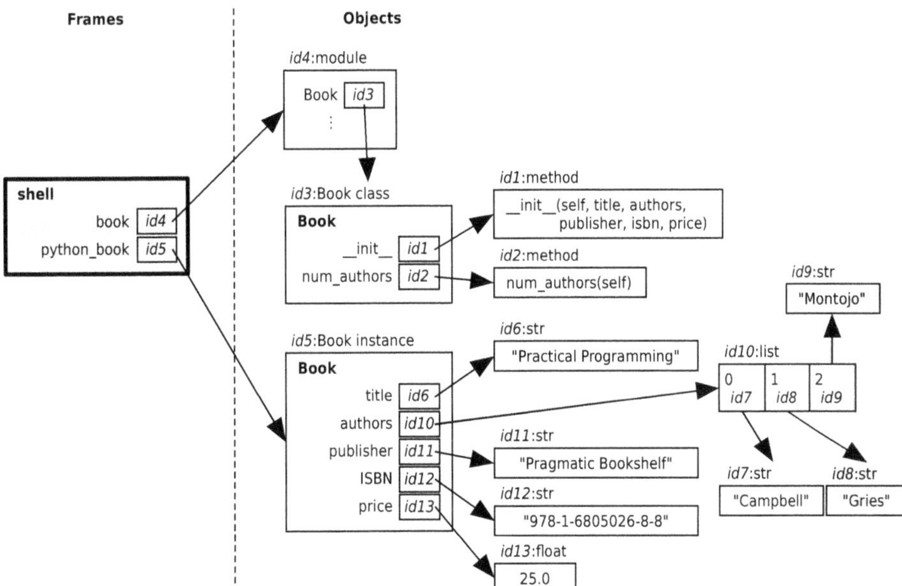

Let's trace method call python_book.num_authors. Python first finds the object that python_book refers to and calls its method num_authors. There are no explicit arguments, so Python only passes in the Book object that python_book refers to, assigning that object to the self parameter:

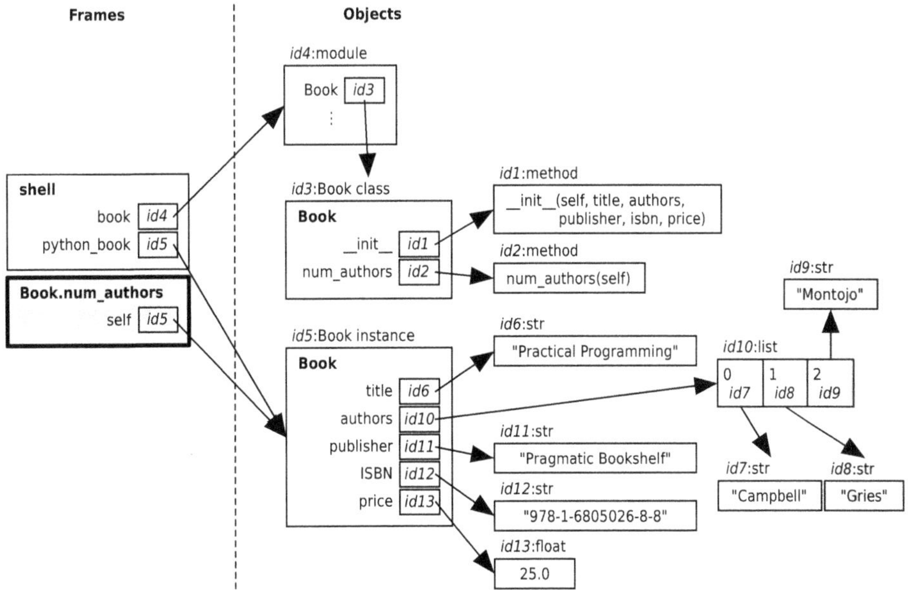

The return statement, return len(self.authors), is then executed. The expression, len(self.authors), is a function call. Python evaluates the argument, self.authors, by finding the object that self refers to and then, in that object, finds the instance variable authors. The variable is a list, and the length of that list is the value that Python returns, as shown here:

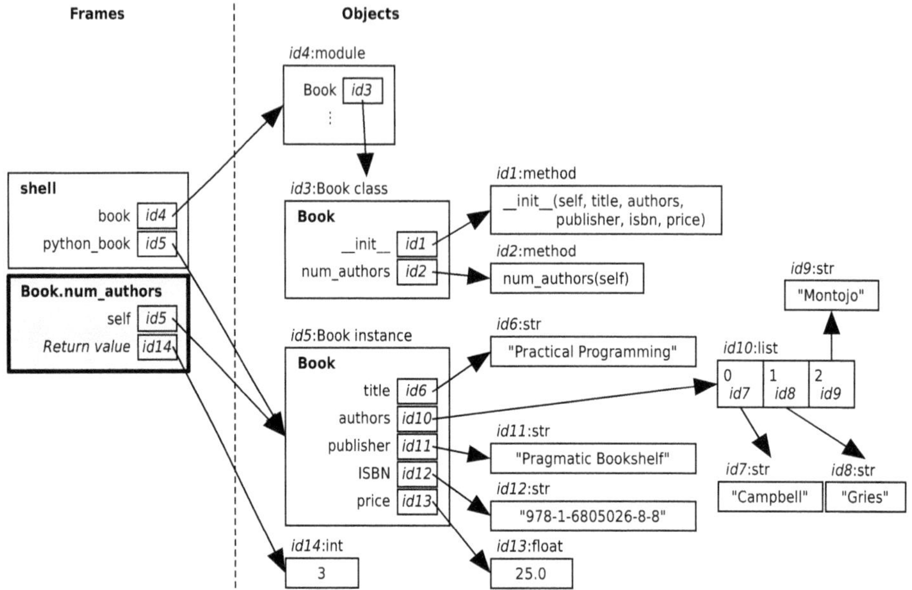

With initializers, methods, and instance variables in hand, you can now create classes that look and work like those that come with Python itself.

Plugging into Python Syntax: More Special Methods

In What Are Those Underscores?, on page 128, you learned that some Python syntax, such as + or ==, triggers method calls. For example, when Python sees 'abc' + '123', it turns that into 'abc'.__add__('123'). When you call print(obj), then obj.__str__ is called to find out what string to print.

> Methods whose names begin and end with two underscores have special predefined meanings in Python

You can do this too. All you need to do is define these special methods inside your classes.

The output Python produces when you print a Book isn't particularly useful:

```
>>> python_book = Book(
...     'Practical Programming',
...     ['Campbell', 'Gries', 'Montojo'],
...     'Pragmatic Bookshelf',
...     '978-1-6805026-8-8',
...     25.0)
```

```
>>> print(python_book)
<book.Book object at 0x7f749d11acf0>
```

What you see is the result of the default conversion of objects to strings: it just shows you where the object is in memory. This behavior is defined in the class object's method __str__, which your Book class has inherited.

If you want to present a more useful string, you need to explore two more special methods, __str__ and __repr__. __str__ is called when an informal, human-readable version of an object is needed, and __repr__ is called when unambiguous, but possibly less readable, output is desired. In particular, __str__ is called when print is used, and it is also called by function str and by string method format. Method __repr__ is called when you ask for the value of a variable in the Python shell, and it is also called when a collection such as list is printed.

Let's define method Book.__str__ to provide informative output; this method goes inside class Book, along with __init__ and num_authors:

```
    def __str__(self) -> str:
        """Return a human-readable string representation of this Book."""

        return f"""Title: {self.title}
Authors: {', '.join(self.authors)}
Publisher: {self.publisher}
ISBN: {self.ISBN}
Price: ${self.price}"""
```

Printing a Book now gives more helpful information:

```
>>> python_book = Book(
...         'Practical Programming',
...         ['Campbell', 'Gries', 'Montojo'],
...         'Pragmatic Bookshelf',
...         '978-1-6805026-8-8',
...         25.0)
>>> print(python_book)
Title: Practical Programming
Authors: Campbell, Gries, Montojo
Publisher: Pragmatic Bookshelf
ISBN: 978-1-6805026-8-8
Price: $25.0
```

Another dunder method, __repr__, is called to get an unambiguous string representation of an object. The string should include the type of the object as well as the values of any instance variables. Ideally, if you were to evaluate the string, it would create an object equivalent to the one that owns the method __repr__. You will see an example of __repr__ in A Case Study: Molecules, Atoms, and PDB Files, on page 300.

The operator == triggers a call to the method _eq_. This method is defined in the class object, and so the class Book has inherited it; object's _eq_ produces True exactly when an object is compared to itself. That means that even if two objects contain identical information, they will not be considered equal:

```
>>> python_book_1 = book.Book(
...     'Practical Programming',
...     ['Campbell', 'Gries', 'Montojo'],
...     'Pragmatic Bookshelf',
...     '978-1-6805026-8-8',
...     25.0)
>>> python_book_2 = book.Book(
...     'Practical Programming',
...     ['Campbell', 'Gries', 'Montojo'],
...     'Pragmatic Bookshelf',
...     '978-1-6805026-8-8',
...     25.0)
>>> python_book_1 == python_book_2
False
>>> python_book_1 == python_book_1
True
>>> python_book_2 == python_book_2
True
```

You can *override* an inherited method by defining a new version in your subclass. Overriding replaces the inherited method so that it is no longer used. As an example, let's define method Book._eq_ to compare two books for equality. Because ISBNs are unique, you can compare books using them; however, you first need to verify whether the object you are comparing to is indeed a Book. Let's add this method to the class Book:

```
def __eq__(self, other: Any) -> bool:
    """Return True iff other is a book, and this book and other have
    the same ISBN.

    >>> python_book = Book( \
            'Practical Programming', \
            ['Campbell', 'Gries', 'Montojo'], \
            'Pragmatic Bookshelf', \
            '978-1-6805026-8-8', \
            25.0)
    >>> python_book_discounted = Book( \
            'Practical Programming', \
            ['Campbell', 'Gries', 'Montojo'], \
            'Pragmatic Bookshelf', \
            '978-1-6805026-8-8', \
            5.0)
    >>> python_book == python_book_discounted
    True
    >>> python_book == ['Not', 'a', 'book']
```

```
    False
    """
    return isinstance(other, Book) and self.ISBN == other.ISBN
```

Here is the new method __eq__ in action:

```
>>> python_book_1 = book.Book(
...     'Practical Programming', ['Campbell', 'Gries', 'Montojo'],
...     'Pragmatic Bookshelf', '978-1-6805026-8-8', 25.0)
>>> python_book_2 = book.Book(
...     'Practical Programming', ['Campbell', 'Gries', 'Montojo'],
...     'Pragmatic Bookshelf', '978-1-6805026-8-8', 25.0)
>>> survival_book = book.Book(
...     "New Programmer's Survival Manual", ['Carter'],
...     'Pragmatic Bookshelf', '978-1-93435-681-4', 19.0)
>>> python_book_1 == python_book_2
True
>>> python_book_1 == survival_book
False
>>> python_book_1 == ['Not', 'a', 'book']
False
```

Here, then, are the lookup rules for a method call obj.method(...):

1. Look in the current object's class. If you find a method with the correct name, use it.
2. If you didn't find it, look in the superclass. Continue up the class hierarchy until the method is found.

Python has many other special methods; the official Python website provides a comprehensive list.

A Book or *the* Book?

When designing classes to model real-world objects, it's essential to distinguish between a concept and a physical instance, such as a *book title* ("War and Peace") and a *book copy* (your paperback on the nightstand).

In OOP terms, the *book title* is an abstraction shared by many copies. It has attributes like the author, title, ISBN, and publisher. The *book copy*, however, is a concrete instance with its unique state: a checkout status, wear and tear, or a barcode in a library.

Failing to make this distinction may lead to design flaws, such as setting a due date on the title rather than on individual copies.

A Little Bit of OO Theory

Classes and objects are two of programming's power tools. They let good programmers accomplish a great deal in very little time, but with them, bad programmers can create a real mess. This section introduces some underlying theory that will help you design reliable and reusable object-oriented software.

Encapsulation

To *encapsulate* something means to enclose it within a container. In programming, *encapsulation* refers to keeping data and the code that uses it in one place, while hiding the details of how they interact. For example, each instance of a fictitious class `file` keeps track of disk reading and writing operations, as well as the current position within the file. The class conceals the implementation details, allowing programmers to use it without needing to understand the underlying mechanisms.

The Single Responsibility Principle

The *Single Responsibility Principle* (SRP) is a guideline from software engineering that states that a class should have only one reason to change. In other words, each class should encapsulate just one kind of responsibility.

For example, the `Book` class keeps track of a book's metadata. It should not manage inventory or customer reviews. Other classes would better handle those.

Following SRP makes programs easier to understand, test, and maintain. This principle applies to methods, too. A method should do one thing, and do it well.

Polymorphism

Polymorphism means "having more than one form." In programming, it means that an expression involving a variable can perform differently depending on the type of object to which the variable refers. For example, if `obj` refers to a string, then `obj[1:3]` produces a two-character string. If `obj` refers to a list, on the other hand, the same expression produces a two-element list. Similarly, the expression `left + right` can produce a number, a string, or a list, depending on the types of `left` and `right`.

Classes support polymorphism: if two classes have methods that work the same way, instances of those classes can replace one another

Polymorphism is widely used in modern programming to reduce the amount of code that programmers need to write and test. For example, it allows you to write a generic function to count non-blank lines:

```
def non_blank_lines(thing):
    """Return the number of nonblank lines in thing."""

    count = 0
    for line in thing:
        if line.strip():
            count += 1
    return count
```

You can apply this function to a list of strings, a file, or a web document halfway around the world (see Files over the Internet, on page 188) or in the cloud. Each of those three types knows how to be the subject of a loop; in other words, each one knows how to produce its "next" element as long as there is one and then say "all done." That means that instead of writing four functions to count interesting lines or copying the lines into a list and then applying one function to that list, you can apply one function to all those types directly.

Inheritance

New classes can be defined by inheriting features from existing ones

Implementing the same methods in several classes is one way to make them polymorphic. Still, it suffers from the same flaw as initializing an object's instance variables from outside the object. If a programmer forgets just one line of code, the whole program can fail for reasons that will be difficult to track down. A better approach is to utilize a third fundamental feature of object-oriented programming called *inheritance*, which enables you to reuse code more effectively.

Whenever you create a class, you are using inheritance: your new class automatically inherits all of the attributes of the class `object`, much like a child inherits attributes from their parents. You can also declare that your new class is a subclass of some other class.

Here is an example. Let's say you're managing people at a university. There are students and faculty. (This is a gross oversimplification for purposes of illustrating inheritance; you're ignoring administrative staff, caretakers, food providers, and more.)

Both students and faculty have names, postal addresses, and email addresses; each student also has a student number, a list of courses taken, and a list of courses they are currently enrolled in. Each faculty member has a faculty number and a list of courses they are currently teaching. (Again, this is a simplification.)

You'll have a Faculty class and a Student class. You need both of them to have names, addresses, and email addresses, but duplicate code is generally a bad thing; so, avoid it by also defining a class, perhaps called Member, and keeping track of those features in Member. Then make both Faculty and Student subclasses of Member:

```
class Member:
    """ A member of a university. """

    def __init__(self, name: str, address: str, email: str) -> None:
        """Initialize a new member named name, with home address and email
        address.
        """

        self.name = name
        self.address = address
        self.email = email

class Faculty(Member):
    """ A faculty member at a university. """

    def __init__(self, name: str, address: str, email: str,
                 faculty_num: str) -> None:
        """Initialize a new faculty named name, with home address, email
        address, faculty number faculty_num, and empty list of
        courses.
        """

        super().__init__(name, address, email)
        self.faculty_number = faculty_num
        self.courses_teaching = []


class Student(Member):
    """ A student member at a university. """

    def __init__(self, name: str, address: str, email: str,
                 student_num: str) -> None:
        """Initialize a new student named name, with home address, email
        address, student number student_num, an empty list of courses
        taken, and an empty list of current courses.
        """

        super().__init__(name, address, email)
        self.student_number = student_num
        self.courses_taken = []
        self.courses_taking = []
```

Both class headers—class Faculty(Member): and class Student(Member):—tell Python that Faculty and Student are subclasses of the class Member. That means they inherit all the attributes of the class Member.

The first lines of both Faculty.__init__ and Student.__init__ call the function super, which produces a reference to the superclass part of the object, Member. That means that both of those first lines call the method __init__, which was inherited from the class Member. Notice that you pass the relevant parameters in as arguments to this call, just as you would with any method call.

If you import these into the shell, you can create both faculty and students:

```
>>> paul = Faculty('Paul Gries', 'Ajax', 'pgries@cs.toronto.edu', '1234')
>>> paul.name
Paul Gries
>>> paul.email
pgries@cs.toronto.edu
>>> paul.faculty_number
1234
>>> jen = Student('Jen Campbell', 'Toronto', 'campbell@cs.toronto.edu',
...               '4321')
>>> jen.name
Jen Campbell
>>> jen.email
campbell@cs.toronto.edu
>>> jen.student_number
4321
```

Both the Faculty and Student objects have inherited the features defined in the class Member.

Often, you'll want to *extend* the behavior inherited from a superclass. As an example, you might write a __str__ method inside the class Member:

```
def __str__(self) -> str:
    """Return a string representation of this Member.

    >>> member = Member('Paul', 'Ajax', 'pgries@cs.toronto.edu')
    >>> member.__str__()
    'Paul\\nAjax\\npgries@cs.toronto.edu'
    """

    return f'{self.name}\n{self.address}\n{self.email}'
```

With this method added to class Member, both Faculty and Student inherit it:

```
>>> paul = Faculty('Paul', 'Ajax', 'pgries@cs.toronto.edu', '1234')
>>> str(paul)
'Paul\nAjax\npgries@cs.toronto.edu'
>>> print(paul)
Paul
Ajax
pgries@cs.toronto.edu
```

That isn't quite enough, though: for class Faculty, you want to *extend* what the Member's __str__ does, adding the faculty number and the list of courses the faculty member is teaching, and a Student string should include the equivalent student-specific information.

Use super again to access the inherited Member.__str__ method and to append the Faculty-specific information:

```
    def __str__(self) -> str:
        """Return a string representation of this Faculty.

        >>> faculty = Faculty('Paul', 'Ajax', 'pgries@cs.toronto.edu', '1234')
        >>> faculty.__str__()
        'Paul\\nAjax\\npgries@cs.toronto.edu\\n1234\\nCourses: '
        """

        member_string = super().__str__()

        return f'''{member_string}
{self.faculty_number}
Courses: {' '.join(self.courses_teaching)}'''
```

With this, you get the desired output:

```
>>> paul = Faculty('Paul', 'Ajax', 'pgries@cs.toronto.edu', '1234')
>>> str(paul)
'Paul\nAjax\npgries@cs.toronto.edu\n1234\nCourses: '
>>> print(paul)
Paul
Ajax
pgries@cs.toronto.edu
1234
Courses:
```

A Case Study: Molecules, Atoms, and PDB Files

Molecular graphic visualization tools allow for interactive exploration of molecular structures. Most read PDB-formatted files, described in Multiline Records, on page 201. For example, Jmol (shown shown at the top of the facing page) is a Java-based, open-source 3D viewer for these structures.

In a molecular visualizer, every structure—atoms, molecules, bonds, and so on—has a location in 3D space, represented by *x*, *y*, and *z* coordinates. All of these structures can be rotated and translated. Here is how ammonia can be described in PDB format:

```
COMPND      AMMONIA
ATOM      1  N  0.257  -0.363   0.000
ATOM      2  H  0.257   0.727   0.000
ATOM      3  H  0.771  -0.727   0.890
ATOM      4  H  0.771  -0.727  -0.890
END
```

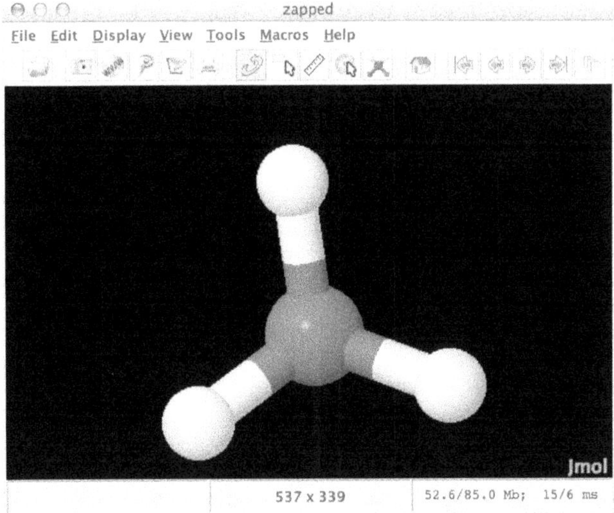

In the simplified PDB format, a molecule is made up of numbered atoms. In addition to the number, an atom has a symbol and (x, y, z) coordinates. For example, one of the atoms in ammonia is nitrogen, with symbol N at coordinates (0.257, -0.363, 0.0). In the following sections, you will explore how to translate these ideas into object-oriented Python.

Class Atom

You might want to create an atom like this using information you read from the PDB file:

```
nitrogen = Atom(1, "N", 0.257, -0.363, 0.0)
```

To do this, you'll need a class called Atom with an initializer that creates all the appropriate instance variables:

```
class Atom:
    """ An atom with a number, symbol, and coordinates. """

    def __init__(self, num: int, sym: str, x: float, y: float,
                 z: float) -> None:
        """Create an Atom with number num, string symbol sym, and float
        coordinates (x, y, z).
        """

        self.number = num
        self.center = (x, y, z)
        self.symbol = sym
```

To inspect an Atom, you'll want to provide _repr_ and _str_ methods:

```
def __str__(self) -> str:
    """Return a string representation of this Atom in this format:

        (SYMBOL, X, Y, Z)
    """

    return f'{self.symbol}, {self.center[0]}, {self.center[1]}, '\
        f'{self.center[2]}'

def __repr__(self) -> str:
    """Return a string representation of this Atom in this format:

        Atom(NUMBER, "SYMBOL", X, Y, Z)
    """

    return f'Atom({self.number}, "{self.symbol}", {self.center[0]}, '\
        f'{self.center[1]}, {self.center[2]})'
```

You'll use those later when you define a class for molecules.

In visualizers, one common operation is translation, or moving an atom to a different location. You'd like to be able to write this to instruct the nitrogen atom to move up by 0.2 units:

```
nitrogen.translate(0, 0, 0.2)
```

This code works as expected if you add the following method to the class Atom:

```
def translate(self, x: float, y: float, z: float) -> None:
    """Move this Atom by adding (x, y, z) to its coordinates.
    """

    self.center = (self.center[0] + x,
                   self.center[1] + y,
                   self.center[2] + z)
```

Class Molecule

Remember that you read PDB files one line at a time. When you reach the line containing COMPND AMMONIA, you know that you're building a complex structure: a molecule with a name and a list of atoms. Here's the start of a class for this, including an add method that adds an Atom to the molecule:

```
class Molecule:
    """A molecule with a name and a list of Atoms. """

    def __init__(self, name: str) -> None:
        """Create a Molecule named name with no Atoms.
        """

        self.name = name
        self.atoms = []
```

```
    def add(self, a: Atom) -> None:
        """Add a to my list of Atoms.
        """

        self.atoms.append(a)
```

As you read through the ammonia PDB information, you add atoms as you find them; here is the code from Multiline Records, on page 201, rewritten to return a Molecule object instead of a list of lists:

```
from molecule import Molecule
from atom import Atom
from typing import TextIO

def read_molecule(r: TextIO) -> Molecule:
    """Read a single molecule from r and return it,
    or return None to signal end of file.
    """
    # If there isn't another line, we're at the end of the file.
    line = r.readline()
    if not line:
        return None

    # Name of the molecule: "COMPND   name"
    key, name = line.split()

    # Other lines are either "END" or "ATOM num kind x y z"
    molecule = Molecule(name)

    line = r.readline()
    while line and not line.startswith('END'):
        key, num, kind, x, y, z = line.split()
        molecule.add(Atom(int(num), kind, float(x), float(y), float(z)))
        line = r.readline()

    return molecule
```

If you compare the two versions, you can see that the code is nearly identical. It's just as easy to read the new version as the old—more so even, because it includes type information. Here are the __str__ and __repr__ methods:

```
def __str__(self) -> str:
    """Return a string representation of this Molecule in this format:
        (NAME, (ATOM1, ATOM2, ...))
    """

    res = ''
    for atom in self.atoms:
        res += f'{atom}, '

    # Strip off the last comma.
    res = res[:-2]
    return f'({self.name}, ({res}))'
```

```
def __repr__(self) -> str:
    """Return a string representation of this Molecule in this format:
      Molecule("NAME", (ATOM1, ATOM2, ...))
    """

    res = ''
    for atom in self.atoms:
        res += f'{repr(atom)}, '

    # Strip off the last comma.
    res = res[:-2]
    return f'Molecule("{self.name}", ({res}))'
```

Add a translate method to Molecule to make it easier to move:

```
def translate(self, x: float, y: float, z: float) -> None:
    """Move this Molecule, including all Atoms, by (x, y, z).
    """

    for atom in self.atoms:
        atom.translate(x, y, z)
```

And here, call it:

```
ammonia = Molecule("AMMONIA")
ammonia.add(Atom(1, "N", 0.257, -0.363, 0.0))
ammonia.add(Atom(2, "H", 0.257, 0.727, 0.0))
ammonia.add(Atom(3, "H", 0.771, -0.727, 0.890))
ammonia.add(Atom(4, "H", 0.771, -0.727, -0.890))
ammonia.translate(0, 0, 0.2)
```

Classifying What You've Learned

In this chapter, you learned the following:

- In object-oriented languages, new types are defined by creating classes. Classes support encapsulation; in other words, they combine data and the operations on it so that other parts of the program can ignore implementation details.
- Classes support polymorphism. If two classes have methods that work the same way, instances of those classes can replace one another without the rest of the program being affected. Polymorphism enables "plug-and-play" programming, in which one piece of code can perform different operations depending on the objects it is operating on.
- Finally, new classes can be defined by inheriting features from existing ones. The new class can override the features of its parent and/or add new features.

- When a method is defined in a class, its first argument must be a variable that represents the object the method is being called on. By convention, this argument is named self.
- Some methods have special predefined meanings in Python; to signal this, their names begin and end with two underscores. Some of these methods are invoked when constructing objects (__init__) or converting them to strings (__str__ and __repr__); others, such as __add__ and __sub__, are used to implement arithmetic operations.

Exercises

Here are some exercises for you to try on your own.

1. In this exercise, you will implement the class Country, which represents a country with a name, a population, and an area.

   a. Here is a sample interaction from the Python shell:

   ```
   >>> canada = Country('Canada', 36991981, 9984670)
   >>> canada.name
   'Canada'
   >>> canada.population
   36991981
   >>> canada.area
   9984670
   ```

   This code cannot be executed yet because the class Country does not exist. Define Country with an initializer (method __init__) that has four parameters: a country, its name, its population, and its area.

   b. Consider this code:

   ```
   >>> canada = Country('Canada', 36991981, 9984670)
   >>> usa = Country('United States of America', 342034432, 9826675)
   >>> canada.is_larger(usa)
   True
   ```

   In the class Country, define a method named is_larger that takes two Country objects and returns True if and only if the first has a larger area than the second.

   c. Consider this code:

   ```
   >>> canada.population_density()
   3.704877677479576
   ```

   In the class Country, define a method named population_density that returns the population density of the country (people per square kilometer).

d. Consider this code:

```
>>> usa = Country('United States of America', 342034432, 9826675)
>>> print(usa)
United States of America has a population of 342034432 and is 9826675
square km.
```

In class Country, define a method named __str__ that returns a string representation of the country in the format shown here.

e. After you have written __str__, this session shows that a __repr__ method would be useful:

```
>>> canada = Country('Canada', 36991981, 9984670)
>>> canada
<exercise_country.Country object at 0x7f2aba30b550>
>>> print(canada)
Canada has population 36991981 and is 9984670 square km.
>>> [canada]
[<exercise_country.Country object at 0x7f2aba30b550>]
>>> print([canada])
[<exercise_country.Country object at 0x7f2aba30b550>]
```

Define the __repr__ method in Country to produce a string that behaves like this:

```
>>> canada = Country('Canada', 36991981, 9984670)
>>> canada
Country('Canada', 36991981, 9984670)
>>> [canada]
[Country('Canada', 36991981, 9984670)]
```

2. In this exercise, you will implement a Continent class, which represents a continent with a name and a list of countries. Class Continent will use class Country from the previous exercise. If Country is defined in another module, you'll need to import it.

   a. Here is a sample interaction from the Python shell:

```
>>> canada = country.Country('Canada', 36991981, 9984670)
>>> usa = country.Country('United States of America', 342034432,
...                       9826675)
>>> mexico = country.Country('Mexico', 132452034, 1943950)
>>> countries = [canada, usa, mexico]
>>> north_america = Continent('North America', countries)
>>> north_america.name
'North America'
>>> for country in north_america.countries:
        print(country)

Canada has a population of 36991981 and is 9984670 square km.
```

```
United States of America has a population of 342034432 and is 9826675
square km.
Mexico has a population of 132452034 and is 1943950 square km.
>>>
```

The code cannot be executed yet, because class Continent does not exist. Define Continent with an initializer (method _init_) that has three parameters: a continent, its name, and its list of Country objects.

b. Consider this code:

```
>>> north_america.total_population()
511478447
```

In class Continent, define a method named total_population that returns the sum of the populations of the countries on this continent.

c. Consider this code:

```
>>> print(north_america)
North America
Canada has a population of 36991981 and is 9984670 square km.
United States of America has a population of 342034432 and is 9826675
square km.
Mexico has a population of 132452034 and is 1943950 square km.
```

In class Continent, define a method named _str_ that returns a string representation of the continent in the format shown here.

3. In this exercise, you'll write _str_ and _repr_ methods for several classes.

   a. In class Student, write a _str_ method that includes all the Member information and in addition includes the student number, the list of courses taken, and the list of current courses.

   b. Write _repr_ methods in classes Member, Student, and Faculty.

   Create a few Student and Faculty objects and call str and repr on them to verify that your code does what you want it to.

4. Write a class called Nematode to keep track of information about *C. elegans*, including a variable for the body length (in millimeters; they are about 1 mm in length), gender (either hermaphrodite or male), and age (in days).

   Include methods _init_, _repr_, and _str_.

5. Consider this code:

```
>>> segment = LineSegment(Point(1, 1), Point(3, 2))
>>> segment.slope()
0.5
```

```
>>> segment.length()
2.23606797749979
```

In this exercise, you will write two classes, Point and LineSegment, so that you can run this code and get the same results.

a. Write a Point class with an __init__ method that takes two numbers as parameters.

b. In the same file, write a LineSegment class whose initializer takes two Points as parameters. The first Point should be the start of the segment.

c. Write a slope method in the class LineSegment that computes the slope of the segment. (Hint: The slope of a line is rise over run.)

d. Write a length method in class LineSegment that computes the length of the segment. (Hint: Use x ** n to raise x to the nth power. To compute the square root, raise a number to the (1/2) power or use math.sqrt.)

CHAPTER 15

Testing and Debugging

How can you tell whether the programs you write work correctly? Following the function design recipe from Designing New Functions: A Recipe, on page 49, you include an example call or two in the docstring. The final step of the recipe is to call your function and ensure it returns the expected result. But are one or two calls enough? If not, how many do you need? How do you pick the arguments for those function calls? In this chapter, you'll learn how to choose good test cases and how to test your code using Python's unittest module.

Finally, what happens if your tests fail, revealing a bug? (See What's a Bug?, on page 4.) How can you tell where the problem is in your code? This chapter will also teach you how to find and fix bugs in your programs.

Why Do You Need to Test?

Quality assurance (*QA*) is the set of processes that ensure software is built to meet defined requirements and quality standards. Over the last half-century, programmers have learned that quality isn't magic pixie dust you can sprinkle on a program after it's written. Quality must be built in from the start, and software must be carefully designed, reviewed, and tested throughout its development.

The good news is that investing in QA makes you more productive overall. The later you find a bug, the more expensive it is to fix, so catching issues early reduces effort in the long run. The reason can be seen in Boehm's curve, shown at the top of the next page.

This idea—that early testing pays off—is why modern software development places a strong emphasis on testing, particularly automated testing.

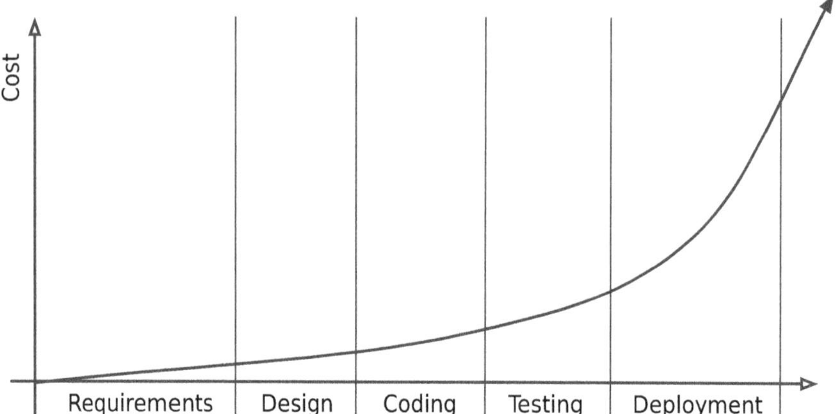

Finding and fixing bugs early reduces overall effort

Most good programmers today don't just test their software while writing it; they build their tests so that other people can rerun them months later and across a dozen time zones. Building tests takes a little more time upfront but makes programmers more productive overall, since every hour invested in preventing bugs saves two, three, or ten frustrating hours tracking bugs down.

In Testing Your Code Semiautomatically, on page 116, you learned how to run tests using Python's doctest module. As part of the function design recipe (see Designing New Functions: A Recipe, on page 49), you learned to include example calls on your function in the docstring. You can then use the module doctest to execute those function calls and have it compare the expected output with the actual output produced by that function call.

Case Study: Testing above_freezing

The first function that you'll test is above_freezing from Testing Your Code Semiautomatically, on page 116:

```
def above_freezing(celsius: float) -> bool:
    """Return True iff temperature celsius degrees is above freezing.

    >>> above_freezing(5.2)
    True
    >>> above_freezing(-2)
    False
    """

    return celsius > 0
```

In that section, you ran the example calls from the docstring using the doctest module. But you're missing a test—what happens if the temperature is zero? In the next section, you'll write another version of this function that behaves differently at zero, and we'll discuss how your current set of tests is incomplete.

Choosing Test Cases for above_freezing

Before writing your testing code, you must decide which test cases to use. Function above_freezing takes one argument, a number, so for each test case, you need to choose the value of that argument. There are billions of numbers to choose from, and you can't possibly test them all, so how do you decide which values to use? For above_freezing, there are two categories of numbers: values below freezing and values above freezing. Pick one value from each category to use in your test cases.

Looking at it another way, this particular function returns a Boolean, so you need at least two tests: one that causes the function to return True and another that causes it to return False. That's what you already did in the example function calls in the docstring.

In the docstring of above_freezing, the first example call uses 5.2 as the value of the argument, and since that value is above freezing, the function should return True. This test case represents temperatures above freezing. Choose that value from among the billions of possible positive floating-point values; any one of them would work just as well. For example, you could have used 100.6, 29, 357.32, or any other number greater than 0 to represent the "above freezing" category.

The second example call uses -2, which represents temperatures below freezing. As before, you could have used -16, -294.3, -56.97, or any other value less than 0 to represent the "below freezing" category, but let's chose to use -2. Again, your choice is arbitrary.

Are you missing any test case categories? Imagine that you had written your code using the >= operator instead of the > operator:

```
def above_freezing_v2(celsius: float) -> bool:
    """Return True iff temperature celsius degrees is above freezing.

    >>> above_freezing_v2(5.2)
    True
    >>> above_freezing_v2(-2)
    False
    """

    return celsius >= 0
```

Both versions of the function produce the expected results for the two docstring examples; however, the code differs from before, and it won't produce the same result in all cases. You neglected to test one category of inputs: temperatures at the freezing mark. Test cases like the one at the freezing mark are often referred to as *boundary cases*, as they lie on the boundary between two distinct possible behaviors of the function (in this case, between temperatures above freezing and those below freezing). Experience shows that boundary cases are much more likely to contain bugs than other cases, so it's always worth identifying them and testing them.

Sometimes there are multiple boundary cases. For example, if you had a function that determined the state of water—solid, liquid, or gas—then the two boundary cases would be the freezing point and the boiling point.

To summarize, the following table displays each category of inputs, the value you chose to represent that category, and the value you expect the function to return in that case:

Test Case Description	Argument Value	Expected Return Value
Temperatures above freezing	5.2	True
Temperatures below freezing	-2	False
Temperatures at freezing	0	False

Now that all categories of inputs are covered, you need to run the third test. Running the third test in the Python shell reveals that the value returned by above_freezing_v2 isn't False, which is what you expected:

```
>>> above_freezing(0)
False
>>> above_freezing_v2(0)
True
```

It took three test cases to cover all the categories of inputs for this function, but three isn't a magic number. The three tests had to be carefully chosen. If the three tests had all fallen into the same category (say, temperatures above freezing: 5, 70, and 302), they wouldn't have been sufficient. It's the quality of the tests that matters, not the quantity.

Testing above_freezing Using unittest

Once you decide which test cases are needed, you can use one of two approaches that you've learned about so far to test the code. The first one is to call the functions and read the results yourself to see if they match your expectations. The second is to run the functions from the docstring using the module doctest. The latter approach is preferable because the comparison of the actual value returned by the function to the expected value is done by the program, not by a human, making it faster and less prone to errors.

In this section, you'll study another of Python's modules, unittest. A *unit test* exercises just one isolated component of a program. As you did with doctest, you'll use the unittest module to test each function in your module independently of the others. This approach contrasts with *system testing*, which examines the system's behavior as a whole, just as its eventual users will.

Test your functions by writing subclasses of the unittest's TestCase class

In Inheritance, on page 297, you learned how to write classes that inherit code from others. Now, you'll write test classes that inherit from the unittest.TestCase class. Your first test class tests the function above_freezing:

```
import unittest
import temperature

class TestAboveFreezing(unittest.TestCase):
    """Tests for temperature.above_freezing."""

    def test_above_freezing_above(self):
        """Test a temperature that is above freezing."""

        expected = True
        actual = temperature.above_freezing(5.2)
        self.assertEqual(expected, actual,
            "The temperature is above freezing.")

    def test_above_freezing_below(self):
        """Test a temperature that is below freezing."""

        expected = False
        actual = temperature.above_freezing(-2)
        self.assertEqual(expected, actual,
            "The temperature is below freezing.")

    def test_above_freezing_at_zero(self):
        """Test a temperature that is at freezing."""

        expected = False
        actual = temperature.above_freezing(0)
        self.assertEqual(expected, actual,
            "The temperature is at the freezing mark.")

unittest.main()
```

The name of your new class is TestAboveFreezing, and it's saved in the file test_above_freezing.py. The class has three methods, one for each test case. Each test case follows this pattern:

```
expected = «the value you expect will be returned»
actual = «call on the function being tested»
self.assertEqual(expected, actual, "Error message in case of failure")
```

In each test method, there is a call to the assertEqual method, which has been inherited from the unittest.TestCase class. To *assert* something is to claim that it is true; here, you are asserting that the expected value and the actual value should be equal. Method assertEqual compares its first two arguments (which are the expected return value and the actual return value from calling the function being tested) to see whether they are equal. If they aren't equal, the third argument, a string, is displayed as part of the failure message.

At the bottom of the file, the call to the unittest.main method executes every method that begins with the name test.

When the program in test_above_freezing.py is executed, the following results are produced:

```
...
----------------------------------------------------------------------
Ran 3 tests in 0.000s

OK
```

The first line of output has three dots, one dot per test method. A dot indicates that a test was run successfully—that the test case *passed*.

The summary after the dashed line indicates that unittest found and ran three tests, completed the task in under a millisecond, and all results as successful (OK).

If your faulty function above_freezing_v2 were renamed above_freezing and your test_above_freezing unit test program was rerun, instead of three passes (as indicated by the three dots), there would be two passes and a failure:

```
.F.
======================================================================
FAIL: test_above_freezing_at_zero (__main__.TestAboveFreezing)
Test a temperature that is at freezing.
----------------------------------------------------------------------
Traceback (most recent call last):
  File "test_above_freezing.py", line 30, in test_above_freezing_at_zero
    "The temperature is at the freezing mark.")
AssertionError: False != True : The temperature is at the freezing mark.

----------------------------------------------------------------------
Ran 3 tests in 0.001s

FAILED (failures=1)
```

The F indicates that a test case *failed*. The error message indicates that the failure occurred in the method test_above_freezing_at_zero. The type of the error is AssertionError, which suggests that when you asserted the expected and actual values should be equal, you were incorrect.

The expression False != True comes from your call on assertEqual: variable expected was False, variable actual was True, and of course, those aren't equal. Additionally, the string that was passed as the third argument to assertEqual is part of that error message: "The temperature is at the freezing mark."

Notice that the three calls on assertEqual were placed in three separate methods. You could have put them all in the same method, but that method would have been considered a single test case. That is, when the module was run, you would see only one result; if any of the three calls on assertEqual failed, the entire test case would have failed. Only when all three passed would you see the coveted dot.

As a rule, each test case you design should be implemented in its own test method.

Now that you've seen both doctest and unittest, which should you use? We prefer unittest, for several reasons:

- For large test suites, it is nice to have the testing code in a separate file rather than in a very long docstring.
- Each test case can be in a separate method, so the tests are independent of each other. With doctest, the changes to objects made by one test persist for subsequent tests, so more care needs to be taken to properly set up the objects for each doctest test case to ensure they are independent.
- Because each test case is in a separate method, you can write a docstring that describes the test case tested so that other programmers understand how the test cases differ from each other.
- The third argument to assertEqual is a string that appears as part of the error message produced by a failed test, which helps provide a better description of the test case. With doctest, there is no straightforward way to customize the error messages.

Case Study: Testing running_sum

In Case Study: Testing above_freezing, on page 310, you tested a program that involved only immutable types. In this section, you'll learn how to test functions involving mutable types, like lists and dictionaries.

Suppose you need to write a function that modifies a list to contain a running sum of its values. For example, if the list is [1, 2, 3], the list should be mutated so that the first value is 1, the second value is the sum of the first two numbers, 1 + 2, and the third value is the sum of the first three numbers, 1 + 2 + 3, so you expect that the list [1, 2, 3] will be modified to be [1, 3, 6].

Following the function design recipe (see Designing New Functions: A Recipe, on page 49), here is a file named sums.py that contains the completed function with one (passing) example test:

```
def running_sum(L: list[float]) -> None:
    """Modify L so that it contains the running sums of its original items.

    >>> L = [4, 0, 2, -5, 0]
    >>> running_sum(L)
    >>> L
    [4, 4, 6, 1, 1]
    """

    for i in range(len(L)):
        L[i] += L[i - 1]
```

The structure of the test in the docstring is different from what you've seen before. Because there is no return statement, running_sum returns None. Writing a test that checks whether None is returned isn't enough to know whether the function call worked as expected. You also need to check whether the list passed to the function is mutated in the way you expect it to be. To do this, follow these steps:

- Create a variable that refers to a list.
- Call the function, passing that variable as an argument to it.
- Check whether the list that the variable refers to was mutated correctly.

Following those steps, you created a variable, L, that refers to the list [4, 0, 2, -5, 0], and then called the running_sum(L). You confirmed that L now refers to [4, 4, 6, 1, 1].

Although this test case passes, it doesn't guarantee that the function will always work—and, indeed, there is a bug. In the next section, you'll design a set of test cases to test this function and identify the bug more thoroughly.

Choosing Test Cases for running_sum

Function running_sum has one parameter, which is a list[float]. For your test cases, you need to decide both on the size of the list and the values of the items. For size, you should test with the empty list; a short list with one item, and another with two items (the shortest case where two numbers interact); and a longer list with several items.

When passed either the empty list or a list of length one, the modified list should be the same as the original.

When passed a two-number list, the first number should be unchanged and the second number should be changed to be the sum of the two original numbers.

For longer lists, things get more interesting. The values can be negative, positive, or zero, so the resulting values might be bigger than, the same as, or less than they were initially. Let's divide the test of longer lists into four cases: all negative values, all zero, all positive values, and a mix of negative, zero, and positive values. The resulting tests are presented in the table below:

Test Case Description	List Before	List After
Empty list	[]	[]
One-item list	[5]	[5]
Two-item list	[2, 5]	[2, 7]
Multiple items, all negative	[-1, -5, -3, -4]	[-1, -6, -9, -13]
Multiple items, all zero	[0, 0, 0, 0]	[0, 0, 0, 0]
Multiple items, all positive	[4, 2, 3, 6]	[4, 6, 9, 15]
Multiple items, mixed	[4, 0, 2, -5, 0]	[4, 4, 6, 1, 1]

Now that you've decided on your test cases, the next step is to implement them using unittest.

Testing running_sum Using unittest

To test running_sum, you'll use this subclass of unittest.TestCase named TestRunningSum:

```
import unittest

class TestRunningSum(unittest.TestCase):
    """Tests for sums.running_sum."""

    def test_running_sum_empty(self):
        """Test an empty list."""

        argument = []
        expected = []
        sums.running_sum(argument)
        self.assertEqual(expected, argument, "The list is empty.")

    def test_running_sum_one_item(self):
        """Test a one-item list."""

        argument = [5]
        expected = [5]
        sums.running_sum(argument)
        self.assertEqual(expected, argument, "The list contains one item.")
```

```
    def test_running_sum_two_items(self):
        """Test a two-item list."""

        argument = [2, 5]
        expected = [2, 7]
        sums.running_sum(argument)
        self.assertEqual(expected, argument, "The list contains two items.")

    def test_running_sum_multi_negative(self):
        """Test a list of negative values."""

        argument = [-1, -5, -3, -4]
        expected = [-1, -6, -9, -13]
        sums.running_sum(argument)
        self.assertEqual(expected, argument,
            "The list contains only negative values.")

    def test_running_sum_multi_zeros(self):
        """Test a list of zeros."""

        argument = [0, 0, 0, 0]
        expected = [0, 0, 0, 0]
        sums.running_sum(argument)
        self.assertEqual(expected, argument, "The list contains only zeros.")

    def test_running_sum_multi_positive(self):
        """Test a list of positive values."""

        argument = [4, 2, 3, 6]
        expected = [4, 6, 9, 15]
        sums.running_sum(argument)
        self.assertEqual(expected, argument,
            "The list contains only positive values.")

    def test_running_sum_multi_mix(self):
        """Test a list containing mixture of negative values, zeros and
        positive values."""

        argument = [4, 0, 2, -5, 0]
        expected = [4, 4, 6, 1, 1]
        sums.running_sum(argument)
        self.assertEqual(expected, argument,
            "The list contains a mixture of negative values, zeros and"
                         + "positive values.")

unittest.main()
```

Next, run the tests and see only three of them pass (the empty list, a list with several zeros, and a list with a mixture of negative values, zeros, and positive values):

```
..FF.FF
======================================================================
FAIL: test_running_sum_multi_negative (__main__.TestRunningSum.\
      test_running_sum_multi_negative)
Test a list of negative values.
----------------------------------------------------------------------
```

```
Traceback (most recent call last):
  File "testdebug/test_running_sum.py", line 37, in\
       test_running_sum_multi_negative
    self.assertEqual(expected, argument,
    ~~~~~~~~~~~~~~~~^^^^^^^^^^^^^^^^^^^^
        "The list contains only negative values.")
        ^^^^^^^^^^^^^^^^^^^^^^^^^^^^^^^^^^^^^^^^^^
AssertionError: Lists differ: [-1, -6, -9, -13] != [-5, -10, -13, -17]

First differing element 0:
-1
-5

- [-1, -6, -9, -13]
+ [-5, -10, -13, -17] : The list contains only negative values.

======================================================================
FAIL: test_running_sum_multi_positive (__main__.TestRunningSum.\
      test_running_sum_multi_positive)
Test a list of positive values.
----------------------------------------------------------------------
Traceback (most recent call last):
  File "testdebug/test_running_sum.py", line 54, in\
       test_running_sum_multi_positive
    self.assertEqual(expected, argument,
    ~~~~~~~~~~~~~~~~^^^^^^^^^^^^^^^^^^^^
        "The list contains only positive values.")
        ^^^^^^^^^^^^^^^^^^^^^^^^^^^^^^^^^^^^^^^^^^
AssertionError: Lists differ: [4, 6, 9, 15] != [10, 12, 15, 21]

First differing element 0:
4
10

- [4, 6, 9, 15]
+ [10, 12, 15, 21] : The list contains only positive values.

======================================================================
FAIL: test_running_sum_one_item (__main__.TestRunningSum.\
      test_running_sum_one_item)
Test a one-item list.
----------------------------------------------------------------------
Traceback (most recent call last):
  File "testdebug/test_running_sum.py", line 21, in \
       test_running_sum_one_item
    self.assertEqual(expected, argument, "The list contains one item.")
    ~~~~~~~~~~~~~~~~^^^^^^^^^^^^^^^^^^^^^^^^^^^^^^^^^^^^^^^^^^^^^^^^^^^
AssertionError: Lists differ: [5] != [10]

First differing element 0:
5
10

- [5]
```

```
+ [10] : The list contains one item.

======================================================================
FAIL: test_running_sum_two_items (__main__.TestRunningSum.\
      test_running_sum_two_items)
Test a two-item list.
----------------------------------------------------------------------
Traceback (most recent call last):
  File "testdebug/test_running_sum.py", line 29, in \
       test_running_sum_two_items
    self.assertEqual(expected, argument, "The list contains two items.")
    ~~~~~~~~~~~~~~~~^^^^^^^^^^^^^^^^^^^^^^^^^^^^^^^^^^^^^^^^^^^^^^^^^^^^
AssertionError: Lists differ: [2, 7] != [7, 12]

First differing element 0:
2
7

- [2, 7]
+ [7, 12] : The list contains two items.

----------------------------------------------------------------------
Ran 7 tests in 0.002s

FAILED (failures=4)
```

The four that failed were a list with one item, a list with two items, a list with all negative values, and a list with all positive values. To find the bug, let's focus on the simplest test case, the single-item list:

```
======================================================================
FAIL: test_running_sum_one_item (__main__.TestRunningSum.\
      test_running_sum_one_item)
Test a one-item list.
----------------------------------------------------------------------
Traceback (most recent call last):
  File "testdebug/test_running_sum.py", line 21, in \
       test_running_sum_one_item
    self.assertEqual(expected, argument, "The list contains one item.")
    ~~~~~~~~~~~~~~~~^^^^^^^^^^^^^^^^^^^^^^^^^^^^^^^^^^^^^^^^^^^^^^^^^^^
AssertionError: Lists differ: [5] != [10]

First differing element 0:
5
10

- [5]
+ [10] : The list contains one item.
```

For this test, the list argument was [5]. After the function call, you expected the list to be [5], but the list was mutated to become [10]. Looking back at the function definition of running_sum, when i refers to 0, the for loop body executes the statement L[0] = L[-1] + L[0]. L[-1] refers to the last element of the list—the 5—and L[0] refers to that same value. Oops! L[0] shouldn't be changed, since the running sum of L[0] is simply L[0].

Looking at the other three failing tests, the failure messages indicate that the first different elements are those at index 0. The same problem described for the single-item list also occurred in these test cases.

So, how did those other three tests pass? In those cases, L[-1] + L[0] produced the same value that L[0] originally referred to. For example, for the list containing a mixture of values, [4, 0, 2, -5, 0], the item at index -1 happened to be 0, so 0 + 4 evaluated to 4, and that matched L[0]'s original value. Interestingly, the simple single-item list test case revealed the problem, whereas the more complex test case involving a list of multiple values hid it!

To fix the problem, you can adjust the for loop header to start the running sum from index 1 rather than from index 0:

```
def running_sum(L: list[float]) -> None:
    """Modify L so that it contains the running sums of its original items.

    >>> L = [4, 0, 2, -5, 0]
    >>> running_sum(L)
    >>> L
    [4, 4, 6, 1, 1]
    """

    for i in range(1, len(L)):
        L[i] += L[i - 1]
```

When the tests are rerun, all seven tests pass:

```
.......
----------------------------------------------------------------------
Ran 7 tests in 0.000s

OK
```

In the next section, you'll see some general guidelines for choosing test cases.

Choosing Test Cases

Having a set of tests that pass is good; it shows that your code performs as expected in the situations you've considered. However, for any large project, there will be situations that *don't* occur to you. Tests can reveal the absence of many bugs, but they cannot confirm that a program is entirely correct.

It's essential to ensure you have good *test coverage*: your test cases should thoroughly cover critical situations. In this section, we provide some heuristics to help you develop a comprehensive set of test cases.

Now that you've seen two example sets of tests, we'll give you an overview of things to think about while you're developing tests for other functions. Some of them overlap, and not all will apply in every situation, but they are all worth thinking about while you are figuring out what to test.

- *Think about size.* When a test involves a collection such as a list, string, dictionary, or file, you need to do the following:
  - Test the empty collection.
  - Test a collection with one item in it.
  - Test a general case with several items.
  - Test the smallest interesting case, such as sorting a list containing two values.

  Consult the story A Software Tester Walks Into A Bar..., on page 322, for more inspiration!

- *Think about dichotomies.* A *dichotomy* is a contrast between two things. Examples of dichotomies are empty/full, even/odd, positive/negative, and alphabetic/nonalphabetic. If a function deals with two or more different categories or situations, make sure you test all of them.

- *Think about boundaries.* If a function behaves differently around a particular boundary or threshold, test exactly that boundary case.

- *Think about order.* If a function behaves differently when values appear in different orders, identify those orders and test each one of them. For the sorting example mentioned earlier, you'll want one test case where the items are in order and one where they are not.

When choosing test cases, you should consider size, dichotomies, boundary cases, and order

If you carefully plan your test cases according to these ideas and your code passes the tests, there's a very good chance that it will work for all other cases as well. Over time, you'll commit fewer and fewer errors. Whenever you find an error, figure out why it happened; as you mentally catalog them, you'll subsequently become more conscious of them. And that's the whole point of focusing on quality. The more you do it, the less likely it is for problems to arise.

A Software Tester Walks Into A Bar...

by: Random Guy on Reddit

A software tester walks into a bar. Runs into a bar. Crawls into a bar. Dances into a bar. Flies into a bar. Jumps into a bar. *And orders* a beer. 2 beers. 0 beers. 99999999 beers. A lizard in a beer glass. -1 beer. "Qwertyuiop" beers. *Testing complete.*

A real customer walks into the bar and asks where the bathroom is. The bar goes up in flames.

Hunting Bugs

Bugs are discovered through testing and program use, although the latter is what good testing can help avoid. Regardless of how they are found, tracking down and eliminating bugs in your programs is part of every programmer's life. This section introduces some techniques that can make debugging more efficient and give you more time to do the things you'd rather be doing.

Debugging a program is like diagnosing a medical condition. To find the cause, you start by working backward from the symptoms (or, in a program, its incorrect behavior). Then, you come up with a solution and test it to ensure it fixes the problem.

> To debug software, you have to know what it is supposed to do and be able to repeat the failure

At least, that's the right way to do it. Many beginners make the mistake of skipping the diagnosis stage and attempting to cure the program by making random changes. Renaming a variable or swapping the order in which two functions are defined might fix the program, but millions of such changes are possible. Trying them one after another in no particular order can be an inefficient waste of many, many hours.

Here are some rules for tracking down the cause of a problem:

1. *Make sure you know what the program is supposed to do.* Sometimes, this means doing the calculation by hand to verify the correct answer. Other times it means reading the documentation (or the assignment handout) carefully or writing a test.

2. *Repeat the failure.* You can debug things only when they go wrong, so find a test case that reliably causes the program to fail. Once you have one, try to find a simpler one; doing this often provides enough clues to allow you to fix the underlying problem.

3. *Divide and conquer.* Once you have a test that causes the program to fail, try to identify the first point at which something goes wrong. Examine the inputs to the function or block of code where the problem first becomes visible. If those inputs are not what you expected, look at how they were created, and so on.

4. *Change one thing at a time, for a reason.* Replacing random bits of code on the off-chance they might be responsible for your problem is unlikely to do much good. (After all, you got it wrong the first time...) Each time you make a change, rerun your test cases immediately.

5. *Keep records.* After working on a problem for an hour, you won't be able to remember the results of the tests you've run. Like any other scientist, you should keep records. Some programmers use a lab notebook; others keep a file open in an editor. Whatever works for you, make sure that when the time comes to seek help, you can tell your colleagues exactly what you've learned.

Bugs We've Put in Your Ear

In this chapter, you learned the following:

- Finding and fixing bugs early reduces overall effort.
- When choosing test cases, you should consider size, dichotomies, boundary cases, and order.
- To test your functions, you can write subclasses of unittest's TestCase class. The advantages of using unittest include keeping the testing code separate from the code being tested, allowing tests to be independent of one another, and enabling the documentation of each test case.
- To debug software, you have to know what it is supposed to do and be able to repeat the failure. Simplifying the conditions that make the program fail is an effective way to narrow down the set of possible causes.

Exercises

Here are some exercises for you to try on your own.

1. Your lab partner claims to have written a function that replaces each value in a list with twice the preceding value (and the first value with 0). For example, if the list [1, 2, 3] is passed as an argument, the function is supposed to turn it into [0, 2, 4]. Here's the code:

```
def double_preceding(values: list[float]) -> None:
    """Replace each item in the list with twice the value of the
    preceding item, and replace the first item with 0.

    >>> L = [1, 2, 3]
    >>> double_preceding(L)
    >>> L
    [0, 2, 4]
    """

    if values != []:
        temp = values[0]
        values[0] = 0
        for i in range(1, len(values)):
```

```
        values[i] = 2 * temp
        temp = values[i]
```

Although the example test passes, this code contains a bug. Write a set of unittest test cases to identify the bug. Explain what the bug in this function is, and fix it.

2. Your job is to come up with tests for a function called line_intersect, which takes two lines as input and returns their intersection. More specifically:

   - Lines are represented as pairs of distinct points, such as [[0.0,0.0], [1.0, 3.0]].
   - If the lines don't intersect, line_intersect returns None.
   - If the lines intersect at one point, line_intersect returns the point of intersection, such as [0.5, 0.75].
   - If the lines are coincident (that is, lie on top of each other), the function returns its first argument (that is, a line).

   What are the six most informative test cases you can think of? (That is, if you were allowed to run only six tests, which would tell you the most about whether the function was implemented correctly?)

   Write out the inputs and expected outputs of these six tests, and explain why you would choose them.

3. Using unittest, write four tests for a function called all_prefixes in a module called TestPrefixes.py that takes a string as its input and returns the set of all nonempty substrings that start with the first character. For example, given the string "lead" as input, all_prefixes would return the set {"l", "le", "lea", "lead"}.

4. Using unittest, write the five most informative tests you can think of for a function called is_sorted in a module called TestSorting.py that takes a list of integers as input and returns True if they are sorted in nondecreasing order (as opposed to strictly increasing order, because of the possibility of duplicate values), and False otherwise.

5. The following function is broken. The docstring describes what it's supposed to do:

```
def find_min_max(values: list):
    """Print the minimum and maximum value from values."""

    least = None
    largest = None
    for value in values:
```

```
        if value > largest:
            largest = value
        if value < least:
            least = value

    print(f'The minimum value is {least}')
    print(f'The maximum value is {largest}')
```

What does it really do? What line(s) do you need to change to fix it?

6. Suppose you have a dataset of survey results where respondents can optionally provide their age. Missing values are read in as None. Here is a function that computes the average age from that list:

```
def average(values: list[float]) -> float:
    """Return the average of the numbers in values.  Some items in values are
    None, and they are not counted toward the average.

    >>> average([20, 30])
    25.0
    >>> average([None, 20, 30])
    25.0
    """

    count = 0  # The number of values seen so far.
    total = 0  # The sum of the values seen so far.
    for value in values:
        if value is not None:
            total += value

        count += 1

    return total / count
```

Unfortunately, it does not work as expected:

```
>>> import test_average
>>> test_average.average([None, 30, 20])
16.666666666666668
```

a. Using unittest, write a set of tests for the function average in a module called test_average.py. The tests should cover cases involving lists with and without missing values.

b. Modify the function average so it correctly handles missing values and passes all of your tests.

CHAPTER 16

Mastering Iteration Tools

Python treats many data collections as ordered sequences. The most common are lists (mutable), tuples (immutable), and strings (immutable). You learned in Processing Items in a List, on page 153 how to iterate through a sequence item by item in a loop. Loops over sequences are so essential to modern idiomatic (or "Pythonic," as further explained in *Pythonic Programming [Zin21]*) programming that the language provides a family of iteration tools that hide low-level loop bookkeeping and help you write clear, efficient programs.

Being Pythonic

The adjective "Pythonic" refers to Python code that follows the language's idioms, philosophy, and design principles, rather than just using Python's syntax to write code that resembles another language. It emphasizes readability, simplicity, and the use of built-in features effectively to write clear, efficient, and maintainable programs.

Core Idioms

Consider the following task: given a list or tuple of words from a social media post, extract a list of hashtags (items that begin with #) and return them as "normal" words without the "hash." For example, the input `['#Mary', 'had', 'a', 'little', '#lamb']` should produce the output `['Mary', 'lamb']`.

You can build the result incrementally in a loop. Note: as tempting as it is to compare the first character of an item with `'#'` (in other words, `item[0] == '#'`), that's unsafe: some items on the list might be empty strings, and indexing would raise an error. The function `startswith` handles empty strings correctly.

```
data = ['#Mary', 'had', 'a', 'little', '#lamb']
result = [] # Initialize an empty list
```

```
for item in data:
    if item.startswith('#'): # Check the condition
        result.append(item[1:]) # Strip the leading '#' and append

print(result) # ['Mary', 'lamb']
```

This style is known as *imperative programming*: it works at a lower level of abstraction (Programs and Programming, on page 2) and emphasizes how a result is produced, often focusing on implementation details as much as on the outcome itself. By contrast, *comprehensions* are a higher-level, *declarative programming* construct: they describe the transformation from inputs to outputs and typically abstract away the underlying implementation.

Comprehensions

The hashtag extraction task is a special case of a common *Filter–Map–Reduce* pattern in data processing (you can read more about the pattern in *Functional Programming Patterns in Scala and Clojure [Bev13]*). The pattern typically involves three steps: filtering (selecting items that meet a condition), mapping (transforming each selected item), and reducing (aggregating results).

Design Patterns

A *design pattern* is a general, reusable solution to a recurring problem in software design. It is not a complete solution but a blueprint that must be adapted and implemented in code. Read more about design patterns in *Design Patterns: Elements of Reusable Object-Oriented Software [GHJV95]*.

Python supports the Filter–Map–Reduce pattern with three types of comprehensions: list, set, and dictionary. The two general *list comprehension* forms are:

```
[«expr» for «var» in «data»]
[«expr» for «var» in «data» if «cond»]
```

In the first form, expr is evaluated for every var in data, and the results are collected into a list. If data is ordered (a tuple, a list, or a string), the result preserves that order. As an example, consider computing the lengths of each item in data:

```
data = ['#Mary', 'had', 'a', 'little', '#lamb']

result = [len(item) for item in data]
print(result) # [5, 3, 1, 6, 5]
```

In the second form, expr is evaluated only for the items that satisfy the condition cond. All other items are filtered out. In the following example, the parts of the comprehension that correspond to the filter, map, and reduce actions are placed on separate lines for clarity.

```
result = [
    item[1:]                # map
    for item in data
    if item.startswith('#') # filter
]                           # reduce (implicit list construction)
print(result) # ['Mary', 'lamb']
```

How to "Comprehend" Comprehensions

Read a comprehension aloud by starting at the keyword for: "for every item in data, if item.startswith('#')..." ("filter").

Go back to the beginning and prepend "calculate" before the expression: "...calculate item[1:]" ("map").

Add "...and assemble the results" ("reduce").

This mirrors the execution order and often makes complex comprehensions easier to understand.

If you omit the if clause in a comprehension, there is no filtering; every item is included. The expression at the front can also be trivial (just the loop variable) or even a constant. You can use the latter form to count values that satisfy the condition:

```
result1 = [item for item in data if item.startswith('#')]
print(result1) # ['#Mary', '#lamb']
result2 = [1 for item in data if item.startswith('#')]
print(result2) # [1, 1]
print(len(result2)) # 2
```

Last but not least, if the expression is just a variable and there is no condition, the comprehension makes a copy of the original sequence, serving as an expensive equivalent of data[:].

```
result = [item for item in data]
print(result == data[:]) # True
```

A *set comprehension* uses curly braces {} instead of square brackets [] and produces a set. Think of it as essentially an application of set to a list comprehension:

```
result = {item[1:] for item in data if item.startswith('#')}
print(result) # {'Mary', 'lamb'}
```

Storing hashtags in a set dramatically improves the performance of membership tests because Python sets use hash tables internally (see Hash Tables and Why They Matter, on page 230).

```
present = 'Mary' in result
print(present) # True
```

Quite expectedly, a *dictionary comprehension* produces a dictionary. As such, for every dictionary item, it needs a key and a value, separated by a colon:

```
{«key_expr»: «value_expr» for «var» in «data»}
{«key_expr»: «value_expr» for «var» in «data» if «cond»}
```

Now, you can precompute a mapping from hashtags to their lengths. To facilitate lookups, convert the keys to lowercase (or any other standard form):

```
result = {item[1:].lower() : len(item[1:])
          for item in data if item.startswith('#')}
print(result) # {'mary': 4, 'lamb': 4}
```

If a hashtag happens in `data` more than once, the duplicates will be merged during the dictionary construction.

One limitation of comprehensions is that each produces only one output collection. If you want to split items into two groups (those that meet a condition and those that don't), you must have two comprehensions with complementary conditions, iterating over the same data twice.

```
hashtags  = {item[1:].lower() : len(item[1:])
             for item in data if     item.startswith('#')}
justwords = {item.lower() : len(item)
             for item in data if not item.startswith('#')}
```

This approach is inefficient, particularly for large datasets. A single-pass `for` loop is a better alternative:

```
hashtags = {}
justwords = {}
for item in data:
    if item.startswith('#'):
        hashtags[item[1:].lower()] = len(item[1:])
    else:
        justwords[item.lower()] = len(item)
```

Generators

Comprehensions create the entire output collection in memory, even if you need it piecewise, item by item.

Suppose you want the average length of the words in data. A straightforward approach involves building a list of lengths and then calculating the average:

```
lengths = [len(item) for item in data]
average = sum(lengths) / len(data)
print(average) # 4.0
```

Note that the list lengths exists only to be immediately reduced to a single number by summation. If data is large, so is lengths, even though the built-in function sum needs items one at a time, not all at once. Having a comprehension-like expression that produces items as needed would make this code more memory-efficient.

Enter generators. A *generator expression* yields ("generates") values on demand. It looks like a list comprehension, but it is enclosed in parentheses ():

```
lengths = (len(item) for item in data)
print(type(lengths)) # <class 'generator'>
```

Generator expressions yield items lazily (on demand), which saves memory for large datasets

The value returned by a generator expression is an object of class generator. A generator uses *lazy evaluation*: it doesn't return the results themselves but a "promise" to produce them later. That "promise" can be fulfilled explicitly by calling the built-in function next (beware that each call to next consumes the next generated value and may exhaust the generator before it is otherwise used):

```
>>> data = ['#Mary', 'had', 'a', 'little', '#lamb']
>>> lengths = (len(item) for item in data)
>>> next(lengths)
5
>>> next(lengths)
3
>>> next(lengths)
1
>>> next(lengths)
6
>>> next(lengths)
5
>>> next(lengths)
Traceback (most recent call last):
  File "<python-input-7>", line 1, in <module>
    next(lengths)
    ~~~~^^^^^^^^^
StopIteration
```

At the end of the sequence, the generator raises a StopIteration exception.

Alternatively, pass the generator to an aggregating function, such as sum:

```
average = sum(lengths) / len(data)
print(average) # 4.0
```

Generator expressions may be slightly slower than plain list comprehensions, and they can't be reused: they must be re-created to iterate again. However, for large datasets, they are often essential, making the difference between feasible and infeasible list processing.

Enumerating and Zipping

Python offers iterator-centric helpers beyond basic loops.

In addition to generator expressions and custom-made generators (see below), Python provides several other built-in objects that can be used as iterators. An *iterator* represents a stream of data and can be used wherever you would iterate over a sequence—for example, in a for loop or a list comprehension, just like a generator. In fact, all generators are iterators, but not all iterators are generators. For example, the built-in functions enumerate and zip return iterator (but not generator) objects of their respective classes.

The built-in function enumerate returns an object that "promises" to yield (index, value) tuples from the sequence data. The first tuple is (0, data[0]), then (1, data[1]), and so on, as illustrated in the following:

```
>>> enumerated = enumerate(data)
>>> next(enumerated)
(0, '#Mary')
>>> next(enumerated)
(1, 'had')
>>> next(enumerated)
(2, 'a')
>>> next(enumerated)
(3, 'little')
>>> next(enumerated)
(4, '#lamb')
>>> next(enumerated)
Traceback (most recent call last):
  File "<python-input-7>", line 1, in <module>
    next(enumerated)
    ~~~~^^^^^^^^
StopIteration
```

You can apply the list constructor, list, to the iterator to extract all tuples at once and build a list, but this transformation defies the purpose of on-demand generation.

```
result = list(enumerate(data))
print(result) # [(0, '#Mary'), (1, 'had'), (2, 'a'), (3, 'little'),
              #  (4, '#lamb')]
```

Instead, use enumerate objects directly in for loops, comprehensions, or generator expressions—for example, to print the words with human-adjusted (1-base) indices:

```
for i, word in enumerate(data):
    print(f'{i + 1}: {word}')
# 1: #Mary
# 2: had
# 3: a
# 4: little
# 5: #lamb
```

Built-ins enumerate and zip pair indexes with values or walk multiple sequences in lockstep

The built-in function zip is a powerful generalization of the enumerate function. While enumerate pairs a single sequence with consecutive integer numbers, zip returns an object that combines N sequences into a sequence of N-tuples: the first tuple is (data1[0], data2[0], ...), the second is (data1[1], data2[1], ...), and so on, stopping at the shortest input sequence. In particular, zipping a sequence with an appropriate range of numbers produced by the range function (see Generating Ranges of Numbers, on page 156) is equivalent to using enumerate:

```
indexes = range(len(data))
zipped = zip(indexes, data)
print(list(zipped)) # [(0, '#Mary'), (1, 'had'), (2, 'a'), (3, 'little'),
                    #  (4, '#lamb')]
```

Possibly the most efficient application of zip is managing parallel lists (see Processing Parallel Lists Using Indices, on page 160). Parallel lists store different attributes of the same items. For example, the item at index 0 of metals corresponds to the value at index 0 of weights. Such lists are easy to desynchronize if you insert or delete an item in one list but not in the others. Using zip allows you to iterate over the lists in lockstep, reducing the risk of mismatched data (compare this example with the code fragment on page 160):

```
>>> metals = ['Li', 'Na', 'K']
>>> weights = [6.941, 22.98976928, 39.0983]
>>> for name, weight in zip(metals, weights):
...     print(name, weight)
...
Li 6.941
Na 22.98976928
K 39.0983
```

It is still your responsibility to ensure that the original parallel constituents are correctly aligned.

Packing and Unpacking

Multiple assignment, introduced in Packing and Unpacking, on page 334, is a special case of *packing/unpacking*. Python packs multiple RHS expressions into a tuple and then unpacks the tuple into the LHS targets, provided that the number of items on both sides of the assignment match.

But what if it doesn't? For general unpacking, you can use a *starred target*, a variable prefixed with an asterisk *, which captures all items that don't fit into explicitly specified targets. A starred target can appear anywhere on the LHS (at the beginning, middle, or end). Here, the first character of 'Mary' is assigned to head, and the list of the remaining characters goes into tail:

```
>>> head, *tail = '#Mary'
>>> head
'#'
>>> tail
['M', 'a', 'r', 'y']
```

Conversely, in the following assignment, the last character is assigned to the explicit tail, the middle characters are assigned to rest, and the leading hashtag marker (#) is assigned to the conventional throwaway variable (_).

```
>>> _, *rest, tail = '#Mary'
>>> rest
['M', 'a', 'r']
>>> tail
'y'
```

Throw It Away!

Use the throwaway variable _ (a single underscore) when Python requires a variable, but you don't intend to use its value. The name has no special meaning; it's simply a widely used convention. Incidentally, Python's interactive interpreter also assigns the most recent result to _:

```
>>> 1 + 2
3
>>> print(_)
3
```

Unpacking can happen on the RHS as well. If a function requires several parameters, you can pass them as a starred sequence of the matching size. In this example, the function distance calculates the Euclidean distance between two points in the plane. The function requires two pairs of coordinates as four arguments. However, if you represent points as (x, y) tuples, you can pass them directly and let Python unpack each tuple into two arguments:

```
>>> from math import sqrt, pow
>>> def distance(x1: float, y1: float, x2: float, y2: float) -> float:
...     """Return the euclidean distance between the points `(x1,y1)`
...     and `(x2,y2)`.
...     """
...     return sqrt(pow(x1 - x2, 2) + pow(y1 - y2, 2))
...
>>> origin = (0, 0) # x1, y1
>>> other = (3, 4)  # x2, y2
>>> distance(origin[0], origin[1], other[0], other[1]) # Good
5.0
>>> distance(origin[0], origin[1], *other) # Better
5.0
>>> distance(*origin, *other) # Best
5.0
```

Adding an asterisk to a parameter name in a function definition makes that parameter a "catch-all" (starred) parameter. It packs all remaining positional arguments (but not keyword arguments) into a tuple. Using a starred parameter allows the function to accept a variable number of arguments. For example, the following function returns the count of its positional arguments:

```
>>> def count_args(*args: Any) -> int:
...     """ Return the number of positional arguments passed to the function.
...
...     >>> count_args(1, 2, 'hello', True, None)
...     5
...     """
...     return len(args)
...
>>> count_args(1, 2, 'hello', True, None)
5
```

Some arguments may be fixed (and required). They are bound to their respective parameters first; any leftover positional arguments are collected in the starred parameter:

```
>>> def count_opt(required: Any, *optional: list[Any]) -> int:
...     return len(optional)
...
>>> count_opt(1)
0
>>> count_opt(1, 2, 'hello', True, None)
4
```

A slightly more useful example computes the average of all its parameters:

```
>>> def average(*numbers: list[float]) -> float:
...     """Return the average of all positional arguments or 0 if
...     called without parameters.
...     """
...     if len(numbers) > 0:
...         return sum(numbers) / len(numbers)
...     return 0
...
>>> average(1,2,3,4)
2.5
>>> average()
0
```

Returning 0 (or None) as the "average" of an empty input is generally not recommended. When called without arguments, the function should raise an exception (for example, ValueError). See Chapter 17, Handling Exceptions, on page 351 for how to do this.

Functional Programming

Given the importance of sequence processing, Python includes comprehensive, higher-level support for sequence operations, which provides for functional tools and lambda functions.

Functional Tools

You have already seen how to apply an existing function (built-in or external) to items in a sequence using for loops, list comprehensions, and generator expressions. These constructs are explicitly iterative, emphasizing the "for each" mechanism: "*for each* item matching a condition, transform it, and add to the result."

Functional tools let you work with sequences as higher-level, abstract (opaque) objects.

The built-in function map creates an iterator that calls another function func using arguments taken from one or more sequences. The number of sequences must match the number of parameters expected by func, and at least one sequence is required.

A call to map(func, data0, data1, ...) is equivalent to the generator expression:

```
(func(*args) for args in zip(data0, data1, ...))
```

That is:

1. Combine the sequences with zip.
2. Iterate through the resulting sequence of tuples.
3. Call func on each unpacked tuple.

However, map is more concise and keeps the focus on the operation rather than on the implementation details. Like any iterator, the result of map can be expanded into a list or used in a for loop, a comprehension, or a generator expression.

In the next example, the built-in function len is applied to each word in the list. The resulting iterator is zipped with the original words to produce (word, length) tuples, which are then used to build a dictionary of words and their lengths:

```
>>> data = ['#Mary', 'had', 'a', 'little', '#lamb']

>>> lengths = map(len, data)
>>> dict(zip(data, lengths))
{'#Mary': 5, 'had': 3, 'a': 1, 'little': 6, '#lamb': 5}
```

The mapped function does not have to be built-in; it can be user-defined. Suppose you are automating grading for a six-question true/false quiz. The expected (correct) answers are in expected, and the submitted answers are in real. You can define a function that returns whether a question was answered correctly, and map it over the two lists:

```
>>> expected = [True, False, False, True, True,  False]
>>> real     = [True, True,  True,  True, False, False]
>>> def success(x: bool, y: bool) -> bool:
...     """Return True if and only if x equals y
...
...     >>> success(True, False)
...     False
...     """
...     return x == y
...
>>> all(map(success, expected, real))
False
```

The built-in functions all and any (the latter not used in the example) return True if all or any elements of the argument list are True.

The built-in function filter, another functional tool, returns an iterator that yields those items from the input sequence data for which the argument function func is True. Here is a Pythonic way to find the words that are not hashtags (the predicate method str.isalpha checks if the argument string consists only of alphabetic characters), and then measure their lengths by combining the power of filter and map:

```
>>> data = ['#Mary', 'had', 'a', 'little', '#lamb']
>>> words = filter(str.isalpha, data)
>>> list(words)
['had', 'a', 'little']
>>> words = filter(str.isalpha, data)
>>> list(map(len, words))
[3, 1, 6]
```

Note that filter expects a function that takes one argument. There is no standard one-argument predicate that tests whether the first character is a hashtag, so you can write your own and obtain the familiar result:

```
>>> def ishashtag(s: str) -> bool:
...     """Return True if and only if a string starts with a hashtag marker
...
...     >>> ishashtag('#lamb')
...     True
...     >>> ishashtag('')
...     False
...     """
...     return s.startswith('#')
...
>>> hashtags = filter(ishashtag, data)
>>> list(hashtags)
['#Mary', '#lamb']
```

While writing a one-line throwaway function may feel wasteful, the next section demonstrates a convenient way to handle such cases. Meanwhile, you can find more functional tools in the standard library module functools.

Lambda Functions

A *lambda function* is essentially a function without a name. As an additional restriction, it must consist of a single expression and have no statements. The value of the expression is returned implicitly. The general form of a lambda function is:

Lambda functions are useful for quick predicate checks and simple transformations

```
lambda «args»: «expr»
```

Here, args is a possibly empty comma-separated parameter list. Lambda functions are commonly passed as arguments to higher-order functions such as map, filter, and sorted.

Lambda Calculus and Amazon Lambda

Lambda functions are named after the *lambda calculus*, a formal system for describing computation introduced by Alonzo Church in the 1930s. In the lambda calculus, a lambda abstraction is written as (λx.M), where x is a parameter and M is the body (an expression). The exact reason Church chose the symbol λ is not definitively documented.

Amazon Web Services (AWS) Lambda is a *function-as-a-service* (FaaS) offering that runs your code on managed infrastructure in response to events. The name "Lambda" alludes to the lambda calculus and, by extension, *functional programming.*

Assigning a lambda function to a variable is usually pointless because it is equivalent to defining a "normal," named function. Lambdas work best for small, one-off tasks (for example, testing whether a word is a hashtag or stripping the first character) that you pass to functional tools and then discard:

```
>>> hashtags = filter(
... lambda w: w.startswith('#'), # A predicate
... data)
>>> clean_hashtags = map(
... lambda w: w[1:], # A transformer
... hashtags)
>>> list(clean_hashtags)
['Mary', 'lamb']
```

Writing Your Own Generators

Python functions are typically *stateless*: unless they read or write *global* variables (defined outside functions), they do not "remember" previous calls. Once a function returns, its local variables go out of scope (see Using Local Variables for Temporary Storage, on page 39) and their values are discarded. In the absence of global variables (whose use is strongly discouraged, because they introduce intricate, hard-to-track relationships between code fragments), a function's result depends only on the arguments passed to the function.

Some programming languages (for example, C and C++) solve the problem of preserving function state across calls by declaring *static* variables. Generators are a common Pythonic way to maintain iteration state.

A *generator function* is a function that contains at least one yield statement (introduced later in this section). Calling a generator function doesn't run the body immediately; instead, a call returns a generator object. The generator remembers its execution state (including all local variables). When the generator yields a value (for example, via next or a for loop), it suspends execution and returns that value to the caller. On the next request, the generator resumes immediately after the last yield and continues until the next yield (or until it finishes by executing the return statement).

To understand generator functions better, let's write one that implements a down-counter: it yields a sequence of decreasing positive integer numbers starting from an initial value. The generator function make_down_counter initializes an internal state variable value, then yields it, and decrements it, until value reaches zero. Once exhausted, the generator must be reinitialized. Since all iterators are also generators, you can choose either Iterator or Generator type hint to annotate the function.

```
>>> from collections.abc import Iterator
>>> def make_down_counter(initial: int) -> Iterator[int]:
...     """ Yield a countdown from `initial` down to 1 (inclusive).
...
...     The argument is converted to an integer using `int(initial)`.
...     If the resulting value is <= 0, the generator yields nothing.
...
...     >>> list(make_down_counter(3))
...      [3, 2, 1]
...     """
...
...     value = initial
...     while value > 0:
...         yield value
...         value -= 1
...     return
...
>>> down_counter = make_down_counter(3)
>>> next(down_counter)
3
>>> next(down_counter)
2
>>> next(down_counter)
1
>>> next(down_counter)
Traceback (most recent call last):
  File "<python-input-6>", line 1, in <module>
    next(down_counter)
    ~~~~^^^^^^^^^^^^^^
StopIteration
```

You can use the generator either explicitly (as above) or in a loop:

```
>>> down_counter = make_down_counter(3)
>>> for val in down_counter:
...     print(val)
...
```

```
3
2
1
```

A *pseudo-random number generator* (PRNG) is a practical application of generators. A PRNG is a special case of random number generators: sources of random (that is, unpredictable) numbers. Random numbers are extensively used in cryptography, algorithm design, and computer simulations. Unfortunately, truly unpredictable randomness is difficult to obtain, so in many cases, pseudo-random numbers—deterministic yet hard to predict—are acceptable.

No Pseudo in Crypto!

Never use pseudo-random numbers for cryptography or computer and Internet security tasks because they are deterministic. For example, if a web app uses a PRNG for password-reset tokens, an attacker who can observe a few tokens may predict the next token and take over accounts.

Python provides the `random` module, which is based on the pseudo-random *Mersenne Twister algorithm.*[1] Among other functions, the module includes `randint` and `random` for generating integer and floating-point numbers in the ranges `[a, b]` and `[0, 1)`, respectively:

```
>>> import random
>>> random.randint(0,55)
35
>>> random.randint(0,55)
48
>>> random.randint(0,55)
39
>>> random.random()
0.38402282929624554
>>> random.random()
0.0033172813689996694
>>> random.random()
0.7797058697769986
```

As an alternative, let's write a *linear congruential generator* (LCG), one of the oldest and simplest PRNG algorithms. The algorithm starts with a *seed number* x_0 and computes the next value using a piecewise-linear function: $x_{n+1} = (A * x_n + C) \% M$. The numbers `A`, `C`, and `M` are fixed parameters; their choice is outside this book's scope. The implementation of the generator function is on the next page.

1. https://en.wikipedia.org/wiki/Mersenne_Twister

```
from collections.abc import Iterator
def make_lcg(seed: int) -> Iterator[int]:
    """ Yield a pseudo random number from 0 to M - 1 (inclusive).

    >>> next(make_lcg(0))
    52
    """

    # Define generator parameters
    A, C, M = 83, 52, 101

    # Initialize the initial state (cannot be 24)
    if seed != 24:
        state = seed
    else:
        state = seed + 1

    # Yield PRNs
    while True:
        state = (A * state + C) % M
        yield state
```

Note that the choice of seed is not completely unrestricted: depending on A, C, and M, some seeds can lead to a degenerate sequence (producing the same value repeatedly).

You can test the generator with different seeds inferred from the current time in seconds (computed by time.time from the namesake module):

```
import time

lcg = make_lcg(int(time.time()))
print(next(lcg)) # 96
print(next(lcg)) # 41
print(next(lcg)) # 21
print(next(lcg)) # 78
print(next(lcg)) # 62
```

The results look random enough!

Built-In and Standard Library Helpers

Python's built-in sequence tools don't cover every need. In this section, you'll meet additional iteration utilities: the itertools module and the built-in functions sorted (first seen in Operations on Lists, on page 139) and reversed (first seen in The Readlines Technique, on page 184). The function reversed and most of the functions in itertools return iterators that you can use in for loops, list comprehensions, and generator expressions, or pass to other functions that consume sequences. The function sorted returns a list, not an iterator.

Iterating with itertools

The `itertools` module provides more than a dozen functions for iterating over one or more input sequences. We will apply several of them: `combinations`, `chain`, and `takewhile`—to analyze text and perform simple *text summarization*. You will also encounter a few functions from the `operator` and `collections` modules.

> You can prototype simple text "summaries" by chaining `itertools` tools

While text summarization is generally a hard problem, it can be approximated by identifying the most frequently co-occurring pairs of words. The first step toward counting word pairs is *tokenization*: split the text into sentences (*sentence tokenization*) and sentences into words, also known as *tokens* (*word tokenization*). Both tasks are challenging for natural languages such as English, Russian, Chinese, and Arabic. For more accurate results, use specialized libraries such as `nltk` (*Natural Language Toolkit*).[2]

As a simple first step toward sentence tokenization, convert the text to lowercase to make counting case-insensitive, replace common sentence terminators (for example, ? and !) with periods, and split on periods.

```
text = '''This book is about Python programming. Python is a popular and
efficient programming language. A Python programmer is thoughtful and
pragmatic. Be like a Python programmer.'''
sentences = text.lower().replace('?', '.').replace('!', '.').split('.')
print(sentences)
# ['this book is about python programming',
# ' python is a popular and\nefficient programming language',
# ' a python programmer is thoughtful and\npragmatic',
# ' be like a python programmer']
```

Split each sentence on whitespace and remove *stopwords*: frequently occurring determiners, pronouns, prepositions, modal verbs, and other parts of speech that typically don't convey objects, actions, or properties. Now, you have a list of streams of tokens (filter iterators), one stream per sentence. Do not try to inspect the streams (for example, by converting them to lists): doing so will consume them and cause all further variables to be empty.

```
stops = {'and', 'the', 'in', 'this', "don't", 'was', 'that', 'to', 'a',
         'its', 'as', 'had', 'about', 'is', 'be'}
tokens = [filter(lambda word: word not in stops, s.split())
          for s in sentences]
print(tokens)
# [<filter object at 0x7f34eb4862c0>, <filter object at 0x7f34eb485a50>,
#  <filter object at 0x7f34eb4860b0>, <filter object at 0x7f34eb486170>,
#  <filter object at 0x7f34eb4861a0>]
```

---

2. https://www.nltk.org

Next, generate pairs from each token stream. The function itertools.combination yields *combinations*: n-element tuples of items from data without replacement. For pairs, pass 2 as the second argument. Then the itertools.chain.from_iterable function flattens the sequence of pair sequences into a single sequence, all_pairs, ready for counting.

```
from itertools import combinations, chain, takewhile

pairs = map(lambda words: combinations(words, 2), tokens)
all_pairs = chain.from_iterable(pairs)
print(all_pairs)
# <itertools.chain object at 0x7f9fb6b119f0>
```

all_pairs is yet another stream (iterator). Inspecting it will consume it!

One way to count pairs is to build a dictionary mapping each pair to its count (as explained in Dictionary Example, on page 226). A better way is to use the Counter class from the collections module. The latter solution based on reuse is better: it already exists, it is correct, and it is more efficient than the dictionary-based one. A Counter is a subclass of dict that stores items as keys and their counts as values. The Counter.most_common method returns all items sorted by decreasing count.

```
from collections import Counter

counts = Counter(all_pairs)
print(counts)
# Counter({('python', 'programming'): 2, ('python', 'programmer'): 2,
# ('book', 'python'): 1, ('book', 'programming'): 1, ('python', 'popular'): 1,
# ('python', 'efficient'): 1, ('python', 'language'): 1,
# ('popular', 'efficient'): 1, ('popular', 'programming'): 1,
# ('popular', 'language'): 1, ('efficient', 'programming'): 1,
# ('efficient', 'language'): 1, ('programming', 'language'): 1,
# ('python', 'thoughtful'): 1, ('python', 'pragmatic'): 1,
# ('programmer', 'thoughtful'): 1, ('programmer', 'pragmatic'): 1,
# ('thoughtful', 'pragmatic'): 1, ('like', 'python'): 1,
# ('like', 'programmer'): 1})
items = counts.most_common()
print(items)
# [(('python', 'programming'), 2), (('python', 'programmer'), 2),
#  (('book', 'python'), 1), (('book', 'programming'), 1),
#  (('python', 'popular'), 1), (('python', 'efficient'), 1),
#  (('python', 'language'), 1), (('popular', 'efficient'), 1),
#  (('popular', 'programming'), 1), (('popular', 'language'), 1),
#  (('efficient', 'programming'), 1), (('efficient', 'language'), 1),
#  (('programming', 'language'), 1), (('python', 'thoughtful'), 1),
#  (('python', 'pragmatic'), 1), (('programmer', 'thoughtful'), 1),
#  (('programmer', 'pragmatic'), 1), (('thoughtful', 'pragmatic'), 1),
#  (('like', 'python'), 1), (('like', 'programmer'), 1)]
```

The itertools.takewhile function yields items from data until the Boolean predicate function becomes false. In the example below, the predicate keeps items whose count (the second element of each (words, count) pair) is greater than 1—in other words, pairs that occurred at least twice in the original text. The result is yet another stream.

```
popular = takewhile(lambda item: item[1] > 1, items)
print(popular)
# <itertools.takewhile object at 0x7f3f941a4800>
```

Finally, let's display the popular tuples more humanely by dropping the counts. The itemgetter function from the module operator is a *higher-order function*: it returns another nameless function that, in turn, yields the nth element from its input:

```
>>> zerogetter = itemgetter(0)
>>> print(zerogetter)
operator.itemgetter(0)
>>> zerogetter(['zero', 'one', 'two'])
'one'
```

Applying itemgetter(0) to each "popular" tuple yields just the word pairs: the "summary" of the text:

```
from operator import itemgetter

print(list(map(itemgetter(0), popular)))
# [('python', 'programming'), ('python', 'programmer')]
```

Trying to write a solution in a single statement, a *one-liner*, is a fun challenge —and a great way to grow your Python skills. One-liners start from the input data (usually a sequence) and progressively apply functions, generator expressions, and comprehensions to build new sequences until the desired result is produced. One-liners are often "write-only": powerful and fun to write, but harder to read and modify. One-liners often lead to *software maintenance* problems in the future. Use them responsibly: when in doubt, don't. Here's the text-summarization one-liner corresponding to the code above:

```
print(list(map(itemgetter(0),
               takewhile(lambda item: item[1] > 1,
                         Counter(chain.from_iterable(
                             map(lambda words: combinations(words, 2),
                                 (filter(lambda word: word not in stops,
                                         s.split()) for s in
                                  text.lower().split('.')))))
                    .most_common()))))
# [('python', 'programming'), ('python', 'programmer')]
```

Other itertools functions worth exploring include permutations, product, groupby, and cycle. We leave them for you to discover.

Advanced Sorting

Sorting and reversing sequences are frequently occurring operations. They are supported by the built-in functions sorted and reversed.

The reversed function flips the existing order, while sorted orders by value

The function reversed yields the items in data in reversed order, from last to first. It does not sort the items:

```
>>> items = [1, 'a', None, True]
>>> reversed_items = reversed(items)
>>> type(reversed_items)
<class 'list_reverseiterator'>
>>> list(reversed_items)
[True, None, 'a', 1]
```

If you want to sort a sequence by value (from smallest to largest, or in reverse), you need the sorted function:

```
>>> items_sortable = [1, -4, float('-inf'), 3.14159, float('inf'), 5]
>>> sorted(items_sortable)
[-inf, -4, 1, 3.14159, 5, inf]
>>> sorted(items_sortable, reverse=True)
[inf, 5, 3.14159, 1, -4, -inf]
```

Notice how the function correctly handles float('inf') (positive infinity) and float('-inf') (negative infinity). These values are defined by the *IEEE 754* standard for floating-point numbers. Interestingly, division by infinity is allowed (for example, 1.0/float('inf') yields 0.0), but division by 0 raises a ZeroDivisionError exception, making Python's native number system mathematically inconsistent.

A Number That's Not

The IEEE 754 floating-point number standard defines a special value that is not even a number and is appropriately called nan (float('nan'), "not-a-number"). The result of any arithmetical operation that involves nan is nan. The result of any relational expression that involves nan is False, except operator !=: float('nan') != x is True for any x. This makes nan the only object that is and is not equal to itself!

You can use nan as a placeholder for a number that must be provided but is not. Such "ghost" numbers are referred to as *missing values* and are common in real-world data processing. If you want to know whether a data item x is a "ghost," use the predicate function math.isnan(x) which returns True if and only if x is a nan.

What about sorting heterogeneous sequences? In Python 3, order comparisons between unrelated types are not supported:

```
>>> items = [1, 'a', None, True]
>>> sorted(items)
Traceback (most recent call last):
  File "<python-input-1>", line 1, in <module>
    sorted(items)
    ~~~~~~^^^^^^^
TypeError: '<' not supported between instances of 'str' and 'int'
>>> sorted(items, reverse=True)
Traceback (most recent call last):
  File "<python-input-2>", line 1, in <module>
    sorted(items, reverse=True)
    ~~~~~~^^^^^^^^^^^^^^^^^^^^^
TypeError: '<' not supported between instances of 'NoneType' and 'bool'
```

The function sorted relies on the < operator to compare elements. The operator can compare "apples to apples" (for example, strings to strings) and "oranges to oranges" (for example, numbers to numbers), but not "apples to oranges" (for example, strings to numbers). If you must sort fruit salad, provide your own key function. The key function maps each element to a comparable value (for example, a number or a string). In the following examples, items are compared by their identities (see Identities: How Python Keeps Track of Values, on page 35) or by their printable string representations:

```
>>> sorted(items, key=lambda a: id(a))
[True, None, 1, 'a']
>>> sorted(items, key=lambda a: str(a))
[1, None, True, 'a']
```

The first result appears arbitrary; the second is more interpretable. If you need a more meaningful ordering, provide an appropriate key function!

Let's Reiterate

In this chapter, you learned the following:

- Generator expressions yield items lazily (on demand), which saves memory for large datasets; pass them directly to aggregators like sum rather than materializing intermediate lists.
- Python offers iterator-centric helpers beyond basic loops. Most itertools functions and reversed return iterators you can feed into for loops, comprehensions, or other consumers, while sorted returns a list.

- Built-ins like enumerate and zip are iterators that pair indexes with values or walk multiple sequences in lockstep, handy for labeled iteration and managing parallel lists.
- Lambda functions passed to map and filter are useful for quick predicate checks (for example, "starts with #") and simple transformations (for example, "strip the first char").
- You can prototype simple text "summaries" by chaining itertools tools: tokenize, make word-pairs with combinations, flatten with chain.from_iterable, count with Counter.most_common, and keep frequent pairs with takewhile.
- For ordering, reversed just flips the existing order, while sorted actually orders by value. Python won't sort heterogeneous types unless you supply a key function.

Exercises

Here are some exercises for you to try on your own.

1. Given a list of string tokens data, produce a single output string that reverses the order of tokens in the list, and reverses the characters within each token. You may use any iteration tools you like. Example:

```
data = ['#Mary', 'had', 'a', 'little', '#lamb']
# You code should produce 'bmal# elttil a dah yraM#'
```

2. Solve the previous problem, but if a token begins with #, keep the # at the start of that token in the final result. In other words, reverse each token's characters except a leading #, which should remain in front. Example result:

```
data = ['#Mary', 'had', 'a', 'little', '#lamb']
# You code should produce '#bmal elttil a dah #yraM'
```

3. Write a single expression that uses the dir function (see Module __builtins__, on page 110), the filter function, and a custom lambda to count the number of functions defined in the module itertools whose names *do not* start with an underscore _.

4. You are given a list heights that contains numbers and positive infinities. The float('inf') entries indicate measurements that were too large to be recorded. Example:

```
heights = [1, 2.2, 7, float('inf'), 1.1, 2, float('inf')]
```

Write a code fragment that returns a new list in which every `float('inf')` is replaced with the largest finite value found in the original list. For the example above, the result should be:

```
[1, 2.2, 7, 7, 1.1, 2, 7]
```

Use the function `math.isfinite` to test whether a value is finite. Solve the problem two ways: using a list comprehension, and using the `map`/`filter` tools. Assume the list contains at least one finite value.

5. Implement the generator function `my_enumerate` that mimics `enumerate` without calling `enumerate`. The function should yield `(index, item)` pairs, with the index starting at `0` and increasing by 1 for each element. Use code on page 333 as a guide. Assume `data` is a sequence that supports `len`. Test the function.

6. Write a function `most_frequent_three` that returns the three most frequent characters in `text`, treating letters case-insensitively. Ignore whitespace characters (spaces, tabs, newlines); to detect them, use `str.isspace`. Count all other characters (letters, digits, punctuation). Assume that `text` contains at least three distinct non-whitespace characters. Test your function on a substantial text sample (for example, a Shakespeare play).[3]

7. Write a function `swap_two` that uses multiple assignment to swap the first two elements of the list `l`. Do not use a temporary variable. Assume the list has at least two elements.

8. An RGB ("red–green–blue") color is written as a hash sign (#) followed by six characters. Think of them as three two-character codes placed back-to-back: the first pair controls the amount of red, the second pair controls the amount of green, and the third pair controls the amount of blue. Each pair encodes an integer intensity from 0 (none of that color) to 255 (maximum intensity). In Python, you can convert each pair to an integer with `int(pair, 16)`. For example, the color *#DF2073* (pink) has `int('DF', 16)` of red (=223), `int('20', 16)` of green (=32), and `int('73', 16)` of blue (=115).

   Assume the brightness of a color is a weighted sum of the three component intensities: `(3 * R + 10 * G + B) / 14`.[4] Write a function `brightness` that returns the brightness of a well-formed color string `#RRGGBB`. Use this function as a key to sort a list of colors from darkest to brightest, as shown in the following example:

3. https://shakespeare.mit.edu/
4. https://stackoverflow.com/a/79404122/4492932

```
>>> colors = ['#4526FA', '#0000FF', '#E34530']
>>> sorted(colors, key=brightness)
['#0000FF', '#4526FA', '#E34530']
```

9. Solve the previous problem without defining a named function by using a lambda.

10. Implement a generator function `signals` that yields a sequence of `n` traffic-light signals cycling in this order: "red", "green", and "amber", then repeats as needed. For example, `signals(5)` should yield "red", "green", "amber", "red", "green." Use a `for` loop to demonstrate the correctness of the function.

CHAPTER 17

Handling Exceptions

When it comes to programming styles, we often contrast *pessimists* and *optimists*. Optimists believe that potential errors in program behavior can be avoided by carefully checking preconditions (see Dealing with Situations That Your Code Doesn't Handle, on page 63).

- Don't divide by zero! (Check the divisor.)
- Don't read a nonexistent file! (Check if the file exists.)
- Don't access the 10th character in a 5-character string! (Check the string length.)
- Don't append to a tuple! (Check if the target is mutable.)

> Errors are inevitable. Robust programs anticipate and handle them gracefully

This strategy generally works—until the preconditions become too expensive or impossible to verify. That's when the pessimists step in. They assume that errors are inevitable, so let them happen and deal with them afterward.

Fortunately, violations of preconditions are exceptional situations. When one rarely occurs, Python *raises an exception*: it alerts the program to the specific problem and invokes a special block of code known as an *exception handler*, designed to keep the situation under control.

Handling exceptions is essential for writing robust programs that don't crash unexpectedly and can gracefully handle real-world input and edge cases. Let's take a closer look at how Python manages exceptions.

Core Idioms

Python handles exceptions using the `try/except` statement. Its general form looks like this:

```
try:
    «try_block»
except «optional_error_list»:
    «except_block»
else:
    «optional_else_block»
finally:
    «optional_finally_block»
```

The try block is a sequence of arbitrary statements (and may even include other exception-handling statements). As a *pessimist*, you assume that something inside this block or something it calls might raise an exception. Instead of executing the block blindly, you "try" to execute it.

- If the try block runs successfully, control passes to the optional_else block (if present), or skips to after the try statement (otherwise).
- If it fails, control passes to the except block. This block is not optional, even if it's empty. In that case, it may contain only a no-op pass statement, which does nothing and serves as a placeholder, much like the _ variable described in the sidebar on page 334.

In the following example, we tried to print a nonexistent variable named ghosts and got an error:

```
>>> print(ghosts, end='')
Traceback (most recent call last):
  File "<python-input-0>", line 1, in <module>
    print(ghosts, end='')
          ^^^^^^
NameError: name 'ghosts' is not defined
```

We then wrapped the statement in a try/except block, raising the error from a *syntax* problem to a *philosophical* one:

```
>> try:
...     print(ghosts, end='')
... except:
...     print("Ghosts aren't real") # This!
... else:
...     print(' and goblins')
...
Ghosts aren't real
```

Encouraged, we defined the missing variable and successfully produced the first line of a Halloween sing-along song for children:

```
>>> ghosts = 'Ghosts'
>>> try:
...     print(ghosts, end='')
```

```
... except:
...     print("Ghosts aren't real")
... else:
...     print(' and goblins') # This!
...
Ghosts and goblins
```

Trying to access an undefined variable is uncommon in Python. A more realistic example involves trying to read from a file that does not exist. Suppose data.txt is missing:

```
>>> try:
...     with open('data.txt') as infile:
...         data = infile.read()
... except:
...     print("Failed to read data from 'data.txt'")
...
Failed to read data from 'data.txt'
```

The example above illustrates the power of the pessimistic approach. You could try to check whether the file exists, whether it's readable, and whether the call to read succeeds, but none of that really matters. What you ultimately care about is whether the variable data was successfully initialized. The try/except construct answers exactly that question, letting your code stay focused on what matters.

Keep "try" blocks small and "except" blocks specific. Separate problem-solving from error handling

As a rule of thumb, you should wrap code in a try/except block when you expect it might fail and want to separate problem-solving from error handling. Because error handling is specific to the code inside try, it is important to keep the try block compact; ideally, it should raise only one type of exception (for example, just file-related errors). A common mistake is to wrap your entire program in a single try/except. This moves all error handling, even syntax error handling, into the except block, and if it is not present, suppresses all errors by sweeping them under the rug until you realize your program simply doesn't work.

Keep Your Exception Handlers Specific

Do not wrap your entire program in a single try/except block! Doing so will hide all errors, even syntax errors, and make a broken program appear to work correctly.

An even better approach is to avoid generic, "catch-it-all" exception handlers and associate different handlers with different types of exceptions by specifying the optional_error_list, a comma-separated list of exception types. Inheritance (Writing a Method in Class Book, on page 286) plays a factor here. For example,

ArithmeticError exception handler will catch ZeroDivisionError because a ZeroDivisionError is a subclass of ArithmeticError and every division by zero is also an arithmetic error.

In the following example, the try/except statement has three clauses, each monitoring the progress of the operation and responding to a different condition. Here, we are interested only in the 11th character of the file, illustrating handling an IndexError (this and the following examples intentionally do not use a with block):

```
>>> try:
...     infile = open('data.txt')
...     data = infile.read()[10]
... except FileNotFoundError:
...     print('File data.txt does not exist')
... except PermissionError:
...     print('File data.txt is not readable')
... except IndexError:
...     print('File data.txt is too short')
...
File data.txt is too short
```

You'll see more built-in exception types in Common Built-in Exceptions, on page 357.

To construct a multiclause handler, you need to examine your code carefully, identify every possible exceptional condition, and decide if and how you want to handle it. The task can feel daunting, but the payoff is worth it: a robust, fault-tolerant program that can handle unexpected situations gracefully instead of crashing. Remember that at most one except clause is invoked per execution of the try block. The first matching handler would be called and the rest would be skipped.

The last optional block, optional_finally, if present, is executed after all other blocks, regardless of whether the operation succeeded or failed, even if one of the preceding blocks contains a return or raise (explained later in Raising and Chaining Exceptions, on page 358) statement. You may use finally to clean up resources acquired in the try block—for example, to close files or network connections, as shown below:

A "finally" block ensures that your program always cleans up resources, no matter what happens

```
>>> infile = None
>>> try:
...     infile = open('data.txt'):
...     data = infile.read()[10]
... except FileNotFoundError:
...     print('File data.txt does not exist')
```

```
... except PermissionError:
...     print('File data.txt is not readable')
... except IndexError:
...     print('File data.txt is too short')
... finally: # Clean up
...     if infile:
...         infile.close()
...
File data.txt is too short
>>> infile.closed
True
```

A with block is preferred alternative to try/finally for working with open files. It guarantees that the file is closed when the block ends, even if an exception occurs. A hand-written finally block can fail to close the file if it raises another exception before the close call runs.

Accessing Exception Details

A *traceback*, also known as a *stack trace*, is a report generated by the Python interpreter when an *unhandled* exception occurs in a program. From a debugging perspective, a traceback is a treasure trove of information: it provides a detailed account of the sequence of function calls that led to the error, helping you pinpoint its source.

In the following example, we define a function average that computes the average of a numerical sequence seq, and a helper function divide that, for no particular reason, divides a by b. We test average on an empty sequence, which predictably raises a ZeroDivisionError:

```
>>> from typing import Sequence
>>> def divide(a: float, b: float) -> float:
...     """Return the ratio of the numbers `a` and `b`. """
...     return a / b
...
>>> def average(seq: Sequence[float]) -> float:
...     """Return the average of the items in the sequence. """
...     return divide(sum(seq), len(seq))
...
>>> avg = average([])
Traceback (most recent call last):
  File "<python-input-2>", line 1, in <module>
    average([])
    ~~~~~~~^^^^
  File "<python-input-1>", line 2, in average
    return divide(sum(seq), len(seq))
  File "<python-input-0>", line 2, in divide
    return a / b
```

```
          ~~^~~
ZeroDivisionError: division by zero
```

Unlike the previous examples, the exception here is not raised by the call to average, but by the deeper call to divide, as clearly indicated by the traceback.

For each function call, the traceback shows the file name where the function is defined, the function name, and the code snippet that caused the exception (with the line number). Since this code was entered interactively, the file names (<python-input-N>) are phony, and the top-level function <module> refers to the code executed at the command line. Here's the previous traceback, parsed out:

File	Line	Function	Code Snippet
<python-input-2>	1	<module>	average([])
<python-input-1>	2	average	return divide(sum(seq), len(seq))
<python-input-0>	2	divide	return a / b

Given the traceback, you can follow the history of the program's execution from the line where the top-level function was called back through the chain of function calls to the point where the exception was raised (hence the name *traceback*).

The try/except statement can also provide an *exception object*, which you can capture by using the as keyword in the except block. This object contains useful information about the error, such as its type and any additional arguments that accompany it. These arguments are stored in the args attribute, a tuple that you can inspect for more details. In this example, we use the most general exception type, Exception, but more specific types (like ZeroDivisionError) can be used for finer-grained handling.

```
>>> try:
...     avg = average([])
... except Exception as eo:
...     for arg in eo.args:
...         print(arg)
...     print(type(eo))
...
division by zero
<class 'ZeroDivisionError'>
```

You will learn more about exception arguments in Raising and Chaining Exceptions, on page 358.

Except That eo Is Local

The scope of the exception object (eo in the example on page 356) is limited to the except block. If you need to use it elsewhere in your code (for example, to log the error or pass it to another function), you must assign it to a variable with a broader scope before the block ends.

Common Built-in Exceptions

Python provides a rich set of built-in exception types (71 at the time of writing; see Obtaining the List of Built-in Exceptions, on page 357). All of them are subclasses of the built-in class BaseException (subclasses are explained in the section Function isinstance, Class object, and Class Book, on page 283), but using except BaseException itself is generally a bad idea. If necessary, go for except Exception if you need a catch-all and need access to the details.

Obtaining the List of Built-in Exceptions

To retrieve the list of built-in exceptions for your current Python version, start by importing the built-in module builtins. The module has a dictionary of its contents, accessible as builtins.__dict__, where keys are item names and values are the corresponding objects. Iterate through the dictionary and select only those items that are instances of the built-in class type and subclasses of BaseException, using the built-in functions isinstance and issubclass, respectively.

```
>>> import builtins
>>> exceptions = sorted(name for name, value in builtins.__dict__.items()
...        if isinstance(value, type) and issubclass(value, BaseException))
>>> len(exceptions)
71
```

The following table lists the most frequently used built-in exceptions. An asterisk (*) next to an exception name indicates that the exception has not appeared in examples earlier in the book.

Exception Name	What Happened?
AssertionError	An assertion you made failed.
*FileExistsError	The file or directory you tried to create already exists.
FileNotFoundError	The file you tried to access does not exist.
*ImportError	The module you attempted to import was not imported successfully.
IndentationError	Your code is incorrectly indented (for example, you mixed spaces and tabs).

Exception Name	What Happened?
IndexError	You tried to access a list or tuple element with a nonexistent index.
KeyError	You tried to access a dictionary item with a nonexistent key.
*KeyboardInterrupt	You pressed Ctrl-C (or a similar key chord) to interrupt the program in the console window.
*ModuleNotFoundError	The module you tried to import does not exist in the *system path* (sys.path, a list of directories to search).
NameError	You referred to an undefined variable or function.
*OSError	The operating system failed to complete the operation you requested (for example, file handling, networking, or process management).
PermissionError	You attempted to access a file or resource without sufficient permissions.
StopIteration	Your generator has yielded all of its values.
SyntaxError	Your program contains a syntax error.
TypeError	You provided a value of the wrong type (for example, adding a string to a number).
ValueError	You passed an argument of the correct type but with an inappropriate value.
ZeroDivisionError	You attempted to divide by zero.

A well-designed function should raise appropriate exceptions to signal different error conditions. A well-written program, in turn, should handle these exceptions gracefully.

Raise the most appropriate exception and include helpful context to make errors easier to understand and fix

In the following sections, you'll learn how to raise your own exceptions and define custom exception types to make your programs more robust and expressive.

Raising and Chaining Exceptions

Raising an exception in Python is as simple as using the raise keyword. The raise statement takes an exception object, either built-in or user-defined (and, in exceptional situations, objects of other types), and immediately stops normal execution at that point.

```
>>> raise ZeroDivisionError
Traceback (most recent call last):
  File "<python-input-0>", line 1, in <module>
    raise ZeroDivisionError
```

```
ZeroDivisionError
>>> raise Exception
Traceback (most recent call last):
  File "<python-input-1>", line 1, in <module>
    raise Exception
Exception
>>> raise Exception()
Traceback (most recent call last):
  File "<python-input-2>", line 1, in <module>
    raise Exception()
Exception
```

You should raise exceptions in a function as soon as an error becomes detectable. For example, the function below multiplies a list by a given number of copies. Before doing so, it checks whether the number is positive. If it isn't, the function raises a ValueError.

Without this check, the function would silently return an empty list, which is likely not what the caller intended:

```
>>> def multiply_list(l: list, n: int) -> list:
...     """Return list `l` replicated `n` times."""
...     if n <= 0:
...         raise ValueError
...     return n * l
...
>>> multiply_list([1, 2, 3], 0)
Traceback (most recent call last):
  File "<python-input-12>", line 1, in <module>
    multiply_list([1, 2, 3], 0)
    ~~~~~~~~~~~~~^^^^^^^^^^^
  File "<python-input-11>", line 3, in multiply_list
    raise ValueError
ValueError
```

Here, ValueError is the appropriate exception to raise, not TypeError. We assume that n has the correct type (int), but its value is invalid. If the type itself is incorrect, Python's multiplication operator will raise a TypeError on its own.

You can also pass arguments to an exception when you raise it. These arguments are stored in the exception object's args attribute (see Accessing Exception Details, on page 355) and provide additional context during debugging:

```
>>> def multiply_list(l: list, n: int) -> list:
...     """Return list `l` replicated `n` times."""
...     if n <= 0:
...         raise ValueError(n)
...     return n * l
...
```

```
>>> multiply_list([1, 2, 3], -10)
Traceback (most recent call last):
  File "<python-input-26>", line 1, in <module>
    multiply_list([1, 2, 3], -10)
    ~~~~~~~~~~~~~^^^^^^^^^^^^^^^^
  File "<python-input-25>", line 3, in multiply_list
    raise ValueError(n)
ValueError: -10
```

Beyond simple error reporting, raise can also be used for *exception chaining*: a mechanism that lets you preserve the original cause of an error while raising a new, more abstract, higher-level one. This is especially useful when translating low-level exceptions into higher-level errors without losing valuable debugging information.

Exception chaining preserves the original cause of an error, giving you better insight for debugging

Consider the following example. The function load_data tries to open a file and anticipates a FileNotFoundError. Instead of handling that exception directly, it raises a new exception, IOError, with an additional message argument, chaining the new exception to the original:

```
>>> def load_data(filename: str) -> str:
...     """Return the contents of the file `filename`."""
...     try:
...         with open(filename) as infile:
...             return infile.read()
...     except FileNotFoundError as eo:
...         raise IOError(f'Could not load data from {filename}') from eo
...
>>> import traceback
... try:
...     load_data('missing.txt')
... except IOError as eo:
...     print(eo)
...     print(f'Original cause: {eo.__cause__}')
...     traceback.print_exception(eo)
...
Could not load data from missing.txt
Original cause: [Errno 2] No such file or directory: 'missing.txt'
Traceback (most recent call last):
  File "<python-input-2>", line 3, in load_data
    with open(filename) as infile:
         ~~~~^^^^^^^^^^
FileNotFoundError: [Errno 2] No such file or directory: 'missing.txt'

The above exception was the direct cause of the following exception:

Traceback (most recent call last):
  File "<python-input-5>", line 3, in <module>
    load_data('missing.txt')
```

```
    ~~~~~~~~~^^^^^^^^^^^^^^^
  File "<python-input-2>", line 6, in load_data
    raise IOError(f'Could not load data from {filename}') from eo
OSError: Could not load data from missing.txt
```

This design accomplishes three important goals:

- It shifts responsibility for handling the error to the caller, which is presumably in a better position to decide what to do next.
- It repackages a low-level, implementation-specific FileNotFoundError as a higher-level, more abstract IOError, which might make more sense in the broader context of the program.
- It preserves the tracebacks of the original errors so you can see the full caller chain later.

The from eo syntax in the raise statement copies details from the original exception object (eo) into the new one, where you can access them through the _cause_ attribute. The function traceback.print_exception shows the full call stack for post-mortem analysis.

Use exception chaining when you want to abstract away implementation details from the caller but still retain them for debugging, logging, or troubleshooting.

Defining Custom Exceptions

In the example on page 360, choosing IOError as a replacement for FileNotFoundError is functional but not ideal. While it raises the level of abstraction from "file not found" to "input/output error," that abstraction is still too low-level for, say, an enterprise-scale data management system.

A better approach is to define a custom exception type that reflects the problem in domain-specific terms. For example, you could define a new exception type called DataLoadError. Custom exceptions are typically subclasses of the built-in class Exception:

```
>>> class DataLoadError(Exception):
...     """Custom exception for data loading errors."""
...
>>> help(DataLoadError)
Help on class DataLoadError in module __main__:

class DataLoadError(builtins.Exception)
 |  Custom exception for data loading errors.
 |
 |  Method resolution order:
...
```

Inheritance Matters!

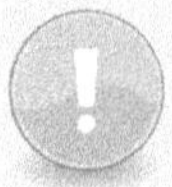

Inherit custom exceptions from Exception, not BaseException. BaseException is for system-exiting errors.

The body of a custom exception class can be empty except for a docstring that documents its purpose (you may want to revisit Designing New Functions: A Recipe, on page 49). Even this minimal definition provides two major benefits:

- Your code communicates intent more clearly.
- Future readers (or your future self) will immediately understand the context and purpose of the exception.

You can now rewrite the previous example in terms of this domain-specific exception:

```
>>> def load_data(filename: str) -> str:
...     """Return the contents of the file `filename`."""
...     try:
...         with open(filename) as infile:
...             return infile.read()
...     except FileNotFoundError as eo:
...         raise DataLoadError(f'Could not load data from {filename}') from eo
...
>>> try:
...     load_data('missing.txt')
... except DataLoadError as eo:
...     print(eo)
...     print('Original cause: {eo.__cause__}')
...
Could not load data from missing.txt
Original cause: [Errno 2] No such file or directory: 'missing.txt'
```

The functionality of the code remains the same, but its readability and maintainability improve significantly. Instead of leaking low-level implementation details (FileNotFoundError), the function communicates a higher-level concept (DataLoadError) that better matches the language of the application or domain.

Exceptionally Important!

In this chapter, you learned the following:

- Errors are inevitable. Robust programs anticipate and handle them gracefully rather than assuming everything will go right.

- Well-designed exception handling means keeping try blocks small and except blocks specific, so you don't accidentally hide real problems.
- Exceptions help separate problem-solving from error handling, letting your core logic stay clean and focused.
- A finally block ensures that your program always cleans up resources, no matter what happens, unless that finally block raises an exception itself.
- You should raise the most appropriate exception, built-in or custom, and include helpful context to make errors easier to understand and fix.
- Exception chaining (raise/from) preserves the original cause of an error when you re-raise it at a higher level, giving you better insight for debugging.

Exercises

Here are some exercises for you to try on your own.

1. Write a program that attempts to open a file specified by the user and read its contents. Handle the cases where the file does not exist, is unreadable, or is empty. Print an informative message for each condition.
2. Write a program that reads data from a file and writes it to another file. Use a finally block to ensure that both files are closed, even if an exception is raised while reading or writing.
3. Write a function that reads a file and parses its contents as an integer number. Catch FileNotFoundError and re-raise a custom DataReadError from it. Then catch ValueError (invalid integer) and re-raise a DataFormatError from it. Print the original causes using the __cause__ attribute.
4. Write a small program with three functions that call one another and deliberately raise an exception in the deepest one. Run it without handling the exception to examine the traceback. Then catch the exception and print its __traceback__ manually to see the call stack details.
5. Deliberately write a program with an except block without a specified exception type that hides a bug. Then rewrite it to catch specific exceptions and explain how that change makes debugging easier.
6. Write a program that tries to convert user input into an integer and then divides 100 by that number. Handle ValueError (invalid input) and ZeroDivisionError (division by zero) with different messages. Use an else block to display the result if no exceptions occur.

Bibliography

[Bev13] Michael Bevilacqua-Linn. *Functional Programming Patterns in Scala and Clojure*. The Pragmatic Bookshelf, Dallas, TX, 2013.

[DEM02] Allen Downey, Jeff Elkner, and Chris Meyers. *How to Think Like a Computer Scientist: Learning with Python*. Green Tea Press, Needham, MA, 2002.

[GHJV95] Erich Gamma, Richard Helm, Ralph Johnson, and John Vlissides. *Design Patterns: Elements of Reusable Object-Oriented Software*. Addison-Wesley, Boston, MA, 1995.

[Hoc04] Roger R. Hock. *Forty Studies That Changed Psychology*. Prentice Hall, Englewood Cliffs, NJ, 2004.

[Hyn06] R. J. Hyndman. *Time Series Data Library*. http://www.robjhyndman.com, http://www.robjhyndman.com, 2006.

[Lak76] Imre Lakatos. *Proofs and Refutations*. Cambridge University Press, Cambridge, United Kingdom, 1976.

[Mat23] Eric Matthes. *Python Crash Course: A Hands-On, Project-Based Introduction to Programming*. No Starch Press, San Francisco, CA, 2023.

[MDWG12] Marilyn Moy, Valery Danilack, Nicole Weston, and Eric Garshick. Daily Step Counts in a US Cohort with COPD. *Respir Med*. 106:962–969, 2012.

[Ost18] Roberto Ostinelli. *Modern Erlang for Beginners*. The Pragmatic Bookshelf, Dallas, TX, 2018.

[Ram22] Luciano Ramalho. *Fluent Python: Clear, Concise, and Effective Programming*. O'Reilly Media, Inc., Sebastopol, CA, 2022.

[Ski23] Rebecca Skinner. *Effective Haskell*. The Pragmatic Bookshelf, Dallas, TX, 2023.

[Sla19] Brett Slatkin. *Effective Python: 90 Specific Ways to Write Better Python.* Addison-Wesley, Boston, MA, 2019.

[Swe19] Al Sweigart. *Automate the Boring Stuff with Python: Practical Programming for Total Beginners.* No Starch Press, San Francisco, CA, 2019.

[Win06] Jeannette M. Wing. Computational Thinking. *Communications of the ACM.* 49[3]:33–35, 2006.

[Wol25] Herbert Wolverson. *Advanced Hands-on Rust.* The Pragmatic Bookshelf, Dallas, TX, 2025.

[Zin21] Dmitry Zinoviev. *Pythonic Programming.* The Pragmatic Bookshelf, Dallas, TX, 2021.

Index

SYMBOLS

- != not equal operator, 86
- " (double quotes)
  - docstrings, 67
  - enclosing strings, 67
  - escaping, 71
  - inside strings, 71
- """ (triple quotes)
  - docstrings, 49
  - enclosing multiline strings, 72
- # (hash sign) for comments, 26
- %
  - modulo operator, 11–12, 15
  - substitution operator, 77–78
- %= augmented modulo assignment operator, 22
- ' (single quotes)
  - enclosing strings, 67
  - escaping, 71
  - inside strings, 71
- ''' (triple quotes), enclosing multiline strings, 72
- () (parentheses)
  - combining comparison operations, 88
  - defined, 5
  - function definition, 39
  - generators, 331
  - line breaks, 25
  - operator order, 15
  - tuples, 216, 219
- * (asterisk)
  - exponentiation operator (**), 12, 15
  - multiplication operator, 10, 12, 15
  - starred parameters, 335
  - starred targets, 334
  - string repeat operator, 70
- ** exponentiation operator, 12, 15
- **= augmented exponentiation assignment operator, 22
- *= augmented multiplication assignment operator, 22
- + (plus sign)
  - addition operator, 10, 12, 15
  - concatenation operator, 68, 140, 146
- += augmented addition assignment operator, 22
- - (minus sign)
  - negation operator, 12
  - subtraction operator, 10, 12, 15
- -= augmented subtraction assignment operator, 22
- . (dot)
  - calling functions from modules, 107
  - calling methods, 123
- .. for directory navigation, 183
- / (forward slash)
  - directory separator, 181
  - division operator, 10, 12, 15
- // (operator), integer division, 11–12, 15
- //= integer division assignment operator, 22
- /= augmented division assignment operator, 22
- : (colon)
  - formatted strings, 79
  - function definitions, 39
- < relational operator, 86
- <= relational operator, 86
- = (equals sign) assignment operator, 16, 18, 86
- == equality operator, 86
- > relational operator, 86, 347
- >= relational operator, 86
- [] (brackets)
  - defined, 5
  - dictionary keys, 222
  - lists, 134, 136
- \ (backslash)
  - directory separator, 181
  - escape character, 71
  - line-continuation character, 25
- ^ for exclusive or, 85
- _ (underscore)
  - module names, 110
  - special methods, 128–130, 292
  - throwaway variable, 334
- {} (braces)
  - defined, 5
  - dictionaries, 222
  - formatted strings, 78
  - set comprehensions, 329
  - sets, 209

A

abs function, 31
abs method, 129
absolute path, 182
Acquire–Use–Release pattern, 180
add method, sets, 211–212
add method, 128
addition
  (+) operator, 10, 12, 15
  augmented assignment (+=), 22
  floats, 13
  operator precedence, 14
  sets, 211
al-Khwarizmi, 235
algorithms
  benchmarking, 244–245
  binary search, 256–261
  defined, 235
  exercises, 246
  finding two smallest values, 235–243
  linear search, 250–256, 261
  P/NP puzzles, 277
  reading files, 193–205
  term origins, 235
  testing, 236, 247
  top-down design, 235–243
aliasing
  defined, 37, 144
  lists, 144–145, 148
alignment, formatted strings, 79
all function, 337
Amazon Web Services (AWS), 339
American Standard Code for Information Interchange (ASCII), 90
and operator, 83, 90
any function, 337
Any return type, 244
append method, 146
append mode (open), 190
arguments
  calling functions as, 32
  defined, 32, 64
  evaluation of, 292
  exceptions, 359
  keyword (kwargs), 75
  lamba functions as, 338
  methods, 287
  number of, 41
  packing/unpacking, 336
  positional, 41, 75
arithmetic
  combining with other operators, 87–90
  expressions, 9–12
  operator precedence, 14
  operators, 9–12
ASCII (American Standard Code for Information Interchange), 90
assertEqual method, 314
AssertionError, 314, 357
assertions
  errors, 357
  preconditions, 64
  unit testing, 314
assignment
  (=) operator, 16, 18, 86
  augmented, 21
  errors, 23
  execution of, 16, 18
  exercises, 29
  function header, 75
  initializing, 287
  lists, 139
  multiple, 219, 334–336
  reassignment, 19–21
  simultaneous, 205
  syntax, 18
  using, 16–23
asterisk (*)
  exponentiation operator (**), 12, 15
  multiplication operator, 10, 12, 15
  starred parameters, 335
  starred targets, 334
  string repeat operator, 70
attributes, classes, 284
augmented assignment, 21
Automate the Boring Stuff with Python, xiv

B

backslash (\)
  directory separator, 181
  escape character, 71
  line-continuation character, 25
banker's rounding, 34
base, 257
BaseException class, 357, 362
benchmarking algorithms, 244–245
Big O notation, 277
binary files, defined, 177
binary operators, 12
binary search, 256–261
binary sorting, 268–271
bisect module, 261, 271
bisect_left function, 261
bisect_right function, 261
bits, 189
Boehm's curve, 309
bool type, 83
Boole, George, 84
Boolean expressions
  bool type, 83
  combining with other operators, 87–90
  exercises, 100–103
  operators, 83–85
  order of precedence, 83
  predicate functions, 125
  reusing variables, 98–99
  short-circuit evaluation, 90
  truth tables, 85
boundary cases, 311, 322
braces ({})
  defined, 5
  dictionaries, 222
  formatted strings, 78
  set comprehensions, 329
  sets, 209
brackets ([])
  defined, 5
  dictionary keys, 222
  lists, 134, 136
break statement, 168–170, 172
bubble sort, 277
bugs, *see also* debugging; testing
  Boehm's curve, 309
  boundary cases, 311
  defined, 4
  term origins, 4
builtins module, 110, 357
bytes, 189
bytes type, 188
Böhm–Jacopini theorem, 170

C

capitalize method, 122, 126
carriage return (\r), escaping, 72
carriage return character (\r), escaping, 72

case, string methods, 122, 126–127
cause attribute, 361
chain function, 343
characters, lexicographic ordering, 91
chr function, 91
Church, Alonzo, 339
class keyword, 284
class object, 289
classes, *see also* methods
 attributes, 284
 data descriptors, 286
 defined, 121
 defining, 284–286
 design, 282
 encapsulation, 296
 errors, 284
 inheritance, 284, 297–300, 353, 362
 as instance of object, 283
 instances, 283
 methods, writing in, 286–292
 object-oriented programming case study, 300–304
 object-oriented programming focus, 282
 objects, creating, 285
 polymorphism, 296
 real-word modeling, 295
 Single Responsibility Principle, 296
 subclasses, 283, 298
 superclasses, 283, 299
 TestCase, 313
 types represented by, 282
clear method, 146, 211–212, 225
close, 180
collections, *see also* dictionaries; lists; sets; tuples
 comparing, 229
 exercises, 232–234
collections module, 343–344
collisions, 228
colon (:)
 formatted strings, 79
 function definitions, 39
columns, printing information in, 73
combinations function, 343–344
comments
 algorithm design, 238, 242
 role of, 26
comparisons, *see also* Boolean expressions; relational operations
 chaining, 88
 combining comparison operations, 87–90
 _eq_, 294
 exercises, 100–103
 sequences, 347
 short-circuit evaluation, 90
 strings, 90–92
comprehensions, 328–330
Computational Thinking, 3
computational thinking, 3
computers, 7
concatenation
 + operator, 68, 140, 146
 lists, 140, 146
 strings, 68–70, 77
conditions
 explicitness in loops, 169
 if statements, 92–97
 reusing variables, 98–99
 while loops, 165–167
constants, 107
constructors, 122, 289
continue statement, 168, 170
control flow, *see also* Boolean expressions; comparisons; loops
 Böhm–Jacopini theorem, 170
 statements, 83
control symbols, formatted strings, 79
count method, 126, 146
Counter class, 344
CPUs, 7
crashes, bugs and, 4
CSV files, splitting, 149
curly braces, *see* braces ({})
current working directory, 182
cycle function, 346

D

data, *see also* files; reading
 dictionary of dictionaries as database, 233
 heterogeneous data and lists, 137
 missing values, 195–197
 ragged, 164
 whitespace-delimited, 197–200
data descriptors, 286
DataLoadError, 362
debugging, *see also* testing
 chaining exceptions, 360
 defined, 117
 exercises, 324–326
 records of, 324
 stack trace, 355–357, 361
 strategies, 323–324
 vs. testing, 117
decimal mode, 14
declarative programming, 328
decoding, 189
decrement operator, 23
def keyword, 39, 109–116
default parameter values, 75
del operator, 141, 223
deleting
 dictionary items, 223, 225
 list items, 141, 146, 238
 sets, 211
description, function design recipe, 51, 53, 55, 59
design, *see also* function design recipe
 algorithms, 235–243
 object-oriented programming, 282
 patterns, defined, 328
 Single Responsibility Principle, 296
 top-down, 235–243
Design Patterns, 328
dichotomies, 322
dictionaries
 adding items to, 223
 comparing with other collections, 229
 comprehensions, 328, 330
 creating, 222
 dictionary of dictionaries, 233
 empty, 222
 exercises, 232
 inverting, 228
 key order, 226
 loops, 224, 226, 228

mapping pairs for text summarization, 344
membership, checking, 223, 229
mutability, 221
names, 226
operations, 224
removing items from, 223
updating, 223
using, 220–227

dictionary ordering, *see* lexicographic ordering
difference method, 211
digital signal processors (DSPs), 9
Dijkstra, Edsger, 248
directories
changing, 182
current working directory, 182
organization, 181–183
parent, 183
root, 181
specifying, 182

directory separator, 181
division, *see also* integer division
/ operator, 10, 12, 15
augmented assignment (/=) operator, 22
errors, 357
floor, 11
operator precedence, 14
rounding, 11

DNA, 71
__doc__ variable, 130
docstrings
defined, 49
exercises, 65
format, 49
testing, 116

doctest module, 310, 312, 315
doctests
doctest module, 310, 312, 315
exercises, 247
methods, 289
sorting, 266

document strings, *see* docstrings
documentation, *see also* docstrings
function design recipe, 53
functions, 49

dot (.)
calling functions from modules, 107
calling methods, 123

DSPs (digital signal processors), 9
dunder methods, 130, 292–295
Dutch National Flag problem, 248

E

editors, xiii, *see also* IDLE
EDU-SIG: Python in Education, xiv
Effective Python, xiv
elements, list, 135
elif clause, 95–97
encapsulation, 296
encoding, 90, 189
end parameter, string methods, 124
endswith method, 125–126
__enter__ method, 181
enumerate function, 332
__eq__ method, 294–295
equal sign (=), assignment operator, 16, 18, 86
equality
equality operators, 85
sets, 210

errors, *see also* exceptions
about, 23
assignment, 23
bugs, 4
built-in modules, 110
classes, 284
dictionaries, 222
HTTP, 190
indentation, 37, 357
infinite loops, 167
local variables, 40
preconditions, 64, 351
repeating failures, 323
strings, 69–70
syntax, 24, 284, 352–353, 357
testing error messages, 314
types, 23–24, 69

escape character (\), 71
escape sequences, 71, 73
examples
function design recipe, 50, 52, 54, 58, 191
writing in StringIO, 191

Exception class, 284, 361
exception object, 356
Exception type, 356
exceptions, *see also* errors
built-in, 357
chaining, 360
defining custom, 361
exception handlers, 351, 353–354
exception object, 356
exception types, 353
exercises, 363
inheritance, 353, 362
multiclause handlers, 354
preconditions, 351
printing, 361
raising, 358–363
stack trace, 355–357, 361
try/except statements, 351–355

exclusive or, 84
exercises
algorithms, 246
assignment statements, 29
Booleans, 100–103
collections, 232–234
comparisons, 100–103
debugging, 324–326
dictionaries, 232
doctests, 247
exceptions, 363
expressions, 29
files, 206
functions, 65–66
if statements, 102
iteration, 348–350
lists, 150–152
loops, 173–175
methods, 131
modules, 119
object-oriented programming, 305–308
reading, 206, 247
searching, 277
sets, 232
sorting, 277
strings, 80
syntax errors, 29
testing, 324–326
tuples, 232
writing, 206

exit method, 181
exponentiation
    ** operator, 12, 15
    augmented assignment (**=) operator, 22
    pow function, 32, 34
expressions
    arithmetic, 9–12
    defined, 9
    evaluating, 9
    exercises, 29
    operator precedence, 13–15
    short-circuit evaluation of, 90
extend method, 146

F

f-strings, *see* formatted strings
False value, 83, 86, 89
FDR, *see* function design recipe
file cursor, 180
file mode, 180
file path, 181–182
FileExistsError, 357
FileNotFoundError, 357, 360, 362
files, *see also* reading
    algorithms for, 193–205
    appending, 190
    closing, 180, 355
    data with missing values, 195–197
    defined, 177
    empty, 178
    errors, 357, 360, 362
    exercises, 206
    file path, 181–182
    format specifications, 177
    headers, reading, 186
    headers, skipping, 186, 193–195
    Internet, 188
    long term storage, 177
    metadata, 178
    mock files for testing, 191
    opening, 179–183
    organization, 181–183
    running programs in, 61
    specifying, 182
    splitting CSV files, 149
    types, 177–179
    writing, 189
filter function, 337
Filter–Map–Reduce pattern, 328
find method, 126
find_min function, 266
float function, 33, 70
float type
    converting int to, 10, 33
    defined, 10
floating-point numbers, *see* floats
floats
    adding, 13
    comparison operators, 86
    converting, 10, 33, 86
    defined, 10
    formatted strings, 79
    IEEE 754 standard, 346
    integer division, 12
    modulo operator (%), 12
    omitting zero in, 10
    operators, 12–13
    precision, 13–14
    pseudo-random number generation, 341
    rounding, 33
    string representation, 70
Fluent Python, xiv
For Line in File technique, 185
for loop
    dictionaries, 224, 226, 228
    execution, 154
    linear search, 253, 256
    lists, 153–155, 242
    sets, 214
    strings, 155
format method, 77
format specifiers, formatted strings, 79
formatted strings, 77–79
FORTRAN, 160
forward slash (/)
    directory separator, 181
    division operator, 10, 12, 15
    integer division (//), 11–12, 15
frames, memory model, 42
from_iterable function, 344
frozenset function, 215
function design recipe
    algorithms, 237
    birthday examples, 52–60
    description, 51, 53, 55, 59
    examples, 50, 52, 54, 58
    exercises, 65
    function body, 51, 53, 56, 59
    function header, 50, 53, 55, 59
    object-oriented programming, 282
    questions, 49
    testing, 51, 53, 56, 60, 116
    using, 49–60
    writing example calls in StringIO, 191
function headers
    assignment statements, 75
    defined, 38
    format, 39
    function design recipe, 50, 53, 55, 59
function objects, modules, 106
function-as-a-service (FaaS), 339
functional programming, 336–342
functions, *see also* arguments; function headers; generators; methods
    as algorithms, 235
    body of, 37, 39, 50–51, 53, 56, 59
    built-in, 31–35
    calling, 41–48
    calling as arguments, 32
    constructors, 122
    default parameters values, 75
    defined, 31, 64
    defining, 36–39, 49–51
    design questions, 49
    design recipe for, 49–60
    documentation, 49
    execution of, 32
    exercises, 65–66
    grouping into modules, 118
    helper, 198, 200
    higher-order, 345
    identities, 35
    importing modules, 106–108
    as instance of object, 283
    instances, 283
    lambda, 338, 350

    listing module functions with help, 33
    local variables, 39
    memory model, 41–48
    in modules, 105
    names, 39, 50
    order of evaluation in, 32
    parameters, 39–40, 75
    preconditions, 63
    predicate, 125
    reload, 111
    return statement, 38
    return statement, omitting, 62, 145
    sequence operations, 336–342
    syntax, 31, 39
    unit testing, 312–315, 317–321
functools module, 338

G

generators
    exercises, 350
    as iterators, 332
    using, 330–332
    writing, 339–342
get method, 225, 227
getcwd function, 182
getvalue method, 192
global variables, 339
Google Python Class, xiv
graphics processing units (GPUs), 9
greater than (>) relational operator, 86, 347
greater than or equal to (>=), relational operator, 86
groupby function, 346
_gt_ method, 129
Guo, Philip, 18

H

hanging and infinite loops, 167
Harvard Mark II, 4
hash sign (#) for comments, 26
hash tables, 230, 330
hashing, 214, 230
hashtags, storing in sets, 330
headers in files, reading, 186, 193–195
headers, HTTP, 190
headers, function, *see* function headers
heap sort, 272
help function, 33
helper functions, 198, 200
higher-order functions, 345
Hopper, Grace, 69
How to Think Like a Computer Scientist, xiv
HTTP requests, 190

I

i variable for indices, 159
id function, 35
identifiers, memory addresses, 17
identities, functions, 35
IDLE
    about, xiii, 9
    killing programs, 167
    prompt (>>>), 9
    running programs in, 61
IEEE 754 standard, 346
if statements
    elif clause in, 95–97
    exercises, 102
    flowchart, 94
    multiple, 94–97
    nested, 98–99
    terminating loops early, 169
    using, 92–97
iff (if and only if), 87
immutability
    comparing collection types, 229
    dictionary keys, 222
    hashing sets, 214
    numbers, 139
    strings, 139
    tuples, 216
imperative programming, 124, 328
import statement, 105–112
import* statement, 108
ImportError, 357
importing
    errors, 357
    modules, 105–116
    modules, running code on import, 112–116
    name conflicts, 108
importlib module, 111–112
in operator
    dictionaries, 223
    lists, 141, 229
    strings, 91
inclusive or, 84
increment operator, 23
indentation
    errors, 37, 357
    functions, defining, 37, 39
    if statements, 93
    loops, 154
    multiline statements, 26
    readability, 26
IndentationError, 357
index method, 146, 249–256
IndexError, 357
indices
    errors, 357
    lists, 135–137, 146, 148, 158–161
    negative, 135
    nested lists, 148
    numbering conventions, 135
    parallel lists, 160
    ranges, 157
    searching algorithms examples, 235–243
    selection sort, 265
    slicing lists, 142
infile variable, 180
infinite loops, 166
inheritance
    exceptions, 353, 362
    object-oriented programming, 284, 297–300
    overriding inherited method, 294
init method, 130, 287, 289
initialization
    init method for, 130, 287, 289
    loops, 241
    methods, 287
input function, 76, 93, 167
insert method, 146
insertion sort, 267–271, 276
insort_left function, 261, 271
insort_right function, 261
installing Python, 9
instance variables, 285, 290
instances, classes, 283
int function, 33, 70

int type
  converting to float, 10, 33
  defined, 10
integer division
  // operator, 11–12, 15
  augmented assignment (//=) operator, 22
  binary search, 259
integers
  comparison operators, 86
  converting, 10, 33, 86
  formatted strings, 79
  int type, 10
  interning, 37
  precision, 14
  pseudo-random number generation, 341
  rounding, 34
  string representation, 70
interning, 37
interpreters
  execution of programs, 8
  running programs, 61
intersection, sets, 211
intersection method, 211
invariants
  linear search, 251
  sorting, 262
IOError, 360
isinstance function, 283, 357
islower method, 126
isnan method, 346
isnumeric method, 126
issubclass function, 357
issubset method, 211
issuperset method, 211
isupper method, 126
itemgetter function, 345
items method, dictionaries, 225
iteration, *see also* loops
  about, 327
  built-in and standard library helpers, 342–347
  comprehensions, 328–330
  enumerating, 332
  errors, 357
  exercises, 348–350
  functional programming, 336–342
  generators, 330–332, 339–342
  packing/unpacking, 334–336
  text summarization, 343–346
  zipping, 332
itertools module, 343–346

J

j variable for indices, 160
Jmol, 300

K

k variable for indices, 160
KeyboardInterrupt, 357
KeyError, 357
keys
  dictionaries, 221, 225, 228
  dictionary comprehensions, 330
  errors, 357
  hash tables, 230
  immutability, 222
  order, 226
keys method, 225
keywords
  defined, 40
  keyword arguments (kwargs), 75
  list of, 40
al-Khwarizmi, 235
kwargs, 75

L

L[i] syntax, 135, 138
lambda calculus, 339
lambda functions, 338, 350
languages, programming
  defined, 3
  learning additional, xiv, 4
lazy evaluation, generators, 331
LCGs (linear congruential generators), 341
len function, 68, 139
len method, 130
less than (<) relational operator, 86
less than or equal to (<=), relational operator, 86
lexicographic ordering, 91
line breaks, multiline statements, 25
line-continuation character (\), 25
linear congruential generators (LCGs), 341
linear search, 250–256, 261
linear sort, 276
list function, dictionaries, 225
lists
  aliasing, 144–145, 148
  assignment, 134, 136, 139, 148
  binary search, 256–261
  built-in functions, 139
  comparing with other collections, 229
  comprehensions, 328
  concatenating, 140, 146
  creating, 134
  defined, 133
  deleting items, 141, 146, 238
  empty, 134, 136
  exercises, 150–152
  heterogeneous data, 137
  indices, 135–137, 146, 148, 158–161
  linear search, 250–256
  loops, 153–155, 158–161, 163–164, 242
  membership, checking, 141
  merge sort, 272–276
  methods, 145
  modifying, 138
  multiple assignment, 219
  multiplying, 141
  as mutable, 138
  nested, 147–149, 163–164
  None and, 147
  number of items in, 139
  operations, 139–141
  parallel lists, 160, 333
  ragged, 164
  ranges, 157
  reversing, 184
  searching, 249–261
  searching algorithms examples, 235–243
  slicing, 142–143
  sorted lists, searching, 250, 256
  sorting, 139, 146, 185, 240, 261–271
  splitting strings, 149
  syntax, 134
  type annotations, 137
  using, 133–137
  zipping, 161, 333
literals, defined, 24

loading, errors, 362
local variables
    defined, 64
    namespaces, 41
    reusing names, 43
    scope, 41, 339
    using, 39
logarithms, 257
loops
    body, 241
    Böhm–Jacopini theorem, 170
    components of, 241
    conditions, explicit, 169
    dictionaries, 224, 226, 228
    execution of, 154
    execution of, controlling, 168–172
    exercises, 173–175
    infinite, 166
    linear search, 250–256
    lists, 153–155, 242
    lists, nested, 163–164
    lists, parallel, 160
    lists, ragged, 164
    lists, with indices, 158–161
    loop condition, 241
    nested, 161–164, 170, 221
    ranges, 156–158
    sets, 214
    skipping ahead with continue, 168, 170
    step size, 157
    strings, 155
    terminating with break, 168–170, 172
    user input, 167
    while loops, 165–167, 252, 256
lower method, 126
lstrip method, 125–126

M

machine learning, 14
map function, 336–338
maps, *see* dictionaries
max function, 65, 139
membership, checking, 91, 141, 223, 229, 330
memory
    comprehensions, 330
    model of, 17
    tracing function calls in, 41–48
    volatile memory vs. secondary storage devices, 177
memory addresses
    identities, 35
    lists, 135
    variable assignment, 17–23
memory model
    aliasing, 144
    classes, 285, 289, 291–292
    dictionaries, 222
    frames, 42
    function calls, 41–48
    lists, 134, 138, 140, 142
    looping lists, 158
    methods, 289
    nested lists, 147
    object-oriented programming, 285, 289, 291–292
    sets, 210
    slicing, 142
    tools, 18
    tuples, 217–218
    using, 17
    variables, 17–23
merge sort, 272–276
Mersenne Twister algorithm, 341
metadata, files, 178
methods, *see also* functions
    arguments, 287
    calling, 122–124, 286–292
    defined, 121
    design, 282
    doctests, 289
    dunder methods, 130, 292–295
    execution of, 124
    exercises, 131
    inheritance, 297–300
    initializing assignments, 287
    list methods, 145
    overriding inherited, 294
    polymorphism, 296
    procedural, 288
    separating test methods, 315
    sets, 211–213
    Single Responsibility Principle, 296
    special, 128–130, 292–295
    strings, 122–128
    syntax, 123
    testing, 289
min function, 65, 139, 238
minus sign (-)
    negation operator, 12
    subtraction operator, 10, 12, 15
mocks, 191
module type, 105
ModuleNotFoundError, 357
modules
    built-in, 110
    defined, 105
    defining, 109–116
    errors, 110, 357
    exercises, 119
    functions, listing with help, 33
    grouping functions, 118
    importing, 105–116
    importlib, 111
    name conflicts, 108
    names, 110
    reloading, 111–112
    restoring, 112
    running, 111–116
    running, on import, 112–116
    size of, 118
    testing, 116
    unittest, 312–315, 317–321
modulo
    augmented assignment operator (%=), 22
    operator (%), 11–12, 15
molecular visualizers, 300–304
most_common method, 344
multiline records, reading, 201–203
multiline statements, 24–26
multiline strings, 72
multiplication
    (*) operator, 10, 12, 15
    augmented assignment (*=) operator, 22
    lists, 141
    operator precedence, 14
mutability
    aliasing and, 144
    comparing collection types, 229
    dictionaries, 221

- lists, 138
- sets, 209, 212

N

- \n (newline character)
  - escaping, 72
  - printing strings, 74
- _name_ keyword, 112–116
- NameError, 357
- names
  - compound types, 231
  - dictionaries, 226
  - errors, 357
  - functions, 39, 50
  - modules, 110
  - name conflicts, 108
  - parameters, 51, 53
  - readability, 26–27
  - reusing, 43
  - self parameter, 287
  - variables, 15, 26–27, 43, 99
- namespaces
  - defined, 41
  - memory model, 41–48
- nan (not a number), 346
- negation (-) operator, 12
- negative indices, 135
- negative operands, modulo and integer division, 11
- nested if statements, 98–99
- nested lists, 147–149, 163–164
- nested loops, 161–164, 170, 221
- _new_ method, 289
- newline character (\n)
  - defined, 74
  - escaping, 72
  - printing strings, 74
- newlines
  - reading files, 184, 186–187
  - strings, 72, 74
  - writing files, 190
- next function, generators, 331
- nltk library, 343
- None
  - Boolean operators, 89
  - lists, 147
  - return values, omitting, 62
  - testing and, 316
- normalizing strings, 74
- not equal (!=) operator, 86
- not operator, 83
- NP/P puzzles, 277
- numbers, *see also* floats; integers
  - comparison operators, 86
  - converting to strings, 69
  - as immutable, 139
  - interning, 37
  - loops, 156–158
  - nan (not a number), 346
  - precision, 13–14
  - pseudo-random number generators (PRNGs), 341–342
  - seed, 341
  - using with Boolean operators, 89
- numerical analysis, 14

O

- object class, 283
- object-oriented programming
  - about, 281
  - defined, 124
  - encapsulation, 296
  - exercises, 305–308
  - inheritance, 297–300
  - instances, 283
  - methods, creating, 286–292
  - PDB files case study, 300–304
  - phases, 282
  - polymorphism, 296
  - problem domain, 282
  - special methods, 292–295
  - testing, 282
  - theory overview, 296–300
- objects
  - about, 128, 283
  - creating, 285, 289
  - exception object, 356
  - ids, obtaining, 35
  - instance variables, 285, 290
  - lists as, 134
  - in memory, 17
  - memory objects, 17
  - real-word modeling, 295
- one-liners, 345
- open function, 180, 182, 189
- operating systems, 7
- operations
  - dictionaries, 224
  - lists, 139–141
  - sequence, 336–342
  - sets, 211–213
  - strings, 68–70
- operator module, 343, 345
- operators
  - arithmetic, 9–12
  - augmented assignment, 22
  - binary, 12
  - Boolean, 83–85, 89
  - combining, 87–90
  - overloaded, 12
  - precedence of, 13–15, 87–90
  - relational, 85–90
  - spaces and readability, 27
  - unary, 12, 83
- optional_else block, 352
- optional_finally block, 354
- or operator, 83, 90
- ord function, 91
- order
  - Boolean operators, 83
  - comparison operators, combining, 87–90
  - comprehensions, 329
  - dictionaries, 222, 226
  - dictionaries, inverting, 228
  - functions, 32
  - lexicographic ordering, 91
  - lists, 135
  - nested if statements, 98
  - operator precedence, 13–15
  - testing, 322
- os module, 182
- OSError, 357
- OverflowError, 167
- overloaded operators, 12
- overriding inherited methods, 294

P

- P/NP puzzles, 277
- packing, 334–336
- parallel lists
  - loops, 160
  - zipping, 333
- parameters
  - aliasing, 144
  - catch-all (starred), 335
  - default parameter values, 75
  - defined, 64
  - function design recipe, 51

functions, 39–40, 75
methods, testing, 289
names, 51, 53
preconditions, 63
as variables, 39–40, 144
parent directory, 183
parentheses (())
combining comparison operations, 88
defined, 5
function definition, 39
generators, 331
line breaks, 25
operator order, 15
tuples, 216, 219
pass statement, 352
patterns
Acquire–Use–Release pattern, 180
defined, 328
Filter–Map–Reduce pattern, 328
PDB files, 233, 300–304
PEP-8 style guide, 27
perf_counter function, 244, 255
performance
benchmarking, 244–245
Big O notation, 277
comprehensions, 331
generators, 332
searches, 255–256, 261, 272, 276
sorting, 262, 268–271
permutations function, 346
plus sign (+)
addition operator, 10, 12, 15
concatenation operator, 68, 140, 146
polymorphism, 296
pop method, 146, 225, 232
pow function, 32, 34
precision, numeric, 13–14
preconditions, 63, 351
predicate functions, 125
print function
running programs, 61
strings, 73–76
printing
exceptions, 361
running programs, 61
strings, 73–76
without new line, 75
problem domain, 282
procedural method calls, 288
processors, execution of programs, 7
product function, 346
programming, *see also* object-oriented programming
declarative, 328
defined, 3
functional, 336–342
imperative, 124, 328
programs
as algorithms, 235
benchmarking, 244–245
defined, 2
execution of, 7–9
killing, 167
running, 60
understanding in debugging, 323
prompts
IDLE (>>>), 9
for user input, 77, 93
pseudo-random number generators (PRNGs), 341–342
.py extension, 61
Python
advantages, xiii
installing, 9
Pythonic adjective, 327
resources on, xiv
uses, xiii
versions, 5, 9
Python Crash Course, xiv

Q

QA (quality assurance), 309
quick sort, 272
quotes
""" for docstrings, 49
docstrings, 67
enclosing strings, 67
inside strings, 71
multiline strings, 72

R

\r (carriage return character), escaping, 72
ragged lists, 164
raise, 358–363
randint function, 341
random function, 341
random module, 341
randomness, pseudo-random number generators (PRNGs), 341–342
range function, 156–158
range type, 211
ranges
loops, 156–158
sets, 211
zipping, 333
read method, 183, 188
Read technique, 183
readability
exceptions, 362
floats, 11
helper functions, 200
indentation, 26
loops, 169, 172
multiline statements, 24–26
names, 26–27
spaces, 27
reading
algorithms for, 193–205
exercises, 206, 247
files, basics, 183–189
files, into a string, 180
handling missing values, 195–197
looking ahead, 203–205
multiline records, 201–203
object-oriented programming example, 302
skipping headers, 186, 193–195
user input, 76
readline function, 186–188, 193–195
readlines function, 184
records, reading multiline, 201–203
relational operators
combining with other operators, 87–90
defined, 85
table of, 86
relative path, 182
reload function, 111–112
reloading modules, 111–112
remove method
lists, 146, 238
sets, 211–212
replace method, 126
__repr__ method, 293
resources for this book
design patterns, 328
directory paths, 183
memory models, 18
Python, xiv

restarting, shell, 61, 112
restoring, modules, 112
return statement
  functions, defining, 38–39
  omitting, 62, 145
reverse method, lists, 146
reversed function
  iteration, 342
  lists, 184
  sequences, 346
reversing
  dictionaries, 228
  lists, 146, 184
  sequences, 346
root directory, 181
round function, 33
rounding, 11, 14, 33
rstrip method, 125–126, 187
running
  code on import, 112–116
  programs, 60

S

Scheme, 4
scope
  exception object, 357
  local variables, 41, 339
searching
  binary search, 256–261
  exercises, 277
  insertion sort, 276
  linear search, 250–256, 261
  linear sort, 276
  lists, 249–261
  performance, 255–256, 261, 272, 276
  selection sort, 276
  sentinel search, 254–256
  sorted lists, 250
  testing, 260
secondary storage devices, 177
security and pseudo-random numbers, 341
seed numbers, 341
selection sort, 263–271, 276
self, 287
semantic errors, 23
sentence tokenization, 343
sentinel search, 254–256
sep argument, 149
sequences
  operations, 336–342
  reversing, 346
  sorting, 346
set function, 210
set type, 209
setdefault method, dictionaries, 225
sets
  comparing with other collections, 229
  comprehensions, 328
  creating, 210
  empty, 210
  exercises, 232
  frozen, 215
  hashing, 214
  loops, 214
  membership, checking, 229
  multiple assignment, 219
  as mutable, 209, 212
  operations, 211–213
  subsets, 211
  supersets, 211
  using, 209–215
Shannon, Claude, 84
shell
  interacting with interpreter, 8
  killing programs, 167
  restarting, 61, 112
short-circuit evaluation, 90
Simula, 124
simultaneous assignments, unpacking, 205
Single Responsibility Principle, 296
slicing lists, 142–143
solid-state drives, 7, 177
sort method
  lists, 146, 240, 262
  performance, 268–271
sorted function
  algorithm example, 240
  iteration, 342
  lists, 139, 185, 240, 262
  sequences, 346
sorted lists, 250, 256
sorting
  binary sort, 268–271
  bubble sort, 277
  exercises, 277
  heap sort, 272
  insertion sort, 267–271, 276
  invariants, 262
  linear sort, 276
  lists, 139, 146, 185, 261–271
  merge sort, 272–276
  performance, 262, 268–272
  quick sort, 272
  selection sort, 263–271, 276
  sequences, 346
  testing, 266
  understanding, 261–263
spaces and readability, 27
sparse vectors, 234
special characters, strings, 71
special methods, 128–130, 292–295
split method
  lists, 149
  strings, 126, 149
square brackets, *see* brackets ([])
stack trace, 355–357, 361
starred target, packing/unpacking with, 334
start parameter, string methods, 124
startswith method, 125–126
statements, *see also* assignment
  conditionally executing, 92–97
  defined, 7
  multiline, 24–26
  return statement, 39
static variables, 339
step size, 157
StopIteration, 357
stopwords, 343
storage devices, 177
str function, 69
__str__ method, 130, 293
str type, 67
StringIO, writing example calls, 191
strings
  aliasing, 144
  assigning to variables, 70
  Boolean operators, using with, 89
  capitalizing, 122, 126
  case, 126–127
  comparing, 90–92

comparing with other collections, 229
concatenating, 68–70, 77
converting numbers to, 69
creating, 67
defined, 67
empty, 68, 70, 89, 327
encoding, 90
escaping characters in, 71, 73
exercises, 80
format method, 77
formatted, 77–79
as immutable, 139
input, reading, 76
length of, 68
loops, 155
lowercasing, 123
membership, checking, 91
methods, 122–128
methods, table of, 124–125
multiline, 72
normalizing, 74
operations, 68–70
order of operations, 69
reading files, 180
repeating, 70
representing as int or float types, 70
special characters, 71
splitting, 126, 149
substitution operator (%), 77
substrings in, 126
whitespaces in, stripping, 125–126

strip method, strings, 125–126
style
optimistic, 351
pessimistic, 351–353
readability, 24–26
style guides, 27
subclasses, 283, 298
subexpressions
operator precedence, 15
order of evaluation, 33
subsets, 211
substitution operator (%), 77–78
subtraction
(-) operator, 10, 12, 15
augmented assignment (-=), 22
operator precedence, 14
sum function, 139
superclasses, 283, 299
supersets, 211
swapcase method, 126–127
symmetric_difference method, 211
syntax
defined, 24
errors, 23–24, 284, 352–353, 357
exercises, 29
for loops, 154
functions, 31, 39
lamba functions, 338
methods, 123
multiline statements, 24–26
Python advantages, xiii
SyntaxError, 284, 357
system testing, 312

T

tab character (\t)
escaping, 72
printing strings, 73
takewhile function, 343, 345
TestCase class, 313
testing, *see also* doctests
algorithms, 236, 247
binary searching, 260
boundary cases, 311, 322
case studies, 310–316
vs. debugging, 117
defined, 117
dichotomies, 322
docstrings, 116
error messages, 314
exercises, 324–326
function design recipe, 51, 53, 56, 60, 116
importance of, 309
methods, 289
modules, 116
None and, 316
object-oriented programming, 282
order, 322
searching, 260
separating test methods, 315
size and, 322
sorting, 266
system, 312
test cases, choosing, 311, 316, 321
test coverage, 321
tips for, 322
with unittest module, 312–315, 317–321
text files, defined, 177, *see also* files
text summarization, 343–346
TextIO, writing files, 190
time module, 244, 255
timeit module, 246
token, 343
tokenization, 343
top-down design, 235–243
tracebacks, 355–357, 361
True value, 83, 86, 89
truth tables, 85
try/except statements, 351–356
tuple type, 216
tuples
comparing with other collections, 229
creating, 216
empty, 216
exercises, 232
immutability, 216
membership, checking, 229
multiple assignment, 219
sets, 211
substitution operator (%), 78
using, 215–220
Turing machines, 69
Turing, Alan, 69
type annotations
creating, 229–232
defined, 50
dictionaries, 226
function design recipe, 51
lists, 137
TypeError, 357, 359
TypeError message, 69
types, *see also* floats; functions; integers; lists; strings
Any return type, 244
classes representing, 282
conversion functions for, 10, 33
defined, 10, 12
errors, 69, 357, 359
exception types, 353
object-oriented programming focus, 282
type contracts, 51

U

unary operators, 12, 83
underscore (_)
  module names, 110
  special methods, 128–130, 292
  throwaway variable, 334
Unicode, 91, 189
Uniform Resource Locators (URLs), 188
union, sets, 211
union method, 211
unit testing, 312–315, 317–321
unittest module, 312–315, 317–321
unpacking, 205, 334–336
update method, 225
upper method, 126
urllib module, 188
urlopen function, 188
URLs (Uniform Resource Locators), 188
user input
  loops, 167
  prompts for, 77, 93
  reading, 76
User-Agent header, 190
UTF-8, 189

V

ValueError, 357, 359
values
  dictionary comprehensions, 330
  errors, 357, 359
  interning, 37
  inverting dictionaries, 228
  key-value pairs and dictionaries, 221, 225
  memory, 17
  placeholder for missing, 346
  preconditions, 63
  reading data with missing values, 195–197
  True or False, 83, 86, 89
values method, dictionaries, 225
variables, *see also* local variables
  aliasing, 144
  assigning class objects, 289
  assigning inner lists to, 148
  assigning list items to, 136
  assigning lists to, 134
  assigning strings to, 70
  assigning, understanding, 16–23
  defined, 15
  global, 339
  grouping into modules, 118
  instance variables, 285, 290
  memory, 17
  in modules, 105, 107
  multiple assignment, 219
  names, 15–16, 26–27, 43, 99
  parameters as, 39–40, 144
  reassignment, 19–21
  reusing in Boolean expressions, 98–99
  reusing names, 43
  scope, 41, 339
  static, 339
  underscores enclosing, 130
vectors, sparse, 234
versions, Python, 5, 9
virtual machines, execution of programs, 8

W

while loops, 165–167, 252, 256
whitespaces
  defined, 24
  reading files, 186–187
  reading whitespace-delimited data, 197–200
  stripping, 125–126
Wing, Jeannette, 3
with statement, 180, 355
word tokenization, 343
working directory, 182
write method, 189
write mode (open), 189
writing
  example calls, 191
  exercises, 206
  files, 189

X

XML files, 178

Y

yield statement, generators, 339

Z

zero, omitting in floats, 10
ZeroDivisionError, 357
zip function, 161, 332

Thank you!

We hope you enjoyed this book and that you're already thinking about what you want to learn next. To help make that decision easier, we're offering you this gift.

Head on over to https://pragprog.com right now, and use the coupon code BUYANOTHER2026 to save 30% on your next ebook. Offer is void where prohibited or restricted. This offer does not apply to any edition of *The Pragmatic Programmer* ebook.

And if you'd like to share your own expertise with the world, why not propose a writing idea to us? After all, many of our best authors started off as our readers, just like you. With up to a 50% royalty, world-class editorial services, and a name you trust, there's nothing to lose. Visit https://pragprog.com/become-an-author/ today to learn more and to get started.

Thank you for your continued support. We hope to hear from you again soon!

The Pragmatic Bookshelf

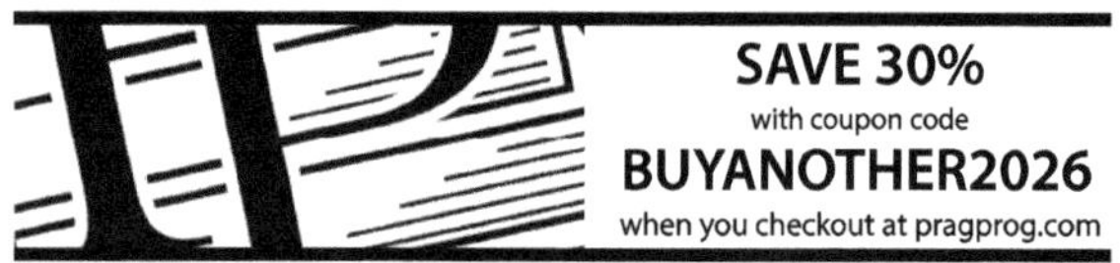

A Common-Sense Guide to Data Structures and Algorithms in Python, Volume 1

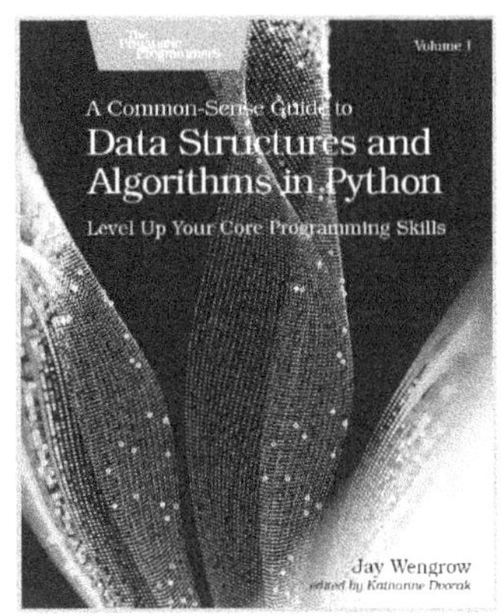

If you thought data structures and algorithms were all just theory, you're missing out on what they can do for your Python code. Learn to use Big O notation to make your code run faster by orders of magnitude. Choose from data structures such as hash tables, trees, and graphs to increase your code's efficiency exponentially. With simple language and clear diagrams, this book makes this complex topic accessible, no matter your background. Every chapter features practice exercises to give you the hands-on information you need to master data structures and algorithms for your day-to-day work.

Jay Wengrow
(502 pages) ISBN: 9798888650356. $57.95
https://pragprog.com/book/jwpython

A Common-Sense Guide to Data Structures and Algorithms in Python, Volume 2

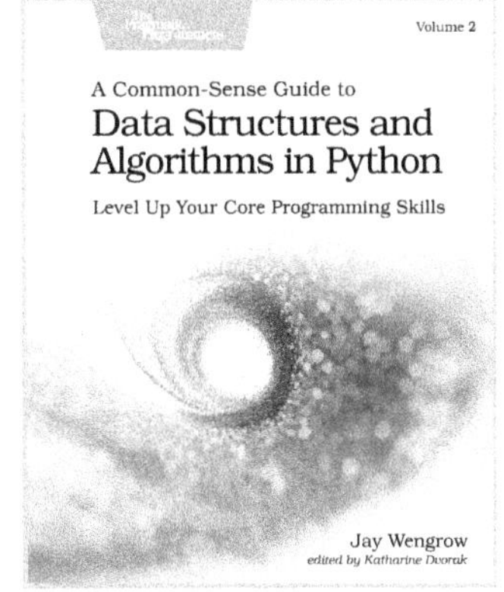

Want to write code that pushes the boundaries of speed, space savings, and scalability? Then you need more advanced data structures and algorithms. Go beyond Big O notation and evaluate the true efficiency of each algorithm you design. Pull out data structures such as B-trees, bit vectors, and Bloom filters to wrangle big data. Wield techniques like caching, randomization, and fingerprinting to tame even the most demanding applications. With simple language, clear diagrams, and practice exercises and solutions, this book makes these topics easy to grasp. Go beyond the basics and use these next-level concepts to build software that's ready to take on the challenges of the real world.

Jay Wengrow
(500 pages) ISBN: 9798888651322. $75.95
https://pragprog.com/book/jwpython2

Pythonic Programming

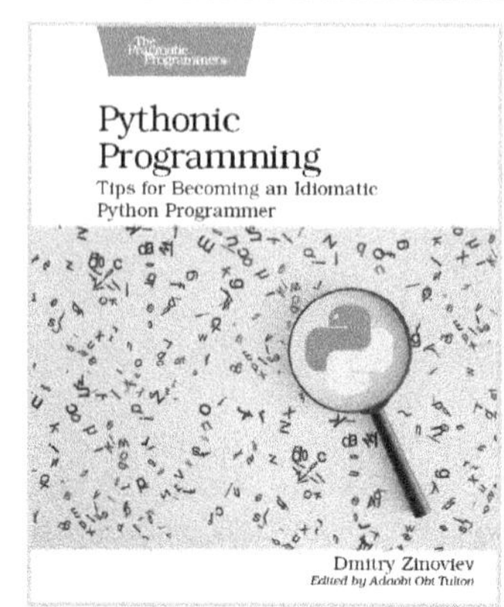

Make your good Python code even better by following proven and effective pythonic programming tips. Avoid logical errors that usually go undetected by Python linters and code formatters, such as frequent data look-ups in long lists, improper use of local and global variables, and mishandled user input. Discover rare language features, like rational numbers, set comprehensions, counters, and pickling, that may boost your productivity. Discover how to apply general programming patterns, including caching, in your Python code. Become a better-than-average Python programmer, and develop self-documented, maintainable, easy-to-understand programs that are fast to run and hard to break.

Dmitry Zinoviev
(150 pages) ISBN: 9781680508611. $26.95
https://pragprog.com/book/dzpythonic

Python Brain Teasers

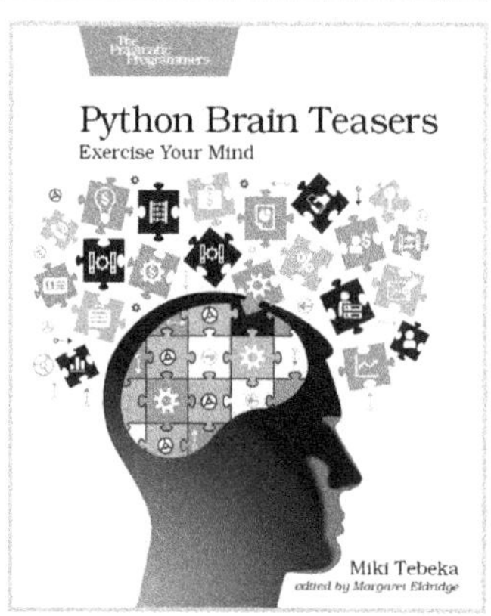

We geeks love puzzles and solving them. The Python programming language is a simple one, but like all other languages it has quirks. This book uses those quirks as teaching opportunities via 30 simple Python programs that challenge your understanding of Python. The teasers will help you avoid mistakes, see gaps in your knowledge, and become better at what you do. Use these teasers to impress your co-workers or just to pass the time in those boring meetings. Teasers are fun!

Miki Tebeka
(116 pages) ISBN: 9781680509007. $18.95
https://pragprog.com/book/d-pybrain

Data Science Essentials in Python

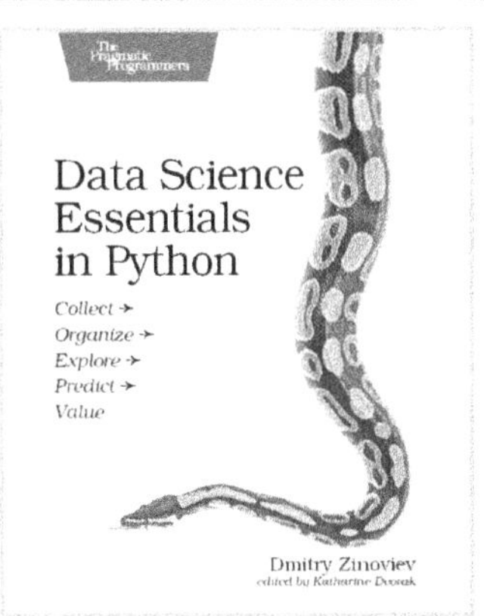

Go from messy, unstructured artifacts stored in SQL and NoSQL databases to a neat, well-organized dataset with this quick reference for the busy data scientist. Understand text mining, machine learning, and network analysis; process numeric data with the NumPy and Pandas modules; describe and analyze data using statistical and network-theoretical methods; and see actual examples of data analysis at work. This one-stop solution covers the essential data science you need in Python.

Dmitry Zinoviev
(224 pages) ISBN: 9781680501841. $29
https://pragprog.com/book/dzpyds

Python Testing with pytest, Second Edition

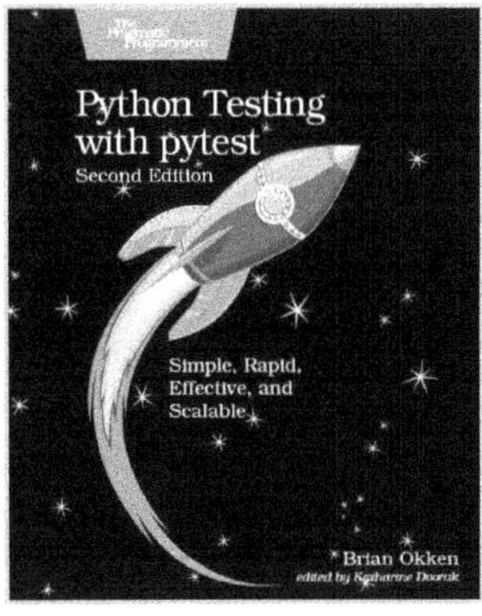

Test applications, packages, and libraries large and small with pytest, Python's most powerful testing framework. pytest helps you write tests quickly and keep them readable and maintainable. In this fully revised edition, explore pytest's superpowers—simple asserts, fixtures, parametrization, markers, and plugins—while creating simple tests and test suites against a small database application. Using a robust yet simple fixture model, it's just as easy to write small tests with pytest as it is to scale up to complex functional testing. This book shows you how.

Brian Okken
(272 pages) ISBN: 9781680508604. $45.95
https://pragprog.com/book/bopytest2

The Pragmatic Bookshelf

The Pragmatic Bookshelf features books written by professional developers for professional developers. The titles continue the well-known Pragmatic Programmer style and continue to garner awards and rave reviews. As development gets more and more difficult, the Pragmatic Programmers will be there with more titles and products to help you stay on top of your game.

Visit Us Online

This Book's Home Page

https://pragprog.com/book/gwpy4

Source code from this book, errata, and other resources. Come give us feedback, too!

Keep Up-to-Date

https://pragprog.com

Join our announcement mailing list (low volume) or follow us on Twitter @pragprog for new titles, sales, coupons, hot tips, and more.

New and Noteworthy

https://pragprog.com/news

Check out the latest Pragmatic developments, new titles, and other offerings.

Save on the ebook

Save on the ebook versions of this title. Owning the paper version of this book entitles you to purchase the electronic versions at a terrific discount.

PDFs are great for carrying around on your laptop—they are hyperlinked, have color, and are fully searchable. Most titles are also available for the iPhone and iPod touch, Amazon Kindle, and other popular e-book readers.

Send a copy of your receipt to support@pragprog.com and we'll provide you with a discount coupon.

Contact Us

Online Orders:	*https://pragprog.com/catalog*
Customer Service:	*support@pragprog.com*
International Rights:	*translations@pragprog.com*
Academic Use:	*academic@pragprog.com*
Write for Us:	*http://write-for-us.pragprog.com*

www.ingramcontent.com/pod-product-compliance
Ingram Content Group UK Ltd.
Pitfield, Milton Keynes, MK11 3LW, UK
UKHW051940150726
7214IPUK00020B/352